ALSO BY RICHARD NOLL

The Jung Cult

THE ARYAN CHRIST

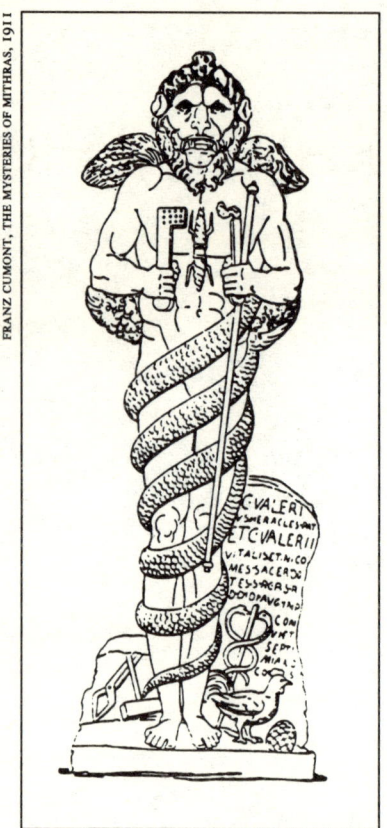

Aion, the Mithraic lion-headed god that Jung became in a visionary ecstasy in December 1913. At the time, the Mithraic mysteries were considered the most ancient form of Aryan spirituality.

RICHARD NOLL

THE ARYAN CHRIST

The Secret Life of Carl Jung

MACMILLAN

First published 1997 by Random House Inc., New York, and simultaneously in
Canada by Random House of Canada Ltd., Toronto

First published in Great Britain 1997 by Macmillan
an imprint of Macmillan Publishers Ltd
25 Eccleston Place, London SW1W 9NF
and Basingstoke

Associated companies throughout the world

ISBN 0 333 66618 6

Copyright © Richard Noll 1997

The right of Richard Noll to be identified as the
author of this work has been asserted by him in accordance
with the Copyright, Designs and Patents Act 1988.

All rights reserved. No part of this publication may be
reproduced, stored in or introduced into a retrieval system, or
transmitted, in any form, or by any means (electronic, mechanical,
photocopying, recording or otherwise) without the prior written
permission of the publisher. Any person who does any unauthorized
act in relation to this publication may be liable to criminal
prosecution and civil claims for damages.

1 3 5 7 9 8 6 4 2

A CIP catalogue record for this book is available from
the British Library.

Printed by Mackays of Chatham PLC, Chatham, Kent

In every man . . . there is one part which concerns only himself and his contingent existence, is properly unknown to anybody else and dies with him. And there is another part through which he holds to an idea which is expressed through him with an eminent clarity, and of which he is the symbol.

—Wilhelm von Humboldt, "Autobiographical Fragment," 1816

Contents

Introduction   xi

PART ONE: GENESIS
 1. The Inner Fatherland   3
 2. Summoning the Spirits   22
 3. Hidden Memories   42
 4. Religion Can Only Be Replaced by Religion   53

PART TWO: MYSTERIA
 5. Polygamy   69
 6. Sun Worship   98
 7. The Mystery of Deification   120
 8. Zurich 1916: Abraxas and the Return of the Pagan Gods   148

PART THREE: ACTS OF THE APOSTLES
 9. Fanny Bowditch Katz—"Analysis Is Religion"   165
10. Edith Rockefeller McCormick—The Rockefeller Psychoanalyst   200
11. The Passion of Constance Long   236

PART FOUR: REVELATIONS
12. From Volkish Prophet to Wise Old Man   263

Acknowledgments   281
Notes   285
Index   321

Introduction

Sifting through the private literature of the past, the letters and diaries intended only for those now dead, is like listening to a conversation at the next table as we pretend to be lost in thought. Inevitably, we gather only bits of detritus that we—like magpies—weave into something meaningful. We construct—not really reconstruct—stories about the past for the purposes of the present. We imagine that the dead have returned, move about, gossip. We try to convince our readers that they have joined us, to sip tea nonchalantly and strain to hear the tales being told nearby.

If one thinks about it this way, the craft of the historian seems almost Dadaist. The dead are astoundingly dead. How can we really hear what they're saying? Why the delusion that the dead said what they said, wrote what they wrote, *for us*? Yet we always feel that these things are so. For better or worse, we personalize the past. The dead become ours. And we become upset, disturbed, when our preferred tales of the dead are heard differently—and retold differently—by others.

I relate the following tale of Carl Gustav Jung under the cloud of such vexation.

"The cradle rocks above an abyss," Vladimir Nabokov wrote at the outset of his autobiography, "and common sense tells us that our existence is but a brief crack of light between two eternities of darkness."[1] But with biography, when the subject is someone other than ourselves, the situation is often reversed. We seem to see an illuminated path of events that lead up to the birth of an individual and, with the omniscience of a blind god, foresee what happened afterward. The historian or biographer often discovers that the arc between birth and death is frustratingly obscured in shadow. Data are often missing—or deliberately fudged by the subject or intimates—that are necessary for the proper calculation of the trajectory. And, of course, to tell a proper story we always want to know *why* A led to B and not C.

I can state with confidence that Carl Gustav Jung was born on July 26, 1875, and died on June 6, 1961. Born near Basel, Switzerland, over the last sixty years of his life he lived and worked—and died—near the banks of Lake Zurich. We know the dates of many of his travels to foreign lands, his publications, his public lectures, and a few other factual items. We have the letters he sent to Sigmund Freud and vice versa; consequently, we have a consistently useful record of many of his inner and outer concerns from 1907 to 1913. We can consult two published volumes of letters he wrote from age thirty-one until his death, heavily edited and selected by his estate for a favorable depiction of him. We have the twenty-plus volumes of his *Collected Works* and published transcripts of some of the seminars he taught. As a scientist, psychiatrist, and psychoanalyst, he achieved world renown while still in his thirties, and today he is regarded as the most famous man that Switzerland has ever produced. His face adorns a Swiss postage stamp.

At this point, the trail of evidence fades. Upon careful consideration, we are led to the surprising conclusion that very little about the historical Jung—particularly the first sixty years of his life (until 1936)—is known to us. Jung's life remains largely a mystery.

The book you hold before you is not a biography of Carl Gustav Jung. I sincerely doubt an authentic, comprehensive biography of Jung's entire life will be written any time soon. To do so would require that the heirs of Jung's estate open up *everything* to a scholar—Jung's private diaries, all the letters he wrote and received, his famous "Red Book" of paintings of his visions and discussions with the Dead,[2] and of course all the personal papers and letters of his wife and collaborator, Emma Jung, who many forget had an interesting and full life independent of her husband's. What we know about Emma Jung would barely fill two or three pages of text, and this will remain the case unless her personal papers are made available to scholars. The Jung family would also have to allow access to any diaries or papers from Jung's collaborator and lover, Antonia Wolff, that may be in the archives, along with documents belonging to Jung's early associate, J. J. Honegger, to which Jung's heirs have no discernible legal claim. As we shall learn, the Honegger papers are of paramount importance for making judgments about Jung's character and intellectual honesty.[3] Regrettably, the surviving members of the Jung family and the administrators of the Jung estate have shown little interest in contributing to the historical record.

We do have, however, the posthumously published "autobiography" known as *Memories, Dreams, Reflections* (hereafter *MDR*), which purports to be an honest statement from Jung himself about his own life. This is only partly true. As the scholar Alan Elms was the first to document, this book is less an autobiography than a patchwork of material brilliantly integrated by Aniela Jaffé, Jung's assistant in his last years, with copious editorial assistance from the American editors at Pantheon, who brought out the English edition before a German one appeared.[4] Although Jung wrote the initial draft of the first three chapters and a later one entitled "Late Thoughts," in which he speculated on life after death, these were not intended to be the first chapters of an autobiography, despite what the published volume would lead one to think. Furthermore, against Jung's own wishes, his words in these chapters were altered or deleted to conform to the image preferred by his family and disciples. Jaffé took Jung's own contributions, transcripts of his old lectures, and her own notes of discussions with him, put them into the first person, and allowed this to be passed off on an unsuspecting public as an autobiography. Unflattering material was, of course, left out, and even the usual sort of factual material that one expects in a biography or an autobiography is missing, leaving the strange story of an extraordinary individual who somehow lived outside of time and escaped history.

The Jung portrayed in *MDR* is a clairvoyant sage, a miracle worker, a god-man who earns his apotheosis through his encounter with the Dead and with God. His is a morality tale of mystical evolution, as his life becomes the exemplum of his theories, the heroic saga of an "individuated" man who survived a terrifying encounter with extramundane beings (the archetypes) from a transcendent reality (the collective unconscious). Unfortunately, *MDR* has served as the basis for all subsequent "biographies" of Jung since its first publication in 1962. Until recently, the truthfulness of this preferred version of Jung's "myth" has gone unquestioned. There is great resistance to altering the myth, which would mean tangling Jung in time and space and restoring him to his German cultural milieu, a humiliating descent from mythopoesis into history.

MDR, rightly or wrongly, has become one of the primary spiritual documents of the twentieth century. As the story of Jung's spiritual rebirth, it has inspired awe and hope in its readers, reenchanting their worlds. It is a powerful book, and I recall my bewildered reaction to it at age seventeen after the first of what was to become many readings. As I have subsequently learned from years of critical readings of Jung and historical research into his life, *MDR* and its imitators have actually obscured the story of a Jung who is much more interesting—and at times terrifyingly flawed—because of his humanity, not his semidivinity.

In this volume I have no desire to diagnose Jung or to continue the tradition of idealizing him as a god-man. There are hagiographies and hatchet jobs enough. In the pages that follow, with the guidance of the voices of the dead who spoke to me while I read through crumbling letters and diaries in archives throughout the United States and Europe—extracts from which appear in this book for the first time—my project is to supply some of the missing chapters in the story of Jung's life.

In a departure from the style, though not the substance, of my earlier scholarship on Jung, this volume is written as a sort of narrative history. Composing history in this style is much like writing a novel about people and events that we know and can document—"dead certainties," as the historian Simon Schama calls them. Unlike most narrative history, however, this is not the retelling of Jung's entire life and career, but instead a series of stories behind the official story. These episodes give form to an alternate myth of the unfolding of Carl Gustav Jung. At the core of Jung's life—and he is consistently clear about this—was always an obsession with existential issues, with the coin toss of life's meaning or meaninglessness, with mystery and with things sacred. Regarded by Jung himself as rooted in eternal currents, outside of time, outside of history, and represented as such by the many authors of his "autobiography," his subjective experiences in *MDR* are less a revelation than an occultation. The man himself, the historicity of his spirituality, and the roots of his ideas in German cultural soil all vanish from view.

Many who encounter Jung do so within the community of the spirit, and some look to the personal myth of C. G. Jung in *MDR* as a contemporary gospel that contains the kerygma of a new dispensation. To those readers I say: You may consider the book you now hold in your hands as its apocryphon. It is the apocryphon of a historian, however, and the rejected secrets in these pages have more to do with history than mystery.

This is not an easy story to tell. The Carl Jung I discovered is not too different in one respect from the Carl Jung in *MDR*: I am convinced by the historical evidence that Jung believed himself to be a religious prophet with extraordinary powers. I further believe that despite his multiple professional personas of physician, psychotherapist, and social critic, he consciously devoted his life to promoting the growth of a religious community centered on his personality and his teachings. This was his calling, and many in his earliest circle of disciples in Zurich during the First World War followed him because they believed he was "the new light," a charismatic prophet of a new age. In later life, after studying the ancient mystery cults and alchemy, Jung openly told more than one person that he—and those who follow his methods—were chosen to be the redeemers of God. "He spoke of his mission," said Eugen Bohler, a Swiss scholar who knew Jung intimately from 1955 on. "He regarded his life as a mission: to serve the function of making God conscious. He had to help God to make himself conscious, and not for our own sake, but for the sake of God."[5] I believe this is at the core of what Jung was about. Most persons who consider themselves Jungians would not disagree with this, and many openly acknowledge their participation in such a mystery. Some, worried about how this reflects on the public perception of their secular professional identity, which they have bound totemically with Jung's name, have grave reservations.

I will risk controversy with an additional observation. Through years of reflection on Jung's considerable impact on the culture and spiritual landscape of the twentieth century, I have come to the conclusion that, as an individual, he ranks with the Roman emperor Julian the Apostate (fourth century C.E.) as one who significantly undermined orthodox Christianity and restored the polytheism of the Hellenistic world in Western civilization. I realize this is quite an incautious statement, reflecting the hubris of the historian who succumbs to the fantasy of being a demiurge. Nevertheless, I believe that, for a variety of historical and technological factors—modern mass media being the most important—Jung has succeeded where Julian failed. For the first sixty years of his life—the period of his "secret life" largely lost to history—Jung was openly hostile to Judeo-Christian orthodoxies, particularly Judaism and Roman Catholicism. Contemporaneously, the patriarchal monotheism of the orthodox Judeo-Christian faiths has all but collapsed. Filling that void, however, we increasingly find Protestants, Catholics, and Jews adopting alternative, syncretic belief systems that often belie a basis in Jungian "psychological" theories.

I place the term "psychological" in quotation marks because I believe—and argue in this book—that this twentieth-century mask was constructed deliberately, and somewhat deceptively, by Jung to make his own magical, polytheist, pagan worldview more palatable to a secularized world conditioned to respect only those ideas that seem to have a scientific air to them. I make this judgment about Jung without being either Christian or Jew or Moslem—or Freudian. From the perspective of the history of religions, I find Jung and Jungism a remarkable phenomenon—that is all.[6] Not surprisingly, Jung's polytheism and extremely uncritical relativism have made him the perfect source of quotations for a new generation of postmodern literary critics and classicists.

Evidence—and there is much of it—reveals Jung to have been an acutely self-conscious heresiarch, much like Julian the Apostate, with whom Jung believed he was an initiate into a fourth-century mystical brotherhood. Like Julian, for many years Jung presented himself as a

Christian but in private practiced paganism. Further, even late in life Jung looked upon the orthodoxies of Judeo-Christianity as his enemy and as the enemy of life itself. R.F.C. Hull, the principal translator of Jung's *Collected Works* into English, expressed outrage over how the Jung family and Aniela Jaffé removed or softened so many of Jung's outspoken views "concerning Christian theology" in his handwritten contributions to *MDR*. Hull, who knew Jung well in his later years, said, "I am absolutely sure everything vital and creative came to him out of the depths of his pagan unconscious."[7]

Nevertheless, whatever the disposition of Jung's many students and intimates, nearly all studies of him and his work have overlooked the historical container in which his amalgam of ideas about pagan antiquity was distilled: namely, the German cultural context of his time, tellingly illustrated by the beliefs widely held by the classicists Jung respected, regarding the place of Indo-European pagans and Hellenistic Gnostics within the evolution of the Aryan race.

This brings me back to the challenges of storytelling. The success of the tale that follows pivots on your willingness to attempt an understanding of the story of Jung as an actor living entirely within the categories of the world as he knew it. His perspective on reality was framed by a concrete belief in a spirit world and in the ability to communicate directly with the Dead or discarnate entities of mysterious origin—not an easy leap of faith for many. Less difficult to imagine is a world where a belief in myth is more important than fact-based history and where intuition and feeling are valued above a reliance on rational thought. Those familiar with the popular philosophies of the American mythologist Joseph Campbell or Eugen Drewerman of Germany will understand these latter categories of mythic or mystic perception. But the most troublesome part of this story comes from asking you, the reader, to do the morally impossible: to imagine a world—fin-de-siècle German *Kultur*—in which the words "Hitler" and "Nazi" and "Holocaust" do not exist, a world in which spirituality is fused with blood and soil and the sun, a world in which an Aryan Christ could find apostles—and sincerely promise redemption to his redeemers.

PART ONE

Genesis

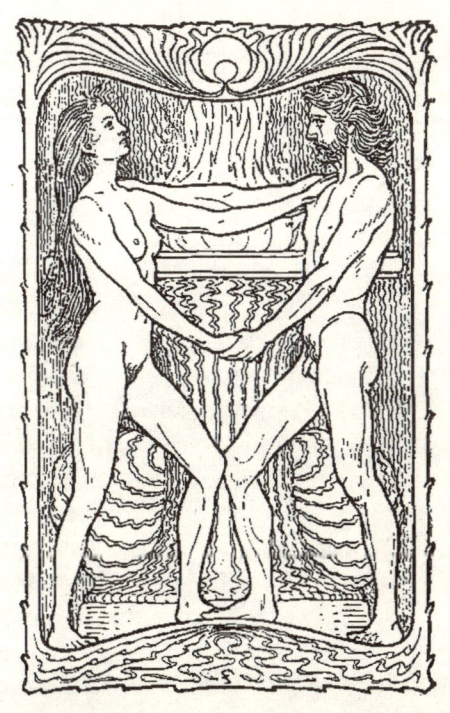

(*preceding page*) Fidus, "Liebe" ("Love"), 1916.

ONE

The Inner Fatherland

Along the banks of upper Lake Zurich, on a silent patch of land in Bollingen, the stone structure known as Jung's *Turm* (Tower) remains a site of pilgrimage. Jung began building the small, primitive refuge in 1923 as a round container for his solitude. Later, with additions, it became a tower and a sacred space where he could paint his visions on the walls and preserve them in carved stone. It also became a sexual space, a pagan sin altar where, removed from his wife and family in Küsnacht and his disciples in Zurich, he could enjoy his intimate companion, Toni Wolff, with orgiastic abandon. An unsettling mural that covers the entire wall of the bedroom depicts his spirit guide, Philemon, the transpersonal entity whom Jung met in visions during the First World War. Philemon is an interloper from the Hellenistic period, an old man with a long white beard and the wings of a kingfisher.[1] It is from his discussions with Philemon, or so the story goes in *MDR,* that Jung received his most profound insights about the nature of the human psyche. Jung's most famous ideas—the collective unconscious, which he first described in print in 1916, and the archetypes (its "gods"), which were added shortly thereafter—would not have been possible without guidance from Philemon.[2] It is from this Gnostic-Mithraic guru, who lives in a timeless space that Jung called the Land of the Dead, that Jung received instruction in "the Law," the esoteric key to the secrets of the ages. Jung inscribed these lessons in his "Red Book."

Privileged visitors who are invited by members of the Jung family are allowed to see this icon of Philemon. Another painting, in another part of the Tower, is revealed only to intimates. Usually concealed, perhaps to protect the eyes of the uninitiated from witnessing the sacred mysteries it portrays, is the image of a thin crescent ship, like those that carry the dead in Egyptian iconography, with male and female figures facing each other. In the center of Jung's vision is a large, reddish solar disk that brings to mind the frightful passage of souls to the underworld in the Egyptian Book of the Dead.

Outside in the courtyard, adjacent to the Tower, stand three stone tablets upon which, as Jung tells it in *MDR,* "I chiseled the names of my paternal ancestors."[3] The imaginal world of the ancestors, Jung's inner fatherland, was a living presence in Jung's everyday experience. *Ahnenerbe,* "ancestral inheritance," is the ground of all subjective experience within every individual, according to Jung. We find this idea at the epicenter of his worldview from a very early age, in an alien part of his childself that he called his "number two personality"—an elderly gentleman of the eighteenth century—allowing him to imagine he was "living in two ages simultaneously, and being two different persons."[4] He is an individual, yet a second heart beats in his breast, a sacred heart that squeezes the lifeblood of the ancestors through his veins. This, too, has origins in the nostalgic culture of his day, an era when heredity and *Kultur* and the landscape were merged with one's soul in the timeless and deeply resonant concept of *Volk* (a much fuller term than our poor derivative "folk"; the German spelling will be kept throughout to maintain this distinction).

"When I was working on the stone tablets," Jung confided, "I became aware of the fateful links between me and my ancestors. . . . It often seems as if there were an impersonal karma within a family, which is passed from parents to children. It has always seemed to me that I had to answer questions which fate had posed to my forefathers, and which had not yet been answered, or as if I had to complete, or perhaps continue, things which previous ages had left unfinished."[5]

What questions did Jung's paternal ancestors leave unanswered? What did Jung feel compelled to complete or to continue? What was the family karma that bound Jung to a specific fate? These questions already contain the seeds of their answers. What we must listen for here are the assumptions behind the queries, the brand of reality that would allow the possibility of such statements or questions in the first place. It is an arcane reality that Jung was destined to keep alive for millions in the twentieth century.

1817: The *Thing* at the Wartburg

What no one could forget were the bells. Joyously ringing their welcome to the young men who had come from afar, the bells of Eisenach would be forever etched in their memories.[6] Having gathered just outside the red-tiled buildings of this medieval German town, the young men lit torches and began their solemn procession up to the castle, yellow and red autumn leaves blanketing their path. Some of the young men referred to this congregation at the Wartburg castle as a *Thing*—what the ancient Germans called their annual tribal gatherings. Some of the young men were in ancient German dress, but most wore the *Trachten*, or traditional folk dress, of their native regions. They were urged to do so by the event's organizers, one of whom was Friedrich Ludwig Jahn, the famous "*Turnvater* Jahn," best remembered for founding gymnastics societies (*Turnvereinen*). There was no Germany in 1817, only several dozen principalities united by language, culture, and their common history of being recently overrun by Napoléon's armies. Jahn's gymnastics societies were designed to kindle the sparks of German nationalism in a defeated, fragmented, and often sleepy population. (Many of the foreign travelers through these lands in the nineteenth century described the Germans as rather indifferent, dreamy folk, all too glad to share their bread, wurst, and beer—not as seething tribes of warriors.)

Many of the young men marching with torches to the Wartburg castle that day were members of these proud gymnastics societies. The rest belonged to student fraternities, some of them secret known as *Burschenschaften*. Most were from the university in Jena. These student fraternities had only just come into being, but they would play an important role in German cultural life in the nineteenth century.[7] Some of them were also affiliated with an older secret society, the Freemasons, for whom the rose and the cross were blended into a meaningful occult symbol. Some of the participants at the Wartburg festival wore cloth bands around their torsos in the colors that comprise the flag of today's Germany—black, red, and gold.

It was no coincidence that these rituals of nascent German national fervor played out in the shadow of the mighty Wartburg fortress on an October night. It was here that Martin Luther gave Jesus a German accent. Luther's translation of the New Testament into German catalyzed nationalist sentiment and revolutionized the German world of letters. Heinrich Heine captures so many of the contradictions in the German soul in his often quoted description of Luther as "not merely the greatest but also the most German man in our history, so that in his character all the virtues and failings of the Germans were united in the most magnificent way." Luther was "the tongue as well as the sword of his age . . . a cold scholastic word-cobbler and an inspired, God-drunk prophet who, when he had worked himself almost to death over his laborious and dogmatic distinctions, in the evening reached for his flute and, gazing at the stars, melted in melody and reverence."[8] For many of the young men, the commanding walls of the Wartburg fortress rose above them like the brooding, corpulent specter of Martin Luther himself.

In October of 1517 a defiant Martin Luther hammered his theses of protestation to a church door. October also was celebrated as the anniversary of the defeat of Napoléon at Leipzig in 1813. The feeling of being German swelled whenever these victories of the *Volk* were recounted.

"Feelings" of being German were all that one could have, for "Germany" was a word for an ideal, not a reality. German-speaking peoples lived in a loose confederation of dozens of autonomous states of varying sizes and significance bound only by a weakly ruled political entity called the Holy Roman Empire of the German Nation. They shared no common currency or legal system, and travel and commerce between many of them was a gauntlet of complex taxes, customs fees, and unanticipated local restrictions on personal freedoms.

At the foot of the Wartburg, the men built a huge, blazing bonfire and other pillars of fire that could be seen by the people of Eisenach. Encircling the central fire, with an excitement driven by a sense of the sacred and the dangerous, the men sang the traditional hymn *"Eine Feste Burg"* ("A Mighty Fortress Is Our God"). One of the leaders then offered a few inspirational remarks about justice and invoked the important symbol of the German forest of oaks. The mighty oak was sacred to the ancient Teutons and indeed was the "cross" upon which Wotan (Odin) underwent his revelatory self-sacrifice. Nostalgic references to it recur throughout more than a century of German spiritual longing.

More songs were sung and a patriotic sermon was delivered. Then, before a final hymn to end the formal segment of their ritual, the young men joined hands around the fire and took a collective oath of allegiance to one another and to their group (*Bund*). They also pledged to preserve the purity of the *Volk*. Before the Wartburgfest concluded, for the first time in recorded German history "un-German books" were denounced and burned in the great central fire.

Karl Gustav Jung—the grandfather of Carl Gustav Jung—considered his participation in the Wartburgfest one of the purest and most meaningful experiences of his life. He was twenty-three. He carefully preserved his black, red, and gold wrap from his days of student activism, and it became one of his grandson's most cherished possessions.

"Where Jung was, there was life and movement, passion and joy"

Karl Gustav Jung was born in Mannheim in 1794 to a physician, Franz Ignaz Jung, and his wife, Maria Josepha, rumored by later generations to have submitted, like Europa, to a most remarkable infidelity. Little is known about Karl's childhood. The Jungs were Roman Catholics from Mainz and distinguished by their heritage of German physicians and jurists. In a diary Karl kept in his later years, we know that his father had always remained something of a stranger to him and that his mother was inclined toward bouts with depression. (A similar parental constellation is described by Karl's grandson in the early chapters of *MDR*.) The Jung family cannot be traced prior to its residence in Mainz, for the public archives were burned in 1688 during the French occupation. Franz Ignaz Jung served in a lazaretto during the Napoleonic wars. His brother, Sigismund von Jung, was a high-ranking Bavarian official who was married to the youngest sister of perhaps the most famous religious and nationalist figure in Germany at that time, Friedrich Schleiermacher.

In a drawing of Karl dated February 1821, we see a young man with longish curls, seductive, heavy-lidded eyes, and a truly aquiline nose; he resembles a Teutonic Byron.[9] In his youth he was, simultaneously, political activist, poet, playwright, and physician. In his lifetime he would give thirteen children to three wives. Energetic, extraverted, full of passion for living, his boundless energy thrilled and, at times, crushed others. At his burial in 1864, his friend the chemist Schoenbrun said, "Where Jung was, there was life and movement, passion and joy."[10] At the 1875 opening of the Vesalianum, the anatomical institute at the University of Basel, the elderly Wilhelm His remembered Jung's "continual optimism and unbending high-spirits, which were not broken by difficult family sorrows." These sorrows were the early deaths of most of Jung's children, as well as of his first two wives. One of the few progeny that survived into adulthood was his last child, the lucky thirteenth, Johann Paul Achilles Jung, who would live to sire a son, Carl Gustav, in 1875 and a daughter, Gertrud, in 1884.

Like his father and grandson, Karl Gustav Jung was a physician. He was trained at Heidelberg, that famous university town, an important center of alchemy and a symbol in Rosicrucian lore. He earned his medical degree in 1816, then moved to Berlin to practice as a surgical assistant to an ophthalmologist. Berlin changed him forever.

Place, landscape, soil—to understand the imaginal world of Jung it is important to identify these nodal spaces where meaning condenses, the earthen crossroads upon which history rains. Such a place was the home of the Berlin bookseller and publisher Georg Andreas Reimer, an intimate friend of Schleiermacher. Reimer served as the host of the Reading Society, a patriotic club that met in his home. Ernst Moritz Arndt, one of the founding fathers of the nationalist Volkish movement (*Volkstumbewegung*) in Germany, befriended Schleiermacher here. To avoid prosecution for anti-French activity in the occupied German heartland, Arndt fled to Berlin, the capital of Prussia, and lived in Reimer's home from 1809 to 1810.[11] In 1816 and 1817, so did Karl Gustav Jung.

At Reimer's, Jung found himself in one of the central incubators of German Romanticism and nationalism. He came into contact with a steady flow of ideas from determined men—some of them political fugitives—who were convinced of the idea of a *Volksgeist,* the unique characteristics or genius of the German people as a single nation, determined by language, climate, soil or landscape, certain economic factors, and, of course, race. These ideas found form in the essays of J. G. Herder, Arndt, Jahn, and the sermons of Schleiermacher. Here Jung met the Schlegel brothers—Friedrich and August Wilhelm—and Ludwig Tieck, all noted writers and founders of the Romantic movement. Jung underwent a transformation not only of political consciousness, as evidenced by his contributions to the *Teutsche Liederbuch* anthology of German nationalist poem-songs (*Lieder*), but of religious consciousness as well. As confirmed in the baptismal certificate signed by Schleiermacher—another proud possession of the grandson[12]—Karl Gustav Jung renounced the Roman Catholic faith and became an Evangelical Protestant in the Romantic and nationalist mode.

The aftershocks of the grandfather's renunciation of his ancestral faith can still be felt by those touched by the life and work of the grandson. The sudden conversion of the grandfather, his act of apostasy, his angry rejection of Rome, would arguably prove to be one of the most powerful determinants of the destiny of C. G. Jung. The importance of this familial mark of Cain cannot be overstated.[13]

"Religion of the heart"

Religion mated with German nationalism in the eighteenth century and produced a fever in the people called Pietism.[14] Schleiermacher had been visited by this fever in his youth, and although he forged his own path as a theologian and philosopher, he said his ideas remained closest to this "religion of the heart." To Schleiermacher, the highest form of religion was an "intuition" (*Anschauung*) of the "Whole," an immediate experience of every particular as part of a whole, of every finite thing as a representation of the infinite. This was the perfect theology for an age of nature-obsessed Romanticism, and at times Schleiermacher's rhetoric, adorned with organic metaphors of the whole derived from nature, shaded into pantheism and mysticism. By 1817, he most certainly infected Karl Jung with it, as he did that entire generation of young patriots through his sermons, his writings, and especially his revisions of the Reformed Protestant liturgy, making it more simple, festive, and Volkish. Additionally, in the decade before he met Jung, he had published translations of Plato and, by his own admission, had become quite influenced by Platonism. This, too, must be remembered when we fantasize about what the older spiritual adviser imparted to the enthusiastic young convert.

German Pietism was loosely related to contemporaneous religious movements, such as Quakerism and enthusiastic Methodism in England and America and Quietism and Jansenism in France. Pietism, however, was to play a key role in developing Volkish self-consciousness and a sense of nation in the politically fragmented German lands. In the spirit of Luther, Pietism was born of disgust with orthodoxies, dogmas, and church hierarchies in the traditional Protestant denominations, making it a form of radical Lutheranism. Pietists dared to question authority and to be suspicious of foreign interpreters of Christianity. They called it a *Herzensreligion*, a "religion of the heart," a spiritual movement that emphasized feeling, intuition, inwardness, and a personal experience of God.[15] The function of thinking, indeed reason itself, was disparaged and could not be trusted. To experience God, the intellect must be sacrificed. (For example, according to Count Nikolaus Ludwig von Zinzendorf, a prominent eighteenth-century Pietist who influenced Schleiermacher and twentieth-century figures Rudolph Otto and Hermann Hesse, only atheists attempted to comprehend God with their mind; the True sought revelation.)[16]

Pietists' mystical enthusiasm is reflected in some of their favorite incendiary metaphors for their ecstatic experiences. It was the fire of the Holy Spirit that must burn within; indeed, it was often said that "the heart must burn." They emphasized the burning experience of "Christ within us" instead of the inanimate, automatic belief in the dogma of a "Christ for us." Such subtle distinctions had profound implications for German nationalism, for the belief arose in the feeling of group identity bound by common inner experience, a mystical blood-union of necessity, rather than as something external existing *for* an individual. Hence, the Pietist emphasis on service to others as a method of serving God.

Prussia, the most absolutist of the many German political entities, welcomed the Pietists to Berlin. Attracted to Pietism's rejection of the Lutheran clerical hierarchy—which threatened the overriding legitimacy of the state—the eighteenth-century rulers of Prussia adopted Pietism's religious philosophy and offered sanctuary to many of its exiled leaders. As populist movements, Pietism and pan-German nationalism were as threatening to the royal rulers of the dozens of German states as to Lutheran clerics, for they challenged the political status quo. Prussia, however, as the strongest of the German states, already presaged its manifest destiny as the unifier of Germany, and so its short-term goals coincided with those of such movements. Nicholas Boyle, one of Goethe's biographers, described the immense significance of this convergence of affinities for the next two centuries of German religious life and political history:

> The particular feature of Pietism which makes it of interest to us is its natural affinity for state absolutism. A religion which concentrates to the point of anxiety, not to say hypochondria, on those inner emotions, whether of dryness or abundance, of despair or of confident love of God, from which the individual may deduce the state of his immortal soul; a religion whose members meet for preference not publicly, but privately in conventicles gathered round a charismatic personality who may well not be an ordained minister; a religion who disregards all earthly (and especially all ecclesiastical) differentiation of rank, and sees its proper role in the visible world in charitable activity as nearly as possible harmonious with the prevailing order . . . —such a religion was tailor-made for a state system in which all, regardless of rank, were to be equally servants of the one purpose; in which antiquated rights and differentiae were to be abolished; and in which ecclesiastical opposition was particularly unwelcome, whether it came from assertive prelates or from vociferous enthusiasts unable to keep their religious lives to themselves.[17]

By the middle of the eighteenth century, German nationalism had become so intertwined with Pietism that the literature of the time blurs distinctions between inner and outer Fatherlands.[18] The "internalized Kingdom of Heaven" became identical with the spiritual soil of the German ancestors, a Teutonic "Land of the Dead." In these patriotic religious tracts the sacrificial deaths of Teutonic heroes such as Arminius (Hermann the German, who defeated the Romans in the Teutoberg forest) and the mythic Siegfried are compared to the crucifixion of Christ, thus equating pagan and Christian saviors. By the early 1800s, this identity became even more explicit. To Ernst Moritz Arndt, the subjective experience of the "Christ within" was reframed in German Volkish metaphors. In his 1816 pamphlet *Zur Befreiung Deutschlands* ("On the Liberation of Germany"), Arndt urged Germans, "Enshrine in your hearts the German God and German virtue."[19] They did. By the end of the nineteenth century the German God had reawakened and was moving to reclaim his throne after a thousand-year interregnum.

The primary literature of Pietism consisted of diaries and autobiographies, most driven by the psychological turn inward so valued as the path to reaching the kingdom of God. These confessional texts emphasize the spiritual evolution of the diarist. Each account peaks dramatically with the description of what Schleiermacher called the "secret moment," the tremendous subjective experience that completely changed the life course of an individual and became the central, vivid milestone of his or her faith. This experience was known as the *Wiedergeburt,* the "rebirth" or "regeneration." Sometimes this experience was preceded or accompanied by visions. Several of the more famous texts, such as the autobiography of Heinrich Jung-Stilling, became part of the canon read by educated nineteenth-century Germans.

Several of these spiritual autobiographies were in the library in C. G. Jung's household when he was growing up, and he cites some of them (such as the work of Jung-Stilling) in *MDR* and in his seminars.[20] While *MDR* is highly unlike usual biographies or autobiographies, its story of Jung's spiritual journey is similar in many ways to the *Wiedergeburt* testimonies of the Pietists. *MDR* is indeed the story of Jung's rebirth, but the book diverges from the tradition in one uncanny respect: Rather than recording the renewal of Jung's faith as a "born-again Christian," *MDR* is a remarkable confession of Jung's *pagan* regeneration.

Prison and exile

Two years after the Wartburgfest, Karl Jung was arrested by Prussian authorities after a friend of his assassinated a government official. Charged with being a political demagogue, Jung spent the next thirteen months in a Berlin prison.

Sitting in his filthy cell, the stench of human waste ever present, he lamented the sad fact that his medical career in his beloved Fatherland was over before it really began. Losing hope as the months continued to pass, he struggled to resist the temptation to interpret his long prison term as the Creator's revenge for his strident apostasy. His intense desire to participate in the political, cultural, and spiritual union of his *Volk,* his hatred of the

Pope and the Papists, his Pietistic rebirth in the hands of Schleiermacher—all of these newly flowering branches were suddenly and cruelly chopped from the trunk of his living soul, abandoning him to a lifetime of torturous fantasies that swirled around questions never answered, heroic tasks never completed.

Expelled from Prussia, unable to work in most of the German principalities due to his criminal record, in 1821 Karl Jung fled to Paris, the capital of the recent oppressors of the German peoples. This must have seemed like the ultimate capitulation, but his retreat into the heart of his enemy, this embrace of the negation of all that he thought he was and wanted to be, would bring unintended rewards. Jung tempered his Volkish romanticism and his nationalist activism and redirected his attention and vitality to the practice of medicine. The religious zeal of the new convert that energized him in Berlin was, by necessity, submerged in Roman Catholic France. He married a Frenchwoman and learned to become more cautious politically. Career and home replaced Volkish utopianism as his primary concerns.

In Paris he had the good fortune to meet Alexander von Humboldt, next to Goethe perhaps the most famous German man of science of his age.[21] Humboldt was impressed by the young physician, and upon his recommendation Jung was able to procure work as a surgeon at the famous Hôtel Dieu. In 1822, Humboldt wrote a letter recommending Jung to the medical faculty at the University of Basel in Switzerland, where Jung went on to assume the chair in surgery, anatomy, and obstetrics, rising from *Dozent* (lecturer) to *Ordinarius* (professor) within the year.

The position Jung assumed was not exactly one of the most coveted in Europe. Between 1806 and 1814, the University of Basel only produced one doctorate in medicine. For many years there was only one instructor in the medical faculty, and often lectures were given to only a single medical student and a few barber-surgeons who only required a little training in bloodletting, nail clipping, and haircutting. To his credit, Jung succeeded in modernizing medical education and research at this institution, and his lasting fame in Basel derives from this pioneering effort. By 1828, Jung was made rector of the university. He became a legendary figure in Basel, and there were many still alive who knew old Professor Doctor Karl Jung when his grandson grew up in Basel and received his own medical training at the university in the late 1890s.

But in 1822 the soul of Karl Jung was still profoundly rooted in his German homeland, and initially he felt alien among the Swiss. He was homesick most of the time, and because the people of Basel spoke their own Swiss-German dialect, he had difficulty understanding and being understood. He came to Switzerland as an exile, knowing in all likelihood he could never go home again. Although geographically close to Germany, Basel was psychologically remote, almost otherworldly, "in a corner of the world, across from the Fatherland." Perhaps most painful was his loss of national identity: "I am no longer a German," he lamented.[22]

As he threw himself into the building of new hospitals and clinics (including one for the mentally alienated), Karl Jung forged new relationships and became a prominent citizen and a relatively wealthy man. To rekindle the spirit of belonging to a brotherhood of idealists, which he missed dearly, Jung joined a powerful secret society. In time, he became its supreme leader in Switzerland.

Reconstructing the Temple of Solomon with Philosopher's Stones

Karl Jung first became acquainted with Freemasonry during his student days. There were many thriving lodges in Paris, but as a German he had little chance of joining. Opportunities were plentiful in Switzerland, however. As a stranger in a strange land, Jung gravitated naturally toward the local Masonic community as a way of assimilating into Swiss society. Then, as now, Freemasonry provided unique opportunities for making friends and advancing one's career through a network of individuals from a variety of occupations and social, political, and religious backgrounds. In Switzerland, as elsewhere, Masonic lodges were places where men could gather outside their family, their church, and bodies of government. Often driven by the ethical idealism of the Enlightenment, Masonic lodges were places where nationalists could congregate and conspire, where antipapists could vent their spleens, and where philanthropic projects could be planned and carried out. Jung's own hospital and clinic projects in Basel were no doubt expedited by his relationships with the secret Masonic brotherhood.[23]

There was another side to Freemasonry, however: its esoteric approach to religion. Behind the not-so-secret rites and rituals, grades and degrees, breathed a very different order. Spiritual growth, Freemasons believed, was best nurtured in a secret society of those farther along the illuminated path who initiated those less enlightened.

When Karl Jung first encountered Freemasonry in Germany, it was a movement still recovering from its 1784 banning by the Bavarian government, which claimed to have discovered a radical republican conspiracy within the Illuminati, the exalted inner circle of the Masons. Bavaria made it a capital crime to recruit others to this secret society, and most of the other German governments followed suit. In Germany and in Switzerland, Freemasons continued to assemble and enact rituals under the ruse of being patriotic clubs or philanthropic societies. Not surprisingly, during the Napoleonic wars they became efficient vehicles for organizing resistance to the French.

Traditionally, the German Freemasons were split into two sometimes contentious camps. One advocated the organizational goal of fostering Enlightenment virtues of liberty, equality, and ethical universalism in the German peoples. Its ideological rival, a faction that generally referred to itself as Rosicrucian, saw itself as the bearer of the torch for the ancient theology handed down to the first Freemasons from the *prisci theologi,* the "pristine theologians," from whom all wisdom is derived.[24] Although Freemasonry did not emerge with any force in Germany until the 1740s, the Masonic Rosicrucians claimed that they were the keepers of occult knowledge passed to them by the ancient Rosicrucians, whose symbol was the Christian cross wrapped in roses. The wisdom of the ancients was passed from man to man in secret through a series of initiatory steps or grades or degrees. The Grand Masters were the true adepts, experts in the arcane, even allegedly gifted with healing powers and second sight.

From its inception in the mid-1600s, Freemasonry has been related to the mythology of the Rosicrucians, although there is no evidence that such a secret society ever existed.[25] The fascination with Rosicrucianism can be traced to the appearance of two anonymous pamphlets published in Cassel, the German *Fama* (1614) and the Latin *Confessio* (1615); and to a German book by Johann Valentin Andreae called the *Chymische Hochzeit Christiani Rosencreutz* (The chemical wedding of Christian Rosenkreutz), which appeared in 1616. The two manifestos tell the story of "Father C.R.C.," also known as "Christian Rosenkreutz," the founder of an ancient order or brotherhood—symbolized by a red cross and a red rose—that had been secret but now wanted new members. The appearance of these mysterious invitations ignited considerable speculation, and soon copycat secret societies were formed, many claiming to be the true keepers of the Rosicrucian flame. It was out of this Rosicrucian mania that Freemasonry was born.

The legend that Karl Jung learned in the early nineteenth century is still very much the basis of arcane Masonic lore today: the first Freemasons were the stonemasons who built the Temple of Solomon in Jerusalem. During the construction, some of the masons were initiated into cosmic mysteries related to geometry and mathematics and, it was later said, alchemy. Each stone they used to build the Temple was not an ordinary stone, but an alchemical Philosopher's Stone. This knowledge was passed secretly from mason to mason through the ages to the men in the medieval guilds who built the magnificent cathedrals. Together, the esoteric goal of each of the Masonic brethren was to metaphysically rebuild the sacred Temple of Solomon within each Masonic lodge. In Masonic lore, the Philosopher's Stone has many names. Sometimes it is called the Word of God, and the path of illumination is described as the search for the lost Ark of the Covenant. Throughout, we find the collective fantasy of a mutual journey, a quest, a search for the Holy Grail in its myriad manifestations. Above all, the ability to keep a secret was the key to the spiritual advancement of each individual.

In truth, Freemasonry probably did arise out of guilds of masons, and master masons did have secret handshakes and coded knowledge that apprentices would not know. Out of these guilds of skilled craftsmen emerged secret societies that transmitted philosophies about the moral and mystical interpretation of building. Eventually, these "speculative masons" ritualized the passage of knowledge within the masonic-guild structure and the practice of keeping secrets that allowed masters to recognize their members.

Unlike their brethren to the north, the Swiss lodges did not close down in the purges of the late 1780s and so were a haven for German Freemasons, both Illuminatist and Rosicrucian. When Karl Jung knew them, each, to a greater or lesser degree, continued the traditions of Freemasonry: as vanguard proponents of Enlightenment civic virtues and as an occult brotherhood united by the symbols of the rose and the cross. The secret rituals of initiation demanded the wearing of special caps and aprons, the recitation of special arcane incantations, and the mastery of the esoteric interpretations of symbols of transformation that were hewn from Hermeticism, Neoplatonism, and especially alchemy—occult philosophies thus quite familiar to Grand Master Jung. Even his personal image of God as the "eternal Space" conjures up Masonic images of the interior of the Temple of Solomon. In fact, his identity as a Freemason was so important to him that he added such traditional Masonic symbols as an alchemical gold star to the Jung family coat of arms. In the twentieth century, his grandson would paint these Masonic emblems from the family crest on the ceiling of his Tower in Bollingen. Other arcane symbols familiar to his grandfather would be carved into walls and special monuments, each stone worked by his own hands in the old way.

The rose, the cross, and the mysteries

Goethe enters our story at this point, less as an apparition than as a visitation from a god.

There were many affinities between these two contemporaries, Karl Gustav Jung and Johann Wolfgang von Goethe. Goethe was also a Freemason, but unlike Jung, he did not remain ardent about the veiled brotherhood for very long.

While in Weimar, Goethe applied for membership to the Amalia lodge, as it was called, in 1780. By 1782, he had risen rapidly to become a Master Mason, and in February 1783 he rose to the exalted inner circle of Illuminists. Having mastered all the secret handshakes, the Masonic myths of origin, the alchemical metaphors for personal transformation and growth, the progression of occult symbols associated with each grade—such as a casket with the Seal of Solomon on it and an image of the Ark of the Covenant—he expressed dissatisfaction, indeed annoyance, that he had been so naive to believe that some great secret would be revealed to him if he could only reach the lofty inner circle. A few weeks after finally reaching this circle, Goethe said to a friend, "They say you can best get to know a man when he is at play and now I have reached the ark of the covenant I have nothing to add. To the wise all things are wise, to the fool foolish."[26]

Goethe later blended portions of the arcane knowledge and symbolism introduced to him through Freemasonry in *Faust,* but two pieces of literature in particular were more directly influenced by his gaming with the "brethren." One was a Masonic comedy, *Der Gross-Cophta* (The grand kophta), which he wrote in 1790. The protagonist of this play, a young knight, joins a special brotherhood that claims to be dedicated to only the most spiritual and noblest of aims. Indeed, this altruistic brotherhood believes its work is the salvation of a misguided humanity. However, the young knight soon realizes that he has been deceived and that the brotherhood has much more base and pecuniary motives. With his missionary zeal to save the souls of his fellow humans destroyed, he wonders what to do with his misspent idealism. Wisely, the young knight realizes, "Fortunate he, if it is still possible for him to find a wife or a friend, on whom he can bestow individually what was intended for the whole human race."[27]

Goethe's disillusionment with his Masonic involvement is nakedly revealed in the hard-earned wisdom of the young knight. However, his humanistic idealism and his earlier hopes for a true Holy Order of the Rose and the Cross that would unite humankind in spiritual brotherhood appear in a second work, never completed, that he called *Die Geheimnisse* (The mysteries).[28] Both Jungs, grandfather and grandson, committed it to their hearts.

The work begins, as all initiations do, with a quest. A certain Brother Markus is traveling through the mountains during Holy Week and seeks a place to sleep in an unfamiliar monastery. As the sun sinks behind the mountain peaks, the bells of the monastery suddenly start to ring, filling him with hope and consolation. As he nears the gates he sees a Christian cross. Suddenly, he realizes it is not the usual crucifix, but a remarkable sight that he has never seen before: a cross tightly wound with roses. "Who delivered these roses to the cross?" he wonders. The tower gate opens and Brother Markus is greeted and invited inside by a wise old man whose openness, innocence, and gestures make him seem like a man from another world. Soon Brother Markus is welcomed by a community of gray-haired knights who are too old for adventure but are proud men who have all lived life to the fullest. They have chosen to spend their remaining years in peaceful contemplation, and they accept no new brother if he is still "young and his heart has led him to renounce the world too soon."

Yet all is not in harmony at the monastery. Their founder and master, Brother Humanus, has informed his brethren that he will be leaving them soon. Brother Markus hears wondrous tales about the childhood of Humanus, which is filled with such miracles as making a spring flow out of dry stone with the touch of a sword. He is entranced by the wisdom of Humanus ("the Holy One, the Wise One, the best man I've ever laid eyes on"), but hears him relate something incomprehensible:

> *Von der Gewalt, die all Wesen bindet,*
> *Befreit der Mensch sich, der sich ueberwindet*

> From the force that binds all beings,
> The man frees himself who overcomes himself.

Brother Markus is led to a great hall and is shown something rarely seen: a ritual room—resembling a chapel—in which thirteen seats line the walls, one for the master of the order and twelve for the knights. Behind the seat of each knight hangs a unique coat of arms with unfamiliar symbols of faraway lands. Brother Markus sees that the seats are arranged around a cross with rose branches wound around it. Swords and lances and other weapons are also scattered about the chamber. It is a holy place, but unlike any chapel he's ever seen.[29]

That night, Brother Markus gazes out of his window and sees "a strange light wandering through the garden." He then is astounded by the sight of three young men with torches, clad in white garments, off in the distance. Who are they? We'll never know, for here Goethe's fragment comes to its premature end.

Goethe decided to publish it as is, but in response to queries on April 9, 1816, in the prominent newspaper *Morganblatt*, he published a description of how *Die Geheimnisse* would end. The twelve knights were to each represent a different religion and nationality, and each would have then had his turn to narrate a tale about the remarkable life of Humanus. Together these stories would comprise the entire range of human religious experience, the unity of which is symbolized by this Order of the Rosy Cross. Goethe revealed that the poem would climax with the Easter death of Humanus, who then would be replaced by Brother Markus, of course, as grand master of the order.

Exactly one hundred years after *Die Geheimnisse* appeared in print, Carl Gustav Jung stood before a historic gathering of his disciples in Zurich and delivered an inspirational address that spoke almost exclusively of spiritual matters: of self-deification, of overcomings, of disturbing the Dead, and of this poem.[30] The occasion of his talk was the founding of the Psychological Club, based on the new psychological theories he derived from the insights he received from his own visions and encounters with Philemon, his spiritual master.

To describe the essence of their collective purpose, as he saw it, he invoked the Grail-knights imagery of Wagner's *Parsifal* and the Rosicrucian brotherhood in Goethe's fragmentary fantasy. Jung framed the Psychological Club within these ancient German motifs of holy orders of knights in search of occult knowledge, healing powers, and especially spiritual redemption. By mentioning this poem, and by invoking the spirit of Goethe, Jung was also paying homage to his ancestors, to his ancestral soul. I mean this in several senses: as homage to the Dead, to his own fathers, and to the ancestors of the Fatherland as spirits who have traveled the same paths on the same Grail quest. Further, there is good reason to believe that as he delivered this inaugural address, Carl Jung believed that his grandfather, Karl Gustav Jung, was the bastard son of the great Goethe. In an age and culture obsessed with the commanding influence of heredity and race on an individual, the possibility that Goethe was his great-grandfather was a very powerful fantasy.

Near the end of his life, however, Jung changed the story. No longer was he merely the blood-kin of the greatest genius the German *Volk* had produced. He believed instead that he was an eternal recurrence, an avatar, a revenant. Carl Jung believed himself to be, literally, the reincarnation of Johann Wolfgang von Goethe.

Atavisms and Illuminati

The family fable—discounted by everyone with an amused smile, including by Carl Jung himself sometimes—lives in the tradition of all myths of erotic union between mortal women and the gods. Many within the Jung family and without would occasionally tell the story furtively, relishing the role of an insider privy to celebrity gossip, that the mother of Professor Doctor Karl Jung had a "spring to the side" as they say in German, an extramarital tryst with Goethe that resulted in Karl, so the story goes. True or not, Carl Jung enjoyed telling this anecdote throughout his life. Its origins are not known, but there is good reason to suspect it was alive even during Karl Jung's lifetime. Jung said he first heard this story from strangers when he was a schoolboy, which must have only reinforced the possibility that it might be more than a frivolous family story.

Carl Jung marveled at the similarities between his grandfather and Goethe. Both were vital, energetic, productive men who dominated, intellectually and temperamentally, most people. Both were scientists as well as poets, influenced by Pietism in their youth and disaffected from it in their maturity. Both were Germans and Freemasons—Illuminati, in fact— and above all, true Romantics until the end. They both seemed larger than life, daemonic, godlike, more like forces of nature than men.

Carl Jung knew that he shared many of the temperamental qualities of his grandfather (and therefore, by extension, of Goethe). By his own admission, it was the legend of his grandfather, not the living example of his father, against which Jung constantly measured himself as a young man.

In a seminar he gave in Zurich in 1925, Carl Jung expressed his belief in the idea of "ancestor possession"—that is, that certain hereditary units would become activated under certain circumstances in one's life, allowing the spirit of one's ancestor to then "take over" one's actions. Jung gave the example of an "imaginary normal man" who, on the surface, never indicated a capacity for leadership but in whom, when put in a position of power, the "ancestral unit" of a leader somewhere in the family past was awakened.[31] These ancestral units were a far cry from anything resembling genetics but were in sympathy with nineteenth-century biological theories that were on the verge of dying out. Jung also used this concept in a spiritualist sense. It is hard not to imagine him fantasizing about his own grandfather, and perhaps Goethe, in these terms. During the first sixty years of

Jung's life, biology and spirituality were fused in ways difficult—indeed, distasteful—for us to imagine. And so, the scientist in Jung no doubt found support in the surviving Lamarckian currents in German biology to keep the possibility open that the inherited personality characteristics of his great-grandfather, those blinding rays of Goethe's genius, were radiating from his own personality.

But the scientist in Jung would always remain just his "number one personality," his day side, his compromise to a skeptical world that insisted on erasing magic from life, a feat as impossible to the night side of Jung's personality as removing the stars from the evening sky. His belief in reincarnation is one of many renditions of a melody of eternal recurrence that plays throughout Jung's inner and outer lives.

Jung felt a special kinship with Goethe by age fifteen, after his first of many readings of *Faust*. "It poured into my soul like a miraculous balm," he recalled.[32] Faust, the learned scholar who has many doctorates but is "no wiser than before," is the seeker of truth who sacrifices the realm of the intellect to turn to the magical invocation of spirts for occult wisdom. Jung regarded Goethe's *Faust* as a new dispensation, a product of revelation, a contribution to the world of religious experience as a new sacred text. In 1932 he wrote in a letter, "*Faust* is the most recent pillar in that bridge of the spirit which spans the morass of world history, beginning with the Gilgamesh epic, the *I Ching*, the Upanishads, the *Tao-te-Ching*, the fragments of Heraclitus, and continuing in the Gospel of St. John, the letters of St. Paul, in Meister Eckhardt and in Dante."[33] In his eyes, Goethe became "a prophet," especially for confirming the autonomous reality of "evil" and "the mysterious role it played in delivering man from darkness and suffering."[34]

The public expression of Jung's position on reincarnation, to be found in the chapter "On Life After Death" in *MDR,* is that he keeps "a free and open mind" and is not "in a position to assert a definite opinion," while at the same time several cryptic pages are devoted to "hints" of his past lives. In fact, Jung says at one point, "Recently, however, I observed in myself a series of dreams which would seem to describe the process of reincarnation in a deceased person of my acquaintance." After remarking that he has "never come across any such dreams in other persons," he has no basis for comparison and therefore chooses "not to go into it any further." He does admit, however, that "after this experience I view the problem of reincarnation with somewhat different eyes."[35] But we know from archival sources that his private opinion was that these dreams confirmed to him that he had been Goethe in a previous incarnation.[36]

"I know no answer to the question of whether the karma which I live is the outcome of my past lives, or whether it is not rather the achievement of my ancestors, whose heritage comes together in me," Jung confessed in *MDR*. "Am I a combination of the lives of these ancestors and do I embody these lives again? Have I lived before in the past as a specific personality, and did I progress so far in that life that I am now able to seek a solution? I do not know."[37]

Yet reincarnation implies *many* existences, and Jung did not end his metaphysical antecedents with Goethe. In replies to questions about his possible past lives, Jung sometimes claimed he was Meister Eckhardt.[38] Eckhardt, born in Erfurt in 1260, was considered one of the most profoundly philosophical and original of all the Christian mystics. Eckhardt (like Jung) used poetical expression and paradox to convey the meaning of his beliefs about God, which can be easily interpreted as pantheism. In 1329, Pope John XXII condemned portions of his writings as heretical.

The addition of Eckhardt to Goethe brings Jung's inner fatherland into focus. The fact that he believed in an immortal soul or life after death or even reincarnation is no revelation to those who read him, or who read between the lines of *MDR*. As Jung himself maintained, beliefs about such matters are always deeply subjective and inordinately personal, which is precisely why Jung's speculations about his own past lives are so revealing—and so difficult to accept unless we first understand the worlds in which he lived, both inner and outer fatherlands.

The ethnic pattern of his incarnations is what is so important. His own logic mirrors that of his culture, and is consistent, indisputable, and racial: Jung is the perfected result of the evolution of his ancestors, whose heritage converges in him. And it is always German genius, the genius of his *Volk*.

TWO

Summoning the Spirits

One month before he turned twenty, and just two after he was officially matriculated into medical school, Carl Jung began his first formal dialogues with the Dead. In June 1895, he and a circle of female kin—like a coven of white witches—first gathered in secrecy to contact the spirit world. He had already reached the commanding height and bulging weight that framed him throughout most of his life. His hair was cropped military short in the Prussian style. While youthful and unsure of himself, to most people he seemed stiff, perhaps a bit arrogant. Those who knew him well considered that behind his severe, sometimes contemptuous, pronouncements on people and events and his dismissive remarks—particularly to and about women—lay a sensitive boy playing at being a man. Girls were enthralled by his height and broad shoulders, his piercing intellect and delightful wit, his promise as a man and as a mate. And women who were a bit older than this wunderkind admired all this and more, for they sensed his acute emotional sensitivity, an alluring quality—almost an aura—that set him apart from most men. For his part, Jung himself was more comfortable in the company of women than in the company of men, and from this important month onward Jung often found himself presiding over groups of women, many of whom adored him.

Although Jung concealed many of the details of these youthful meetings in his published work (sometimes contradicting himself), his experiences with spiritualism were far more important to his later worldview and psychotherapeutic techniques than he would have wished those outside his inner circle to know.[1] By the time of the First World War, when Jung was developing the concepts of his psychological theories, spiritualism was resurging in popularity, but to many—particularly to academics and medical professionals—it still bore the taint of its history of frauds and scandals. Hence, his own public statements on the subject were always framed within the safe containers of psychiatric or philosophical jargon. He would later claim the philosophies of Kant and Schopenhauer and William James, or the psychiatric theories of Pierre Janet, Théodore Flournoy, or Sigmund Freud had shaped his own theories, but these were only intellectual masks for inexplicable paranormal phenomena that he himself had directly, vividly, experienced.

Jung's early encounters with the spirit world bore fruit in his later psychiatric career (especially after his final break with Freud in January 1913), but the influence of spiritualism on his early thought is apparent in the lectures he gave to his medical-school fraternity, the Zofingia, to which his father had also belonged as a student. As the noted historian of psychiatry Henri Ellenberger observed, "The germinal cell of Jung's analytic psychology is to be found in his discussions of the Zofingia Students Association and in his experiments with his young medium cousin, Hélène Preiswerk."[2] Therefore, the events of 1895 marked the opening of a door that never completely closed, an invitation to countless discarnate voices and prescient entities that Jung would consult—and teach others to consult—for the rest of his life. Spiritualist techniques of visionary-trance induction not only introduced Jung to his deceased ancestors but also to the spirits and gods of the Land of the Dead, who, under various pseudonyms of psychological jargon, remained his traveling companions along the trails of life. Jung never lost his "will to believe," to use the words of William James, and this attracts disciples to him even now.

But June 1895 altered Jung's fate in other ways. It brought him his first sweet, bitter tastes of lust and love. And soon, too, of death. Jung invited four female relatives to participate in an experiment at his home outside Basel, where his father was a pastor. As the cabal gathered for its first spiritualist séance, the Reverend Paul Jung lay mortally ill in bed like the long-suffering King Amfortas in Wagner's *Parsifal*. By autumn he would take to his bed for the last time. Unlike Amfortas, Paul Jung never received the healing touch of a savior knight and, on January 28, 1896, he finally expired. Six months earlier, in September 1895, also after a period of illness, death came to Rudolph Preiswerk, the protective older brother of Jung's mother. Uncle Rudolph was the father of two of the young participants in the séances. The lingering deaths of Rudolph Preiswerk and Paul Jung were omens that presaged the dissolution of the thin barrier that separates the living from the dead.

Perhaps it was the impending demises of Rudolph Preiswerk and Paul Jung that motivated the group to experiment with spiritualism at that time, or maybe it was simply the fact that the table-tipping fad had piqued the curiosity of a group of people who already believed in the immortal soul and in a world of spirits and then sought direct proof of its existence. Certainly, the members of this particular group were ripe for such experiments, and Jung was eager to show them the way.

By the age of nineteen, as Jung claims in *MDR,* he had experienced remarkable divisions within his own subjective sense of self, knowing—or guessing—that in addition to his everyday nominal "self" or "number one personality," a deeper, older, indeed ancient, personality lay within him. This wiser and older "number two personality" was somehow connected with the ancestors, with the Dead, and with spiritual mysteries. Was it a part of his present self, a previous incarnation, or the spirit of a deceased man who possessed him? Jung was intrigued by his inner experiences of multiplicity and conquered his fears of them by earnestly seeking answers, first through books, then through his own spiritualist practices.

At forty-seven, the oldest member of the séance circle was Carl Jung's mother, Emilie Preiswerk Jung, whom Jung said had at least two distinct personalities. When Emilie met Paul Jung, the Preiswerks, like the Jungs, were among the most prominent families in Basel. Unlike the Jungs, who had been in Switzerland only since 1821, the Preiswerks could boast of roots going back five centuries. Yet Carl Jung's German cultural identity superseded the civilizing influences of his Swiss and Christian upbringing.[3] In an age when heredity was destiny, he was biologically guided to fulfill his karmic fate as a descendant of an important German family and as a member of the *Volk.* But however prominent the inherited legacy of his male ancestors, it was through the rejected mother-world, through his Swiss mother and relatives, that Jung believed he was granted the gift of second sight. From the Preiswerks he learned the techniques for his own form of mediumship, a practice he would legitimize in Zurich in 1916 with the term "active imagination."

Jung's maternal grandfather, the Reverend Samuel Preiswerk, was a man of many talents.[4] He was chief of the Protestant clergy of Basel, a professor of Old Testament exegesis and oriental languages at the Evangelical Institution in Geneva, an acclaimed Hebrew scholar, a poet, a composer of religious hymns, and a man who regularly spoke to spirits. The spirits of the Dead were everywhere among the living and could be addressed, but only if one knew their language. He believed that Hebrew was the language of heaven (he was not alone in this regard!), and he fully expected to speak to the Old Testament prophets and his savior in their divine tongue. In order to fulfill biblical prophecy, Samuel Preiswerk actively sought the return of the Jews to a homeland of their own in Palestine, and Theodor Herzl acknowledged him as an early Zionist. According to the family legends, he would talk to the spirit of his deceased first wife in weekly séances while locked in his study, much to the dismay of his second wife and the fascination of his children, including his favorite, Emilie. He taught her and his other children to stand behind him and chase away the spirits when he gave his sermons, for he and the family earnestly believed that the air around them was crowded with the chattering masses of the Dead. Emilie believed herself to have second sight, and throughout her life had precognitive dreams and other paranormal experiences that she attributed to messages from the Dead. She kept a diary, now in the possession of the Jung family, of these clairvoyant episodes.[5] Carl Jung never made any secret of the fact that, in addition to being a hysteric, his mother was also a psychic, and a good one at that.

Emilie was the youngest of the twelve children of Samuel Preiswerk's second wife, Augusta Faber, a clairvoyant and spirit-seer in her own right, whose psychic abilities appeared at the age of twenty after a dissociative crisis in which she lay for thirty-six hours in a deathlike cataleptic trance. Consistent with the treatment methods of that time, she awoke from her absent state when the tip of a red-hot iron poker was applied to the crown of her head. Upon waking, she was said to immediately begin babbling prophecies. This pattern of falling into trance and then awakening to reveal information from the world beyond was repeated throughout her life. Carl Jung believed that his mother and his daughter Agathe had inherited their psychic abilities from his grandmother Augusta.

Emilie Preiswerk Jung was closest to her brother Rudolph, and he became the official godfather of Carl Gustav Jung, Emilie's first surviving child. Rudolph himself spawned children in the double digits, including two daughters who were members of Jung's spiritualist circle: Louise (nicknamed "Luggy"), who was twenty-one when the first séance was held, and Hélène, who was thirteen and a half.

Hélène Preiswerk—known throughout her life as "Helly"—was born in 1881, the eleventh of Rudolph's fifteen children. It was apparent to everyone that she was somehow different from the lot. She was a dreamy child, difficult at times, detached yet canny. High-strung and spritelike, she had large, captivating brown eyes that held the gaze of others with an almost hypnotic urgency. Given the magical atmosphere created by the grandparents, it is not surprising that many within the Preiswerk family would have an interest in the spiritualism fad that had begun in the 1850s. Helly's encounter with spiritualism changed her life.

"We have a gifted medium in our midst"

In her 1975 book, *C. G. Jungs Medium,* Stephanie Zumstein-Preiswerk—Helly's niece—combines information from unpublished family documents with the reminiscences of her father (Helly's older brother), her mother (a school friend of Helly) and others in the Preiswerk and Jung families to construct a semifictional narrative of her aunt's career as C. G. Jung's Trilby to his Svengali. The essential information in the book fits with what we know about the histories of the Preiswerk and Jung families and seems to be a more reliable account of Jung's life between 1895 and 1903 than has previously been reported; in fact, it is more consistent with the known facts than any of Jung's own published remarks on this episode in his life.

On that fateful night in June 1895, the first séance proved more remarkable than anyone could have dreamed. Jung sat in the ring of women around the large, round wooden table, presiding nervously. As was the custom in table-tipping groups, he placed a water glass in the center. It would be disturbed if, any minute, imperceptible levitation of the table occurred. He instructed everyone to rest their hands gently on the table, and hold hands by lightly touching fingertips. After a few moments in complete silence, the air suddenly felt thick, electric. Without warning, the water glass on the table began to shake violently. Despite himself, Jung was as terrified as the rest. With great difficulty he exclaimed, "We have a gifted medium in our midst."[6] At that point, young Helly blanched and slumped back in her chair. To everyone's amazement, she began to speak.

"Grandfather visits us," she said eerily, as if she were a stranger to herself and those around her. "I must set off on a journey. Ask where he sends me. It is my place to accept." Her body then went slack, and she fell to the floor. Scared out of their wits, Jung and Luggy lifted her up and placed her on a sofa.

Jung was the first to come to his senses. "Where's Helly?" he asked the entranced girl. "Answer me, you spirit, you kidnapped her!"

Suddenly the girl sat up. Her eyelids fluttered open, and she began to respond. But her voice sounded like that of an old man. "Don't be afraid!" huskily commanded the voice. "I am with you every day, your father

Samuel, who lives with God. Pray to the Lord and ask him to please make sure my grandchild reaches her goal, as she finds herself now over the North Pole in icy heights. That is the shortest way to America." Grandfather Preiswerk, the old reverend, now possessed the thirteen-year-old body of his granddaughter. Grandfather Preiswerk would be the primary spokesman during each of the first three 1895 séances, acting as a sort of spirit guide or "control" for Helly.

"Why America?" asked Jung in all seriousness. The answer he received made it apparent that, like the shamans of old, Helly's soul had left her body and had embarked on a "magical flight" in order to save the soul of another.

"Soon Helly will reach São Paulo. She is now flying over the Isthmus of Panama. She is to stop the Blacks (the Mestizos) from taking hold of Bertha [the older sister of Emilie and the aunt of Jung, Helly, and Luggy]."

But it was too late. Helly's soul didn't reach Brazil in time to help Bertha. In a deep voice, Grandfather Preiswerk urged them all to pray for Bertha because she had already "given birth to a little nigger" ("Berthi hat soeber ein kleines Negerlein geboren"). In 1893, Bertha had emigrated to Brazil and had, in fact, given birth to a black baby after marrying a man of mixed race. Allegedly, Helly had no knowledge of any of this prior to her first trance.

Although two Jung-Preiswerk patriarchs were fatally ill, the possible birth of "a little nigger" to Bertha—the introduction of a "degenerate" strain into the family line—appeared to be the greater family trauma. Now, Grandfather Preiswerk, a good Christian soldier even beyond the grave, returned on that first evening to urge those there to pray for God to forgive his fallen daughter.

A second séance was held in July. To prevent Helly from entering another deep trance in which her soul would once again fly far from her body, Jung changed the technique. This time he devised a kind of a letter board, much like the Ouija boards of today. An empty water glass would act as a planchette, moving from the center of the table onto the surrounding circle of little slips of papers containing letters and numbers. Words were spelled out letter by letter until the message became clear. Helly warned Jung that, for the second experiment, "I no longer want to travel so far." She had been exhausted after the initial séance, and this time when "Grandfather" appeared, she wanted the others to make her wishes clear to him. Helly was afraid that she would die during one of these trances if the thin thread that connected her soul to her body snapped inadvertently.

This time Helly planted two fingers of her right hand on the overturned container. The glass suddenly began to dance across the table, moving quickly from letter to letter as Jung transcribed. Once again, Grandfather Preiswerk introduced himself and told them not to be afraid. This time he brought along "Carl's grandfather, Professor Jung," who remained silent throughout the proceedings.

Following this last message, Helly sank back in her chair in a semiconscious state. Jung moved her to the sofa, where he took the pale medium's pulse. After a while she told everyone in her own voice that she had seen Grandfather Preiswerk and Grandfather Jung arm in arm in conversation like two old friends. Jung was provoked to remark, "I thought these two spirits couldn't stand one another when they were alive and that they barely knew one another."

Helly then began a bizarre narrative about seeing spirits all around her, including one that placed roses in her hands. Then she woke up fully, miffed, telling Jung he should leave, and that "He doesn't deserve the flowers." The second séance was finished. On the whole it had been much less dramatic than the first, but following Jung's urging, the group agreed to meet again.

A week later, on a hot Saturday evening in July, the spiritualist circle once again congregated around the old wooden table at the parsonage in Kleinhüningen that had belonged to Grandfather Preiswerk. At this sitting Helly almost immediately fell—literally—into a trance. Jung put her on the sofa. Soon she lifted her head and said that he should leave the room. "I must report something which is not meant for his ears."

Not wishing to give in totally to her demands, Jung removed himself from the room but stood just near the door, out of sight. Helly stood up and, accompanied by vivid gesturing, claimed that her older sister Dini (Celestine) had sinned mightily and had fallen deeply from grace. (She had recently married but was about to give birth to a child scandalously soon after the ceremony.) Having made this pronouncement, Helly began to lose consciousness. With a sigh she fell into a deep sleep, lying rigidly on the sofa after becoming cadaverously pale. But she wasn't done.

"Will you forgive your sister?" intoned Helly in the voice that everyone now recognized as that of Grandfather Preiswerk. "Her body has sinned, not her spirit." Helly's grandfather then made an awful prophecy: "But the child must die. I can't save it." This proved to be uncannily true (at least according to the family legend), for near the end of August 1895 Dini gave birth to a physically defective child who died soon after birth. After a second such tragedy the following year, it was revealed that Dini had syphilis. Unable to accept this, Dini insisted that she had been bewitched by her mother-in-law.

This third séance would prove to be the last for the next two years.

After Helly's father died in September, her uncle Samuel (the first child of the old reverend) had learned of Jung's experiments and forbade Helly's participation. The excuse was Helly's religious instruction for confirmation, a long process in those days. During the typical two-year period that climaxed with the reception of first communion, piety was expected to replace youthful frivolity, and special religious instruction precluded simple entertainment, let alone acting as a medium at a séance. Helly received this instruction from Samuel, who was a strict Pietist. He was also violently opposed to dabbling in spookery and did not share the fascination with contacting the dead that occupied most of his family and his disagreeable nephew, Carl.

Jung was furious. He had carefully planned the strategy of the séances and had been keeping detailed notes. To have his experiments cut off in midstream seemed tremendously unfair. Despite—or perhaps because of—the fact that his father was a pastor, Jung rarely attended Sunday church services himself and instead spent the day of rest reading. But his choice of reading material was, as we shall see, highly unorthodox.

Mostly, Jung read the literature of spiritualism and of psychical research (the British Society for Psychical Research had existed since 1882 to promote the scientific study of such phenomena). Using this literature as his model, Jung's practice of scrupulously documenting the séances with Helly points to his intention to use or publish the material. The interruption of the séances compromised this long-term goal.

Helly, for her part, had wanted to continue the sessions with Jung and in the long interim found herself prone to quasi-trance states and intuitive pronouncements about poltergeists in the Jung household. To feed the flames of their interest in spiritualism, Jung sent Helly and Luggy many books on the subject, inscribing them with the date and with encouraging messages. Jung wasn't going to let go of his cousins too soon. Helly he needed as his medium; Luggy he had fallen in love with. But as she was his first cousin, this was one flower that could not fully bloom.

Other events, however, eclipsed these setbacks.[7] Jung began attending medical-school classes and Zofingia fraternity meetings in the latter half of 1895. In January 1896, his father died, leaving him, his mother, and his young sister without any source of income. Although he never acknowledged it in *MDR*, he received significant financial support for medical school from the Preiswerk family, who made sure he had opportunities to make money—such as selling off one Preiswerk's antiques—to pay back what they had loaned him. When a new pastor was found in April to replace Paul Jung, the family had to leave the parsonage of Kleinhüningen. Eduard Preiswerk, himself a pastor in St. Leonhard, saved the family from homelessness by placing them in a house he owned at Bottminger Mill. The Jungs lived there with Emilie's sister Auguste, Jung's "Aunt Gusteli," who was said to be like a second mother to him. Jung remained there until he moved to Zurich in December 1900.

Reading philosophy, seeking spirits

There is no doubt that during his medical-school years Jung believed in the potential of human beings to communicate with discarnate or otherworldly entities. Yet the usual grounding of spiritualist practices in Christian beliefs left him cold. His disillusionment with Christian dogma and ritual fueled his skepticism about the veracity of the all-too-Christian messages that were usually sent from beyond the grave. Could there be a non-Christian spirit world? And if so, what would this say about the true nature of religion and its place in the everyday lives of human beings? How could the monotheism of his own Judeo-Christian civilization be reconciled with evidence of a polydaemonic spirit world? And what would the greater implications of such evidence be for the nature of individual human existence? His relentless curiosity about these questions in his early twenties led him along some unusual paths.

Jung realized that he needed to put the mediumistic phenomena of Helly into a wider intellectual context outside traditional Christian thought. He began to read ravenously on a variety of subjects that were clearly far beyond the medical texts he was required to study. Particularly after the death of his father in January 1896, Jung read widely in the traditional Protestant theology of his day, heterodox theological works (David Friedrich Strauss and Ernest Renan on the "historical Jesus"), Christian mysticism (Meister Eckhardt, Jakob Boehme, Nicholas Cusanus, the eighteenth-century spiritualist theology of Emanuel Swedenborg, the romantic mysticism of Gustav Fechner), Pietist autobiographies (Jung-Stilling), philosophy (Immanuel Kant, Arthur Schopenhauer, Eduard von Hartmann, Plato, Plotinus, Heraclitus, Empedocles, and, by 1898, Friedrich Nietzsche), German Romantic natural philosophy (Goethe, Carl Gustav Carus, Josef Goerres, F.W.J. Schelling), and evolutionary biology (Lamarck, Darwin, Ernst Haeckel).

Psychiatric texts—especially the works of French alienists of the "dissociationist" school who studied hypnosis, hysteria, and multiple personalities, men such as J. M. Charcot, Pierre Janet, Théodule Ribot, Alfred Binet, and Théodore Flournoy—were a small part of his extracurricular reading. Of course, they became a special area of focus after December

1900, when Jung's psychiatric career formally began at the time he assumed a position in Zurich at the Burghölzli hospital for mental disorders.

Jung's most extensive readings, however, were in occultism, mesmerism, psychical research, and spiritualism, all areas that touched upon deep personal concerns. The existence of the human soul and its survival after death were open questions that still required answers, and during his medical-school days his heroes were psychical researchers who approached this problem scientifically, such as William Crookes, J.C.F. Zoellner, Cesare Lombroso, F.W.H. Myers, and William James.[8] All of them speculated about a medium outside of the known constraints of time, three-dimensional space, and causality that would account for such phenomena as thought transference and precognition. Some argued that evidence for such phenomena also supported the hypothesis of postmortem survival or the existence of other realities coexistent with our own. Zoellner, for example, in *Transcendental Physics* (1879), hypothesized the existence of a "fourth dimension" of reality as a place from which "four dimensional beings" occasionally entered our experiential world through the filter of the symbolic contents of our own memories and mind, an idea that Jung reworked again and again throughout a lifetime of speculation on parapsychological phenomena.[9] Indeed, we can only conclude that Jung's encounter with his spiritual guru Philemon during the First World War derived from his youthful desire to communicate with the sorts of fourth-dimensional beings that Zoellner claimed were likely to exist.

Jung was single-minded in his pursuit of a particular kind of knowledge. It appears that even his extensive readings in philosophy were guided primarily by his quest for a true understanding of the human soul and the conditions under which postmortem survival was possible. Jung felt that the opinions of respected philosophers legitimized the unconventional obsessions that set him apart from many of his fellow students and from the majority of the scientific community. Although he claimed throughout his life that Kant and Schopenhauer were major influences on his ideas about the nature of the unconscious mind, it is primarily their writings on the spirit world that he had in mind, not their major works that are traditionally studied. Jung was never a very sophisticated student of philosophy, and most of his philosophical knowledge was absorbed secondarily and only as it pertained to the survival of the human soul beyond the body and the three dimensions of conscious human experience.

Kant's analysis of the prophetic experiences of the Swedish clairvoyant Emanuel Swedenborg, a little book entitled *Dreams of a Spirit-Seer* (1766),[10] was a particular favorite of Jung's during these years, and he mentioned it in his Zofingia lectures and in his earliest publications. Kant's discussion of how experiences of the future can be obtained in the present even though they violate the known a priori categories of experience of space, time, and causality became the basis of all subsequent discussions of paranormal phenomena throughout the nineteenth century. As for Schopenhauer, the one work that Jung seemed to be most familiar with was his *Essay on Spirit-Seeing* (1851), which affirmed the validity of hypnotic phenomena and clairvoyance. Schopenhauer offers the theory that all visions of future events are "allegorical or symbolical"[11]—that is, they are filtered through the personal memories and symbolic system of the individual clairvoyant. Furthermore, according to Schopenhauer, all visions of the Dead are merely clairvoyant visions of a "past reality," an ability he calls "retrospective second sight," and are not to be regarded as proof of a living spirit world.[12] Yet based on evidence that the "will" operates independently of time and space and can affect others at a distance, Schopenhauer leaves open the possibility of a spiritual existence not dependent on the body.

Jung-Stilling, animal magnetism, and the spirit world

The theory of animal magnetism and the practice of trance induction and of magnetic healings and exorcisms flourished in the popular culture of France and Germany at this time. Many early nineteenth-century German natural philosophers, often physicians by training, experimented with mesmerism to learn about the forces of nature and the cosmos without embracing the spiritualist uses of such techniques. However, the more widely read researchers did explore the spirit world through mesmerism, and this literature was familiar to Jung during his student years. As we know from his own published statements and the recollections of colleagues from that time, two books from this genre were of singular importance to him.

The first of these was written by Johann Heinrich Jung, the Pietist, under his pseudonym Heinrich Jung-Stilling, and appeared in 1808 as *Theorie der Geister-Kunde* (roughly, The theory of spiritualism).[13] It is a curious book, blending Christian dogma and speculations about the spirit world in a way that echoes the works of Swedenborg. Anecdotal, almost folkloric, fully three quarters of it is filled with wondrous tales of second sight, prophecies that came true, precognitive dreams, and, especially, ghost stories. The rest focuses on his own encounter with animal magnetism, and fifty-five propositions that he derived from his researches.[14]

Jung-Stilling reports on his experiments with animal magnetism, putting subjects into trances and observing the resulting phenomena. For

Jung-Stilling, a Pietist and an old hand at the psychological techniques of directing his attention to his internal fantasy world, the "magnetic visions" induced through mesmerist procedures had the ring of familiarity. Many still considered animal magnetism a viable scientific theory to explain certain psychophysical phenomena that fit with new knowledge about galvanism, electricity, magnetism, and the luminiferous ether that excited the scientific community. As Carl Jung would also argue in an 1897 lecture, Jung-Stilling points to the scientific evidence of mesmeric and paranormal phenomena as evidence that the human soul could exist independent of the body. Proposition nine of Jung-Stilling's grand theory states that "Animal Magnetism undeniably proves that we have an inward man, a soul, which is constituted of the divine spark, the immortal spirit possessing reason and will, and of a luminous body which is inseparable from it."[15] In proposition thirteen he assures his readers that all of his propositions are scientific because they are derived from "certain inferences which I have drawn from experiments with animal magnetism." Furthermore, "these most important experiments undeniably show that the soul does not require the organs of sense in order to see, hear, smell, taste and feel, in a much more perfect state; but with this great difference, that in such a state, it stands in much nearer connexion with the spiritual than the material world."[16] Human experience, even of the transcendent, is mediated through our psychic reality of the five senses, according to Jung-Stilling, and so spirits and other extramundane "beings" of "the created world" do not appear to us in their true state (as they are "organized" differently), but reflect our own psychophysical "organization" of reality. However, Jung-Stilling did warn in propositions twenty-three and twenty-four that it was a sin to use these trances to foretell the future or to communicate with spirits, even though such trances made this possible. By the time he began his own experiments with spiritualism, its alleged "sinfulness" would have been no real concern to Carl Jung.

Jung-Stilling distinguishes the "real" experience of apparitions of the Dead from mere "visions," which are waking dreams that exist only in the imagination and hence are "unreal." However, as Jung would also argue a century later, there are some people who are predisposed to visions, but their inclination also opens a door to other dimensions of reality that allow them to see apparitions and divine the future. "Hysterical and hypochondriacal persons are inclined to visions," Jung-Stilling wrote. "They have them either with or without fits . . . [They] develop their faculty of presentiment, so that they easily come into connexion with the invisible world. Every thing is then jumbled together, and much knowledge and experience is necessary to distinguish a vision from a real apparition."[17]

When psychiatrists and psychologists began to study spiritualist mediums at the end of the nineteenth century within the prevailing medical theories, terms such as "hysteria," "hypnosis," "dissociation," and "doubling of personality" were used to explain the pathological basis of the mediums' personalities and trances. Even Jung, who in 1902 devoted his doctoral dissertation to this issue, believed that spiritualist mediums may or may not have genuine psychic abilities, but they all share an affliction with hysteria. It is clear that Jung had made these connections between hypnosis, hysteria, and spiritualism long before he ever read a single psychiatric textbook.

The Seeress of Prevorst

Jung-Stilling's long-forgotten book is an important clue to Jung's earliest beliefs about the nature of personal reality. Yet of the vast, strange literature on spiritualism it was Justinius Kerner's extensive case history of a young clairvoyant woman in the German town of Prevorst that became Jung's model for his very first publication as an alienist. This book, *Die Seherin von Prevorst* (1829), also became Helly's training manual for mature trance mediumship.[18] Jung had given it to his cousin for her fifteenth birthday in 1896. Although not much of a reader, Helly reread Kerner's account of the most famous medium of the early nineteenth century many times.

It is not hard to see why Carl Jung and his cousin were so fascinated by this book. Kerner employs language that has a psychological ring to it. In his detailed descriptions of the "inner world" of the Seeress and her "inner eyes" or "spiritual eyes" that allowed her to witness apparitions, we find precursors to Jung's later attempts to reductively psychologize paranormal experiences in public statements, while in private pursuing the possibility of communication with the Dead. Many of Jung's later paradoxical opinions concerning the tension between the nature of "psychic reality" (our experienced psychological reality) and the actual reality of spirits and the spirit world can be traced directly to this book, although its contents are virtually unknown to most people interested in Jung and his ideas.

Justinius Kerner, the impresario of the seeress, was the appointed city physician of the town of Weinsberg in the German state of Württemberg. He was also a minor Romantic poet and the host of a salon that brought philosophers, theologians, writers, poets, and even royalty to his home for stimulating conversations. As part of his medical therapies he on occasion "magnetized" his patients and, if they were deemed to be spiritually possessed, he performed his own exorcisms.

On November 25, 1826, a twenty-five-year-old married woman, Frau Friedericke Hauffe, was brought to Kerner at his home, gravely ill: skeletal, pale, barely breathing, and wrapped in a white gown like that of a nun. He had treated her once before in her own town of Prevorst, but with no real success. For the previous five years she had suffered from a multitude of physical and psychological complaints of unknown cause: intermittent headaches and other bodily pains, paroxysmal "spasms" of writhing in her bed, fevers, night sweats, diarrhea, crying fits, gums that bled to the point that she lost all her teeth, reclusiveness, and, most mysteriously, somnambulisms or trancelike episodes. During these latter "magnetic" episodes of illness she would regularly see the spirits of the Dead near her, particularly family members and people from her village. Sometimes she had visions that presaged the deaths of others, in one instance seeing an image of a coffin with her paternal grandfather in it six weeks before his death. She foretold her own death in a similar vision three weeks before it happened. The "magnetic passes" of the hands of local physicians over her body and trials of homeopathic remedies calmed her for a while, but then misfortune intervened. In February 1823, she gave birth to her first child, but it died in August, plunging her into a depression that rendered her almost comatose, indeed being "so much afflicted, that she became cold and stiff as a corpse." Bathing and other standard treatments of the day helped to revive her, but, according to Kerner, "she always lay as in a dream."[19]

In the three-year period just prior to being brought to Kerner, Hauffe began to develop the talents that would eventually evolve into the later manifestations that made her famous as the Seeress of Prevorst. For example, as she lay in bed in her home she claimed that "she heard and felt what happened at a distance," and since she had become "so sensible to magnetic influences" the nails in the walls of her room had to be removed because they irritated her. She also became hypersensitive to light and avoided it at all costs, traveling only in enclosed carriages. It was also during this period that she developed the gift of ghost-seeing, and "for the first time, she began to see another person behind the one she was looking at," often viewing the Dead in the company of the living in the roles of guardians or "protecting spirits."[20] She claimed to have no organic strength of her own but instead survived only by "magnetically" drawing life force from others through her eyes and fingertips. "She admitted that she gained most strength from the eyes of powerful men."[21] Others felt themselves being drained of energy in her presence, as if they were victims of a psychic vampire.

After other physicians treated her "magnetically" and gave her special powders and amulets—all to no avail—Kerner was finally summoned.

Suspicious of all the previous medical attempts, especially magnetic ones, he immediately ordered that such methods be stopped until he could observe her at length. He had come reluctantly to Prevorst because he had long heard the gossip about her and doubted that he could help her, as he believed she was a hopeless malingerer. "I had never seen her," Kerner wrote, "but I had heard many false and perverted accounts of her; and I must confess that I shared the world's opinions, and gave credit to its lies."[22] Kerner came and went, leaving instructions with a local physician for a new regimen of treatments. It soon became clear that the special tonics he had ordered were not working. Her friends attempted their own exorcism of the "demoniacal influence" through long prayer vigils. Finally, said Kerner, "much against my will, they brought her to Weinsberg to see if anything could be done for her there."

Friedericke Hauffe remained at Kerner's consulting room for almost three years. No one could have predicted the curious therapeutic relationship that developed between the doctor and his patient, an experience that transformed both healer and patient and made them two of the most famous people of the nineteenth century.

The story of their celebrated collaboration began with a therapeutic innovation by Kerner that later became a standard psychotherapeutic technique: allowing the patient to express her own thoughts and needs. One day when Hauffe had lapsed into a dissociative trance state, Kerner suspected that he could communicate with an intelligent source within the patient despite the deep disturbance in her sense of self. Simply, he asked her what course of treatment she thought might be helpful, and thus began the pattern of the Seeress prescribing her own treatments. Not surprisingly, she often recommended mesmeric treatments, which then seemed to lead to a recovery of strength the next day. Kerner carefully recorded her reactions to various materials, such as magnetized and unmagnetized water, a spider's web, metals, laurel leaves, minerals, plants, precious gems, and even animal parts thought to have healing properties, such as the hoof of an elephant (which produced an epileptic fit in her), the nipples of a horse, and the tooth of a wooly mammoth.

The few details we know about Hauffe's personal history do not provide many clues to the origins of her later career. Kerner tells us that she was the daughter of a gamekeeper in Prevorst. She had little formal education other than what she gleaned from her Bible and psalm book. Kerner points this out because the Seeress's sophisticated prophecies and verse compositions are seemingly inconsistent with this lack of significant formal education. To Kerner and others this seemed compelling evidence for the ability of trance states to give people access to ancient spiritual mysteries or to higher forms of knowledge. (Jung made similar, if less plausible, disclaimers about his own patients' lack of formal education or prior exposure to occult symbolism or mythological themes when arguing for the existence of an impersonal or collective unconscious that he believed was the true source of such symbols.)

Hauffe's strange ability to diagnose the physical conditions of others by looking into their left eye and then to prescribe successful courses of treatment brought a steady stream of people to her for consultations. Although practically bedridden, she enjoyed the repeated visits of the theologians David Friedrich Strauss and Friedrich Schleiermacher, as well as meetings with philosophers such as Friedrich Schelling, Josef Goerres, Franz von Baader, Adam Carl August von Eschenmayer, and Gotthilf von Schubert. Many of these visitors later wrote about their impressions of the Seeress and, accepting her phenomena as genuine, several contributed their own theories on the origins and significance of what they observed. Jung read, and in most cases owned, these commentaries.

One of the more interesting psychological theories put forth by the Seeress herself was the notion that subjective emotional states could be externalized and perceived, symbolically, as apparitions. Hauffe insisted that everyone had a "protecting spirit" who stood behind them at all times—in her case, her deceased grandmother. However, when she saw apparitions hovering around another person, "sometimes this appeared to be his protecting spirit, and at others the image of his inner self."[23] Later, in his formal public statements, Jung always adopted a "psychological" explanation for ghosts and apparitions and seemingly clairvoyant visions. But in private Jung spoke quite differently.

Among the most mysterious pronouncements of the Seeress of Prevorst were her decidedly unorthodox metaphysical theories about the spiritual nature of human beings. Borrowing a compass from Kerner one day, she drew a series of elaborately designed concentric circles to represent the shades of spiritual existence and the passage of time. Of these were eight idiosyncratic "sun circles" and one "life circle," which represented her own life. The rings of the circles corresponded, in part, to areas of "magnetic" influence over the body. In many respects they resembled diagrams of the planetary orbits of the solar system, or cross-sections of the Earth. These diagrams made a powerful impression on both Helly Preiswerk and her older cousin, and similar illustrations appeared in Jung's publications throughout the next sixty years.

On August 5, 1829, after failing to recover from one of her many physical crises, the Seeress of Prevorst died. The following night, Justinius Kerner saw her and two other female forms in a dream, relieved that in the spirit world she had "apparently perfectly recovered."[24] An autopsy revealed abnormalities in the heart, liver, and gall bladder, but Kerner was quick to emphasize to his readers that the postmortem found absolutely no abnormalities in her brain or nervous system.

Kerner's descriptions of the extraordinary states of consciousness of the Seeress—states of mind that seemed to offer the promise of direct contact with the Dead or, perhaps, access to genius—tempted the curious and the bored, believers and doubters, to open the same doors of perception.[25] Some—like Helly Preiswerk and Carl Jung—opened doors that they quickly discovered they could never close again.

A return to the "border zones"

In autumn 1897, the spirits returned to the Jung household.

Confirmed as a Christian in good standing, Helly was able to resume the most important role of her young life. She was especially eager to once again be the center of Jung's attention. She didn't hesitate when he approached her about resuming the séances, although there was considerable pressure from her uncle and her mother to keep away from such things. This time additional deception was required. According to her niece, Helly used the excuse that she was going to the Jung home to work in the garden.[26]

Although the early trials were experimental, exploratory, Jung had mastered the spiritualist literature and had received just enough scientific training to see the greater possibilities inherent in this project. In fact, Jung had already given two lectures to the Zofingia fraternity that demonstrated his budding theoretical views on spiritualist phenomena.[27] He felt confident enough in the reality of spiritualist phenomena and in his opinions about their great religious and scientific significance that he zealously defended such ideas in a community of his peers. Jung turned the séances from a parlor game into a more serious affair, at times inviting his medical-student colleagues to witness Helly's phenomena and to make their own judgments.

In the new series of séances, Helly's trances took on an entirely new character. Grandfather Preiswerk receded in importance as Helly's "control" spirit, and instead a crowd of deceased personages took turns speaking to the group. Some of these were based on actual historical persons, others claimed to be barons and baronesses who seemed to have fictitious names. At one point, Helly mediumistically produced the great-grandmother of Jung's who had been seduced by Goethe.

Over and above this flood of new contacts, the spirit known as "Ivenes" eventually took over Helly's trances. Ivenes was described as a small, sensitive, dark-haired Jewish woman who was morally pure ("snow white"), a wise, mature personality. A novel feature of these new communications from Ivenes was the theory of reincarnation. Ivenes, through Helly, claimed to be the Seeress of Prevorst, as well as a fifteenth-century woman who she said was burned at the stake as a witch, a female Christian martyr executed in Rome during the reign of Nero, and a paramour of King David. She claimed to have had numerous children in all of these incarnations, and in her "romances," as Jung later called them, she created detailed genealogies and marvelous tales of her past lives. Ivenes even claimed that she traveled between the stars and had visited Mars, and she described in great detail the Martians and their highly developed civilization. Helly now began to arouse Jung's suspicions.

A popular book of the 1890s was Camille Flammarion's pseudoscientific speculations on the Martian civilization that had created the famous canals that many astronomers claimed to see on the red planet's surface.[28] When Jung realized that Helly was concocting her romances from things she had heard or read, everything he had believed about the spirit world through the séances was thrown into confusion.

Jung realized that much of the personality of Ivenes was based on the figure of the Seeress of Prevorst in Kerner's book. By giving Helly a copy of the book, Jung had inadvertently created Ivenes. He learned a valuable lesson about the power of "hidden memories" and textual material to reemerge in an entirely novel form in consciousness. In fact, material that one has "forgotten" can reappear in thoughts, fantasies, or dreams and have all of the emotional force and visual clarity of actual memories. At the turn of the century, this quite normal phenomenon was called "cryptomnesia," literally "hidden memories." With Helly, Jung saw for the first time that amalgams of forgotten memories can, under certain circumstances, be reorganized into alternate personalities that seem to have an authentic life of their own independent of the ego of an individual. Despite his awareness of the influence of cryptomnesia on Helly's performances while he observed them, however, he did not use such psychological terminology to characterize them until he completed his medical training. More significant, he was later to deny seemingly clear cases of cryptomnesia that if acknowledged would threaten his most central theories.

Miraculous explosions, acts of love, acts of fraud

In the autumn of 1898, the table around which Jung and Helly led their spiritualist séances suddenly cracked down the middle.[29] Within weeks, a bread knife, inherited by Jung's mother from her father, suddenly exploded into four pieces. Jung later mounted these pieces and kept them in a safe in his home as a lifelong reminder of the powerful forces he and his kin had summoned during their séances.

The séances came to an abrupt halt for several reasons. First, according to Jung, Helly had fallen in love with him, and it became clear to him that she was faking many of the manifestations of her trances in order to keep him interested in her.[30] Second, Jung's own increasing sophistication in the natural sciences was leading him to reevaluate his extreme antimaterialism. In nineteenth-century concepts such as a "vital force," he began to see a more biologically based starting point for his own thinking about spirituality.[31] But third, and most important, after one of these final séances Helly's mother was startled at her daughter's exhaustion and feared for her health. She accused Jung and his mother of harming Helly. After a period of depression, Helly left Basel to learn dressmaking in Montpellier, France, and then in Paris. Although Jung spent time with Helly in Paris in 1902, he would never completely patch up his relationships with the Preiswerks and later wrote derisively of them.

Helly died of tuberculosis a few days before her thirtieth birthday, in November 1911. Although Jung later claimed that in the last few months of her illness her mind slowly disintegrated, regressing her to the level of a two-year-old, the Preiswerks denied this. According to her niece Stephanie Zumstein-Preiswerk, "she died of a broken heart"[32]—a heart that Carl Jung broke, as we shall see, in more ways than one.

What, then, are we to make of this early spiritualist period in the life of Carl Jung? Some things seem abundantly clear.

Jung took these spiritualist experiments so seriously that the ideas from them held sway over him longer than most of the instruction he received in medical school. Unquestionably, he felt that through Helly's mediumistic trances he was receiving knowledge from an intelligent source beyond Helly herself. Whenever they appeared, Jung acknowledged the various personalities that emerged during Helly's performances as real and always attempted to engage them in dialogue. At least for a time, Jung regarded some of these experiences as authentic contact with discarnate entities.[33] Eventually, he realized that much of this may have been merely the cryptomnesiac products of Helly's own mind. But Jung's very personal approach to Helly's personifications or splinter personalities—or spirits—later characterized his conception of the unconscious human mind. Whereas Freud approached the products of the unconscious mind as hieroglyphs to be deciphered, Jung always regarded them as the starting point for a dialogue. For Jung the unconscious would always be a source of higher knowledge beyond the confines of time and three-dimensional space, and one could establish a personal relationship with the voices and images of one's unconscious, one's inner Land of the Dead.

But long before the First World War, when Jung again led others into the Land of the Dead, he endured several years of scientific doubt and relative skepticism about the reality of spirits. During these first years of Jung's psychiatric career, a career cruelly built on the sacrifice of Helly's social reputation, the spirits were transformed. Jung renamed them. The spirits became "complexes," and the spirit world became "the unconscious." Until when, in Zurich in 1916, once again the unconscious became the home of the ancestors, the inner fatherland, the realm of the gods.

THREE

Hidden Memories

Die Kunst blüht, die Kunst ist an der Herrschaft,
die Kunst streckt ihr rosenumwundenes Zepter
über die Stadt hin und lächelt. . . .
         München leuchtete.

Art blossomed, art reigned, art extended its
rose-covered scepter over the city, and smiled.
    . . . Munich was radiant.
      —Thomas Mann, "Gladius Dei," 1902

Early December in Munich is always brisk. The royal blue Bavarian sky never seems more open. But the skies were gray and drizzling during the first days of December 1900, when Doctor Carl Gustav Jung emerged from his sleepy *Gasthaus* with the excitement of being in the most bohemian cultural metropolis in the Germanic world west of Vienna.[1]

For only the second time in his life Carl Jung was in a foreign country. (Once, as a gymnasium schoolboy, he had hiked the Alsatian countryside of France, making a special effort to see the military fortification at Belfort designed by Vauban.)[2] But when he stepped off the train in Munich, fresh from passing his state medical exams, he entered a brief but pivotal liminal period, a juncture between two lives.

Up to now he had merely been a student in provincial Basel, living with his mother and sister on the brink of poverty, surviving only by the grace of the Preiswerks' charity. Now, he was in cosmopolitan Munich, away from his old existence, completely a new man. He enjoyed registering as a doctor at his humble lodgings and thrilled at being addressed as such by the proprietor. He looked forward to the tenth of December, when he would be expected to assume his first real job as an alienist at the famous Burghölzli research hospital for mental disorders in Zurich. But first, in Munich, he wanted to indulge his passions for art and archeology.

Then, as now, the traditional heart of Munich lay along the grand

Ludwigstrasse, which is lined with the yellow and tan imperial structures built throughout the nineteenth century by the kings of Bavaria: the royal library, the various royal offices of state, and the university. The upper end of Ludwigstrasse was capped by the Siegestor, the "Victory Arch" that mirrored the design of the Arch of Constantine in Rome. To the north and to the west of the Siegestor was the infamous "artistic" district of Schwabing, filled with young painters and poets and novelists and adventurers who were creating new artistic styles in their studios and hatching utopian schemes in their coffeehouses. During the first decade of the twentieth century, Paul Klee and Rainer Maria Rilke and Stefan George lived there, just blocks from Russian expatriates such as Wassily Kandinsky and Vladimir Ilyich Ulyanov—Lenin—who sometimes could be seen with a cue stick in hand at the old billiards salon on Schellingstrasse. The twenty-five-year-old Jung, a mildly talented illustrator and painter of watercolor landscapes in his own right, was naturally attracted to Schwabing.[3]

Ludwigstrasse ends at Odeonsplatz, next to the royal palace. In the Odeonsplatz is a monument known as the Feldherrnhalle or "Gallery of the Marshalls," a large Florentine arched gallery that encases the statues of two Bavarian military heroes. When Jung visited Munich that winter, among the grandest shows in the city were the military parades, with marching bands, held at noontime thrice weekly in front of the Feldherrnhalle. Fascinated with military fortifications and with the ceremonialism of martial rituals since childhood, Jung's periodic military training in the Swiss army had only increased his love of military parades and music. At the Feldherrnhalle he could see the imperial military prowess of the Kaiser and the relatively new nation of Germany on vivid, muscular display.

West of the Feldherrnhalle sits the cluster of museums at Koenigsplatz. Here, in an edifice resembling an ancient Roman temple, stands the Glyptothek, the world-famous museum that drew Jung so far from home. There Jung was in the presence of the gods.[4] Fantastic, alluring, frightening statues, reliefs, and busts of Assyrian, Egyptian, Greek, Etruscan, and Roman divinities filled every one of the marbled rooms. He recognized some of them from books on archeology he had read since childhood and from the illustrations he had been forced to copy in drawing class as a schoolboy. These were the ancient ones invoked by Goethe and Schiller, Heine and Nietzsche. Yet the old gods had never seemed so real, so *possible*.

In the Hall of Bacchus he saw the famous Greek statue known as the Barberini Faun and compelling hermaphroditic figures and images of Dionysian orgies in which the god led swooning, dancing young madwomen known as maenads in flowing, processional revelry. Here, too, were images of satyrs and the great satyr-god Pan, upon which Christian images of the devil were based. Jung, with his small-town Protestant upbringing, could not but have felt that he was in the presence of something a bit obscene and forbidden—something Nietzschean.[5]

Next, Jung walked north along Arcisstrasse to the art museums known as the Alte Pinothek and the Neue Pinothek. In the Alte Pinothek he saw many famous paintings and drawings by Rembrandt, Michelangelo, Holbein, Raphael, and da Vinci that he had read about. Here, too, he saw the woodcuts and paintings of the revered German artist Albrecht Dürer, including his famous self-portrait of 1500 in which he resembles familiar images of Christ.

In the Neue Pinothek, Jung studied many examples of the contemporary art nouveau, known in Germany as *Jugendstil* or "youth-style" (so named because the Munich cultural journal *Jugend* had popularized it). Here, too, were representative works of some members of the artistic community known as the Munich Secession, whose fantastic and erotic themes signaled a conscious reaction against the traditional Roman Catholic social milieu of Bavaria that had kept freedom of artistic expression to a minimum.[6] The leader of this movement, whose images would long influence Jung, was the Munich painter and sculptor Franz Stuck.[7]

Stuck stunned the public in the 1890s with his decorative Symbolist paintings of mythological themes, many of which were frankly erotic. He played with traditional religious motifs and made them more consonant with the neoromantic and neopagan spirit of the times. In 1891, in a painting called *Pieta* (not at the Neue Pinothek in 1900), Stuck added a Volkish twist to the famous image of the grief-stricken Mary standing next to the body of Jesus by depicting him, like Wagner's Siegfried, with blond hair and beard.[8] In 1898 he built a large neo-Classical house (known as Villa Stuck) on the Prinzregentstrasse. Here, in this spiritual container, he lived and loved and gave form to his fantasies. He created his own universe of the imagination, as he termed it, filling the ceilings and walls with his own murals and erecting a marble structure adorned with his art that he called his "Sin Altar." The centerpiece of this pagan altar was a copy of a painting of his that had been the main attraction at the Neue Pinothek in December 1900, the chillingly erotic work entitled *Die Sünde* (Sin).

Bought and displayed by the museum just after he painted it in 1893, *Die Sünde* depicts the shadowy nude upper torso of a woman who gazes out at us, but who is partly obscured by a thick black and green snake that has wrapped itself around her body. Jung mentioned this painting early in the first part of his famous *Wandlungen und Symbole der Libido*,[9] and the Christian lapsarian themes of Stuck's painting reappear in a series of transformative visions Jung experienced in December 1913. This painting, which could only be seen in Munich, had a profound effect on him.

These were the images that later fueled Jung's fantasies as he traveled to Zurich to begin a new life: a phantasmagoria of gods, nymphs, satyrs, and sin.

But for a brief time—a very brief time—he forgot them.

"The monastery of the world"

Jung began his career at the Burghölzli clinic as an asylum psychiatrist on December 10, 1900, and left in the spring of 1909.[10] During this time he lived in an apartment in the large hospital (his new wife, Emma, joining him there in 1903), as did the other four or five physicians on staff there, including the noted chief, Eugen Bleuler, who would first publish the term "schizophrenia" in 1908.[11] Throughout Jung's tenure, foreign physicians rotated through the Burghölzli to learn the latest scientific techniques in psychiatry; these included many exiled Russian doctors and many German, Austrian, Hungarian, British, and American physicians, some of whom became prominent in the psychoanalytic movement in the decades to follow.

Jung assisted Bleuler with the pioneering clinical research at the Burghölzli on dementia praecox (later called schizophrenia), manic-depressive illness, alcoholism, and, later, hysteria. Among the patients were a fair number suffering from something called the "general paralysis of the insane," the psychotic and vegetative disorder caused by the tertiary stages of syphilis. It was here, among the inpatient population of the largest asylum in Switzerland, that Carl Jung received his training in the diagnosis and, later, treatment of mental disorders.

Since many, if not most, mental disorders were considered at that time to be diseases caused in part by hereditary degeneration, Jung and his colleagues were cloistered in a veritable hothouse of human degeneracy twenty-four hours a day. New physicians at such asylums saw things few outsiders could even imagine. Constant exposure to the bizarre delusions and hallucinations of psychotic individuals, to the flotsam and jetsam of human existence, to the sight of raw sexual acts and overt seductions, and to irrational responses to reasonable questions could only have a subtle but seductive destabilizing effect on the rigid, intellectualizing, bourgeois young men who were the standard-bearers in Western European civilization's war against degeneracy. To preserve their virtue and sanity, the clinical staff took vows of abstinence from alcohol and focused their minds on their scientific work in what Jung called "the monastery of the world." Although the transition was difficult, he joined them in "a submission to the vow to believe only in what was probable, average, commonplace, barren of meaning, to renounce everything strange and significant, and reduce anything extraordinary to the banal."[12] Such dedication would make the experimental psychiatric research at the Burghölzli world renowned in the years following Jung's arrival, and, by 1906, by age thirty-one, Jung himself would be famous throughout Europe, England, and America as a promising young scientist.

The central topic that obsessed the researchers at the Burghölzli was human memory. Specifically, they were interested in how certain disorders of memory could be measured through experimental means. After analyzing patterns in the data, they applied this knowledge to the development of techniques for the differential diagnosis of mental disorders. They were on the right track. As so much of modern research in cognitive neuroscience has suggested, the laws governing the processes of human memory are also the keys to unlocking the mysteries of human consciousness. Our conscious experience of a self that is continuous through time is dependent on our memory processes, and any disruption of the normal functioning of human memory may also disrupt our normal sense of identity or self. Since such disruptions were common in all mental disorders, it made perfect sense to focus on them.

Memory was also seen as the central problem of heredity and evolutionary biology. Why do children look like their parents? And why are they also different from them? Biologically, what is "remembered" from one generation to the next? The problem of evolution soon became the problem of distortion in biological memory. Richard Semon, an associate of Jung's at the Burghölzli, began to examine the problem of inherited memories (through a vehicle called the "mneme," akin to our modern notions of a "memory trace") and published his theories in 1904 and 1909.[13] Like Ernst Haeckel and many others, including Freud and Jung, Semon was a Lamarckian who believed in the inheritance of acquired characteristics. He believed that human memory and hereditary mechanisms were two aspects of an underlying process of "organic memory," first theorized in 1870 by the German psychophysiologist Ewald Hering.[14] The common acceptance of the theoretical construct of a gene as the biological unit of hereditary transmission in the nucleus of each cell did not take hold until 1909 or so, and since DNA did not enter the picture until the 1950s, the biological mechanism for the transmission of hereditary information from one generation to another was largely a mystery for most of Jung's life. Jung's speculations about the organic or genetic or hereditary basis of his theories—even that of the collective unconscious (1916)—were thus worked out within the conceptual framework provided by Richard Semon and Ewald Hering.

Within hours after Jung had been met at the train station on December 10, 1900, by Bleuler, he was given the task of learning to use a psychological test that had been employed for at least a decade. This was the famous word-association test in which a subject was asked to give unrehearsed, spontaneous one-word responses to stimulus words.[15] A third person, sometimes a trusted patient, kept notes of the reaction time to each stimulus word with the use of a stopwatch. Additional data were collected by hooking subjects up to devices that measured galvanic skin response (electrical activity on the skin) and breath and heart rates—all assumed to be physiological measures of anxiety and arousal. It was thought—and Jung pioneered some of this research—that such tests could have forensic applications, and indeed our modern polygraph tests are based on the technology that was fine-tuned at the Burghölzli. From 1901 until 1909, Jung conducted the program of experimental research using the word-association test, sometimes using himself and his colleagues as "normal" subjects in the published accounts of the experiments.

Jung's research on the disorders of human memory eventually led him back to the experiences with his cousin Helly and the lost world of the spirits.

"So-called" occult phenomena

Before Jung could achieve his new goal of becoming a university professor he needed to write, and have Bleuler approve, a doctoral dissertation. After discussion with his chief, Jung decided to write an analysis of the personality of his cousin Helly as a case study of a spiritualist medium. Since Bleuler himself had a lifelong interest in spiritualism (and, with Jung, was investigating mediums at the Burghölzli), and in light of the interest of many of the major figures in French psychiatry in the "dissociation" of the personalities of many spiritualist mediums, he gave his young assistant his blessing.[16] But while this project eventually became Jung's first publication and helped launch his psychiatric career, it proved disastrous for his cousin.

Jung's dissertation, "On the Psychology and Pathology of So-Called Occult Phenomena,"[17] which appeared in 1902, changed many of the details of the spiritualist séances that he held with Helly, but perhaps the most striking aspect of the work is Jung's devaluing clinical dissection of the so-called pathological personality of the medium "S.W.," the pseudonym for Helly. In this case history she is pictured as suffering from hysteria. Jung interprets all the phenomena of her mediumship—her trances, her changes in voice and character, her fainting spells (which he calls "hysterical attacks"), her "automatisms," and her distortions of identity and memory—as symptoms of a dissociative process, a "splitting" of the normal river of consciousness into several distinct streams. In this regard he compares her ability to assume alternate spirit identities in her trances—particularly the entity known as Ivenes—with the clinical phenomenon of the "dual" or "multiple personality" that was a fad at the end of the last century among French researchers such as Pierre Janet, Théodule Ribot, Alfred Binet, and especially Théodore Flournoy. Jung decided, however, against any analogy with cases of "double consciousness." Instead, he believed that a less serious clinical phenomenon was in evidence with Helly/Ivenes, and that "the mournful features, the attachment to sorrow, her mysterious fate, lead us to the historic prototype of Ivenes—Justinius Kerner's 'Prophetess of Prevorst.' "[18]

According to Jung, "[Helly] pours her own soul into the role of the prophetess, thus seeking to create an ideal of virtue and perfection.... She incarnates in Ivenes what she wishes to be in twenty years—the assured, influential, wise, gracious, pious lady.... [Helly] builds up a person beyond herself. It cannot be said that 'she deceives herself' but that 'she dreams herself into the higher ideal state." Here, in his first publication, Jung introduced the idea that the unconscious mind has a prospective and, at times, prophetic function that can give hints to the conscious mind and its ego about what mental organizations should or will be on the horizon. Jung accepted the opinion that the unconscious mind could have such precognitive power, as did such figures as Schopenhauer, von Hartmann, and many distinguished international authorities on psychical research.

Although his experiences with Helly corresponded with those of Justinius Kerner with the Seeress of Prevorst, and it is clear Jung fancied himself in Kerner's role (he is mentioned throughout the dissertation), psychiatry as we know it did not exist in Kerner's day. Since Jung had to produce a medical treatise based on the current state of psychiatric knowledge, he based the technical analyses in his dissertation on the example provided by Flournoy in his own exhaustive study of a spiritualist medium.

Des Indes à la planete Mars was a clinical case analysis of the fanciful stories and ersatz languages produced during the trances of a medium Flournoy pseudonymously named "Hélène Smith."[19] During her spiritualist séances the medium reported a series of past lives on Earth (as a noble personage from India) and on Mars. At times she spoke in a strange language, which she said was "Martian" but which Flournoy termed "glossolalia" (a phenomenon commonly called "speaking in tongues"). The key to Flournoy's compelling analysis was that he was able to reasonably argue that much of the content of these productions could be traced to "hidden memories." These were memories of information that the medium had previously heard or read but had, in the meantime, "forgotten." Hence, when they reappeared during the séances, these stories seemed quite novel to the medium. She had literally forgotten that she knew this material; in today's terms, she had "source amnesia."

This "cryptomnesia" is today more broadly termed "implicit memory" and is implicated in such contemporary issues as "false memory syndrome" in cases of alleged child abuse, alleged "ritual abuse" at the hands of covens of Satanists, and alleged kidnapping and torture by extraterrestrials.[20]

From 1902 onward, in his professional publications Jung referred to spirits as "unconscious personalities," "splinter personalities," or "complexes." In other words, spirits and other paranormal phenomena became only "so-called," not at all genuine. Since complexes operate unconsciously, the "spirit world" of the mediums is given a new place-name: "the unconscious."

By the term "complex" Jung referred to a cluster of images, affects, and ideas organized around a thematic core that, under certain circumstances, could have a sliver of consciousness all its own and act like an alternate personality, as in cases of multiple personality. In these early years there was nothing transcendent, hereditary, or supernatural about complexes—they comprised the personal experiences of a single individual. His word-association experiments quantitatively documented the phenomena of complexes in the operation of human memory. For example, if a stimulus word triggered a highly charged emotion in a person—perhaps a hidden memory unavailable to consciousness—the psychophysiological instruments attached to the subject would measure changes that correlated with a subjective feeling of anxiety, and the person's reaction time to that particular word would be longer. Such complexes were thought to be quite common in all humans and accounted for the remarkable range of behaviors and attitudes in a single individual. Indeed, the ego itself was thought by Jung and his colleagues to be the most important complex of all. In normal individuals, it was at the core of the field of consciousness and was centered upon body memories and on the personal identity that had developed since birth. The interplay of alternate complexes with the ego was what made each individual human personality dynamic and unique.

Given that this prevailing model of the normal human mind was based on the idea that we were all, down deep, highly integrated multiple personalities, it is not surprising that it would attract Jung, who had experienced tangible divisions between "number one" and "number two" personalities in himself, his mother, and Helly. Although he would diagnose both women as hysterics, he reserved such fears about himself for his private musings. But clearly his choice of clinical pursuits had relevance to searching for the secrets of his own personality.

Scandal and cryptomnesia

For Helly the publication of Jung's thesis was disastrous. It quickly made the rounds in the small circle of "German Mandarins" in Basel, creating a minor scandal that embarrassed and enraged the venerable Preiswerk family. Given that mental illnesses such as hysteria were thought to be the result of "bad blood" in a degenerate family, Helly and her younger relatives were suddenly ostracized.[21] It is said that after a potential marriage prospect for Helly read Jung's case history of her, any talk of marriage was swiftly withdrawn. She never did marry.

We can only speculate on what Helly thought about Jung's dissertation, or what she may have said to him about it. When they met again in Paris after it had been published, their relations were cordial.[22] We have no idea, no unambiguous historical record, as to why Jung exposed her to such trials. For now, his motivations must remain a mystery.

The influence of hidden memories of past experience on present behavior continued to fascinate Jung throughout his years at the Burghölzli. After leaving in 1909, he developed a new theory about the nature of unconscious memories, a theory whose basic assumptions flatly contradicted, indeed discounted, all of his previous research on this process of human memory. But the problem of cryptomnesia would shadow him for the rest of his career.

Despite its obvious role in the production of the content of "spirit communications" by mediums and in the symptoms of hysteria and psychosis, Jung also recognized the powerful contribution of cryptomnesia to creativity. In a 1905 essay, "Cryptomnesia," he argued that much creative work of writers, poets, artists, and so on, was the end product of the unconscious processing of previously learned information.[23] No creative act—even works of genius—appears "out of nothing." A genius, like a hysteric, puts ideas together in unconventional patterns. New combinations of memories of previously experienced events or previously learned material are the wellsprings of creativity. However, even a true genius mistakes his or her novelty as creation and forgets its true source. In essence, Jung proposes that cryptomnesia is the root of all genius.

Cryptomnesia is also responsible for another phenomenon: unconscious plagiarism. In the final section of his dissertation Jung juxtaposes lengthy passages from Nietzsche's *Also Sprach Zarathustra* and an essay by Justinius Kerner to show their striking similarities. Jung reports that he contacted Nietzsche's sister to find out if he had ever read Kerner, and the sister reported that he had in his youth. Jung thus persuasively demonstrates the powerful influence of memories of things read or heard on our thoughts even decades later, long after we have forgotten the original source of the material. Within just a few years Jung himself would "forget" this argument.

"A religious sect, a scientific hypothesis"

Jung's monastic immersion in the world of scientific experimentation at the Burghölzli led him to a new, more mature, skepticism about spiritualism. During these years, with Bleuler's permission, he applied his new scientific rigor to the subject. As he told an audience at the Bernoullianum in his Basel "homecoming" on February 5, 1905, "In the past few years I have investigated eight mediums, six of them women and two of them men." Given the Preiswerk family scandal caused by the publication of his case history of Helly, Jung didn't help matters by adding that "mediums as a rule are slightly abnormal mentally," and that seven of his eight subjects showed "slight" symptoms of hysteria. However, he explained to his audience, he learned virtually nothing from this exercise. He witnessed no magical levitations or clairvoyant demonstrations—indeed, nothing paranormal or supernatural at all. Speaking with the conviction of a skeptical man of science, the twenty-nine-year-old Jung told his audience, "Everything that may be considered a scientifically established fact belongs to the domain of the mental and cerebral processes and is fully explicable in terms of the laws already known to science."

Yet despite all this, the body of Jung's address was a discussion of reports of the extraordinary phenomena of animal magnetism, clairvoyance, precognition, and visions that took these accounts seriously. To Jung, spiritualist phenomena were still a legitimate area for research. Jung maintained this unshakable belief throughout his life, and he was particularly gratified when, in 1934, the American researcher J. B. Rhine published the results of experiments at Duke University supporting the hypothesis of extrasensory perception (ESP).[24]

Spiritualism, however, was unique in human history, Jung explained to his Basel audience. The "sect" of spiritualism was based on a "religious belief in the actual and tangible intervention of the spirit world in our world." The religious practice of this sect then becomes the "practice of communicating with the spirits." Pointing to the vast body of literature purporting to document the reality of communications with the spirit world, the spiritualist sect claims that its religious practice is based on science. Jung says that the sect of spiritualism is unique because of its dual nature: "on the one side a religious sect, on the other a scientific hypothesis."[25]

The lessons learned from studying an influential mass movement, a religious sect whose success derived from its claim of being based on a scientific hypothesis, would not be lost on him.

FOUR

Religion Can Only Be Replaced by Religion

Of all the remarkable persons that he met during his years at the Burghölzli, none is more closely linked to Jung than Sigmund Freud. Jung became aware of the work of Freud shortly after arriving at the Burghölzli in 1900. Jung read Freud's *The Interpretation of Dreams* (1899) during his first year as a clinician, but claimed he didn't understand it.[1] In 1904, he encountered a new patient suffering from hysteria—a young Jewish woman from Russia by the name of Sabina Spielrein—and began experimenting with the methods of "psychoanalysis" as he interpreted them from Freud's descriptions. On September 25, 1905, he wrote his first letter to Freud with a case summary of this patient, referring the case to him for further treatment. The patient's mother never delivered this letter to Freud.[2] The first official contact between the two men, by letter, was in 1906, and they met for the first time in Freud's flat in Vienna on March 3, 1907. By January 1913 they had exchanged letters agreeing to cease their personal relations.

The mythic tale of Freud and Jung is one of the best known of the twentieth century. Most people know the skeleton, if not the flesh, of the truth: that Freud and Jung were famous psychoanalysts; that Freud, the father of psychoanalysis, anointed Jung as his heir apparent; that Jung, perhaps like an ungrateful son, rejected his mentor and went his own way after a terrible clash. Jungians reframe the story by claiming that Jung could not accept

Freud's exclusively sexual theory of life and broke with him to fashion a theory that took into account the essential religious or spiritual nature of people. For those who tend toward the view of history constructed by Freud's disciples, Jung's defection was an apostasy, a rejection of the science of psychoanalysis marked by Jung's lapse into narcissism, psychosis, mysticism, and anti-Semitism. There are elements of truth in all these versions.

It would be impossible to do full justice to the Freud/Jung myth here. This relationship has been discussed in so many other volumes, and usually with more than an ounce of partisanship, that I could not even begin to summarize the viewpoints and sift the evidence, pro and con, for the arguments therein. My personal, idiosyncratic view of the Freud/Jung myth is this: I believe it is time to step out of this important but very limiting intellectual context and free both men from being bound together in history. I believe that this approach is especially important to understand Jung. His psychoanalytic years are best viewed as a transition period, not the central source of his later ideas, as so many have erroneously argued. The period from 1907 to 1913 was an interlude during which issues and concerns that predated his interest in Freud—especially spiritualism, the spirituality of pagan antiquity, and the dissociation psychology of Janet and Flournoy—were briefly syncretized with psychoanalytic thought. After 1913, these issues reemerged with a new vitality that resulted in the theories for which Jung is best known: psychological types (1913, 1921), the collective unconscious (1916), its "dominants" (1916–17) or "archetypes" (1919), and individuation (1916).

As this period in Jung's life marks a transition, so will this chapter break from the narrative history in order to put the foundations of Jung's later career in focus.

I believe that Jung initially became attracted to Freudian psychoanalysis for its clinical utility. After meeting Freud and championing him and the cause of psychoanalysis at professional conferences at a time when Freud's sexual theories were met with great skepticism, psychoanalysis began to take on the function of a *Weltanschauung,* or totalizing worldview, for Jung. Not only the secrets of psychopathology, but of the human personality, of human culture and history—of life itself—were unlocked with the keys Freud provided. In his final years with the psychoanalytic movement, Jung—like so many others—began to see it as a powerful vehicle for social change, for cultural revitalization in a fin-de-siècle world of degeneration and decay.

I believe that this latter interpretation of the psychoanalytic movement best registers its true historical significance in the twentieth century. Jung, however, could not abide by its secular claims: in the psychoanalytic movement he envisioned, for a brief time, a scientific religion of the future.

In the presence of genius

Throughout his life—in autobiographical accounts, seminars, letters, and in filmed interviews in the 1950s—Jung always acknowledged Sigmund Freud's greatness. In many respects, Freud was Jung's first encounter with someone he considered a living genius. There are unmistakable parallels here with Friedrich Nietzsche's relationship with Richard Wagner. In the presence of genius, both Nietzsche and Jung wisely observed, absorbed, and imitated. It is the traditional nature of a genius to be inconstant and mercurial, and after repeated exposure to the genius and his ever-changing ideas, the luster of divinity soon fades. It was the repeated personal contact with Wagner, which reached a climax in the cultlike atmosphere the *Meister* encouraged in his entourage, that drove Nietzsche to leave in disgust. For Jung, who only had intermittent personal contact with Freud in 1907 and 1908, the seven weeks he spent with Freud traveling to and from America in the autumn of 1909 were enough to begin to sour his worship of the sage from Vienna.[3] But, of course, once he recognized the spark of genius in himself, there was no longer any need to remain a disciple.

Why was Jung attracted to Freud and his ideas for eight years, and with such devotion? Other than his obvious attraction to Freud's charisma as a genius, there are several alternatives that are rarely discussed.

Jung was intrigued by the therapeutic possibilities of the psychoanalytic method. Psychoanalysis became a way to circumvent or overcome the stigmata of hereditary degeneration in his institutionalized patients—and perhaps in himself. (He reported in *MDR* that during his early years at the Burghölzli he secretly kept "hereditary" statistics on his colleagues in order to understand the "psychiatric mentality," including, no doubt, his own family's incidence of hysteria.[4])

As the historian of psychiatry Sander Gilman has noted, Freud "repudiated the model of degeneracy" in his theories.[5] This was an advantage of Freud's theory that Jung recognized: it shifted emphasis from hereditary biological factors (such as degeneracy) to psychodynamic ones. "Bad blood" in one's family therefore did not condemn one to a lifetime of disease and suffering. In fact, psychoanalytic treatment promised relief and renewal. This made psychoanalysis especially attractive to those considered "tainted" by their ethnicity, such as Jews.

The Burghölzli was, like other mental hospitals then and now, a place where far too many cases needed constant care and supervision and never seemed to improve. Although with advances in psychopharmacology conditions have improved somewhat, in Jung's day more time was spent making diagnoses than carrying out treatments because so few of them were effective. As a staff physician, Jung ordered treatments such as extended baths, electrotherapy, work therapy, opiates, and barbiturates. Physical restraints were sometimes necessary, such as wrapping patients in wet sheets, or restraining their hands in muffs or their arms in straitjackets.

At the turn of the century, such hospitals were storerooms of human degeneration. Freud's claims about the therapeutic success of his psychoanalytic method must have seemed like a ray of hope to compassionate physicians like Jung who felt as confined to the back wards of the asylums as the patients. Jung is best remembered for his philosophical and theoretical inclinations, but it is often forgotten how determined he was to find practical applications of such ideas in the form of psychotherapeutic intervention. Anything that offered hope for the treatment of dementia praecox (defined as a progressively degenerative disorder),[6] an area of clinical interest for Jung, was considered with great seriousness.

Interestingly, during 1904 and 1905, when Jung was experimenting with psychoanalysis on a female patient who would later become his lover, there was very little in Freud's writings about how to actually do it. Jung and his colleagues had to read between the lines somewhat to practice their own version of what Freud was up to in Vienna. From the very start, the method seemed to be fully understood only by its maker. Bleuler and his staff found themselves increasingly intrigued. In 1904, they began to correspond with Freud, often seeking his advice for the treatment of patients. This only added to the mystery of psychoanalysis and its inventor.

From medical treatment to cultural movement

From the start, Freud conceived of psychoanalysis as a new form of medical treatment that promised a better existence (freedom from symptoms, self-knowledge) for those who were successfully analyzed. The key to such revitalization was full access to memory, encompassing the infantile, the sexual, and, above all, the personal. Hysterics, said Freud and his mentor Josef Breuer in their 1895 book *Studies on Hysteria,* suffered from "reminiscences."[7] Psychoanalysis, as Freud began to develop it starting in 1896, provided a magical vocabulary to contain the power of such affectively charged memories when they were unchained from their unconscious moorings.

Freud has loomed so large during the twentieth century that we tend to forget just how little known he was for most of his early career. Before the First World War, the common citizen of Austria-Hungary would probably not have known his name. (Today in Austria his image appears on a unit of paper currency). For the most part, until 1902, Freud worked in his "splendid isolation" and essentially *was* the psychoanalytic movement. In that pivotal year, four Viennese Jewish physicians (primarily internists) met at Freud's flat as the famous Psychological Wednesday Evening Circle. They were Alfred Adler, Wilhelm Stekel, Max Kahane, and Rudolph Reitler. By the time Freud and Jung began their correspondence, the Wednesday Circle had grown to seventeen participants. Two years later, in 1908, forty participants from six countries attended the first congress of the International Psychoanalytic Association in Salzburg.

The conversion of the Swiss contingent at the Burghölzli legitimized the psychoanalytic movement in Europe. Previously seen as only a Jewish affair, that psychoanalysis aroused the interest of Bleuler and his largely Swiss, Christian staff was a major coup for Freud and broadened its appeal.

Jung was a major organizer of the movement, and when the International Psychoanalytic Association was founded in 1910, he became its first president. He seems to have been attracted to psychoanalysis as an agent of cultural revitalization through its promotion of core Nietzschean themes of uncovering, the breaking of bonds, irrationality, and sexuality. He was not alone.

It was Franz Riklin, Jung's colleague at the Burghölzli, who would inaugurate the transformation of the psychoanalytic movement into a worldview. In 1908, in a publication that he also presented at the Salzburg congress, Riklin used psychoanalytic theory to interpret fairy tales.[8] Remarkably, this was the first time material from patients was not the main focus of analysis. Soon, other works followed that analyzed Wagnerian opera, myths, legends, painters and their paintings, and so on. Psychoanalysis's claim to being a science rested on the application of the method in clinical settings, where analytic hypotheses could be tested against the free associations of living persons. When the theory was applied to fairy tales and other cultural creations, psychoanalysis quickly developed into a worldview through which all of human history could be understood. Art, religion, and music, like the free associations of patients in analysis, became products of the unconscious and therefore were fair game for reinterpretation. After this point more and more individuals involved in the humanities began to take an active interest in psychoanalysis, leading to its chic image among those in literature and in the arts, including Lou Andreas-Salomé, who became a lifelong friend of Freud's.

The problem, of course, in this application of psychoanalytic theory was that the inert material could not talk back. Clinical hypotheses could not be tested as they could in the give-and-take between psychoanalyst and patient. A work of art, a fairy tale, a hero myth, or a Wagnerian opera had only the new, "real" meaning given to it by the psychoanalyst who wrote about it. Any pretense about the verifiability of psychoanalytic judgments broke down irretrievably. For difficulties like this, contemporary critics of psychoanalysis such as Frederick Crews can claim with justification that it has produced more converts than cures.

Psychoanalysis: an uncanny religion?

Right from the start, many American psychologists voiced concerns about the scientific claims of Freud, Jung, and psychoanalysis. They also expressed alarm at the secretive social structure of analytic training and the buoyant, charismatic nature of the movement. To many Americans, no strangers to such things, it seemed like a religious revivalist movement, or even a cult or pseudoscientific religion. John B. Watson, who later revolutionized American psychology with his system of "behaviorism," said in 1912 that psychoanalysis was a "new cult" whose "devotees" failed "to maintain an intellectual freedom in their system" and therefore "have hindered the scientific studies of the methods of Freud and Jung." Although Watson was hopeful that psychoanalysis might prove to further "medical practice, psychology and legal procedure," he nonetheless charged: "The psycho-analyst is using methods in a very crude and unsatisfactory way. He is building an enormous structure without looking carefully at the foundations."[9] Robert Woodworth, the eminent experimental psychologist from Columbia University, charged that Freudian psychoanalysis was an "uncanny religion."[10] Knight Dunlap, another famous psychologist, argued that "psychoanalysis attempts to creep in wearing the uniform of science, and to strangle it from the inside."[11] The atheistic, the materialistic, and, to many, the Jewish nature of Freudian psychoanalysis made it particularly unpalatable.

Just as spiritualism provided Jung with certain hypotheses about an alternative or transcendent reality and methods for contacting it, his experience with Freud and the early psychoanalytic movement provided him with a model of socialization that he adopted after 1913 when founding a movement of his own. Jung's own movement was overtly religious in nature,[12] but before we can even approach Jung's attempts to sacralize psychoanalysis we must ask: Other than Jung, were there any other major figures in Freud's charismatic movement that were self-consciously attuned to its religious or cultlike nature? If psychoanalysis is not a science, in the modern sense of that word, is it—or was it—a religion?

These are intriguing questions that have long been the subject of debate, most notably (and eloquently) in Philip Rieff's *The Triumph of the Therapeutic* (1966) and the fascinating study by Richard Webster, provocatively entitled *Why Freud Was Wrong,* which appeared in 1995.[13] Of the two, Webster faces this difficult question head-on and comes to some surprising conclusions. Webster scoured the autobiographical literature of the early psychoanalysts and found evidence of religious metaphors used to describe the fervor these men felt from their participation in Freud's movement. Given the fact that Freud's Viennese circle was composed almost exclusively of assimilated, agnostic, or atheist physicians of Jewish ethnicity, their borrowed use of the Christian metaphors of the dominant Austro-Hungarian population is understandable, if still surprising. Max Graf (who, like many others, was driven out of the movement as a "heretic," a word Freud employed in 1924 to refer to Jung and Adler)[14] painted the following sectlike image of the Wednesday evening meetings:

> The gatherings followed a definite ritual. First, one of the members would present a paper.... After a social quarter of an hour the discussion would begin. The last and decisive word was always spoken by Freud himself. There was the atmosphere of the foundation of a religion in that room. Freud himself was its new prophet who made the heretofore prevailing methods of psychological investigation appear superficial. Freud's pupils—all inspired and convinced—were his apostles.... However, after the first dreamy period and the unquestioning faith of the first group of apostles, the time came when the church was founded. Freud began to organize the church with great energy. He was serious and strict in the demands he made of his pupils; he permitted no deviations from his orthodox teachings.[15]

For Webster, Freud was quite consciously a "messianic" figure, and he refers to psychoanalysis as a "messianic cult" or as "quintessentially a religion" that "should be treated as such."[16] The power that bound these men together, according to him, came from the fact that Freud and the other analysts at the top of the social structure simply knew too many of the very personal, sexual, and at times sordid details of the others' personal lives. They not unreasonably feared "excommunication" from the movement because it could lead to the public disclosure of such information. It was well known within Freudian circles that several analysts had shared sexual intimacies with their female patients, and such "confidential" information appears regularly as gossip in the letters of Freud, Jung, Ernest Jones, Sandor Ferenczi, Karl Abraham, and others in the inner ring of adepts. The history of the psychoanalytic movement is littered with suicides, and this pressure-cooker atmosphere of implicit blackmail may have played a role in some of them.

Freud's "analytic hour" is referred to as a "confessional ritual" by Webster, drawing a deliberate comparison to the rite used to maintain power relations within the ecclesiastical structure of the Roman Catholic church. It was during the analytic session that potentially scandalous information was collected and noted by those analysts who served as direct conduits to Freud. Webster is blunt in his assessment of the shadow side of the underlying dynamics of "the psychoanalytic church":

> In placing what was, in effect, a confessional ritual at the very heart of the psychoanalytic movement, it seems clear that Freud was not, as he himself believed, engaging in a form of scientific innovation. Rather, he was unconsciously institutionalizing his own profound religious traditionalism at the same time that he was creating for himself a ritual stage on which he could play out his own "God complex" in relation to patients he regarded as inferior and in need of redemption. Just as, through his history of infantile sexuality, he had revised in disguised technical form the doctrine of Original Sin, so he also brought back to life, under a clinical disguise, the most important ecclesiastical ritual which had traditionally helped to sustain that doctrine, and to create psychological dependency among those who burdened themselves in the secrecy of the confessional.[17]

The religious or cultlike social structure and interaction patterns of the psychoanalytic movement from its very inception have been commented on by several psychoanalytic scholars, sociologists, and both proponents and opponents of the movement. Sociologist George Weisz has noted that the fundamental characteristics of the psychoanalytic movement as a social organization "were the group's elitism and sense of exclusiveness, combined with an extreme mistrust of and hostility toward the outside world; an eschatological vision of reality which made adherence to the group an experience approaching religious conversion; and, more important, an exaggerated reverence for the founder which transcended the normal bounds of scientific authoritarianism."[18]

An important Darwin and Freud scholar, Frank Sulloway, notes, "Few theories in science have spawned a following that can compare with the psychoanalytic movement in its cultlike manifestations, in its militancy, and in the aura of a religion that has permeated it." He goes on to charge that, "the discipline of psychoanalysis, which has always tapped considerable religious fervor among its adherents, has increasingly come to resemble a religion in its social organization" with its "secular priesthood of soul doctors."[19]

The sociologists of religion Rodney Stark and William Sims Bainbridge, who pioneered the study of new religious movements and cults worldwide, note that "Cults are particularly likely to emerge wherever large numbers of people seek help for intractable personal problems. The broad fields of psychotherapy, rehabilitation, and personal development have been especially fertile for cults."[20] They go on to say, "A number of psychotherapy services have evolved into cult movements, including those created by some of Freud's immediate followers," including Jung. Later, in a scathing indictment of psychoanalysis, they define it as a "client cult":

> Freud and his followers frequently suggested that all religion was a mass delusion, a communal neurosis, or even a shared psychosis. . . . Of course, Freud's circle consisted of well-educated, highly secular persons who prided themselves on their scientific attitudes. But we suggest that the main reason for this hostility to conventional religion was the fact that Psychoanalysis itself was a client cult, struggling to establish itself at the very border of religion. Surely, it offered a package of compensators, some of which were very general, totally outside the prevailing Christian culture. In attacking conventional religions, Psychoanalysis explicitly sought to replace them. For many of Freud's followers, indeed, for an embarrassingly prominent set of his most famous disciples, Psychoanalysis did develop into a religious cult.[21]

I cite these critics of the psychoanalytic movement not to mount an argument against Freud and his direct descendants (although I share the concerns) but to indicate how easy it would be for someone like the parson's son C. G. Jung—gripped since childhood with existential questions—to generalize the basic model of the psychoanalytic movement to one that was more explicitly religious or spiritualist. Indeed, when compared to the multiyear socialization process to an organization such as Freud's psychoanalytic movement, it becomes easier to understand how Jung could see the need for the prevailing Judeo-Christian orthodox religious to be replaced by something else, something more alive, that was also religious at its very core.

A "religious crush"

After Jung met with Freud in March 1907, his veneration for the older man gradually blossomed into something that even Jung recognized as a kind of falling in love. Jung, as a budding psychoanalyst, was quick to note the sexual basis of such feelings. But what is interesting is that Jung additionally placed this feeling of veneration within a religious context, acknowledging Freud as a godlike figure or spiritual guru.

Jung made this explicit in an often-cited letter to Freud of October 28, 1907. In it, Jung confessed to Freud that, "my veneration for you has something of the character of a 'religious crush.' " This statement alone conveys how Jung cognitively framed his participation in the psychoanalytic movement, but he then revealed to Freud: "Though it does not really bother me, I still feel it is disgusting and ridiculous because of its undeniable erotic undertone. This abominable feeling comes from the fact that as a boy I was the victim of a sexual assault of a man I once worshipped."[22]

Jung's remarkable admission has unfortunately been the source of misleading speculation by some commentators who base their interpretations of this incident on hearsay. Specifically, Jung has been said to have been an adolescent when this sexual encounter occurred and that, considering Jung's impressive physical size and strength, he willingly submitted to a homosexual "seduction."[23] But at least at present, there is no other corroborative evidence from Jung himself that can more accurately determine the true circumstances of this event.

Without direct citation, these commentators are using as a source an interview with Jolande Jacobi, one of his closest disciples and primary pupils in the late 1930s, conducted by the C. G. Jung Biographical Archives Project, a program funded by a now defunct foundation that interviewed and transcribed the reminiscences of 143 persons who knew Jung personally. Jacobi's interview in Zurich in 1969 is without a doubt the most revelatory document in the entire collection.

A large part of the early interview involves a discussion of Jacobi's flirtations with Jung after meeting him in 1927 and includes a long digression into his long-noted inability to form lasting, trusting relationships with other men. In one passage from this interview Jacobi states:

JJ: I discovered why Jung was at the same time afraid of men; to accept men as best friends or as his best pupils. He told me one day that when he was eighteen years old one of the best friends of his family was also his best friend—a man of about fifty, and he was eighteen. He was very proud of this friendship and had the feeling that he had—you know that Jung had difficulties with his father—in this man a fatherly friend with whom he could discuss everything until one day . . . [he] tried a homosexual approach with him. He was so disgusted and so afraid that he immediately broke the relationship. When Freud wanted him to be so near (Freud was twenty years older than Jung), he had the same feeling, "Don't let yourself be caught." I think that all this had a great influence because he repressed it and it influenced also the development of his relationships with men.[24]

In November 1912, Freud confronted Jung with this very fact. After Jung attempted to apologize for accusing him of treachery (the famous "Kreuzlingen gesture" incident), Freud told Sandor Ferenczi in a letter of November 26 that

> I spared him nothing at all, told him calmly that a friendship with him couldn't be maintained, that he himself gave rise to the intimacy that he so cruelly broke off; that things were not at all in order in his relations with men, not just with me but with others as well. He repels them all after a while. All those who are now with me have turned away from him because he threw them out. His referring to his sad experience with Honegger [who had committed suicide in 1911] reminded me of homosexuals or anti-Semites who become manifest after a disappointment with a woman or a Jew.[25]

Jacobi states that Jung told her the story of this "homosexual approach" because she often asked his advice about how to interpret the characters of her homosexual patients. According to her, "Jung always rejected" her requests for help with these patients.

JJ: ... One day he told me this story, which I told you [the interviewer, Gene Nameche] just now. And he also explained to me, when Freud wanted to make him his son and his successor, he had the same feeling, "No, no, no, I don't want to belong to anybody. I don't want to be embraced." That is very interesting because I think that it throws a very strong light on Jung's problem with men, which was for him, maybe, more unconscious than conscious. If it had been conscious, he would never have talked about it. It was the first time he did so with me because of my interest in homosexuality....

INT: Eighteen, and the man was fifty?

JJ: Around that—he told me, I think, between forty and fifty.

INT: Yes, yes. That's quite ...

JJ: So he must have been a friend of his father. He didn't tell me the name—nothing.[26]

After establishing that this event probably took place while Jung was still a student, Jacobi repeats: "And he said he trusted in this man and felt so friendly towards him and it was a terrible shock for him because he had never known about homosexuality at all. You can imagine so in such a pious family."[27]

Jacobi's testimony, which corroborates Jung's letter to Freud, hardly describes a seduction, at least not a sexual one. However, as the remainder of the correspondence between Freud and Jung makes clear, psychoanalysis, for a time, held out to Jung the temptations of a spiritual seduction—temptations that he ultimately could not resist.

"We must . . . infiltrate into people from many centers"

The 1974 publication of the letters between Sigmund Freud and C. G. Jung was a huge event. Scholars, long curious about the true relationship between these two giants, suddenly found themselves confronted with an abundance of new evidence to sift, interpret, and argue over. John Gedo and Peter Homans were two of many who immediately recognized that in several of Jung's letters to Freud, beginning in 1910, Jung clearly expressed a desire to transform psychoanalysis into something like a religious movement that would liberate an entire culture with its powerful insights.[28] The psychoanalytic historian John Kerr has likewise documented this "spiritualizing" trend in Jung and in the Swiss contingent of the psychoanalytic movement, a development that eventually led to the resignation of many Swiss—including Jung, Riklin, and Bleuler—from a movement increasingly dominated by Freud's energetic and very vocal Viennese Jewish contingent.[29] F. X. Charet has amply documented that the tension in the Freud-Jung relationship was, in part, rooted in Jung's continuing interest in spiritualism and paranormal phenomena and Freud's disdain for Jung's macabre fascination with the dead and "occultism."[30] I have documented at length in *The Jung Cult* that Jung did indeed have such intentions and over time succeeded in fashioning a charismatic religious cult centered on his own personality and teachings, offering modern individuals the promise of redeeming themselves "spiritually"—a process he called "individuation"—and offering them the opportunity to become part of a select spiritual elite.

Volumes have been written about the evidence in the Freud-Jung correspondence pointing to Jung's religion-building proclivities. For our purposes, two letters by Jung stand out. Only a little over four months after immersing himself in the study of mythology and archeological sites and texts, on February 11, 1910, Jung responded to a query by Freud. In a letter to Jung on January 13, Freud mentioned that he had received an invitation to join the International Order for Ethics and Culture, which its founder, Albert Knapp, proposed as a forum for making pragmatic changes in human society. It was to be a secular organization designed to fill the ethical and cultural vacuum caused by the demise of the superstitious worldview promoted by Judeo-Christian religions. Freud told Jung that he thought psychoanalysis might benefit from such an association and asked Jung's opinion. Freud could never have anticipated the response he received.

Jung wrote that he, too, had received such an invitation, but that the project appalled him. He complained that Knapp's organization would be an "artificial one," since "religion can only be replaced by religion."[31]

"Is there a new savior in [it]?" he asked. "What sort of new myth does it hand out for us to live by? Only the wise are ethical from sheer intellectual presumption, the rest of us need the eternal truth of myth."

Jung's meaning here is clear: even psychoanalysis can only be authentic if it offers the "eternal truth of myth" to others. Further, Jung believed that the mythic sexual insights of psychoanalysis could be the catalyst for cultural redemption and rebirth, a vivifying replacement for Christianity. "The ethical problem of sexual freedom is really enormous and worth the sweat of all noble souls. But 2000 years of Christianity can only be replaced by something equivalent, an 'irresistible mass movement.' "

Such a mass movement would, of course, be the new religion of modernity: psychoanalysis.

Jung wrote:

I imagine a far finer and more comprehensive task for [psychoanalysis] than alliance with an ethical fraternity. I think we must give it time to infiltrate into people from many centers, to revivify among intellectuals a feeling for symbol and myth, ever so gently to transform Christ back into the soothsaying god of the vine, which he was, and in this way absorb those ecstatic instinctual forces of Christianity for the *one* purpose of making the cult and the sacred myth what they once were—a drunken feast of joy where man regained the ethos and holiness of an animal. That was the beauty and purpose of classical religion.

Had the letter ended there, it would have been stunning enough. But Jung insisted that a biologically and evolutionarily correct ethical development must arise from within Christianity and "must bring to fruition its hymn of love, the agony and ecstasy over the dying and resurgent god, the mystic power of the wine, the awesome anthropophagy of the Last Supper—only *this* ethical development can serve the vital forces of religion." He ended this letter by expressing his desire "to affiliate [psychoanalysis] with everything that is dynamic and alive. One can only let this kind of thing grow."

If we could point to the very moment when Freud should have begun to have grave doubts about Jung as his son and heir apparent, it would have to be shortly after he read this letter. This explosive effusion of Christian and Dionysian imagery and visions of psychoanalysis as an "irresistible mass movement" and as a living replacement for orthodox Christianity could only have reminded Freud of certain Nietzschean, Wagnerian, Volkish neopagan cultural themes that would appeal primarily to Germanic Christians—Aryans.

Freud's response was a reprimand. Jung's zealotry was clearly off-putting. "But you mustn't regard me as the founder of a religion," Freud said. "My intentions are not so far-reaching. . . . I am not thinking of a substitute for religion. This need must be sublimated."[32]

Jung quickly responded on February 20, 1910, asking Freud's forgiveness for "another of those rampages of fantasy I indulge in from time to time."[33] Within the year, however, he returned to his fantasies about turning psychoanalysis into a new religion. In August 1910, he wrote to Freud that the enemies of the psychoanalytic movement were "saying some very remarkable things which ought to open our eyes in several ways."[34] These critics charged that the psychoanalytic movement was more a mystical sect or cult, or a secret society with levels of initiation like the Freemasons, than a medical or scientific program. Jung did not refute these charges. "All these mutterings about sectarianism, mysticism, arcane jargon, initiation, etc., mean something." He agreed that the critics were aiming their criticisms at something that did indeed have "all the trappings of a religion." Rather than deny these charges of cultism, Jung offered a defense of the movement's secret-society social structure.

"[Psychoanalysis] thrives only in a very tight enclave of minds," Jung wrote. "Seclusion is like a warm rain. One should therefore barricade this territory against the ambitions of the public for a long time to come." Only a specially chosen elite who are initiated into the mysteries of psychoanalysis—the analysts themselves—should have full knowledge of its secrets. In Jung's view, the psychoanalytic movement should operate outside the conventional sphere of society, holding out to the public little more than the promise of revitalization or rebirth if they submitted to treatment. As in the Freemasons, where special knowledge exclusive to the Illuminati is only hinted at, Jung argued that "psychoanalysis is too great a truth to be publicly acknowledged as yet. Generously adulterated extracts and thin dilutions of it should first be handed around." Then, after fantasizing about the infiltration of proponents of psychoanalysis into major universities, he exuberantly proclaimed, "thereupon the Golden Age will dawn."

But within less than two years Jung and Freud were not even on speaking terms. And the "irresistible mass movement" that was to unite Viennese and Swiss, Jews and Aryans, shattered into several centers of gravity.

PART TWO

Mysteria

Shall we write about the things not to be spoken of?
Shall we divulge the things not to be divulged?
Shall we pronounce the things not to be pronounced?

>   Julian, *Hymn to the Mother of the Gods*
>   (*fourth century* C.E.)

(*preceding page*) Fidus, "Betender Knabe" ("Worshiping Lad"), 1916. This is an example of Fidus's signature icon: "Lichtgebet" ("Prayer to the Light"), the famous image of Aryan sun worship.

FIVE

Polygamy

There is no doubt that Jung had good reason to be satisfied with his life as he approached his thirty-second birthday in 1907. He had risen to *Oberarzt* at the Burghölzli clinic, just behind Bleuler. His experimental researches using the word-association method had been hailed as a major new advancement, helping to place psychiatry onto a scientific footing. These same experimental reports had been translated into major English, French, and Italian scientific journals, making him world renowned within the field of psychiatry. He had established a relationship with the controversial Sigmund Freud and brought the movement to such prominence that it could no longer be ignored. As confirmed later by vote of its membership, Jung was clearly second in command of the psychoanalytic movement. Freud made it clear to the jealous Viennese that he had extended the right of charismatic succession to Jung if he wanted it. We all know now that he didn't.

By all outward appearances, the spring of 1908 brought a continuation of joyous triumphs in his personal life. He marked his fifth wedding anniversary with his wife, the former Emma Rauschenbach of Schaffhausen, and their two children, Agathe and Gret, in their living quarters at the Burghölzli. By the late spring of 1908, Emma was pregnant again, and their only son, Franz Karl, was born in early December.[1] Jung made occasional trips to Munich to confer with Ernst Fiechter, an architect who was designing a new home for them in Küsnacht on the shore of Lake Zurich. Others would look at the Jung family and see an enviable model of youthful vigor, domestic fulfillment, and financial promise.

Jung, it was true, had successfully created the bourgeois existence that he had been trained to do as a "German Mandarin" and a blood member of the German educated middle class. Yet all was not as it appeared. The events of 1908 would threaten the *embourgeoisement* of Jung's psyche like no other and force him onto a path that would profoundly change his outlook on life. Many of the ideas that would later distinguish him from Freud and others had their roots in this year. And the apparent bourgeois tranquillity of his personal life would soon be in utter chaos.

Most histories traditionally—and mistakenly—point to Freud as the single most influential person in Jung's life. As the new material that has emerged from archives has shown, that honor could go to any one of three individuals who were all patients and colleagues of Jung: Otto Gross, Sabina Spielrein, and Antonia ("Toni") Wolff. Gross was Jung's colleague in the psychoanalytic movement before he became his patient at the Burghölzli in the spring of 1908. Spielrein and Wolff were his patients before becoming his lovers and collaborators. It was Jung's experience with Gross in 1908 that crucially twisted his fate—and thereby also the destinies of Spielrein, whom he knew at the time, and later Wolff.

Together they consciously sought a formula to unleash, like a chemical reaction, the unconscious forces of creativity and even genius within them. They succeeded. This quaternity synthesized every idea we call "Jungian" today from the elements of their personal experience.

Their catalyst was polygamy.

Otto Gross

By all accounts, Otto Gross was one of the most dangerous men of his generation—a threat to the bourgeois-Christian universe of German Europe.[2] He was never violent; indeed, quite the opposite. But he had an uncanny capacity to inspire others to act on wanton, instinctual impulse. Gross was the great breaker of bonds, the loosener, the beloved of an army of women he had driven mad—if just for a short time. He coaxed one lover/patient to suicide, and then another patient died under similar circumstances. His contemporaries described him as brilliant, creative, charismatic, and troubled. He was a Neitzschean physician, a Freudian psychoanalyst, an anarchist, the high priest of sexual liberation, a master of orgies, the enemy of patriarchy, and a dissolute cocaine and morphine addict. He was loved and hated with equal passion, an infectious agent to some, a healing touch to others. He was a strawberry-blond Dionysus.

Sigmund Freud thought him a genius. To Jung he once said, "You really are the only one capable of making an original contribution; except perhaps for O. Gross, but unfortunately his health is poor."[3] Ernest Jones met with him in 1907 and 1908 in Munich to receive his first instruction in the methods of psychoanalysis. To him, Gross was "the nearest approach to the romantic ideal of a genius I have ever met, and he also illustrated the supposed resemblance of genius to madness, for he was suffering from an unmistakable form of insanity that before my very eyes culminated in murder, asylum, and suicide."[4] To Jung he was so much more, but neither Jung nor his followers have acknowledged his importance. As he revised his published works over the course of his life, Jung carefully removed references to colleagues who fell prey to scandal or suicide. Otto Gross was certainly one of them. Nevertheless, Jung's cataclysmic encounter with Gross is a critical episode in the secret history of his life.

The criminal mind

No story of Otto Gross can be told without reference to his antithesis, his father Hans, famous in his own time around the world as the father of modern scientific criminology. Trained as a lawyer, he was for many years a powerful examining magistrate who traveled all over Austria investigating and analyzing criminal evidence. His practical experience hunting criminals taught him the value of the modern scientific techniques offered by chemists, biologists, bacteriologists, toxicologists, physicians (especially psychiatrists), engineers, and firearms experts. He recognized the importance of Jung's work with the word-association test for examining potential criminals and liars. He was a professor of criminal law at Czernowitz, Prague, and Graz. He authored the first modern textbook on the science of crime detection and set up the first multipurpose, multidisciplinary laboratory for analyzing evidence from the scenes of crimes.

At his famous Criminalistic Institute he kept a collection of items of educational value to the modern crime fighter, including an unforgettable display of the skulls of murdered men. He also kept cabinets of deadly poisons, firearms and bullets, sword canes and rifle canes, as well as the dream books, love potions, astrological charts, and magical verses that provided clues to the superstitious criminal mind. Occult interests, Hans Gross believed, were the behavioral stigmata of degeneracy, especially among Gypsies. He spent considerable effort in drawing this public-health issue to the attention of the lay public, and the Romany and Sinti Gypsy populations of Austria-Hungary did not fare well under his recommendations for a more hygienic, civilized society. A Roman Catholic tempered by a scientific education, he investigated the belief that Jews were kidnapping and ritually murdering Christian babies. But his legal handling of such cases raised questions about his impartiality.[5]

In 1914, Hans Gross told a reporter for *McClure's* magazine that the criminalist must be a polymath:

> He should be a linguist and a draftsman. . . . He should know what a physician can tell him, what he should ask him; he must know the wiles of the poacher as well as those of the stock speculator; he should discern how a will was forged, and what was the sequence of events in a railway accident; he must know how professional gamblers cheated, and how a boiler exploded . . . he must understand the jargon of the underworld, must be capable of translating cipher messages, and must know the methods and tools of all artisans.[6]

Footprints, bloodstains, fingerprints, and the tricks of photography should also all be the business of the criminalist, he said.

Hans Gross proselytized his vision for a better world. In it, science should serve as an instrument of power with whose help the state and society could create and maintain law and order.[7]

To many in the years before the First World War this father-son dyad symbolized a grand tension of opposites in the Central European culture. It became a titanic and very public clash between acknowledged leaders of bourgeois-Christian and bohemian worlds, between the ideals of patriarchy and matriarchy, and between the forces of repression and liberation, both sexual and political. Both Freud and Jung entered this fray on the side of the father.

Michael Raub, an expert on the life and work of Otto Gross, has pointed out that in his early career as a physician Otto Gross was very much his father's son. His first book was a straightforward medical manual, and a year later an essay on the "phylogenetic" basis of ethics proposed an evolutionary explanation for what he termed the "anticriminal impulse," the revulsion felt by most normal human beings toward antisocial or criminal activities.[8]

Although Otto Gross rejected his father's views just a few years later, this essay demonstrates an important aspect of his style of thought that dominated much of his later philosophy: the evolutionary basis of most present human behaviors. Neither spiritual nor intellectual existence is dependent upon the free will of the individual, he argued, but both are the results of the phylogenetic development of the instincts. Gross utilized evolutionary theory as an apologia for bourgeois social conventions, and he later appealed to the logic of evolutionary theory and the call of the ancestral blood to cast off such mechanisms of repression, promising both physical and psychological liberation for those who followed his new ethics. Scientific insights, especially those of Nietzsche and Freud, were to be the new instruments of power through which the patriarchal state and society could be overthrown.

Since 1898, Gross had been experimenting with psychoactive substances.[9] On a sea voyage to South America in 1900 and 1901, the boredom was lessened by the drugs he brought with him as the ship's doctor. At first he ingested small amounts of opium and morphine, but by the beginning of 1902 he was taking higher doses of morphine, and by April he needed it at least twice a day just to perform his duties in a psychiatric clinic in Graz. Soon he could not even perform the most basic of duties. He spent his days at a coffeehouse, where he sat and thought and wrote. Through the efforts of his father, Gross was sent to Switzerland for treatment, and by the end of April he was admitted to the Burghölzli Psychiatric Clinic in Zurich. Although Jung was there at the time and must have known of his admission, the records do not indicate who the treating physician was.

At the Burghölzli, Gross was monitored as he withdrew from morphine. According to the existing hospital records, he claimed upon admission that the "cause of his bout of morphinism was unhappy love."[10] His diagnosis was "Morphinism." After observing him for a few months, an unknown member of the medical staff administered a final diagnosis of "severe psychopathy." By July he was discharged.

Soon he was back in the coffeehouses, thinking, writing.

"Dr. Askonas"

Otto Gross developed an interest in the works of Freud as early as 1904. In 1907, after a brief stint in Emil Kraepelin's famous clinic in Munich, he published a book comparing and contrasting Freud's ideas with Kraepelin's concept of "manic-depressive insanity."[11] Gross's small book was favorable to Freud, and he soon found himself being courted by the Viennese psychoanalytic circle. Freud in particular saw Gross as a prime catch, famous and, like Jung, an Aryan.

In 1906, Gross moved to Munich with his wife, Frieda, whom he had married in 1903. In the years to follow, he sank deeper into chronic morphinism and cocaine addiction. Like many of that fin-de-siècle generation, he absorbed the works of Nietzsche and became interested in finding practical methods to change not only the repressed individuals he treated but the entire pathogenic, patriarchal authority structure of society as a whole. For Gross, Nietzsche provided the metaphors, and Freud provided the technique.

In Schwabing, Otto Gross met the writers, artists, and revolutionaries who remembered him even decades later. His "place"—the Café Stefanie—was a nexus of cultural history in those years, and for a time Gross ruled bohemia from his small table in the back, enveloped in the thick ectoplasmic fog of tobacco smoke. Richard Seewald recalled that so many would-be geniuses from all over Europe gathered there in the years before the First World War that it was popularly called *"Cafe Grössenwahn"*—"Café Megalomania."[12] Here Seewald met future Dadaists Emmy Hennings and Hugo Ball, Henri Bing (the cartoonist for the avant-garde journals *Jugend* and *Simplicissimus*), the writers Johannes Becher, Erich Mühsam, and Gustav Meyrink, and "the unhappy Dr. Gross, son of the famous criminal psychologist, his waistcoat sprinkled with cocaine."[13]

Leonhard Frank, who was Gross's friend for many years, said that "The Café Stefanie was his university . . . and [Gross] was a Professor with an academic Chair at a table near the stove."[14] Frank remembered that Gross knew all of Nietzsche by heart. At the Café Stefanie, Gross led nocturnal discussions about the implications of the works of Freud and Nietzsche for the world, as he believed they had paved the way for a new type of human being. Frank remembers that the overthrow of the existing political and social structure, the utopian restoration of prehistoric matriarchy, and the necessity of sexual freedom were frequently discussed at any table that Gross occupied. Gross gave impromptu all-night psychoanalytic sessions, holding his audiences spellbound. Commanding his "patients" with his blue eyes, he relentlessly insisted, *"Nichts verdraengen!"*—"Repress nothing!"

They obeyed.

Erich Mühsam, the archetypal bohemian, writer, anarchist, revolutionary, Asconan orgiast, and bisexual, did not fully overthrow the repressions instilled by a bourgeois upbringing in Lübeck until Gross analyzed him daily for six straight weeks. Mühsam was so thrilled with his experience that he wrote to Freud to thank him for inventing psychoanalysis.[15] Mühsam marveled to Freud that he experienced relief by tracing his symptoms back to their original causes, claiming, "I was able to observe how sometime through a question of the physician and the consequent answer with its associations, suddenly an entire crust of disease fell off." Outside of his sessions, Mühsam said the method he had learned from Gross worked "automatically." Although originally fearing a loss of his creative ability through analysis, the exact opposite happened: his poetry and writing actually improved. His description of his experience in analysis gives us insight into Gross's unorthodox—but apparently effective—clinical style:

> For me as a writer, the functioning of your system was of course of particular interest. I found its value especially in the fact that the task of the physician would be mainly to make the patient himself the physician. The patient is induced to diagnose his illness. On the basis of the diagnosis discovered by himself, he therefore carries out his own cure. He is brought to the point where he is no longer interested in himself as a sufferer but in the suffering itself. He objectifies his condition. He does not put the importance anymore upon himself as a pitiable patient, as the emotionally martyred, as a hysteric seeking cure, but as a physician, as someone who does not feel the sickness anymore but perceives it. The transformation of the subjective sensations into objective values is the process of cure.

Ernest Jones remembered watching Gross in action at the Café Passage, "where the analytic treatments were all carried out."[16] Late in life Jones could recall the man's magic: "But such penetrative power of divining the inner thoughts of others I was never to see again, nor is it a matter that lends itself to description."

Gross soon joined the great migratory circuit of fin-de-siècle bohemian life from Schwabing to Zurich to Ascona, a village in the Italian part of Switzerland that became a spiritual epicenter for the counterculture.[17] Between 1906 and 1913, Gross divided most of his time between it and Schwabing. His activities during these years brought him into contact with writers who would later immortalize him as a character in their novels and short stories. In one by Max Brod, he is portrayed, albeit negatively, in the dictatorial character known as "Dr. Askonas."[18]

Through Otto Gross, psychoanalysis first leapt from the bourgeoisie to the bohemian counterculture, beginning a literary and artistic fascination with Freudian theory that continues to this day. But in 1908, when Jung first became intimate with Gross and his domain, this was a foreign world that was highly objectionable to the bourgeois sentiments of men like Freud and Jung. Freud was not happy about the "crazy artists" and others of "that kind" whom Gross brought into the psychoanalytic fold. Hans Gross went even further, believing that such alternative lifestyles promoted degeneracy and were a greater threat to the survival of a good and just society than criminality. By 1908, he increasingly looked upon his only child, Otto, with these damning eyes.

"Exclusiveness of sexual community is a lie"

The sociologist Max Weber and his wife, Marianne, personally witnessed Gross's charismatic effect on others and were equally repulsed by the theory of cultural revitalization through sexual liberation that he espoused. "It was a delusion to build up certain psychiatric insights into a world-redeeming prophecy,"[19] the Webers warned their friends—unsuccessfully—as they watched marriages bend and break around them.

In 1907, Gross traveled to Heidelberg, where the circle around Max Weber was one of the most vibrant intellectual centers in Germany. Weber was a living model of bourgeois-Christian respectability and regarded by many as one of the best minds in Europe.

Gross usually stayed with Weber's close associate, Edgar Jaffe. (Jaffe's wife, Else, and her sister, Frieda Weekly, are better known to us as the von Richthofen sisters.)[20] Gross established intimate relationships with several people in that circle, some of whom he had met at the Café Stefanie. By this time Gross was preaching a gospel of sexual liberation that he claimed was based on the insights of Nietzsche and Freud. Psychoanalysis—at least in the "wild" manner that Gross conducted it—would remove the chains of repression that an unnatural "civilized" society had imposed on individuals. As products of a long evolutionary process, humans were not adapted for civilized life and social conventions. The creative life-force—sexuality—suffered the most in the artificial environment of the civilized world. The most detailed description of Gross's philosophy is in the memoirs of Marianne Weber:

> A young psychiatrist, a disciple of S. Freud with the magic of a brilliant mind and heart, had gained considerable influence. He interpreted the new insights of the master in his own fashion, drew radical conclusions from them, and proclaimed a sexual communism compared with which the so-called "new ethics" appeared quite harmless. In outline his doctrine went something like this: The life-enhancing value of eroticism is so great that it must remain free from extraneous considerations and laws, and, above all, from any integration into everyday life. If, for the time being, marriage continues to exist as a provision for women and children, love ought to celebrate its ecstasies outside this realm. Husbands and wives should not begrudge each other whatever erotic stimuli may present themselves. Jealousy is something mean. Just as one has several people as friends, one can also have sexual union with several people at any given period and be "faithful" to each one. But any belief in the permanence of feeling for a single human being is an illusion, and therefore exclusiveness of sexual community is a lie. The power of love is necessarily weakened by being constantly directed to the same person. The sexuality on which it is founded requires many-sided satisfaction. Its mo-

nogamous limitation "represses" the natural drives and endangers emotional health. Therefore, away with the fetters that prevent a person from fulfilling himself in new experiences; free love will save the world.

Weber sadly recalls, "The Freudian was successful and his message found believers. Under his influence both men and women dared to risk their own and their companions' spiritual well-being."[21]

What Marianne Weber didn't report in her memoirs was the extent to which Gross personally converted her friends to the practice of polygamy. He had affairs with both von Richthofen sisters, impregnating Else. Frieda was so profoundly changed by her liaison with Gross that she kept his love letters to her and practiced his doctrine of free love throughout the rest of her life, even during her long, nomadic marriage to D. H. Lawrence. Gross's love letters were awash in his Nietzschean life-philosophy (*Lebensphilosophie*): "You know my faith," he wrote, "that it is always out of *decadence* that a *new harmony* in life creates itself."[22] In 1907, both Frieda Gross and Else Jaffe gave birth to sons sired by Otto Gross. Both mothers named their sons Peter.

Although shocked and bewildered by the seemingly mad behavior of their close friends, the Webers did not condemn them for following Gross's destructive "psychiatric ethos." "Indeed," Marianne Weber admits, "we had to admire the courage of those who risked themselves by sinning and then overcame the sin."[23] One who undertook the risk—and thereby underwent a tremendous personal conversion—was C. G. Jung.

Saving psychoanalysis by civilizing Otto Gross
In the spring of 1908, Hans Gross wrote to Bleuler and Jung to beg them to again commit his son to the Burghölzli for treatment. Hans Gross had been communicating with Otto's wife, Frieda, and was greatly concerned about what was happening in Munich. Because he now had a grandson, he feared Otto would ruin this child's life as well. On April 4, he wrote again to Bleuler, reporting that his daughter-in-law had told him that Otto would submit to treatment—meaning psychoanalysis—but not for his addictions; Otto clearly resented Frieda for colluding with his father. Hans Gross asked Bleuler to keep a place reserved for Otto. Bleuler relayed these messages to Jung.[24]

For a while, Jung put him off. And for a good reason: He did not like Otto Gross very much.

They had met in Amsterdam in September 1907 at the Congress for Neuro-Psychiatry, where Jung gave his first public defense of Freud. Afterward, he wrote a letter to Freud that contained some revelatory, if perhaps contradictory, observations on polygamy. Jung first told Freud that he envied the "uninhibited abreaction of the polygamous instinct" of the psychoanalyst and "gasbag" Max Eitington, who was also at the conference. Then Jung turned his attention to Otto Gross.

"Dr. Gross tells me," wrote Jung, "the truly healthy state for the neurotic is sexual immorality. Hence he associates you with Nietzsche." Jung clearly disagreed. As a man who at least nominally considered himself a Christian in 1907 and 1908, and as a physician and politically conservative member of the bourgeoisie, at this point in his life he still regarded civilization as a largely positive process. This soon changed. But at the time, he told Freud: "It seems to me, however, that sexual repression is a very important and indispensable civilizing factor, even if pathogenic for many inferior people. Still, there must always be a few flies in the world's ointment. What else is civilization but the fruit of adversity? I feel Gross is going along too far with the vogue for the sexual short-circuit, which is neither intelligent, nor in good taste, but merely convenient, and therefore anything but a civilizing factor."[25]

Others in the psychoanalytic movement knew of Jung's ill will toward Gross. After he eventually agreed to treat Gross at the Burghölzli, and Gross concurred, Ernest Jones wrote to Freud on May 13, 1908, expressing his concern. Jones at this time was still very fond of Gross. "I hear Jung is going to treat him psychically," he reported, "and naturally feel a little uneasy about that for Jung does not find it easy to conceal his feelings, and he has a pretty strong dislike to Gross; in addition, there are some fundamental differences of opinion between them on moral questions. However, we must hope for the best."[26]

Freud had been urging Jung to cooperate with Hans Gross. They recognized Otto's intellectual gifts and realized the importance of having Hans Gross's son in the psychoanalytic movement. The very first congress of the International Psychoanalytic Association was about to take place in Salzburg. Extraordinary methods to save Otto Gross suddenly became a priority.

Freud convinced Jung to admit Gross to allow him to withdraw from opium and cocaine. Jung could then proceed with an initial psychoanalysis. Freud urged Jung to keep Gross incarcerated until October, when he could be transferred to Vienna, where Freud would handle the deeper psychoanalysis himself.

At the Salzburg congress, Freud and Jung persuaded Otto to enter treatment. Looking thin and a bit unkempt, and probably under the influence of cocaine, Otto Gross nonetheless gave a short talk that everyone agreed was brilliant. Wilhelm Stekel remembered later that, "in his inspiring speech [Gross] compared Freud to Nietzsche and hailed him as a destroyer of old prejudices, an enlarger of psychological horizons, and a scientific revolutionary."[27] Stekel was the only one of Gross's former colleagues to write an appreciation of him after his lonely death on the streets of Berlin in 1920.

On May 11, 1908, Jung reported to Freud that Gross had arrived in Zurich with his wife. He looked terrible. Jung immediately began the gradual process of diluting his opium intake and comforting him during the painful withdrawal phase.

Jung's notes on the patient Otto Gross

Jung interviewed Frieda Gross at length to obtain a detailed medical history of Otto.[28] In the medical history report of "Frau Dr. Gross," Jung recorded that Frieda and Otto had married shortly after his 1902 discharge from the Burghölzli. Not long after the wedding, he began once again to use morphine. In 1904, Frieda wanted to have a child, so Otto went to Ascona and successfully weaned himself off all drugs. After a successful conception (the fate of the child is not mentioned in Jung's report), his use of narcotics resumed. From morphine he went on to opium and cocaine. He snorted a concoction of an anesthetic and cocaine every day and ingested up to fifteen grams of pure opium. His sleep patterns were extremely irregular. Sometimes he would sleep for sixteen hours at a time, and sometimes he wouldn't be able to sleep at all. He could never sit still for very long and often needed to get up and pace about. The worst thing for Frieda was his "incessant theorizing" and his constant questioning. He insisted on analyzing her, but she resisted him, very often proposing her own counterhypotheses. Frustrated, he claimed these were symptoms of her "complex-resistances." In his darker moments he threatened to commit suicide. She left him for weeks at a time just so she could regain her strength.

Frieda complained bitterly about Otto's affair in the past year with the "Jewess" Regina Ullman. Ullman was a writer, and Gross was convinced that he could "liberate her genius through analysis." Frieda resisted the affair vigorously, and it was eventually terminated. At that time he took vast quantities of opium. During his administration of this "treatment" he was always in the greatest excitement. The analysis often lasted throughout the night and he insisted that his entire destiny depended on it. He blamed Frieda for his lack of interest and desire in scientific work. She said that all of his energy went into the nightly coffeehouse sessions, where he analyzed losers (*Declasses*) of all kinds. Finally, Otto promised her that he would seek treatment in an institution. Jung ended his report with the compassionate statement that Otto's decision to enter the hospital for treatment "cost the wife a heroic expenditure of her energy."

Jung's own notes on the course of treatment are sparse but still revealing.[29] We see here already the beginning of Jung's interest in how a patient's artistic productions provide information about the unconscious mind. By 1916, Jung required this therapeutic technique of all his patients.

On May 18, after the initial week of treatment, Jung reported in his first note that, "Until now the opium was kept at a maximum of 6.0 [grams] per day. On the very first night the patient made a great scene when he was told that he could not have any light at night. Then he said he must be going and should be let out immediately. With the greatest meanness he said that someone had locked him in here. . . . Daily many hours of analysis." On May 23, Jung noted that the level of opium had been reduced to three grams per day "without any remarkable withdrawal symptoms" and "with continuing analysis." Furthermore, "only with daily reminders does he wash his hands at least once a day and does not continue to stain his clothes with food and cigarette ashes. Outside of analysis he does nothing but make infantile drawings. He draws 'movement' not wholly indecently, but certainly like a dilettante." To Jung, Gross seemed completely unaware of the low artistic quality of his productions.

The note continued: "He insists he has a great talent for drawing. Inscribes the walls with associations and other notes. Always lies in bed with his clothes and shoes on, and, despite the warm weather, he wears thick underpants and 5–6 undershirts. Snorts cocaine and anaesthesin [an anesthetic] continuously. In his room the greatest disorder always rules. Throws all matches, cigarettes, etc. on the floor. Leaves his intimate personal letters around for anyone to see." Although ideas about treating addictions were certainly different at the turn of the century, the fact that Gross was allowed to continue to snort cocaine and an anesthetic during this time still raises some difficult questions about Jung's judgment in this case.

Jung reported on May 28 that the "opium was discontinued entirely." Jung's letters to Freud during the treatment period always stressed that Gross "voluntarily" agreed to the reduction and eventual discontinuation of doses of opium during the withdrawal. The clinical notes tell a different story. Gross, it seems, wanted opium slipped to him on the side, even if it meant threatening or blackmailing the assistant physician. Jung wrote simply, "No insight that this is impossible in a psychoanalytic relationship."

Jung ended the progress note for this day by adding other details that never appeared in his reports to Freud: "In recent days another terrible outburst, constantly demanded attention, roared like an animal if one didn't come immediately, rolled himself on the ground. The worst withdrawal symptoms often disappeared during conversation and without renewed 'Opiumdosis.' Opium restored with Codein, 4.0 [grams] per day. Once, while in a rage, broke a chair."

From May 28 until June 12, Jung gradually reduced the codeine, producing typical withdrawal symptoms along the way. Gross strongly protested further reduction in his dosage, but to no avail. By June 12, Gross was free of all drugs and feeling much better. Although Jung's letters to Freud during these weeks painted a rich and optimistic picture of his analysis with Gross as an intellectually stimulating engagement between two colleagues, his short clinical notes concerning the analysis provide a more realistic impression of a desperately ill man withdrawing from powerful narcotics. Psychoanalysis is mentioned in the clinical-progress notes as being "administered" to Otto Gross as if it were a powerful therapeutic drug itself.

The relationship between the two men intensified. During these warm June days Jung became more and more intrigued with Otto Gross and at times held around-the-clock analytic sessions with him. "I have sacrificed days and nights to him," he later told Freud."[30] Something was happening to him as well.

"After intensive analysis of complexes [*Komplex-analyse*] the patient accepted the knowledge of his own progressive deterioration," Jung noted on June 2. One week later, Jung triumphantly recorded his first therapeutic success: "Under continual analysis [his] condition has improved markedly. The infantile tantrums [*Aufregungen*] with childish complaints and impulses have now stopped." But his first drug-free days were still difficult. Jung wrote on June 12: "Healthy without withdrawal. Amiable but very labile, cries very easily, and when he speaks or laughs it is with a whining voice. Quick to anger. He is totally convinced that he is cured. Makes the most optimistic plans for the future: a Munich apartment with 4 rooms and a servant, rented in the vicinity of Kraepelin's clinic, 'Dr. Gross, Austrian certified physician, Psychotherapist.' Exhibits infantile delight until financial difficulties are discussed." Jung clearly thought Gross was bordering on grandiosity, and there was an obvious avoidance of the demands of reality. Jung continued: "Illustrated the outer-side of the door to his room with peculiar drawings. If he isn't walking around, he spends the entire day sitting or lying in bed in just about any position imaginable, for example, his head under the pillow or his feet on it. Never productive."

Jung then made an interesting revelation about his own interests at the time: "Returned a thick book on mythology, claimed to have read it." Jung must have loaned him the book, and given that doctor and patient were also colleagues we must assume that Jung saw some relevance of mythology to the understanding of the unconscious mind. This new evidence places his interest in such a connection more than a year earlier than has previously been thought.

However, despite Gross's insistence that he was cured, Jung's notes make it clear that Gross still suffered from severe cognitive impairment and a lack of psychological insight. "He writes all the time, but *never* a letter. Despite numerous requests, he is in no condition to put the results of his analysis in writing. Only once was he able to formulate a couple of sentences with psychological content." Jung again commented on the dirtiness and disorderliness of Gross's room and his disheveled appearance.

On June 14, Frieda Gross visited her husband. "At first he conducted himself in a calm and kindly manner." Soon, however, he became agitated, childish. Efforts were made to prevent a more serious outburst. Frieda visited him again on the following day, but Gross caused "a great scene" because his wife had refused to have him immediately discharged from the hospital. Jung wrote that Gross "considered himself completely cured and said he would develop an anxiety neurosis if he wasn't immediately discharged. He conducted himself like a small child. Finally said to his wife: he *hates* her, and from now on they are separated." Soon, he calmed down.

By the following day, Gross's mood had swung to the opposite pole: "Today," Jung wrote, "he is of one heart and soul with his wife. He is completely convinced that he can change his wife's mind through analysis." Gross maintained that his wife considered herself to be just fine and replied to his attempts to analyze her with a few responses of an "insignificant nature." Jung reported that Gross's mood had picked up, that indeed he was radiant because Gross felt "he had completed an invaluable analysis, had won back his wife, and that now everything was going to be fine." Jung's notes, however, expressed skepticism about this sudden flight into health.

The morning of the seventeenth began with the usual analytic session. Jung reported that Gross "expressed a desire to go on a long journey with a female friend of his after discharge. The proposal that he again spend a half year as a ship's doctor was not accepted. He maintains that he has so much to do and that his head is so full of ideas that such a journey was not possible. Now he must return to work because he is full of productive energy and is in a creative mood. [His mood is] always very labile, speaks with emotion in a shaky voice." This was the last conversation these two men would ever have.

Feeling and looking better, Otto Gross was allowed to take an unsupervised walk on the enclosed hospital grounds. This proved to be a mistake. "At 4 o'clock this afternoon he *escaped* from the A-2 garden over the wall," Jung wrote. "He had been granted free access to the garden. Has no money with him."

Two days later, Jung received a letter from him. He was in Zurich, and he wanted Jung to send him some money. Jung sent a telegram to Frieda informing her of the escape, but no further steps were taken. She reported that Otto turned to his female friend for money and that he was most likely heading toward Munich or Heidelberg. We can only surmise that Frieda thought he was off to Munich to visit his bohemian friends or to Heidelberg to link up with Else Jaffe.

Jung's last note, on June 19, 1908, ended simply, *"Aufenthalt unbekannt"*—"Whereabouts unknown."[31]

But not to Ernest Jones. Jones was in Munich in May and June 1908 to train with Kraepelin—who despised psychoanalysis and had fired the irresponsible Gross. He made the following report to Freud on June 27:

> I don't know how much you know of the Gross affair. He escaped from Burghölzli last week over the wall and came back here this week. I saw him yesterday. He seems to be much worse, quite paranoiac—shut off from the outside world—and had already started taking cocaine again. He wants to provoke a lawsuit to prove the value of psycho-analysis, to drag Kraepelin in and expose his ignorance before the world! He is extremely *euphorisch und aufregregt* [agitated]. It is a bad business altogether. I believe his wife is going to Graz next week.[32]

"In Gross I discovered many aspects of my true nature"

It is clear from Jung's clinical notes that his experience in treating Otto Gross was not always pleasant. Here was a man he did not like in the first place who, while withdrawing from an addiction to powerful narcotics, was behaving in a highly unstable and, at times, hostile manner. Even his personal hygiene was appalling. To make matters worse, the analysis clearly ended in failure as soon as Otto Gross fled. Jung was supposed to save his soul for Freud and the future of psychoanalysis. He failed. Jung's final diagnosis of Gross was dementia praecox—a severely stigmatizing diagnosis that seems based more on spite than clinical acumen.[33]

At any rate, it was Jung, not Gross, who was most transformed by the analysis, as a remarkable reversal in Jung's attitude toward Gross took place. The analysis was not a one-way street. In effect, as we know from Jung's letters to Freud in May and June 1908, the two men analyzed each other for many hours at a stretch, sometimes until they were both nodding off from exhaustion.

Jung was intent on pushing the limits of the psychoanalytic method to bring about a quick cure. He needed to impress Freud with his great personal healing powers. In the end, Jung's zeal to erode all of Gross's resistances only exacerbated his anxiety—as Gross himself tried to warn Jung. At best, Gross was unaffected by Jung's treatment; at worst, Jung may have pushed his patient to the brink of destruction.

Jung, however, was never the same again. "Whenever I got stuck, he analyzed me," Jung told Freud on May 25, quite early in his treatment.[34] "In this way my own psychic health has benefitted." Jung's optimism during this first week seemed unbounded. "[Gross] is an extraordinarily decent fellow with whom you can hit it off at once provided you can get your own complexes out of the way." Amazingly, Jung then told Freud that "I finished the analysis yesterday," and that there were only "minor obsessions of a secondary importance" to be cleaned up. The Burghölzli progress notes indicate none of this and instead depict Gross as a rather degenerate individual teetering at the point of no return.

Jung admitted that his experience treating Gross was "one of the harshest of my life," but also that something inside him had profoundly changed. "In spite of everything, he is my friend," Jung told Freud in a letter dated June 19, "for at bottom he is a very good and fine man with an unusual mind . . . for in Gross I discovered many aspects of my true nature, so that he often seemed like my twin brother—except for the dementia praecox."[35]

From bourgeois-Christian to modern consciousness
Knowing what kind of person Otto Gross was, and keeping in mind Marianne Weber's summary of his worldview, we can construct a likely scenario of his historic conversations with Jung. Gross captivated Jung with his theories of sexual liberation, his Nietzscheanism, and his utopian dreams of transforming the world through psychoanalysis. Jung must have heard stories about a world that he had been too afraid to venture into, a bohemian realm that was antithetical to everything he thought he valued. During these long hours he learned of Gross's sexual escapades in Heidelberg. He heard of the seductions of the von Richthofen sisters, of illegitimate children, of vegetarianism and opium and orgies. He learned of the Schwabing-to-Zurich-to-Ascona countercultural circuit and listened, amazed, as Gross informed him of neopagans, Theosophists, and sun worshipers who had formed their own colonies in Jung's Switzerland.

And then, of course, there was Otto Gross's own brilliant theorizing. We know from his early psychiatric publications that Gross had an interest in the relationship between biological evolution, cultural evolution, and present experience. In the years just prior to his encounter with Jung, Gross had become quite interested in Johann Jakob Bachofen's theory that our distant ancestors had lived freely, instinctively, polygamously, in small nomadic bands that tended to be matriarchal. Bachofen, who claimed to have archeological evidence for his theories, came to have a profound effect on both Gross and Jung.[36]

In the 1850s, Bachofen visited collections of Greco-Roman antiquities in Italy and began to notice certain patterns in the symbolism that no one had addressed. He became convinced he saw evidence of a lost period of human experience that predated all known civilization in Europe. After spending years deciphering the hidden message behind the signs and symbols on funerary monuments and other items, he outlined his theory in a book published in 1861. Entitled *Das Mutterrecht* (The law of mothers), it had only minimal success and was not well known until it was reprinted in the 1890s. These later printings caught the attention of the bohemians of Schwabing and Ascona. Ludwig Klages, a Nietzschean philosopher and graphologist, read Bachofen's book in 1899 and introduced it to his friends in the so-called Cosmic Circle of disciples that surrounded the German poet Stefan George in Munich. Gross knew several of the members of the circle and probably developed his interest in matriarchy and Bachofen through them.

The nineteenth century was the great era of "stage models" of cultural evolution. Friedrich Engels, for example, developed a theory based on Bachofen's work that proposed that the earliest human societies were matriarchal in structure and only evolved later into patriarchy.[37] Bachofen himself hypothesized that the human race passed through at least three stages of cultural evolution:

The first stage was known as "hetairism." Humans in this period of prehistory lived in small nomadic, communist, and norm-free groups. Polygamy (both polyandry and polygyny) was the rule. Both sexes lived instinctively and freely, but also, by modern standards, savagely. There was no agriculture, no marriage or other social institutions, and females did not know who the fathers of their children were. Bachofen called this stage of human history the "tellurian" period and claimed that it was characterized by earth symbolism.

The second stage was known as the authentic phase of matriarchy, or *Mutterrecht*. During this period, agriculture and the domestication of animals appeared, and along with these innovations came the first rudimentary social institutions. The society of these early humans was based on egalitarian values and a worship of Mother Earth, and the worst crime one could commit was matricide. This was an age in which the human body was glorified. Bachofen thought that the famous Eleusinian mysteries of Greece had come about during these times, and that Demeter was a later incarnation of the original earth-mother goddess.

The third stage of human history—in which we live—is characterized by patriarchy. (Bachofen thought that a very brief transitional phase between matriarchy and patriarchy involved the bisexual god Dionysus.) In the period of dominant patriarchy, the intellect and the rule of society by law were exalted. The sun became the dominant symbol, evinced in Greek culture by the form of Apollo. Bachofen believed that once patriarchy was established, all signs of the prior matriarchal period were systematically eliminated. Enough evidence, however, survived to allow Bachofen to divine the actual truth of the matter—or so he believed.

Such theories were quite popular in the counterculture of German Europe at the turn of the century. Within the tenets of a prehistoric matriarchal society that was egalitarian and possibly even polygamous, many saw the basis of a critique of the patriarchal structure of civilized life. Many who fled to Switzerland—and especially to Ascona—to escape conscription dreamed of an egalitarian and pacifist society. It seemed only logical that the reigning patriarchy should be replaced with matriarchy if it meant a return to a more humane existence.

Gross and Jung came to see the justification for Bachofen's theory in evolutionary biology. If it was true that our earliest human ancestors lived in small nomadic and polygamous bands for tens of thousands of years, then modern humans could not possibly have developed all the necessary adaptations to live in urban, industrialized environments. Since adaptations develop only gradually over time, the last five thousand years or so of recorded civilization were insufficient for natural selection to change the entire world's population. Like contemporary sociobiologists and "evolutionary psychologists," both Gross and Jung believed that, when it came to reproductive strategies, humans were biologically still quite primitive.

Polygamy was therefore to be considered a strong ancestral impulse that ruled even modern human beings. Civilization, despite its many wonderful qualities, tended to injure humans by creating social conventions that required them to repress their true savage nature. To restore human beings to physical and psychological health, the compromises they must make to societal norms must be kept to a minimum. Instinctual, creative energy that was lost to the repressive influence of society could be regained by breaking the rules of society, especially when it came to the "creative life-force" of sexuality. The shackles of family, society, and Deity must be broken. To love freely, instinctively, guiltlessly, generously—to live polygamously—would unleash the ancient creative energies of the body and the unconscious mind and bring humans to a new level of being.

This is what Gross believed and Jung abhorred when they began to analyze each other in the Burghölzli in May and June 1908. This is what both believed by the end of the treatment and what both actively tried to bring about in the years to follow. Gross tried to do so by becoming an anarchist and, in the last years of his life, a kind of communist. Jung did so by founding a spiritualist mystery cult of renewal and rebirth—and by advocating polygamy for the rest of his life.

With historical hindsight, we can see that fundamental aspects of Jung's personal life and his professional life changed after this encounter. He recognized attitudes and impulses in himself that he had previously associated with bohemians, not a professional man, a Christian, and head of a family such as himself. During the course of their time together Gross offered Jung forbidden fruit. After a period of tormented consideration, Jung finally bit. Jung's conception of what constituted a "sin" changed: "doing evil" could have a beneficial effect on the personality by freeing one from "one-sidedness" and putting one back in touch with an Edenic instinctual being. Jung came to believe that *not* giving in to a strong sexual impulse could result in illness or even death. These are all ideas that everyone who knew Jung for any length of time would hear him urge on others.

Once Jung submitted to the temptations Gross offered, profound alterations in his concepts of the places of sexuality and religion in life took place. Because they denigrated the body and sexual activity—especially outside of holy matrimony—the repressive orthodoxies of Christianity now seemed to him to be the true enemies of life. Sexuality had to be brought back into spirituality. By 1912, Jung found another model—the spirituality of pagan antiquity—that held sex sacred. Although Gross did not share Jung's fascination with spiritualism or the occult, his "religion" was finding ways to rejuvenate and indeed redeem humankind through the sacrament of uninhibited sex. Jung soon learned of the spiritual sacredness of sex through personal experience and implored others to consider the call of the flesh.

Jung is also indebted to Otto Gross for the concepts of extraversion and introversion. These are the fundamental ideas of his theory of "psychological types," which he first began to develop in 1913 after his break with Freud, and they are terms that are familiar even today.[38] These concepts are also the basis of a hypothesized trait—"extraversion-introversion"—that is the most scientifically valid of all the "Big Five" personality traits thought to be the basis of all human personalities; whenever the genetic basis of personality is evaluated, the bulk of the evidence points to extraversion-introversion as the most genetically based. Understandably, contemporary textbooks on behavioral genetics usually credit Jung for these ideas, but, arguably, they belong to Gross.[39]

Jung said so himself. In his 1921 book, *Psychological Types,* Jung discusses at length a 1902 book by Gross entitled *Die Cerebrale Sekundärfunktion* (The cerebral secondary function), in which the core concepts that Jung later called extraversion and introversion are described. Jung generously concludes, "Even my terms 'extraversion' and 'introversion' are justified in light of his conceptions."[40] Leonhard Frank later claimed that Jung stole Gross's ideas, although this is not entirely supported by the evidence. Still, 1921 was the last time Jung ever publicly referred to Otto Gross in any significant way. As he became increasingly famous for his theory of psychological types, Jung allowed the memory of the contributions of Otto Gross to recede further and further into obscurity.

Gross never did quit using narcotics. His father succeeded in having him arrested in Berlin on December 9, 1913, and forced into an Austrian asylum for treatment. The resulting scandal shook bohemia and made Otto Gross into a kind of martyr. A Viennese cultural society distributed ten thousand leaflets in Munich, Berlin, Vienna, Zurich, and elsewhere, urging, "Free Otto Gross!" Newspapers and political journals commented on the war between the bourgeois father and the bohemian son. Hans Gross, with the help of Frieda Gross (and possibly even Max Weber), successfully found a way to legally become the guardian of Otto's son Peter.

After agreeing to psychoanalytic treatment by Wilhelm Stekel, Gross was released in 1914. During the First World War he served as a physician in the Austro-Hungarian army. Little is known of this period in his life, although in a letter to Freud dated February 5–9, 1918, Sandor Ferenczi indicates that Gross did not let the war stop his sociosexual revolution:

> A young colleague brought me his wife, whom I naturally was unable to accept. He came to psychoanalysis by way of *Dr. Otto Gross.* Dr. Gross is supposed to have worked in the hospital for infectious diseases *in Ungvar* as a physician attached to the Home Guard regiment. Naturally, he also made his circle of disciples there, who, among other things, had the duty without exception to enter into sexual relations with Dr. Gross's lover, named "Mieze." They supposedly classified the young colleague, who found that repugnant, as "morally unreliable" for that reason. Incidentally, the young colleague had some time ago received news of Dr. Gross's *death,* which has, however, not been substantiated. He will still pop up here and there as a "Golem."[41]

Ferenczi was right to dismiss the report of Gross's death. He was soon spotted in Prague, where he made the acquaintance of Max Brod and Franz

Kafka (who had taken law courses with Hans Gross in Prague), and in Berlin, where he wrote anarchist and unorthodox communist articles for political publications and befriended many in the Berlin Dada movement. But one day he was found alone and ill in an abandoned warehouse in Berlin. He died in a sanitorium in Pankow, north of Berlin—probably of pneumonia—on March 13, 1920.

Sabina Spielrein

Jung's personal life had been in turmoil for quite some time before Gross arrived at the Burghölzli. He had become erotically obsessed with a small, dark twenty-two-year-old Jewish woman, an exile from Russia. She was scintillatingly brilliant, extraordinarily sensitive, and sexually preoccupied. She was deeply in love with Jung, and she didn't care if he had a wife. She had been his patient at the Burghölzli, a hysteric, his "first success" as a psychoanalyst, and now she was a medical student. They shared a love for the music of Richard Wagner. She fantasized about having a Jewish-Aryan child by him, a Wagnerian hero-genius whom she would name Siegfried. When Otto Gross skipped over the wall in June 1908, she was there to comfort Jung. And, in fact, Gross had delivered him to her.

At some point in late 1908 or 1909, Spielrein wrote (probably to Freud): "I sat there waiting in deep depression. Now he arrives, beaming with pleasure, and tells me with strong emotion about Gross, about the great insight he has just received [i.e., about polygamy]; he no longer wants to suppress his feeling for me, he admitted that I was his first, dearest woman friend, etc., etc. (his wife of course excepted), and that he wanted to tell me everything about himself."[42]

Whether Jung and Spielrein had engaged in a sexual relationship prior to this time is unknown. But this independent confirmation of Jung's conversion to the life-philosophy of Otto Gross increases the likelihood of such a possibility. The affair was certainly over by 1912. Sabina Spielrein left Zurich by then and married an exiled Russian physician, even though some evidence suggests she may still have been in love with Jung.

Almost all of what we know about Sabina Spielrein comes from a cache of her personal papers that were found in 1977 in the cellar of the Palais Wilson in Geneva.[43] In recent years, more material on Spielrein has emerged. Perhaps the most significant find has been Jung's original clinical case notes from his initial treatment of her in the Burghölzli in 1904 and 1905, as well as a previously unknown letter to Freud in which he summarized her treatment. In this letter, dated September 25, 1905, Jung claimed, "I have fairly completely analyzed her illness using your method," and with "very favorable success."[44]

Jung referred Spielrein to Freud for treatment at the insistence of her mother, who realized that Spielrein had fallen in love with Jung and feared the consequences. Jung does inform Freud that "During the treatment the patient had the misfortune to fall in love with me," and had revealed this to her mother. But in this letter Jung also claims that both the "father and the mother are hysterical, especially the mother," which may explain why Frau Spielrein never passed this letter on to Freud.

No new information about the on-again, off-again affair between Jung and Spielrein appears in these documents. It is clear, however, in his letters to Freud, that after his encounter with Gross, polygamy was very much on Jung's mind. In quite a reversal from the disgust with which he initially greeted Gross's ideas, in a letter to Freud dated March 7, 1909, Jung discussed the Spielrein affair and admitted to his own "polygamous components."[45] He told Freud that he hoped his brush with scandal with Spielrein had secured him "moral qualities which will be the greatest advantage to me in later life." He assured Freud that his relationship with Emma "has gained enormously in assurance and depth." However, by January 3, 1910, he told Freud that his wife was "staging jealous scenes, groundlessly" and that "the prerequisite for a good marriage, it seems to me, is a license to be unfaithful. I in my turn have learned a great deal."[46] Spielrein was still very much on his mind, and soon other female patients and colleagues were as well.

After 1912, Jung exchanged a few letters with Spielrein, but there is no evidence that they ever saw each other after the start of the First World War. As with Gross, he soon stopped talking about her and ceased citing her publications in his own.[47] By 1969 and 1970, out of the 143 persons who were interviewed by Gene Nameche for the C. G. Jung Biographical Archives Project, not one mentioned her. She had apparently disappeared from the oral traditions of the Jungians, lost from memory.[48]

Rx: Polygamy

As the correspondence demonstrates, Jung tended to mislead Freud about the realities of his personal life. Given his need to preserve his bourgeois-Christian persona at this time and his desire to stay in Freud's good graces, Jung's inclination to sweeten the truth is quite understandable. As we now know, Jung's "polygamous components" eventually won out in his personality. From the time he decided to indulge these impulses with Sabina

Spielrein, he would practice polygamy for the rest of his life. Yet as we have learned from the discrepancy between his letters to Freud and his clinical notes on Otto Gross, he also tended to mislead Freud about what he actually said and did with his patients. From at least 1909 onward, he explicitly recommended the central tenet of Gross's philosophy—polygamy—to his male patients.

The first indication of this comes from the case of a patient that Jung mentions in the same fateful letter to Freud of March 7, 1909, in which he admits to his own "polygamous components." After describing his affair with Spielrein, he told Freud: "Fate, which evidently loves crazy games, had just at this time deposited on my doorstep a well-known American (friend of Roosevelt and Taft, proprietor of several big newspapers, etc.) as a patient. Naturally he has the same conflicts I have just overcome, so I could be of great help to him, which is gratifying in more respects than one. It was like balm on my aching wound. This case has interested me so passionately in the last fortnight that I have forgotten my other duties."[49]

This American patient was Medill McCormick, of the prominent McCormick family of Chicago. McCormick's immediate family owned the *Chicago Tribune*. He was treated unsuccessfully by Jung in Zurich in late 1908 and in March 1909. He saw Jung again in September 1909 for a brief consultation in New York City when Jung was attending the Clark University Conference with Freud. McCormick suffered from severe bouts of alcoholism and depression, for which Jung prescribed polygamy as a way of overcoming his despair and saving his soul.

After his later consultation with Jung, McCormick wrote to his wife, Ruth Hanna McCormick, on September 21, 1909: "Jung warned me against being too good and asked particularly if I *felt* free. He rather recommended a little flirting and told me to bear in mind *that it might be advisable* for me to have mistresses—that I was a very dangerous and savage man, that I must not forget my heredity and my infantile influences and lose my soul—if women would save it."[50]

Otto Gross couldn't have said it any better.

Jung may have imparted this advice to many of his male patients and analytic trainees. For example, Aline Valangin, a young woman who was having a relationship problem with an older man whom she did not want to marry, had a few sessions with Jung in 1915 and wrote to him when he was on military assignment. Jung soon farmed her out to an assistant, Dr. Herbert Oczeret, who immediately told her to stop writing to Jung. He wanted her transference all to himself. She left treatment with Oczeret after a few years because he "started to analyze in a really impossible way. At that time he set up a harem out of his women patients. Yes, that was really terrible."[51] Dr. Tina Keller, a later disciple, placed the blame on Jung himself for such actions by his disciples, explaining that when Jung "tried to break conventional bonds, he became exaggerated, and in the early times, also amongst the group around him, new freedoms were misunderstood and led to abuse."[52]

An additional example of this form of treatment can be found in the case of another American, Henry A. Murray, who met Jung in Zurich. He would become a noted psychologist and personality theorist at Harvard University. The historian Forrest Robinson has documented that in 1925 Jung recommended polygamy to Murray as an alternative to divorce.[53] Murray, quite in awe of Jung at the time, then carried on a three-way relationship with his wife and his mistress, Christiana Morgan. With Morgan he acted out a wide variety of sexual fantasies and sex-role reversals in order to develop the psychological components of their personalities. The rationale for this was Jung's theory of "psychological types," which maintained that the road to health involved developing the energies of the opposite sex that were often repressed in oneself.

In later years, mimicking Jung, Murray built his own "Tower" in Massachusetts, which he and Morgan decorated with their own mystical paintings and drawings. They believed that they were performing important spiritual work for all humankind and starting a new form of religion. They created their own new pantheon of gods, in which the sun symbolized the highest deity. They painted the sun in the center of the ceiling of the main ritual room of their tower. Besides orgies of alcohol and sex, they also indulged in detailed magical rituals that involved recitations from Jung's works.[54] In building his tower and keeping an extramarital relationship that spanned decades, Henry Murray was only performing what the "Old Man" (as he called Jung) modeled for him.

By the time Murray met them in 1925, Jung and Toni Wolff had been lovers for more than a decade. And they, too, were convinced that they had founded a new religion. They believed in a new faith in which former sins and evils became necessary for spiritual rebirth. God—no longer One— would emerge from individual visionary experiences and automatic writing as a multitude of natural forces or entities that were both good and evil.

It was a religion conceived through polygamy.

Toni Wolff

In 1910, a twenty-two-year-old woman from one of the oldest families in Zurich was brought by her mother to Jung for treatment, since Jung had treated the son of a family friend. Although only thirty-five, Jung seemed much older to the young woman. Each recognized something precious in the other, something that both soon coveted. In one form or another—as patient, paramour, companion, and collaborator, as a "second wife" in a polygamous threesome—Toni Wolff had an intimate relationship with C. G. Jung for more than forty years. It is safe to say that she knew more sides of him than anyone else ever would and was closer to him than any other friend or wife.

It is commonly thought that Toni Wolff was brought to Jung for depression that followed the death of her father in 1909. Her sister, Susanne Wolff Trüb, discounts this, remembering that "from her early years Toni was a difficult child, even when she was two years old." Indeed, "she was always complicated, all the time. I don't know whether it was more or less the same, after my father's death."[55] Toni's other sister, Erna Wolff Naeff, "read Toni's diaries," according to Susanne, and "thinks she was more complicated afterward."[56]

From 1910 onward, Toni Wolff never created a life for herself outside of Jung's circle. Her sister remembered her as an intellectual person (far more so than Emma Jung or herself), but her only formal education came from Jung. She was particularly fond of Japanese art and culture. But there was something fundamentally wrong with her character, something that never changed, even after analysis with Jung. Throughout her life she had difficulty taking care of herself. "Toni was not at all a practical person," remembered Susanne Trüb. "She never would have been able to live a married life.... But somehow she was never totally in life." She lived with her mother until her mother died in 1940 and then moved into an apartment in the house of her sister, where she remained until her own death in 1953. "She never had to care for herself; other people did it. And later, when she moved to the house of my sister, she took my mother's maid with her."[57]

Wolff was Jung's patient for at least two years. By the late summer of 1911, however, she had become his assistant. She conducted library research for him for the second half of his paper on "Transformations and Symbols of the Libido" (*Wandlungen und Symbole der Libido*), which was published in 1912. His affection for her seemed to grow, and emotionally he turned to her for support after the tragic deaths of his twenty-five-year-old assistant, J. J. Honegger, who committed suicide with an overdose of morphine in the spring of 1911, and his cousin Helly, who died of tuberculosis that November.

Soon Wolff was well on her way to becoming a colleague of sorts. In a letter dated August 29, 1911, Jung joyfully informed Freud that at the upcoming psychoanalytic conference in Weimar in September, "This time the feminine element will have conspicuous elements from Zurich: Sister Moltzer, Dr. Hinkle-Eastwick (an American charmer), Frl. Dr. Spielrein (!), then a new discovery of mine, Frl. Antonia Wolff, a remarkable intellect with an excellent feeling for religion and philosophy, and last but not least, my wife."[58] Sabina Spielrein did not attend the Weimar conference, but in the famous group photograph in which most of Jung's "Zurich school" is clustered to the right of Freud and Jung, we see in the front row the young Toni Wolff two seats from Emma Jung, peering out at us. Of the five women who were to make up the "feminine element" at the 1911 Weimar congress, Jung certainly had sexual relations with at least three of them and possibly four, if certain references to Maria Moltzer are accurate. Only the American, Beatrice Hinkle, did not have an affair with him.

By 1913, Wolff's formal analysis with Jung was finished. Fearing a repeat of the searing pain of his up-and-down love affair with Spielrein, he broke off all relations with her. She became depressed. He fantasized about her constantly. He desperately needed her. In December 1913, he began experimenting with a dissociative technique that he had learned from his experiences with Helly. He began to have powerful, disturbing visions, hear voices, and receive communications from unseen entities. He needed help. He needed Wolff.

At about this time, he dreamed that he and Wolff were hiking in the Alps together. They were in a rock-strewn valley. As they approached a mountain they heard the singing of elves. To his horror, she walked toward this magic mountain and disappeared into it. He woke up in a state of panic.[59]

Knowing he was taking a chance with his marriage and career and risking the delicate psychological state of his former patient, who now, too, was in love with him, he nonetheless contacted her. They began to see each other. They talked, shared the content of their dreams, and nothing more. Jung began to wonder how long he could repress his natural urges. He feared the damage that he might be doing to himself by being too "one-sided." The experience with Spielrein had been painful, but also liberating. He learned mysteries of life he might never have known, and he understood his patients better because of it. Fate had placed yet another young, dark, intellectually alluring young woman in his path, and this one was more like him: she had religious visions, knew how to read astrological charts, and was fascinated with Theosophical publications and their distillations of Western occult wisdom and Eastern philosophies. Spielrein was never like this. Spielrein was too clever, too Jewish.

In his preparatory discussions with Aniela Jaffé for *MDR,* Jung talked a great deal about Toni Wolff. However, despite her importance to Jung, she is never discussed in the book. But in the transcripts of Jaffé's interviews Jung reveals a story that he repeated to his closest disciples to impress upon them the "danger of one-sidedness." During a memorable private session with Dr. Tina Keller, he said:

> He was swimming in the Lake of Zurich. He was an excellent swimmer. However, one day he had a cramp that made him come close to drowning. Then, in a flash of insight he knew that the cramp was the symbolic expression for an act of violence he was doing to himself. As he decided not to suppress the upsurge of life that he had tried to control by will power, the cramp left him. He drew the conclusion that there are situations in which one has no right to set artificial limitations to life's flow.[60]

The moral of Jung's oft-told tale was that if one did not follow one's inner urgings, the "unconscious" would react to this insult by threatening one's life. Jung's sexual relationship with Toni Wolff began almost immediately thereafter, and together they pushed the boundaries of sanity and sexual abandon.

In later years, Jung would tell many of his disciples that it was with Wolff that he first discovered the "mystical" or "spiritual" significance of sexuality. Sometimes, even with new acquaintances, he would be a bit more graphic. John Layard, a British anthropologist who was for a time a disciple of Jung's, told Gene Nameche that Jung talked frankly about Wolff during his very first analytic sessions with him:

INT: What did he tell you about Toni? In your first meetings he talked about her all the time?
JL: Just how marvelous she had been in bed.
INT: Is that right?
JL: Largely, and how splendid she was. I can't remember everything because I was longing to get on with my analysis, and was only passively listening.[61]

Toni Wolff was at Jung's side during the crucial years when he developed all the concepts we now think of as "Jungian": his famous theories of individuation, the collective unconscious and its dominants, which he later called archetypes. It was during these years that the special Jungian vocabulary still used today was developed, terms such as "shadow," "anima," "animus," "persona." She was deeply involved in the development of his personality typology and in the writing of *Psychological Types,* which appeared in 1921.

Wolff had become indispensable to his creative work. She, too, was soon allowed by Jung to analyze others, and she brought the fruit of her labors into their collaboration. They believed they were discovering hidden dimensions of the human spirit. She assisted him with the founding of the Psychological Club in Zurich in 1916, which Jung would later call their "silent experiment in group psychology." In later years, as disciples came from all over the world to be involved in Jung's special initiatory brand of analysis, Wolff called him by her nickname for him, "the Bishop."[62]

Emma Jung, however, fared less well during these years. Her husband was unreachable, emotionally labile, difficult to talk to. Susanne Trüb, who had become her friend, remembered years later, "It was difficult for her in the beginning to understand all of Jung's work on the collective unconscious. It was difficult for her to take part in that. And it is very difficult for a woman with small children." Echoing the folklore that has been passed down in Jungian circles since those early days Trüb added: "And while Jung was working on the collective unconscious, my sister Toni was so important for him. She had an understanding for it. She perhaps was able to encourage him and so gave him the faith. Frau Jung wasn't able to do it. It is impossible when you have five children."[63] Emma Jung did not choose polygamy freely. The situation was presented to her by her husband. At best, she freely chose to adapt to it.

Somehow Jung, Emma, and Wolff came to a mutual understanding that allowed a polygamous arrangement to continue until at least the 1940s. Jung's ill health after a heart attack in 1944 gave Emma more control of her marriage, and for the rest of her life she was able to successfully limit Wolff's access to her husband. But before then, they developed a very bourgeois schedule for their very bohemian situation. Jung would visit Wolff regularly on Wednesday evenings in Zurich, and she would travel to Küsnacht on Sundays to spend the day with Jung and his family in their home. She would sometimes accompany him on short trips without Emma. After Jung built his Tower at Bollingen in the early 1920s, they would regularly spend weeks there alone every summer. Divorce was discussed by both Jung and his wife with their own confidants, but nothing was ever decided.

Throughout their relationship, Jung and Toni Wolff had tremendous arguments and separated from each other for months at a time. Sometimes this was because Jung became interested in other women. In 1925, Jung took a long voyage to Africa to visit the natives of Kenya and Uganda. He was accompanied in the field by Ruth Bailey, a young woman he had met en route. Jung, who was fifty, and Bailey, who was thirty, had a sexual relationship during the course of their safari. Embers continued to glow over the years. After Emma Jung died in 1955, Ruth Bailey moved in with the eighty-year-old Jung to take care of him. As Jung's colleague Carl A. Meier characterized it, "He had a crush for Ruth Bailey for quite a long time and when he was a very old man, well, he may have indulged in some petting or whatnot. In fact, I was told one of these stories by someone who saw it. But he was already an old man by then. Most of these stories are certainly made up by these women [around Jung] for their own prestige."[64] For her part, Toni Wolff is rumored to have only once allowed her feelings for Jung to stray. For a time she developed romantic feelings for Heinrich Steiger, who was once secretary of the Psychological Club.

Apparently there was much gossip—some driven by envy over Wolff's intimacy with Jung—among his disciples in his later years. John Layard reports that one female disciple (probably Jolande Jacobi), "with the natural curiosity of a Viennese" apparently "watched him bathing and said he wasn't very large."[65] It is difficult to imagine gossip like this existing in the circle around Freud.

Polygamy released not only the ancient sexual forces of nature within an individual, but also the energy of the ancestral god, the only true god, the invincible source of all light and heat and libido and life. Without a doubt, once Jung had made the decision to accept the teachings of Otto Gross, his bohemian John the Baptist, he was well along the path to his own death and resurrection.

SIX

Sun Worship

If one honors God, the sun or the fire, then one honors one's own vital force, the libido.
—C. G. Jung, *Psychology of the Unconscious*, 1911

Not even the most recent scientific discoveries . . . which teach us how we live, and move, and have our being in the sun, how we burn it, how we breathe it, how we feed on it—give us any idea of what this source of light and life, this silent traveller, this majestic ruler, this departing friend or dying hero, in his daily or yearly course, was to the awakening consciousness of mankind. People wonder why so much of the old mythology, the daily talk, of the Aryans, was solar:—what else could it have been?
—Friedrich Max Müller,
Lectures on the Origin and Growth of Religion, 1878

What I am now about to say I consider to be of the greatest importance for all things "that breathe and move upon the earth". . . but above all others it is of importance to myself. For I am a follower of King Helios. And of this fact I possess within me, known to myself alone, proofs more certain than I can give. But this, at least, I am permitted to say without sacrilege, that from my childhood an extraordinary longing for the rays of the god penetrated deep into my soul.
—Julian, Emperor of Rome,
"Hymn to King Helios," 362 C.E.

Who can possibly understand the true source of the archaic, rejuvenating energies that pulsed through C. G. Jung in the years following his encounters with Otto Gross and Sabina Spielrein? Not only did sexual energy surge through him with a power that frightened him, but terrifying, decidedly Wagnerian visions of Teutonic figures such as Wotan and Siegfried and of the cosmic dramas of Greek mythology dominated both his waking fantasies and his nocturnal dreams. He had been a man who prided himself on the rational control of his thoughts, of his ability to maintain composure in the face of psychosis, a man who devalued a spontaneous fantasy life as weak, sick, repulsive. But soon he found that he could not regulate the swirling modern chaos in his own psyche.

Between September 1909, when it was clear that the transformational process had begun, and September 1912, when he published his confirmation of his loss of faith in Freud and in the Judeo-Christian god, Jung's attitude toward the unconscious mind changed profoundly. At first believing the unconscious mind to be an entirely personal and individual warehouse of memories, he came to see it as the source of ancestral wishes and tendencies—and even experiences—that were inherited biologically through a type of vitalistic mechanism, a generalized life-force called the libido. By September 1912 he made it clear to Freud and to his own circle in Zurich that this powerful energy of life was not only the sex drive, as Freud had maintained, but should be viewed as a more generalized force of nature whose currents carried ancestral spiritual longings through biological channels.

During these three years, Jung developed the idea that the unconscious mind was the result of a long, phylogenetic, evolutionary process. Just as the human body is a living museum of evolutionary history, so too is the human psyche. And since the most potent ideas of human concern are religious ones, we should discover the spiritual symbols of our ancestors deep within the unconscious mind of each individual. That is, looking at the evolutionary development of the human species, the most recent, and therefore most powerful, influences on present human experience would be racial or tribal ones. In Jung's new view, religious needs were biologically based. The peoples of pagan antiquity, closer to our prehistoric ancestors, celebrated their sexuality in their spirituality and were therefore less plagued by neuroses and psychoses than modern Europeans. Jung forged these insights into the theory that a life could only be meaningful if one's religious beliefs and sexual practices resonated with those of one's racial ancestors.

Polygamy unblocked the rays of this inner source of light and heat that had been eclipsed by centuries of monotheism and the monogamy crushingly demanded by Judeo-Christianity. Otto Gross had taught him that, but Gross fused this knowledge of the morally corrosive effect of polygamy with efforts to bring about an associated change in political consciousness and thereby incite revolution and anarchy. What Jung desired instead were additional psychotherapeutic methods to effect spiritual rebirth. He sought potent new symbols of transformation to bring about changes of consciousness in large numbers of people. He became increasingly certain of his own destiny as the man who would deliver such redemption to humanity but was uncertain of the means of achieving it. After a dream pointed the way, he knew the secret he was looking for was buried in the accounts of pagan regeneration.

Once Jung charged down this intellectual path there was no stopping him. To be sure, a multitude of others had preceded him on this quest. In German Europe at that time legions of scientists and artists, bohemians and bourgeoisie, were fervently seeking much the same thing. And, when we listen carefully to their voices through the cacophony of historical events that took shape beginning in 1933, we can hear the faint singing of their hymns to the sun.

"I often feel I am wandering alone through a strange country"

It all began with a dream aboard the ship that carried Jung and Freud back to Europe after they attended the Clark University Conference in September 1909. Jung found himself descending layer by layer—spatially and temporally—into the foundations of a large old house. As the story is told in *MDR,* Jung left a "rococo style salon" on the top floor for a fifteenth- or sixteenth-century dwelling on the ground floor.[1] He then descended a stone stairway that led to a room from "Roman times," and then farther down to a "low cave cut into the rock" where, at the lowest levels, he found the remnants of a primitive culture: pottery, scattered human bones, and "two human skulls."

In *MDR,* Jung credits this dream for giving him his first idea of a collective unconscious. In a 1925 lecture in which he gave a slightly different version of it, he told his audience that he had "a strongly impersonal feeling about the dream," indicating, at least to him, that it was less a product of his own personal unconscious than something akin to a message from the great beyond.[2] Later in life he told E. A. Bennett something different that calls into question the mystical nature of Jung's interpretation. In Bennett's account, Jung associates the supposedly "impersonal" material from the collective unconscious with some very personal thoughts: "When he reflected on it," wrote Bennett, "later the house had some associations in his mind with his uncle's very old house in Basel which was built in the old moat of the town and had two cellars; the lower one was very dark and like a cave."[3] In any event, the dream did stir something in Jung that put him on a different track entirely.

Immediately after his return home, Jung began to visit archeological sites so that he could observe ongoing excavations. He began an intensive study of mythology and Hellenistic spiritual practices in the classical scholarship of his day. "Archeology or rather mythology has got me in its grip," Jung wrote to Freud on October 14, 1909.[4] This became a familiar theme in their correspondence over the next two and a half years.

As a boy, Jung had wanted to become a classical philologist or an archeologist. His newfound project reawakened these childhood fantasies. "All my delight in archeology (buried for years) has sprung into life again," he told Freud.[5] Soon, however, his study of mythology took on an almost obsessive quality, and mythological figures began to intrude in his daily fantasies and dreams. On February 20, 1910, he told Freud, "All sorts of things are cooking in me, mythology in particular."[6] By April 17, he was afraid of the effect that his researches might have been having on his mental state: "At present I am pursuing my mythological dreams with almost autoerotic pleasure, dropping only meager hints to my friends. . . . I often feel I am wandering alone through a strange country, seeing wonderful things that no one else has seen before and no one needs to see. . . . I don't yet know what will come of it. I must just let myself be carried along, trusting to God that in the end I shall make a landfall somewhere."[7] By February 15, 1912, Jung was in a panic. "I am having grisly fights with the hydra of mythological fantasy and not all its heads are cut off yet. Sometimes I feel like calling for help when I am too hard-pressed by the welter of material. So far I have suppressed the urge."[8]

Jung's efforts were not in vain. Even as early as the end of November 1909 it was clear that he had developed a new theory for psychoanalysis that would have profound racial implications for its future.

The phylogenetic unconscious

In the spring of 1909, Jung had resigned from his post at the Burghölzli and saw patients privately in his consulting room at his new home in Küsnacht, approximately seven miles southeast of Zurich. Although not a move of great distance spatially, it *was* for Jung, psychologically. From his new home on Lake Zurich, in a letter to Sigmund Freud, Jung outlined for the very first time the contours of his new racial theory of the unconscious:

> I feel more and more that a thorough understanding of the psyche (if possible at all) will only come through history or with its help. Just as an understanding of anatomy and ontogenesis is possible only on the basis of phylogenesis and comparative anatomy. For this reason, antiquity now appears to me

in a new and significant light. What we now find in the individual psyche—in compressed, stunted, or one-sidedly differentiated form—may be seen spread out in all its fullness in times past. Happy is the man who can read these signs! The trouble is that our philology has been as hopelessly inept as our psychology. Each has failed the other.[9]

By Christmas, Jung had employed the assistance of one of his young psychiatrists at the Burghölzli, Johann Jakob Honegger. As he told Freud (December 25, 1909), he entrusted to Honegger everything that he knew "so that something good may come of it." By now Jung was even more convinced that he was on the verge of a breakthrough, for he was having "the most marvelous visions, glimpses of far-ranging interconnections which I am at present incapable of grasping." Again he confirmed to Freud the new direction of his thinking: "It has become quite clear to me that we shall not solve the ultimate secrets of neurosis and psychosis without mythology and the history of civilization, for *embryology* goes hand in hand with *comparative anatomy*."[10]

One of Jung's strengths—and indeed his "genius"—was his remarkable ability to synthesize highly complex and seemingly unrelated fields of inquiry. Early in his career, Jung attempted to use the lessons learned from his experimental researches using the word-association test to explain the phenomenon of hysterical "repressions" in psychoanalysis and the alternate personalities of "spirits" that arose during mediumistic trances. His theory that the normal human mind was made up of unconscious complexes—semiautonomous clusters of images, thoughts, and feelings organized around a specific motif or thematic core—was his overarching explanation for these phenomena. Later, when he first consciously identified himself with Freud and the psychoanalytic movement, he tried to integrate that complex theory with psychoanalysis in a wide range of publications, his most famous being a small book on the psychology of dementia praecox.[11]

By November 1909, Jung's clinical experience had stimulated him to cast his intellectual net even wider. What Jung already saw as his intellectual "project" was nothing less than a grand synthesis of psychoanalysis with evolutionary biology, archeology, and comparative philology. If Jung found a way to integrate psychoanalysis with these esteemed sciences, so revered as the finest of German scientific contributions to the world in the late nineteenth century, it would be a coup of major proportions for the psychoanalytic movement. It would confirm Freud and Jung's claims that psychoanalysis was a science that could spur the development of insights in other disciplines. With its analysis of word associations as a method of recovering the past of an individual, the techniques of psychoanalysis perhaps most resemble those of comparative philology, which attempts to recover the original cultural and linguistic forms. And, like psychoanalysis, philologists, too, are interested in how the laws of language seem to be related—or are identical—with the laws governing the operation of the mind. It is no wonder that Freud encouraged Jung along these paths, but it was a project that would ultimately rend psychoanalysis—at least in Switzerland—along ethnic and racial lines.

Jung wasted no time. He gave his psychiatric assistants extensive reading assignments from the works of classicists, archeologists and philologists on the mythological systems of pagan antiquity. Two of them—Spielrein and Jan Nelken—published extensively documented articles making use of their knowledge of mythology to analyze the hallucinations and delusions of patients with dementia praecox. Honegger was the first to present his findings in public at a conference in 1910. A fourth disciple from an asylum outside Zurich, Carl Schneiter, entered the picture a bit later and published a similar vindication of Jung's views in 1914.[12]

Jung assigned his assistants to go into the back wards of their respective asylums and collect mythological material from psychotic patients, almost as if each new hallucination or delusion was an exotic new species of flora or fauna to analyze and catalog. Until Jung assigned them books on mythology, it is a safe bet that these young physicians had little formal training in mythology or archeology. Armed with their new knowledge, they entered the wards and found exactly what Jung told them to look for: ancient pagan gods in the unconscious of their patients.

And the ones they found most often in the most "regressed" psychotic patients—just as Jung said they would—were various pre-Christian solar deities: sun gods.

Wandlungen und Symbole der Libido

Jung's psychiatric assistants funneled new clinical material to him that confirmed the presence of pre-Christian mythological motifs in psychotic patients. Jung immediately put this wealth of evidence into his magnum opus, which would put him and psychoanalysis on the map. First published as two long articles in a psychoanalytic journal in 1911 and 1912, *Wandlungen und Symbole der Libido* (Transformations and symbols of the libido) appeared as one book in the latter year.[13]

It is a strange book. It was judged so in its day and it remains so now. Without the proper keys to unlock the book's argument, the reader is hopelessly lost. However, to Jung's disciples—and to the mystically minded from all quarters of bohemia—it was received as a stunning revelation, a celebration of neopagan life.

Jung's book has at least two separate agendas and can be read in at least two ways: first, as an attempt to syncretize the methodology of psychoanalysis with those of the esteemed sciences of comparative philology, comparative mythology, and evolutionary biology; second, as a blending of different philosophies of regeneration or rebirth. Psychoanalysis thus became not only a science but also a path of cultural and individual revitalization—which, indeed, it had become for Jung by the time he started the book in 1910.[14]

The writing of this book mirrored a transformation process in Jung himself, the result of which was the loss of his Christian identity and the development of a compensating new vital experience of God. Jung's starting point was a small article published by an unusual American woman, Miss Frank Miller, which contained a series of poetic musings and accounts of her personal visions.[15] She had all the gifts of a spiritualist medium, and she knew it. Many of her visions and experiences could even be interpreted as evidence of reincarnation or of a spirit world. However, after studying in Geneva for a time with Théodore Flournoy, she decided to write an article demonstrating that all of the material arising spontaneously from her "creative imagination" could be traced to things she had previously seen, read, or heard. In effect, she was writing to support Flournoy's thesis that all creative productions were the result of new combinations of previously memorized material whose source had long been forgotten—in other words, cryptomnesia.

Jung took Frank Miller's visions and poetry and argued just the opposite: that these could not possibly have been the creation of new combinations of hidden memories but instead were evidence of a phylogenetic layer of the unconscious mind that could produce pre-Christian symbols from pagan antiquity. From the time the first part of *Wandlungen* appeared in a journal in 1911, Jung never again entertained the possibility that mythological content in his patients' dreams or psychotic symptoms were anything but evidence of a phylogenetic or "collective" unconscious layer of the human mind.

Ontogeny recapitulates phylogeny

The basic theory of *Wandlungen* is based on the famous formula "ontogeny recapitulates phylogeny," popularized at the end of the nineteenth century by the German zoologist and evolutionary biologist Ernst Haeckel, who almost single-handedly introduced Darwinism to the German public.

Haeckel actively promoted the notion that evolution was progressive and purposeful. His biological theories were a blend of Darwinism, Lamarckianism, and the old German Romantic biology of Goethe. Haeckel was the first to argue—as Jung would analogously about psychoanalysis—that biology was first and foremost a historical science, involving the historical (not experimental) methodologies of embryology, paleontology, and especially phylogeny.

Jung's favorite areas of study in medical school were comparative morphology and evolutionary theory—areas that Haeckel dominated. Jung's fascination with Haeckel predates medical school, however. In *MDR* he tells of a dream in which he found a great circular pool in a forest clearing. In this pool, "half immersed in the water lay the strangest and most wonderful creature: a round animal, shimmering in opalescent hues, and consisting of innumerable little cells, or of organs shaped like tentacles. It was a giant radiolarian, measuring about three feet across."[16] To Jung, this dream was a prophetic message from beyond, presaging a destiny as a natural scientist and physician. Haeckel's exquisite color illustrations of radiolaria had appeared in popular science books and magazines, and we know that Jung read such magazines as a teenager. He could have picked up his knowledge of radiolaria only from Haeckel.[17]

What is so unusual about this dream, however, is its incongruity with reality, never explained in *MDR* or in any of the scores of Jungian retellings of this magical story. A radiolarian is a tiny sea organism enclosed in an intricate spherical—and beautiful—exoskeleton. But it is a microscopic organism; one cannot see a radiolarian clearly with the naked eye. There are no three-foot long radiolaria as magnified in the sacred monster of Jung's dream. The inflation of a simple natural phenomenon into a giant, otherworldly spectacle is a signature stroke of Jung. His application of Haeckel's "biogenetic law" to stages of cultural evolution and to the evolution of human consciousness is just one more example.

Haeckel's biogenetic law—"ontogeny recapitulates phylogeny"—was derived from his historical researches in biology, and profoundly influenced not only evolutionary biology but also theories of the mind in psychology, psychiatry, and psychoanalysis. The notion that the stages of individual development (ontogeny) could be shown to replicate, in order, the stages of the development of the human race from lower forms of life (phylogeny) was a compelling theory. Both Jung and Freud adopted such thinking in their own work, though they rarely referred to Haeckel.

Jung believed that changes in the libido over time could be discerned through the study of ancient religions and cultures. If he could identify certain stages of transformations of the libido over time that corresponded with the transformations of libido in a developing individual, psychoanalysis could rightly claim it had unlocked the secrets of life and of history. Jung knew he was the man to do it.

Throughout the layers of mythological references in *Wandlungen*, Jung eventually blends Haeckel's ideas with those of Freud and Bachofen into a new model of the human mind: Freud's stages of psychosexual development (the infantile period of polymorphous perversity; the pre-oedipal, incestuous period of strong attachment to the mother; the phallic stage; and then the genital stage) all seem to correspond with the descriptions of Bachofen's stages of cultural evolution (hetairism; matriarchy; the transitional Dionysian period; and then patriarchy). Haeckel's law provides the unifying biological and evolutionary key.

Having outlined the basic skeleton, Jung needed to provide evidence of symbolic content from contemporary patients and from the cultures of the past that would fit each of these stages.

"Whoever has in himself God, the sun, is immortal, like the sun"
Perhaps the defining characteristic of *Wandlungen* is that it seems to be bursting with religious symbolism, much of which refers in one way or another to the sun. If one opens this massive tome arbitrarily, solar myths or sun-hero myths or solar-sexual interpretations are likely to spill forth. Jung viewed these ancient myths as historical records of the transformation of the libido, and maintained that the most apt metaphor for this spiritual-sexual energy or life-force is the sun. "The comparison of the libido with the sun and the fire is really analogous," he argued.[18]

Solar references began to proliferate in part 1 of *Wandlungen*, in the chapter entitled "The Song of the Moth." Here Jung attempted an analysis of a short romantic poem by Miller entitled "The Moth to the Sun." Jung interpreted this poem from a religious perspective, claiming that the longing of the moth for the "star" was in reality the longing of the poetess for God. Jung followed the chain of associations that led to the conclusion that God and star and sun are indeed one, but he went further. His interpretation brought him close to an idea that clearly obsessed him from 1910 until the end of his life: that God is not the distant, transcendent, absolute god of Judeo-Christianity, but instead is the libido that lives *within* us all.

> In the second poem where the longing is clearly exposed it is by no means the terrestrial sun. Since the longing has been turned away from the real object, its object has become, first of all, a subjective one, namely, God. Psychologically, however, God is the name of a representation-complex which is grouped around a strong feeling (the sum of libido). Properly, the feeling

is what gives character and reality to the complex. *The attributes and symbols of divinity must belong in a consistent manner to the feeling (longing, love libido, and so on).* If one honors God, the sun or the fire, then one honors one's own vital force, the libido. It is as Seneca says: God is near you, he is with you, in you.[19]

With this passage Jung echoes the testimonial literature of Pietism. Pietists such as Count Zinzendorf (mentioned in *Wandlungen*) and even Schleiermacher were profoundly interested in the experience of the "god within" as a burning fire. Jung inundates the reader with a dizzying array of similar metaphors of what one would find if one looked inward, claiming that "divine vision is often merely sun or light," and making repeated references to "the inner light, the sun of the other world." Jung even says, "Whoever has in himself God, the sun, is immortal, like the sun."[20] Page after page is filled with analyses of sun-hero myths, like those of Hellenistic paganism or of Teutonic heroes such as Siegfried and Arminius, with rebirth and redemption the eternally recurring themes. Even Christ is analyzed as a sun god and is therefore "identical" with these self-sacrificing Germanic hero-gods.

Near the end of part 1, Jung provides a statement by comparative philologist Ernest Renan, a former theological student who lost his faith through his philological researches and became a celebrity after writing the shocking *Vie de Jésus* in 1863, in which Jesus was treated as a historical figure and not as a god-man. His philological work led him and others to take the spiritual beliefs of pre-Christian peoples quite seriously and argue that the sun worship of ancient peoples was more consistent with a modern scientific world than Judeo-Christian orthodoxies. In the passage from *Dialogues et fragments philosophiques* (1876) that Jung cites, Renan made the following claim: "Before religion had reached the stage of proclaiming that God must be put into the absolute and ideal, that is to say, beyond this world, one worship alone was reasonable and scientific: that was the worship of the sun."[21]

Aryans and Semites

The period between the publication of the first part of *Wandlungen* in the autumn of 1911 and its second part in the autumn of 1912 gave rise to tremendous pressures in the relationship between Jung and Freud. Jung's fascination with the fusion of religious and mythological impulses with the cultural and therapeutic goals of psychoanalysis—so evident in the first part of *Wandlungen*—accelerated the splitting of their union along national, religious, and racial fault lines.

There is no doubt that as an assimilated Jew and atheist living in Christian-dominated Austria-Hungary while political anti-Semitism was on the rise, Sigmund Freud could only see danger in Jung's fantasies about overtly spiritualizing the psychoanalytic movement. Jung, for his part, saw Freud's continued reticence about this—and about issues near to his heart such as spiritualistic and paranormal phenomena—as increasingly oppressive, dogmatic, and authoritarian. Never one for obeying authority, he came to resent Freud and boldly differed with his master in his public statements. By the summer of 1912, a split not only between Jung and Freud but also between Zurich and Vienna was feared by all concerned. Half gestures and cautious peace offerings attempted to patch the differences between the Viennese and the Swiss; they didn't work.

Perhaps one of the most unfortunate results of the split was the heightening of ethnic tensions and the charges of anti-Semitism. Such tribal prejudices exist in the Freudian and Jungian communities even today. To some degree this was to be expected of Freud and Jung. Cultural, linguistic, and—many claimed—biological differences between European Jews and Aryans were supported by the evidence generated by nineteenth-century comparative philology and Lamarckian evolutionary biology. At the time it was widely and firmly believed that these historical factors influenced the psychology of modern individuals. Such racialist thinking dominated the cognitive categories of educated persons and made sense in the world of the fin de siècle, lacking the Hitlerian taint such ideas have today. Volkish propagandists (not only pan-Germanists, but pan-Slavists and Zionists), it is true, perverted the scientific literature for their own ends, but no one—Freud and Jung included—was immune from such assumptions about human nature.

The issue of Aryan and Semitic differences is raised occasionally in the Jung-Freud correspondence. We know that they discussed the topic while on a stroll through New York City's Central Park in 1909. In the voluminous correspondence between Freud and his Jewish colleagues, such as Karl Abraham and Sandor Ferenczi, he reminds them continually that they need the Swiss Christians to further the movement, and that, in any case, he believes Jung to be the man of the future. But it is only after the breach between Jung and Freud seems certain that the psychoanalytic movement begins to be polarized between Christian and Jew, Aryan and Semite.

By July 1912, Freud was becoming aware of how dangerous and divisive Jung's phylogenetic hypothesis had become. By this time Jung had converted most of his Swiss-German and Christian colleagues to the notion that organic memories of ancestral impulses were more important than individual memories. "They are now doubting the influence of infantile complexes and are at the point of already appealing to racial differences in order to explain the theoretical disparity," Freud complained to Sandor Ferenczi on July 28, 1912. "Jung must now be in a florid neurosis. However this turns out, my intention of amalgamating Jews and goyim in the service of [psychoanalysis] seems now to have gone awry. They are separating like oil and water."[22]

Whether neurosis or psychosis was the true culprit, there is no doubt that the writing of *Wandlungen* resulted in a personal and spiritual change in Jung that he had not foreseen. When he finished part 2 in 1912 he was no longer a Freudian. Nor was he a Christian or a monotheist.

This was the beginning of an Aryan science of psychoanalysis in Zurich. It was the beginning of Jung's return to his *Volk*, and to the inner fatherland.

In September 1912, Jung gave a series of lectures at Fordham University in New York City in which he publicly distanced himself from Freud's exclusively sexual libido theory. At the same time, part 2 of *Wandlungen* appeared in a psychoanalytic journal. Freud read it, aghast. Here was not only proof of Jung's defection from the movement, but for the first time Freud began to realize that Jung's development of a theory of the unconscious based on racial or phylogenetic factors had swept him directly into some very dangerous cultural currents.

Part 2 begins innocently enough. Jung picks up the argument exactly where he had left off: solar mythology and sun worship. The prose here is even more expansive, exuberant, mystical. Something has clearly happened. Forgetting for a moment the psychoanalytic nature of the work, he waxes poetic on the first page in the language of a prophet or a religious mystic. And his reference to the sun as a symbol of the "visible god" of this world echoes the "Hymn to King Helios" of Julian the Apostate, using an image borrowed by pantheists—including Giordano Bruno, Goethe, and Haeckel—for centuries thereafter. Jung wrote:

> The sun is, as Renen remarked, really the only rational representation of God, whether we take the point of view of the barbarians of other ages or that of the modern physical sciences. . . . [T]he sun is adapted as is nothing else to represent the visible God of this world. That is to say, that driving strength of our own soul, which we call libido. . . . That this comparison is no mere play of words is taught to us by the mystics. When by looking inwards

(introversion) and going down into the depths of their own being they find "in their heart" the image of the Sun, they find their own love or libido, which with reason, I might say with physical reason, is called the Sun; for our source of energy and life is the Sun. Thus our life substance, as an energic process, is entirely Sun.[23]

To whom was Jung speaking when he used language like this?

In *Wandlungen,* Jung reflects his mastery of the nineteenth-century literatures on comparative philology and classical archeology. These interlocking disciplines were considered the jewels of German science. They were also the academic disciplines that legitimized the argument that there was scientific evidence for the vast cultural, linguistic, and *biological* differences between the Aryan and Semitic races.

It is from the science of comparative philology that the familiar cognitive categories of Indo-Aryan (now Indo-European) and Semitic arose.[24] In the first half of the nineteenth century, before the great advances in the experimental methods of the physical and biological sciences, the systematizing methods of philosophy and, in particular, philology were the models for all other sciences. Philology arose to prominence in Germany as a consequence of the intense cultural fascination that Germans had with all things Greek. As a politically fractured nation united only by *Kultur,* Germans looked to the culture of the ancient Greeks as the crowning achievement of the Aryan peoples and aspired to be their heirs. This Graecophilia, or "tyranny of Greece over Germany" (as scholars have termed it), provided a wealth of pagan "guiding fantasies" to the German Romantics and others throughout German culture.[25] Schoolchildren had to learn the sagas of Greek and Roman mythology as well as ancient German mythology before they could understand the poems of Goethe or Schiller that they had to memorize.

In *MDR,* Jung remembers being "forced to copy prints of Greek gods with sightless eyes" in drawing class.[26] Like thousands of others, Jung struggled through a classical education in which Greek and Latin played a significant role. Ernest Jones confessed in his memoirs, with no small embarrassment, that what struck him most about his initial contacts with Jung and Freud was their frequent and spontaneous quoting of "Latin and Greek passages by memory during their conversations and being astonished at my blank response."[27] The pagan gods resided in the unconsciousnesses of many educated Germans.

In the scientific search for the ultimate origins of the human race, comparative philologists played a central role in the decades before Darwin and Haeckel shifted the focus of this quest to evolutionary biology and ethnology. It was thought that by comparing and analyzing the similarities and the differences between languages that the original families of humankind could be identified. The Indo-Aryan group and the Semitic group were the most researched linguistic and cultural families in the nineteenth century.

Furthermore, comparative philologists such as Renan and Friedrich Max Müller—the two men most responsible for bringing the cultural and linguistic (but not biological) differences between Aryans and Semites to scientific respectability—believed that the very thoughts, feelings, and cultural (especially religious) beliefs of prehistoric groups could be determined through philological analysis. Philologists believed that everyday language contained living relics from our ancestors, as if the image of an event that happened millennia ago could still be fresh today if one could find the linguistic key to unlock the secret code to peer into the past.

Müller claimed to have found this key to wisdom. Jung borrowed it and applied it to the hallucinations and delusions and fantasies and dreams of his contemporaries. "When I finished [*Wandlungen*], I had a peculiarly lucid moment in which I surveyed my path as far as I had come," Jung recalled in 1925. "I thought: 'Now you have the key to mythology and you have the power to unlock all doors.' "[28] There is no way for us now to fully understand Jung's strange book or the basis of the racialist thought it is based on unless we first understand Jung's reliance on the works of Müller and his "solar mythologists."

From 1856 until his death, Müller and his solar mythologists developed a theory—indeed, a "science"—of mythology that dominated late-nineteenth-century thought.[29] As with Freudian psychoanalysis in the twentieth century, Müller's solar mythology was a totalizing worldview and system of interpretation that claimed to find the ancient pagan gods of the sky and the sun alive and well in the very words we speak. "Why, every time we say 'Good morning' we commit a solar myth," said Müller.[30] He and his colleagues argued that the appearance and the disappearance of the sun and its worship as a source of life was the true basis of all mythological systems of the past, but particularly that of the Aryans, the race that they had studied most. Sun worship was the original natural religion of the ancient Aryan peoples. Since the Aryan races had occupied and dominated Europe for the past several thousand years, all native European pre-Christian religions could be traced back to the worship of the sun. This was true even in the Iranian, Indian, Greek, Roman, and Germanic civilizations that predated the first Aryan ones—the "mythopoetic age," as Müller called it.

"Is everything the Dawn? Is everything the Sun?" Müller asked in a famous passage. "This question I had asked many times before it was addressed to me by others . . . but I am bound to say that my own researches lead me again and again to the dawn and the sun as the chief burden of myths of the Aryan race."[31] To Müller, the sun god of the ancient Aryans was in the languages of their descendants.

To Jung, God was in the blood, and this was his rationale for seeking and finding solar myths in the symptoms of psychotic patients at the Burghölzli and in Miss Frank Miller, whom he regarded on the verge of psychosis even though he had never met her. In highly disturbed patients a biologically based disease process eroded the normal covering of repressive defense mechanisms, some of which he thought were biologically inherited in a quasi-Lamarckian fashion from centuries of civilization and Christianity. The erosion of the thick mask of defense mechanisms released archaic material from the deepest strata of the unconscious mind. Given that Jung and most of his patients were of Aryan stock—a group, unlike the older and more "civilized" Semites, who had practiced their natural religion of the sun and the sky until Christianized only one thousand years ago—it is no surprise that symbols of the sun arise again and again. This fact was consistent with the science of philology as he knew it from the books of Renan and Müller. It was also consistent with biology and race.

"He seems to be Christ himself"

Ernest Jones complained to Freud in December 1912 that "Jung is going to save the world, another Christ (with certainly anti-Semitism combined)."[32] Freud concurred. "I thank you for your very just remarks about Jung. In fact, he behaves like a perfect fool, he seems to be Christ himself, and in the particular things he says and does there is always something of the [rascal]."[33]

After the formal break in personal relations between the two men in January 1913, Zurich and Vienna never seemed so far apart. On June 8, Freud wrote to Ferenczi, "You are right. Our dear Swiss have gone crazy." Then, confirming that the source of tension in the movement emanated from a complex fusion of religion and racialism, he observed:

> On the matter of Semitism: there are certainly great differences from the Aryan spirit. We can become convinced of that every day. Hence, there will surely be different worldviews and art here and there. But there should not

be a particular Aryan or Jewish science. The results must be identical, and only their presentations may vary. Certainly my remark about the *Interpretation of Dreams* should be taken in this way. If these differences occur in conceptualizing the objective relations in science, then something is wrong. It was our desire not to interfere with their more distant worldview and religion, but we considered ours to be quite favorable for conducting science. You had heard that Jung had declared in America that [psychoanalysis] was not a science but a religion. That would certainly illuminate the whole difference. But there the Jewish spirit regretted not being able to join in.[34]

By the end of 1913, however, Jung did not share Freud's enlightened opinion that there should not be a specifically Aryan or Jewish science. Psychoanalysis *had* to raise the consciousness of humanity to a higher level through a religious outlook. The only problem was that such a conception of psychoanalysis could no longer have a place for Jews.

The beginnings of an Aryan psychoanalysis

The last psychoanalytic congress that Jung attended—the fourth, in 1913 in Munich, at which he was reelected president of the international movement—confirmed the disintegration of old personal relationships and the birth of new alliances. One personal relationship that ended was the torrid extramarital affair between Lou Andreas-Salomé and the Swedish physician and psychoanalyst Poul Carl Bjerre. They had met through a mutual friend during a visit to Sweden in 1911. Comparing him to her former lover, the poet Rainer Maria Rilke, Andreas-Salomé noted in her private journal, "Both blonde haired, with sensuous mouths, splendid brows, otherwise rather different."[35]

Freud met Bjerre in January 1911 and reported to Jung that the Swede "is rather dry and laconic, but . . . a thorough and serious thinker."[36] By 1916, in a book on the history of psychoanalysis and its techniques, Bjerre openly criticized Freud for exaggerating the importance of sexuality.[37] Although Bjerre helped to found the first Swedish psychoanalytic society, he nonetheless became persona non grata to Freud and the Viennese. Today his works have been forgotten everywhere but in Sweden.

After Bjerre confirmed that he was sympathetic to Jung's side in the war against Freud and the Viennese, their personal relationship heated up. On November 10, 1913, Jung wrote to Bjerre, complaining that Freud had recently attempted to discredit him.[38] Although we do not know exactly what Freud said to Maeder, Jung had sent a sharp letter of complaint to

Freud about it on October 27.[39] Jung continued to complain to Bjerre about being accused of partisanship against the Viennese at the Munich congress and emphasized his wish to raise his efforts to a new level for the benefit of all. Yet the Viennese continue to be a sore point with him.

Near the end of the letter, Jung made a statement that reveals his inner thoughts and sets the tone for much of the way he conducted his own movement in the years that followed, years in which his movement took on the nature of an Aryans-only cult of redemption and rebirth. This is the first piece of hard evidence to surface regarding his racialist outlook during this early period in his career. To Poul Bjerre, Jung said simply: "Ich war zuvor kein Antisemit, jetzt werde ich es, glaube ich."[40]

"Until now I was no anti-Semite, [but] now I'll become one, I believe."

Sun worshipers in German Europe

Jung's massive hymn to the sun could not have come at a more opportune time in German cultural history. All around him, in places such as Bavaria, Thuringia, and Ascona, German-speaking youths were on the march. They were hiking, singing German folk songs, reading Novalis, Goethe, Haeckel, Wilhelm Bölsche, Hesse, and Madame Blavatsky, wearing swastika pendants and runic rings, bathing nude in the sun, and dancing around bonfires on the days of the summer solstice—the ancient German festival of the "changing sun" (*Sonnwendfest*). They carried banners with the ancient Aryan "sun wheel" on them, a symbol of god that could be found in the ancient homelands of the Aryans—Iran and especially India—in the form of circular mandalas. And they sang hymns of praise to the sun.

Because of decades of Volkish speculation about the consequences of the work of philologists such as Müller and Renan, there was an extraordinary revival of interest in not only the symbolism of sun worship but also its practice.[41] The natural religion of the ancient Aryans—and indeed, of all humans if one were to speculate far enough—was revived by a multitude of groups all over Germany, Austria, and especially Switzerland, where cults and heretical sects had blossomed for centuries. Some actually performed group rituals in honor of the sun.

But sun worship was just one element in a confused mass of cultural contradictions that beset Germany in the three decades preceding the First World War. From the racialist right to the anarchist left a culture of "progressive reaction" against industrial capitalism was on the rise. All of the values that formed the foundation of the industrial order—repressive Judeo-Christian antihedonism, utilitarianism, and rational thought—were confronted with new philosophies of life or of pure experiences that exalted myth over history, impulsive action or deed over conscious reflection, and feeling or intuition over rational thought. This progressive reaction, as historian Jost Hermand has termed it, was manifest in a profound sense of loss, a sense that a spiritual connection with nature and the cosmos had been sacrificed with the rise of a more highly mechanized, industrialized, and urbanized civilization.[42]

Much of the sense of loss was expressed in metaphors of degeneration and decay. Civilization had ruined human beings by forcing them into unnatural, cramped, urban environments. Diseases physical and mental were hatched in some places, and the medical science of the day believed that such damage to an individual could be passed down to successive generations. Racial renewal, whether for the individual or society as a whole, was associated with new attitudes toward sexuality and eroticism. There was a cry to recover the *Volk*—that mystical union of a people with its blood and landscape—from the degenerate industrialized masses. The iron cage of "civilization"—Judeo-Christian beliefs and other political and value systems—had to be cast off in order to recover true culture, the primordial ground of the soul, the *Volk*. There was only one solution: recover the "archaic man" within, allowing a rejuvenating return to the chthonic powers of the Edenic, Aryan past.[43]

It is no coincidence that these same ideas are expressed time and again by C. G. Jung, especially in the first sixty years of his life.

The multifaceted Volkish movement (*Volkstumbewegung*) had a broad plan for Germanic society: at the individual level, the taking of cures, abstinence from alcohol, nudism, vegetarianism, the eating of health foods, contact with the ancestors through spiritualist practices, and hiking through Nature were all remedies to erase the sense of profound loss that so many suffered. At the level of culture, a cleansing of the Aryan race through eugenics and deportations was proposed.

Inspired by Herder, Schleiermacher, Ernst Mortiz Arndt, and *Turnvater* Jahn, throughout the nineteenth century the movement grew increasingly influential as the Germans sought their place in the sun. After German unification in 1871, Volkish energies fueled the establishment of a multitude of lodges, clubs, societies, and so on, all devoted to spiritual renewal. Some of these groups were motivated by blood mysticism and fantasies of reform through a return to the worship of the old Aryan gods.

As early as 1814, Arndt had proposed a return to the celebration of the summer solstice as a way to return politically fragmented Germans to their cultural and religious roots. It was left to future leaders to bring his dream into reality. Eugen Diederichs, the famous Jena publisher of many of the new texts of this mystical, Volkish, neoromantic movement, was one of them. He personally led sun-worshiping rituals with his youth-movement disciples beginning in 1904, expressing the beliefs of so many of them when he said, "My view of god is this, that I regard the sun as a source of all life."[44] The youth organization of the *Monistenbund*—inspired and led by Haeckel—sponsored sun-worshiping festivals each summer solstice. Haeckel himself was not a practicing neopagan but loved the spirit of the movement. In 1910, the year Jung got lost in sun-hero myths while researching *Wandlungen,* a *Monistenbund* journal reproduced this hymn to the sun:

> We are all children of the sun. Out of its womb our planet was born. An eternal law of nature compels us to be within its sphere and influence. The immensity of space is cold, still, lifeless—our luminous mother sun, warming and ripening our fruit, appears as the simple, true element of life. Our ancestors knew this in ancient times. Thus their justifiable joy when the sun made its slow victorious spiral across the sky. They then remembered that all those trees, which concealed their greenness in the wintertime, were consecrated to the god, Wotan.[45]

Others wanted a Wagnerian twist to their Volkish neopaganism. They gathered in bearskins and made ritual sacrifices of animals to Wotan, Thor, Baldur, and other Teutonic deities. They studied the symbols of the ancient Norse runes and took visionary journeys to meet with members of an ancient spiritual brotherhood. There were dozens of groups like these, large and small. They convinced themselves that they were chosen, like the grail knights in Wagner's *Parsifal,* to seek and protect the Holy Grail—in this case, the spiritual purity of Aryan blood. The most famous of these was the Tannenberg Foundation of General Erich Ludendorff, war hero and, later, a coconspirator in Adolf Hitler's failed putsch in 1923. The symbol of Ludendorff's organization was the hammer of Thor. Like many in German culture at the turn of the century, Ludendorff wanted to eradicate Christianity and replace it with an Aryan faith. As one commentator on the neopagan movement in Germany revealed, "In line with the Tannenberg program for the restoration of the ancient Germanic religion, General Ludendorff, accompanied by a few young men, would from time to time retire to the forests near Munich, where a bonfire was lighted and a horse sacrificed in honor of Thor, the god of thunder."[46]

Jung was aware of these groups, but it is unlikely that he participated in any of them. After 1913, Jung rarely deviated from the role of the chieftain of his own tribe in Küsnacht and Zurich. But the cult participation of his clinical associates and of the patients they treated in hospital wards and in their consulting rooms, is an open question.

"An attempt to use old cults to achieve new religious possibilities"

On the bohemian circuit and around the world, Jung's *Wandlungen und Symbole der Libido* was such a countercultural success that in the years following the German edition of 1912 and the English translation of 1916 (under the title *Psychology of the Unconscious*), Jung began to receive spiritual pilgrims from around the world who came to him to help them experience the mythic layers of their own unconscious minds.

For Franziska Gräfin zu Reventlow, whom Ludwig Klages called a "pagan saint," the Schwabing-to-Ascona counterculture was "a spiritual movement, a *niveau,* a direction, a protest, a new cult, or rather an attempt to use old cults to achieve new religious possibilities."[47] "Fanny," as she was called, was a friend and possibly a lover of Otto Gross, and the author of a thinly veiled autobiographical novel known as *Herrn Dames Aufzeichnungen.* It was written during the period (December 1911 to summer 1912) that Jung was working on part 2 of *Wandlungen,* and was first published in 1913. As Jung's dreams swirled with images of Dionysus and the terrible Great Mother Goddess and sun heroes such as Siegfried, Fanny Reventlow sat at her desk and called forth an entire decade of personal experiences. In the magic theater of her mind she witnessed the passionate discussions in the cafés of Schwabing over the mystical nature of race and blood—carriers of the "primordial pagan substances" that emerged in the dreams of modern individuals.[48] These were times in which Dionysian bacchantes and Bachofenian hetaira were reincarnated in young women who walked the streets of Munich and danced naked in the sacred groves of Ascona. She remembered pagan costume balls during Fasching and ritual sacrifices to the Great Mother Goddess.

Is it just a coincidence that Jung was obsessed with these very issues at the very same point in history? Is it just a coincidence that this is the time when Jung, too, became a pagan who said the old gods were still alive within us?

The new pagans' artistic prophet was Karl Höppner, better known as Fidus.[49] More than any other artist, Fidus captured the youthful spirit of the counterculture. In Theosophical journals, in *Simplicissimus* and *Jugend,* on postcards and posters, his breathtaking sun-worshiping images seemed to be everywhere in the first quarter of the century. Nude, long-haired, blond young Aryans—sometimes wearing jewelry made of Runic symbols or swastikas—looked skyward and raised their arms to the sun. The image most often associated with Fidus—the motif of the *Lichtgebet* (Prayer to the light), based on the Norse so-called *Lebensrune* or "life rune"—depicts a nude man, legs together, arm upraised in a Y-shaped posture.

Fidus's images tell us much about the neopagan culture in German Europe at the turn of the century. Aryanist sun-worshiping imagery, runic symbols, swastikas, and towering pillars of fire are synthesized with male and female figures, often nude, who symbolized the great cosmic principles of the Masculine and the Feminine. Typically there are polar opposites united within or just under a circle that symbolizes god as the sun—the primordial ground of all being. In one book illustration by Fidus from 1897, the Masculine and the Feminine are united in a Janus-like bust depicting the Aryan ideals of male and female beauty. This syzygy, this union of opposites, is surrounded by solar rays and crowned by an encircled swastika, a solar symbol of regeneration and eternal recurrence. Fidus contributed this and other similar illustrations to a series of publications by the Berlin Theosophist Max Ferdinand Sebaldt von Werth on the sexual magic and sexual religion of the ancient Aryans.[50] The Aryanist and occultist theory popular in bohemian çircles was that the universe had been created from a primordial fiery chaos out of which the first two principles to emerge were the Masculine and the Feminine. Only from the eternal tension between these opposites, the eternal joining and separating of the two, could the creative force, the primal energy of the sun or fire be released. On the individual level, only the integration of the Masculine and Feminine principles within the soul could restore the connection with the internal solar fire. In the writings of Sebaldt and other Volkish mystics, this blazing primal energy was also associated with the blood. Therefore, to release the creative potential of an entire race, eugenics would be necessary to create pure prototypical Aryan males and females who could then produce progressively superior progeny.

Except for the explicit advocacy of eugenics, all these symbols and themes appear in *Wandlungen* and form the metaphoric core of Jung's theory of psychological types, his famous concepts of the anima and the animus, and his ideas concerning the structure and dynamics of the psyche.

Among the Asconans who read Jung—particularly *Wandlungen*—and who were treated by him or his assistants in Zurich were Hermann Hesse and Rudolph von Laban. Laban had read *Wandlungen* and shared it with his colony of Dionysian dancers in Ascona, including Mary Wigman, who would develop an intellectual passion for psychoanalytic literature. Her

"Witches' Dance" spooked audiences in Munich and thrilled pagans in Ascona. The occultist Aleister Crowley also briefly passed through Ascona, read *Psychology of the Unconscious,* and found it useful inspiration for his own writings on ritual magic.[51]

During the war years, and especially after 1916 when word had spread about the new bohemian twist analytical psychology had taken in Zurich, Asconans flooded the consulting rooms of Jung's colleagues. In the creative container that Jung said a therapy session should be, they revealed their dreams and their drawings, their poems and their dances. They were pagans and welcomed for their paganism. In the cafés of Zurich, they gossiped about their analysts, wildly analyzed one another's dreams, offered one another the latest Theosophical or Anthroposophical publications, shared coffee, cocaine, and encouragement.

The prose of Jung's Hymn to the Sun radiated from the pages of his book with a power that could seduce the spiritually hungry. Jung wrote with conviction derived from a personal experience so tremendous, so cosmic, that he could arouse the desire of others to want it, too. But what exactly was this electrifying experience?

SEVEN

The Mystery of Deification

> Awe surrounds the mysteries, particularly the mystery of deification. This was one of the most important of the mysteries. It gave the immortal value to the individual—it gave certainty of immortality. *One gets a peculiar feeling from being put through such an initiation.*
>
> —C. G. Jung, June 8, 1925

There is a significant, *deliberate* omission from Jung's alleged autobiography.[1] The information Aniela Jaffé left out of *Memories, Dreams, Reflections* is crucial to understanding Jung, the metaphors he chose for his method of psychotherapy, and the early development of analytical psychology. Indeed, it forms the core of his "personal myth," elements of which he kept secret but that can now be revealed with a contextual analysis of this important material.

Aniela Jaffé based the chapter in *MDR* known as "Confrontation with the Unconscious" on "a number of passages from a seminar delivered from March to July 1925 in which Jung spoke for the first time of his inner development."[2] (By then Jung delivered his lectures entirely in English.) Extensive notes were kept and typed by Cary F. de Angulo, checked for accuracy by Jung, and then, in November 1925, copied and distributed to the seminar participants. But until a published edition of the complete seminar notes appeared in 1989, those wishing to read this remarkable document needed at least one hundred hours of "approved" analysis and the permission of one's analyst.

What could have been so important in Cary de Angulo's notes that Jaffé chose to keep it out of *MDR* and that it was kept from many of Jung's own disciples for more than sixty years? Why were the secrets about Jung that it contained considered forbidden fruit for so long?

What is missing is an entire episode from Jung's life, and arguably the most important one.

In December 1913, Jung deliberately and repeatedly induced trance states using methods he had learned from his experience with spiritualism. This technique, which he would later call "active imagination," sparked a series of intense visionary experiences that Jung interpreted as his direct mystical initiation into one of the most ancient of the pagan mystery cults of the Hellenistic world.

Jung became an initiate into this brotherhood during an extraordinary epiphany.

His head changed into that of a lion and he became a god. He became the *Deus Leontocephalus,* the lion-headed god whose image is found in the sanctuaries of the mystery cult of Mithras (first to fourth centuries C.E.). Jung became a god known to us as Aion.

Near the end of his life Jung published a book in 1951 on "the phenomenology of the self" named after this god, with a striking frontispiece photograph of *Deus Leontocephalus.* We can only conclude that throughout his life Jung must have been haunted by the mystery of his initiation. To him it was the revelation of his secret self, of the god within, of the great and unspeakable mystery of the *imago dei.*

After Jung underwent the mystery of deification in December 1913, his personal and professional life changed markedly. Within a few months he resigned from the presidency of the psychoanalytic movement and withdrew from his lecturer position at the university. He maintained his private practice in Küsnacht, and his sexual relationship with Toni Wolff intensified. He continued his visionary explorations and researches into mythology and the history of religion. He gathered his core disciples around him and gave them special lectures on "complex psychology," psychological types, and mythology. By 1916, he began to teach his disciples that analysis was an initiation into the mysteries of the impersonal, the transpersonal, or the collective unconscious. By 1917, he transformed the imaginal entities he met in his visions into elements of his new poetic brand of analytical psychoanalysis.

He developed a model for his movement that set him apart from all other forms of psychoanalysis, psychotherapy, or any other secular form of healing. Jung based the social and psychotherapeutic practices of the "Zurich school" on the ancient mystery cults of the Hellenistic world. From Jung, his disciples learned to participate in the most ancient of mysteries, whose roots reached back into the mythopoetic age.

The defining moment in the secret story of Jung's life and movement happened the day that he was deified. We need to understand why this is so and understand the deeper significance of Jung's own interpretation of the ancient mysteries. Stripping away the false mask of idealization constructed by his disciples reveals the dark face of the god he had truly become.

"Why do you worship me?"

At the very heart of *MDR* is the chapter "Confrontation with the Unconscious."[3] For many of his modern readers who regard *MDR* as a gospel or a new spiritual dispensation, this chapter is the holiest of holies. The stories of Jung's visionary journeys of December 1913 and his additional prophetic visions and dreams subtly model the process of transformation that Jung considered necessary before one could truly become an individual. The chapter offers the promise of such magical experiences to others. He insists that such an ordeal is dangerous and that not everyone can survive it. But the official version of Jung's 1913 visions leaves out the most important ingredient in the recipe for individuation, the experience that all of his therapeutic techniques were designed to bring about: a new experience of god through one's own self-deification.

Let us now compare Jaffé's version in *MDR* with Jung's own confession in a 1925 seminar. Jaffé's version is taken largely from the brief remarks Jung made at the end of the lectures on May 11 and June 1, 1925. Jung induced a dissociative altered state of conscious and made a visionary "descent" into the unconscious, which he refers to as the Land of the Dead. Once in this other realm, he met an old man with a white beard and a young girl who was blind. The old man introduced himself as Elijah. Jung was "shocked" to learn that the girl was named Salome. Elijah assured him that this couple "had been together since eternity." With them was a large black snake, which had an affinity for Jung. "I stuck close to Elijah because he seemed to be the most reasonable of the three, and to have a clear intelligence. Of Salome I was distinctly suspicious."[4]

In the fall seminar notes, Jung amplified these figures with references to motifs in mythology and symbolism. He explained that the snake is associated with hero myths. Salome is "an anima figure." Elijah represents "the wise old prophet," and "a factor of intelligence and knowledge." But, Jung added, "it is very much better to leave these experiences as they are, namely as events, experiences."[5]

One point on which these two versions diverge is the important figure of Philemon, Jung's imaginal guru. In *MDR,* he reveals that this figure, a "pagan" having "an Egypto-Hellenistic atmosphere with a gnostic coloration," developed out of the Elijah figure in subsequent fantasies.[6] Besides covering almost an entire wall in Jung's hermetic Tower at Bollingen, images of the wise old Philemon grace the illuminated manuscript pages of Jung's secret transformation diary, the "Red Book." Philemon is not mentioned in the 1925 seminar.

Jung's initial voyage into the underworld was followed by a second: the long suppressed story of Jung's deification.

Jung told his audience that "a few evenings later, I felt that I should continue. So again I tried to follow the same procedure, but it would not descend. I remained on the surface."[7] He felt it was an "inner conflict" that prevented him from going down. After resolving this, he felt he could go on.

Jung looked about him. He saw Elijah on a rocky ridge, a ring of boulders, which he thought was a "Druidic sacred place." Inside, the old man climbed up on a mounded Druidic altar, and then both Elijah and the altar began to shrink while the walls grew larger. Jung noticed a tiny woman, "like a doll," who turned out to be Salome. He also saw a miniature snake and a house.

The walls around Jung kept growing. Suddenly he realized that he had been descending. "I was in the underworld," he said.

When they all reached bottom Elijah smiled at him and said, "Why, it is just the same, above or below."

Then it happened.

"Salome became very interested in me, and she assumed I could cure her blindness. She began to worship me. I said, 'Why do you worship me?' She replied, 'You are Christ.' "

Jung objected. But Salome persisted. She insisted that he was Christ.

Jung told her, " 'This is madness,' " and he said that he "became filled with skeptical resistance." But events would soon prove she was right.

> Then I saw the snake approach me. She came close and began to encircle me and press me in her coils. These coils reached up to my heart. I realized as I struggled that I had assumed the attitude of the crucifixion. In the agony and the struggle, I sweated so profusely that the water flowed down on all sides of me. Then Salome rose, and she could see. While the snake was pressing me, I felt that my face had taken on the face of an animal of prey, a lion or tiger.[8]

Jung then offered to his stunned audience some rather formulaic interpretations of his experiences in terms of his type theory. But in a meaningful shift of focus that must have taken only a few minutes during the spoken lecture, Jung then compared his experience with those of the ancient mysteries. "You cannot get conscious of these unconscious facts without giving yourself to them. . . . These images have so much reality that they recommend themselves, and such extraordinary meaning that one is caught. They form part of the ancient mysteries; in fact, it is such figures that made the mysteries."

Jung's interpretation here is clear: his visions were an initiatory experience into the mysteries of pagan antiquity. These mystery cults provided all the symbols of transformation necessary for a personal renewal or rebirth. Further, they were at the deepest level of the unconscious mind, available to one and all who wished to descend to the ancestral unconscious or to go on a heroic "night sea journey" through its murky depths. The gods awaited one there.

The climax of the initiation into the mysteries, however, was the "mystery of deification," which gave "certainty of immortality." Jung's statement of his own deification is remarkable:

> One gets a peculiar feeling from being put through such an initiation. The important part that led up to the deification was the snake's encoiling of me. Salome's performance was deification. The animal face which I felt mine transformed into was the famous [Deus] Leontocephalus of the Mithraic Mysteries. It is the figure which is represented with a snake coiled around the man, the snake's head resting on the man's head, and the face of the man that of the lion. This statue has only been found in mystery grottoes (the underchurches, the last remnants of the catacombs). The catacombs were not originally places of concealment, but were chosen as symbolical of a descent into the underworld.[9]

After presenting a few historical details concerning Mithraism, Jung told his audience: "It is almost certain that the symbolical rite of deification played a part in these mysteries." He then identified the *Leontocephalus* as "Aion, or the eternal being," which, he said, was derived from an Iranian deity whose name means "the infinitely long duration."

He described a museum piece he had once seen, a Mithraic amphora that bore the image of a flame with a lion on one side and a snake on the other. To him, these were to be interpreted psychologically as "opposites of the world trying to come together with the reconciling symbol between them." Significantly, "The lion is the young, hot, dry July sun in the culmination of light, the summer. The serpent is humidity, darkness, the earth, winter."

Jung closed this remarkable lecture with a return to the initiatory climax of deification in the ancient mysteries: "In this deification mystery you make yourself into the vessel, and are a vessel of creation in which the opposites reconcile."

An unidentified person in the audience then asked Jung the date of this "dream," and Jung replied, "December 1913. All this is Mithraic symbolism from beginning to end."[10]

Before we can understand the true meaning of Jung's initiation, some questions must be answered: What did Jung have in mind when he spoke of the ancient mysteries? How did he come to the notion that, at the absolute climax of the initiatory rites of these ancient mystery cults, the humble human initiate becomes a god? What were the Mithraic mysteries and why would Jung entertain the fantasy of becoming an initiate into them? What was the most likely source of these remarkable visions? Why were the mysteries of Mithras such an important model for his own circle of disciples in Zurich? And what did it mean when Jung mixed Christian and pagan elements in his own deified self?

To find these answers, we must leave our narrative and enter a lost world of fin-de-siècle classical scholarship, which reflected a mentality quite different from our own.

Jung's sources on the ancient mysteries

Perhaps it is best to explore first the most probable source of the contents of Jung's initiation. In the spring of 1925, after Jung finally revealed the story of his 1913 visionary descent to the Land of the Dead and his meetings with otherworldly entities, he said to his audience: "I had read much mythology before this fantasy came to me, and all of this reading entered into the condensation of these figures."[11]

Is Jung inadvertently admitting here that cryptomnesia played a role in generating the content of his visionary experiences and dreams? Is it possible that these experiences were more personal than transpersonal, more mundane than mystical?

Jung's years of maturation were characterized by an unusually potent convergence of familial and cultural preoccupations with the spirituality of Aryan antiquity, with heredity, evolution, memory, the superiority of direct experience or intuition over reason, and the direct contact with ancestors or the Dead. Like many in Jung's generation, becoming a "modern" meant questioning the very foundations of one's bourgeois-Christian identity and even rejecting it.

Jung, of course, knew the general aspects of the ancient Hellenistic mystery cults before he became obsessed with archeology and mythology following his trip to America in September 1909. But much of his imaginings about the rituals of these cults came from the work of six scholars, four of whom were his contemporaries. All of the metaphors Jung later used to describe his theories and methods of treatment and the otherworldly terrain of the collective unconscious and its archetypes had their basis in this literature.

Nietzsche

As a medical student in the 1890s, Jung absorbed the works of Friedrich Nietzsche, who was a professor of classical philology at the University of Basel before turning to philosophy. From him Jung first became intoxicated with the mysteries of blood and sexuality and underground initiation in the ancient cults of Dionysus. Nietzsche was also the source of Jung's first fascination with Zoroastrianism and ancient Iranian spirituality via his depiction of the prophet Zarathustra in *Also Sprach Zarathustra,* which Jung later claimed was a record of "one of the first attempts in modern times to come back to the immediate, individual initiation."[12]

Creuzer

If there can be said to be one central, nonmystical source of Jung's concepts of the phylogenetic and collective unconscious it is the writings of Friedrich Creuzer, who was a professor of ancient literature at Heidelberg University in the nineteenth century.[13] On November 8, 1909, Jung wrote to Freud, "Now I am reading the four volumes of old Creuzer, where there is a huge mass of material."[14]

Creuzer's four-volume *Symbolik und Mythologie der alten Völker besonders der Griechen,* originally published between 1810 and 1812, was the first truly comprehensive scholarly source in German for information concerning the spirituality of antiquity, especially about the Greco-Roman mystery cults. As a result, it contained information that was widely disseminated throughout the nineteenth and early twentieth centuries. Central to Creuzer's work was a hypothesis on which much German scholarship in the nineteenth century was based; namely, that Greek mythology was the best paradigm through which to study *all* pagan religions, regardless of which part of the world they were from. And Creuzer, like so many others, believed that Greek mythology was a corruption of a prehistoric spiritual worldview, the *Urreligion* of all human beings that had existed for thousands of years before languages and cultures diverged. Creuzer (as Bachofen and Blavatsky and so many others) was convinced that a careful study of the surviving artifacts of pagan antiquity could reveal key elements of the hidden "secret doctrine" of the prehistoric ancestors of us all. Jung shared their views and made Creuzer's work required reading for his assistants.

Thus, Creuzer's personal biases framed the type of mythological data collected from the delusions, hallucinations, and dreams of institutionalized patients with psychotic disorders. They also framed the type of material that would be *ignored* as well, because as dutiful assistants Honegger, Spielrein, and Nelken would disregard anything that wasn't "mythological" in the sense that Creuzer (and Jung) maintained.

Albrecht Dieterich

Beginning in the 1890s, there was a renaissance in classical archeology. No doubt reflecting the intellectual climate of the fin de siècle, classicists became interested in the ancient mystery cults and their special brand of personal religion. In part, this new scholarship reflected a cultural interest in the irrational and the experiential, but it also reflected the tremendous interest in ancient mysteries that was stimulated after 1875 by Madame Blavatsky and her Theosophical Society. Blavatsky claimed to have been an initiate into the mysteries of the goddess Isis, and the social structure of the Theosophical movement was set up, like the Freemasons, as a step-by-step process of initiation into ancient occult wisdom. This new scholarship on the ancient mysteries was a method of scientifically investigating the reality of these cults.

Jung borrowed extensively from Albrecht Dieterich. Dieterich's books on the ancient Gnostic god known as Abraxas, on the heroic "night sea journey," on the cult of Mother Earth, and on a fragment from the Greek Magical Papyri known as the Mithraic Liturgy all provided Jung with numerous metaphors that are familiar to Jungians today.[15] It is probably from Dieterich's book on the Mithraic Liturgy that Jung derived his conviction that an initiation into the mysteries of Mithras involved a self-deification process. Dieterich identifies as central liturgical images of the Mithraic mysteries the mystical union of "man in god and god in man" and the *unio mystica* (erotic union) of humans with a god.

No one reads Albrecht Dieterich today, but he clearly must be remembered when we attempt to reconstruct the hidden history of C. G. Jung and find the original sources of so many of his ideas.

Richard Reitzenstein and Franz Cumont

In the introduction to his book *Ancient Mystery Cults,* Walter Burkert, a classical philologist and a leading contemporary authority on ancient Greek religion, credits Richard Reitzenstein and Franz Cumont for "setting the pace" of scholarship on the Hellenistic mysteries at the turn of the century.[16] Of the two, the Belgian scholar Cumont was far more of an influence on Jung.[17] Cumont was not only an authority on the Mithraic mysteries but also on the use of astrology in antiquity. However, he is most famous for his writings on the Mithraic cult, and they were a seminal influence on Jung.[18]

K.H.E. De Jong

Perhaps the most forgotten of the scholars whom Jung absorbed during his intense period of mythological studies was the Dutch classicist Karel Hendrik Eduard De Jong. De Jong, a lecturer at the University of Leiden, produced a book in 1909 that is one of the long-lost classics of the literature on Hellenistic mysteries, *Das Antike Mysterienwesen in religionsgeschichtlicher, ethnologischer und psychologischer Beleuchtung* (The ancient mysteries in light of the history of religion, ethnology, and psychology).[19] This book fascinated Jung, and with good reason: it was a detailed dissertation offering ethnological and psychological interpretations of the experiential phenomena reported by initiates into the ancient mysteries. While reading it, one cannot but be struck by how close De Jong is to the spirit of the works that Jung began producing with *Wandlungen* (in which he cites De Jong).

De Jong's book is a masterpiece of interdisciplinary scholarship, and when it appeared no other work on the ancient mysteries quite like it existed. After reviewing the major Hellenistic mystery cults (those of Eleusis, Isis, Mithras, and Dionysus), he addressed the classical literature on Egyptian and Greek magic. However, the bulk of the book is devoted to his explanation of the extraordinary initiatory experiences of the ancient mysteries in terms of modern phenomena. De Jong was fascinated with the literature on altered states of consciousness, and he reviewed the clinical literature on hypnosis and hysteria to find clues to the behavior of the ancients. He made use of the occultist literature of Theosophy and the literature on psychical research (especially the accounts of the spiritualistic trance performances of mediums). De Jong even cited Jung's 1902 doctoral dissertation concerning Helly Preiswerk.[20] He explored the phenomena of spiritual disciplines and occult sciences such as yoga and the Kabbalah and mined the ethnographic literature on primitive cultures in Africa, Asia, Australia, and North and South America for clues to their religious use of trances, especially by shamans.

In short, De Jong's book was a major stimulus for Jung's own syncretization of psychoanalysis, psychology, spiritualism, primitive religion, and Hellenistic mysteries in the theories he developed after 1913. Jung differed from De Jong in that he turned these insights into a claim about the nature of reality and developed techniques that enabled his patients and colleagues to directly experience the transformative power of the mysteries.

But what exactly were the mysteries?

Mysteria

Mysteria were the secrets of eternity imparted through initiation into a particular mystery cult of the Greco-Roman or Hellenistic world (fourth century B.C.E. to fourth century C.E.). Each mystery cult based the form of its rites of initiation on the narrative elements in its *hieros logos,* or "sacred myth," the central story of its divinity or divinities. This mystery-cult legend usually involved heroic wanderings by the cult divinity that were then ritually reenacted in public processions (such as the majestic state-sponsored procession from Athens to Eleusis) or in dancing (such as by the maenads in the Dionysian mysteries).

Whether the initiation was into the mysteries of Dionysus, Eleusis (the Greek site where Demeter and Persephone resided), the Great Mother, Isis, Mithras, Sabazios, or the Kabeiroi, the goal was essentially the same: the spiritual and psychological transformation, rebirth, or renewal of the initiate and the opportunity for a better life through direct contact with a transcendent realm of gods, sometimes through a ritual descent to the underworld. This underworld was the Land of the Dead, the realm of the ancestors, or, according to nineteenth-century German Volkish scholars, the "inner fatherland." As many twentieth-century classical scholars have suggested, the initiation into the ancient mysteries was a form of personal religion and served a special psychotherapeutic function in the pagan world.[21]

According to Walter Burkert, "Mysteries were initiation rituals of a voluntary, personal and secret character that aimed at a change of mind through an experience of the sacred.... [They] were a form of personal religion, depending on a private decision and aiming at some form of salvation through closeness to the divine."[22] Participation in the mysteries was not obligatory or unavoidable, unlike participation in organized religions as we know them. "Mysteries are to be seen as a special form of worship offered in the larger context of religious practice.... Mystery initiations were an optional activity within polytheistic religion, comparable to, say, a pilgrimage to Santiago di Compostela within the Christian system," explains Burkert.[23]

Mystery initiations were rites of passage during which the initiate became separated (symbolically and physically) from normal social interactions or norms of behavior. During the initiatory process, the candidate was regarded first as in a marginal, threshold state in which the boundaries between the sacred and the profane were blurred. Later, the initiate passed through an aggregation or "reincorporation" stage.[24] He or she then regained community rights and obligations of a clearly defined type that were commensurate with the new identity. What changed for the initiate was his or her *personal* status vis-à-vis a particular deity, not necessarily his or her social position. In many instances the initiations could be repeated in a process of continual rebirth. This was true for the Eleusinian mysteries, for the many centers of the mysteries of Dionysus, and every twenty years or so for the mysteries of the Great Mother.

By seeing the mysteries or having them revealed, the passage is made from one state of being to another. In the words of an individual who had seen the mysteries of Eleusis, "I came out of the Mystery Hall feeling like a stranger to myself." But what these initiates actually saw is itself a mystery, for secrecy was the essential element of these cults, and history attests that the ancients were able to keep secrets to a remarkable degree.

Although the mysteries conveyed to the initiates a sense of a better life, particularly in the underworld, the ancient mysteries were not religions of salvation because they were not religions as we know them. Burkert notes insightfully that "the constant use of Christianity as a reference system when dealing with the so-called mystery religions leads to distortions as well as partial clarification, obscuring the often radical difference between the two."[25] Cumont and Reitzenstein were particularly guilty of this form of distortion. Cumont once referred to the "loss" of the "liturgical books of paganism" as the most regrettable one in the "great shipwreck" that lost so much of the literature of antiquity. Reitzenstein likewise believed that these "oriental religions" were bound together by shared, systematized articles of faith. Although each of the mystery cults was based on a central myth, perhaps even kept in a written form along with sacred ritual instruments in a *cista mystica* ("secret casket"), there is no evidence that such binding credos or pagan theological works ever existed.[26]

Yet the ancient pagan mysteries continued to occupy the imagination of humankind in an only nominal Christian Europe. Throughout the centuries their symbols and initiatory rites, their gods and goddesses, daemons and *genii* all found their way into the occult underground in the traditions of Gnosticism, Hermeticism, alchemy, astrology, the Kabbalah, the Tarot, ritual or ceremonial magic, Freemasonry, Rosicrucianism, and especially in the occult revivals of the nineteenth and twentieth centuries. They live on in the works of C. G. Jung and those who practice therapy in his name.

The Hellenistic mysteries

Most of Jung's scholarship on the ancient mysteries began in earnest in October 1909, and the understanding of them that he carried throughout his life was based on the classical scholarship available around that time. Like most scholars, he read specific literatures in phases throughout his life as his interests changed. Based on his published correspondence, his bibliographic references, and the dates of publication of the books in his personal library, we know that Jung read very little new material on the Hellenistic mystery cults after 1912 or so. Instead, he read more widely in the literature on Gnosticism (primarily the works of the Theosophist G.R.S. Mead),[27] the patristic Christian literature, and ancient Germanic mythology and religion. By the late 1920s, Jung's dominant interest was alchemy, and in his later works alchemical metaphors replace those of Hellenistic *mysteria* that characterized his earlier thought. However, he integrated the core themes of the ancient mysteries into his alchemical studies, believing not only that the symbols were similar, but that both the mysteries and alchemy were, at their core, secret, underground, anti–orthodox Christian spiritual movements that promised individual redemption and rebirth.

Jung studied the ancient Hellenistic mysteries as precursors to the vitalistic movements of his day in which direct experience and the development of intuition were paramount over mere reason. Neither the details of public ritual processions, nor the political, social, and economic context of the Hellenistic mystery cults were of any major interest to him. This fact is indicative of Jung's whole approach to the scholarship of others that he used in his own works. These external details were unnecessary historical facts that hid the true, living, eternal essence of the mysteries. Mystery, not history, was the bread of life.

The aspects of the ancient mysteries that did interest Jung were the initiates' reports of the direct experience of a transcendental realm of gods and the cryptic symbolism associated with such extraordinary experiences. He was particularly fond of a famous passage in the *Metamorphoses* of Apuleius in which he reported the climax of his initiation into the mysteries of Isis. The passage below reveals the passion for secrecy in the mysteries:

> You would probably inquire quite eagerly, attentive reader, what was then said and done. I would tell you, if it were lawful; you would get to know all, were it lawful for you to hear. But both ear and tongue would incur equal guilt through such daring curiosity. Yet you are probably racked by religious longing, so I shall not torture you with prolonged anguish. Listen, then, but *believe,* for my account is true: I approached the boundary of death and treading on Proserpine's threshold, I was carried through all the elements, after which I returned. I saw the sun flashing brightly in the middle of the night [*nocte media vidi solem*]. I approached close to the gods above and the gods below and worshipped them face to face. Behold, I have related things about which you remain in ignorance, though you have heard them.

> Therefore I shall recount only what can be communicated without guilt to the understanding of the uninitiated.[28]

Here we find a motif that greatly interested Jung: the image of a sun (or a star) in the depths as the central image of the god within.

Imagining Mithras

Jung's view of Mithraism was largely Cumont's Christianized one: Mithras was an ancient Iranian solar god (like Helios) and a god of correct behavior and order (like Apollo). He is referred to as *Sol Invictus,* the "invincible sun." Mithraism had survived from the old dualist Mazdean religion of ancient Persia but adapted itself to the Roman empire. Though only men could participate in these mysteries, Mithraism's wide geographical spread "from the banks of the Black Sea to the mountains of Scotland to the borders of the great Sahara Desert" could mean that it was the main rival to Christianity.[29] Cumont thought this was true because both rose in prominence at about the same time. Indeed, he argued, if historical events had gone a little differently, the Western world would be Mithraic and not Judeo-Christian today. There was perhaps even a voluminous Mithraic Liturgy akin to that of the Christian church, but it did not survive antiquity.

There were seven grades to the Mithraic mystery initiations, and they involved sacramental feasts at which bread and water were consecrated and at which blood was offered as a sacrifice in ceremonies involving priests in robes who offered prayers, sang hymns, and rang bells—as in the Roman Catholic church—at the holiest moment of the ritual: the unveiling of the ubiquitous image of Mithras killing a bull, the *tauroctony.*[30] Indeed, practically all of the elements of Mithraism that Jung refers to over his lifetime can be found in the chapter of Cumont's *The Mysteries of Mithras* entitled "The Mithraic Liturgy, Clergy, and Devotees."

Recent scholars have called into question almost all of Cumont's basic assumptions about the Iranian origins and "sacramental" ceremonies of Mithraism. Using the same archeological and textual evidence that Cumont compiled, while hunting down new evidence and deducing new theories, Mithraic scholars now offer very different interpretations of the mysteries. The main difficulty is simple: although there is a wealth of archeological material that is well preserved because the Mithraeums were built underground, there is not a single recorded account of the central myth of Mithraism, nor does Mithraic iconography provide us with the story. Any interpretation of the myth of Mithras, then, is an imagining, a reconstruction.

If Jung broke through to the eternal realm of the phylogenetic or collective unconscious, as he believed, and experienced an authentic Mithraic process of transformation, then non-Cumontian elements might appear in the structure of his December 1913 visions. They do not. All of the elements of Jung's initiation can be derived from Cumont and other scholars Jung read. This once again raises the issue of whether all of his experiences were based on cryptomnesia. If so, the collective unconscious may still be said to exist, but only on the shelves of Jung's personal library.

However, a review of the aspects of Mithraism that touch upon Jung's personal symbols of transformation sheds new light on secrets that Jung never openly acknowledged, secrets so personally profound that he only hinted at them in public. In part, they concern Sigmund Freud.

The sacrifice: killing the bull

Following the standard position of scholars of his day, Jung interpreted Mithras strictly as a sun god. More recent interpretations of Mithras and the Mithraic symbolism of the tauroctony, the bull slaying, suggest an even greater role for Mithras: that of *kosmokrator,* ruler of the entire cosmos, a deity powerful enough to shift the structure of the stars, constellations, and planets. Mithraic scholar David Ulansey argues persuasively for an astronomical and astrological interpretation of Mithraic iconography.[31] According to Ulansey, Mithras was a greater power than the sun, and indeed Mithraic iconography contains many so-called investiture scenes in which the sun god Helios bows on one knee before Mithras.[32] However, there are also many images of Mithras and Helios dining or riding in a chariot together, and since in the Greco-Roman world the role of cosmic ruler was more often attributed to the sun, Mithras and Helios might be equals. In *Wandlungen und Symbole der Libido* Jung compares their relationship to that of Christ and Peter. Jung also made the connection between Elijah and Mithras, noting that both are depicted as ascending in a fiery chariot, and he repeated Cumont's speculation that "early Christian paintings of the ascension of Elijah are based partly on the corresponding Mithraic representations.[33] In this way, he is able to disregard cultural context and equate Mithras and Elijah and Christ as two sides of the same ahistorical coin.

To be fair, Jung did make an attempt at a historical explanation, essentially arguing that Christianity in part deliberately borrowed and renamed pagan motifs as a way to attract disaffected pagans. A reversal of sorts occurred when, for a brief shining moment, paganism overtook Christianity in a final resurgence. When, in 361, Julian the Apostate resurrected polytheistic paganism as the religious philosophy of the Roman empire, he offered the Mithraic mysteries as a substitute for Christianity. At least, so Jung believed. In a letter to Freud of June 2, 1910, Jung wrote that "Julian the Apostate, for instance, reintroduced them as being the equivalent of Christianity."[34] As Jung knew, Julian alluded to knowing secrets about the sun god in his "Hymn to King Helios."

We should remember that in Jung's 1913 visions the figure of Elijah acts as an adviser and a sage but only acts as a *kosmokrator* when he guides Jung through a rapid descent to the bottom of the world. Perhaps the illuminated pages of Jung's mysterious "Red Book" could shed more light on the Elijah/Mithras identity, but we must await further evidence of what Jung himself (or his imaginal spirit guide Philemon) privately thought about these initiatory visions and why they are Mithraic from beginning to end.

Of what significance could the image of Mithras slaying the bull have to Jung and his secret Mithraic identity? Let us first imagine the classical tauroctony, the only image found universally in Mithraic cult sites and the central icon of Mithraism: Mithras is typically depicted as wearing a Phrygian cap (a felt cap that would have represented someone from the eastern reaches of the Roman empire). His left knee is on the back of a bull, pinning it down. With his left hand he is pulling the head of the bull back by its nostrils, and with his right hand he is slaying the bull by plunging a dagger or sword into its neck. Mithras's cape is usually billowing out in a curved shape behind him, and on its interior are sometimes depicted seven stars—the seven planets known to the ancient world. A scorpion is generally depicted attacking the bull's testicles, but other figures are also shown—namely, a snake, a dog, a raven, and sometimes a lion and a cup. The tip of the bull's tail takes on the form of an ear of grain. Two torchbearers, Cautes and Cautopates, are dressed like Mithras and hold torches pointed up and down, respectively.

One intriguing theory of the meaning of the tauroctony is Ulansey's astronomical interpretation. The key component is the fact that the spring and the autumn equinoxes occur within the period of one of the twelve zodiacal constellations and that they proceed backward through the zodiac every 2,500 years or so. Since about 4000 B.C.E. the precession of the spring equinoxes has moved from Taurus to Aries to Pisces and, soon, will move to Aquarius. In brief, the discovery of the precession of the equinoxes led Stoics in Tarsus to "hypothesize the existence of a new divinity responsible for this new cosmic phenomenon, a divinity capable of moving the structure of the entire cosmos and thus a divinity of great power."[35]

The Mystery of Deification 135

Mithras was this deity, and he is seen killing the bull because the act symbolizes the ending of the cosmic age of Taurus just prior to the age in which Mithraism was born.

The Mithraic tauroctony is explored repeatedly in Jung's fateful chapter in *Wandlungen,* "The Sacrifice." This image obviously held deep significance for him. His interpretation was that Mithras was the "sacrificer and the sacrificed," but "it is only his animal nature that Mithras sacrifices, his instinctuality."[36]

Yet the text holds another layer of meaning. In *MDR,* Jung reports that he waited two months before writing this chapter because he knew that his new ideas on the nature of the libido would cost him his relationship with Sigmund Freud. By 1912, Jung had been deeply immersed in attempts to try to make sense of the tauroctony for at least two full years, and the problem had fascinated Freud for the same amount of time. The image was consistent from Scotland to Italy to Anatolia; it clearly meant *something.* The killing of the bull, the scorpion biting the bull's testicles, and so on were symbols that were begging for a psychoanalytic interpretation.

As their correspondence shows, Freud and Jung did not see eye to eye on the meaning of the Mithraic mysteries. And their disagreement over the tauroctony is a telling sign of the dominance of Mithraism over psychoanalysis in Jung's own personal symbolic system. In a letter sent in June 1910, a month after Jung's first public lecture on the psychological interpretation of mythological and Mithraic material, Freud offered Jung his interpretation of the bull slaying: It was "the killing of the animal ego by the human ego, as the *mythological projection of repression,* in which the sublimated part of the human being (the conscious ego) sacrifices (regretfully) its vigorous drives."[37] Jung disagreed. Instead, he told Freud, "there must be something very typical in the fact that the central symbol of fecundity, the useful and generally accepted (not censored) *alter ego* of Mithras (the bull) is slain by another sexual symbol. The self-sacrifice is voluntary and involuntary at once (the same conflict as in the death of Christ)."[38]

Here we see the beginnings of Jung's firm but polite rejection of Freud, dismissing the psychoanalytic role of an unconscious censor that keeps the instincts out of awareness and putting forth instead a more pagan interpretation that views the Mithraic bull as an accepted alter ego of Mithras.

There is yet another, more poignant meaning of the tauroctony for Jung, and, indeed, it forms part of a secret encased in the *cista mystica* of Jung's life and work. Jung notes in this same letter of June 26 that, "the Mithras myth has undergone an adaptation to the calendar."[39] This reveals that Jung has read Cumont and has likewise noted the astronomical and *astrological* basis of Mithraic symbolism. Jung may have initially taken up the study of astrology to decipher Mithraic symbolism. "My evenings are taken up largely with astrology," he wrote to Freud on June 12, 1911, further reporting that, "I make horoscopic calculations in order to find a clue to the core of psychological truth."[40] In 1911, Antonia Wolff had entered Jung's life as his assistant, and she is believed to be the one who taught him astrology.

He knew that the astrological sun sign of Sigmund Freud, born on May 6, 1857, was Taurus, the bull. The centrality of the Mithraic tauroctony in "The Sacrifice" now takes on new meaning: it symbolizes the triumph of Jung's broader concept of libido over the strictly instinctual (sexual or venereal) libido theory of Freud. More important, it symbolized Jung's sacrifice of Freud. His final break with Freud is therefore heralded with every reference to the "killing of the bull" in "The Sacrifice." We know for certain that while writing "The Sacrifice" in early 1912, Jung connected the Mithraic tauroctony with the astrological sign Taurus and with sexuality in a very suggestive footnote to the section in which the tauroctony is discussed in detail: "Taurus is astrologically the Domicilium Veneris."[41] This was no doubt another hint to Jung's readers that this chapter contained veiled references to his knowing sacrifice of his relationship with Freud and Freud's sexual theory of libido.

Did Jung's fascination with the Mithraic image of the slaying of the bull feed into Freud's fears that Jung had a death wish against him? Freud was a master of the language of symbolism and would cast an analytic glance on any obsessions, especially those of a trusted disciple who may have harbored secret desires to slay the father.

Leonthica: Jung the Leo/Jung the *Leontocephalus*

A closer look at the initiatory process in the mysteries of Mithras reveals a fact about Jung's life that has been hidden for more than eighty years.

Based on some remarks by the Christian apologist Jerome and on archeological evidence (primarily from the Mithraeum of Felicissimus at the Roman seaport at Ostia), we know that there were often seven grades of initiation into the Mithraic mysteries. They were, in ascending order, *corax* (raven), *nymphus* (embryo), *miles* (soldier), *leo* (lion), *perses* (the Persian? the son of Perseus?), *heliodromus* (sun runner), and *pater* (father). Most of the references that survive concern *leo* and *pater,* and we know next to nothing of *perses* and *heliodromus*. According to the ancient observer Pallas (cited by Porphyry), while the members of the *corax* level

The Mystery of Deification

of initiates were called "servants," those of the grade *leo*—known as the *leones*—were welcomed as full "participants" in the mysteries. Indeed, as the scholar R. L. Gordon observed, reaching the grade *leo* marked a "large shift in status, from some stage of preparation to 'membership.'"[42]

In light of this information I have reached this conclusion: As late as 1925, twelve years after his first experiments with active imagination, Jung continued to interpret those experiences as an initiation into the *leo* grade of the Mithraic mysteries. This special level of initiation into the Mithraic mysteries was known as the *Leonthica*. Jung, however, never publicly revealed this fact.

To verify that Jung had prior knowledge of the significance of the grade of *leo*, we need look no further than his primary source of inspiration: Franz Cumont. In *The Mysteries of Mithras,* Cumont wrote: "We may conclude from a passage in Porphyry that the taking of the first three degrees did not authorize participation in the mysteries. . . . Only the mystics that had received the Leontics became Participants . . . and it is for this reason that the grade of *Leo* is mentioned more frequently in the inscription than any other."[43] Jung admitted his knowledge of the grade of *leo* in only two places in all of his writings: a footnote in *Wandlungen* (1912) and in his book *Mysterium Coniunctionis* (1955–56) when comparing the Mithraic grades of initiation to the stages in the alchemical opus: "Each of these stages stands for a new degree of insight, wisdom, and initiation, just as the Mithraic eagles, lions and sun-messengers signify grades of initiation."[44]

What did it mean to become one of the *leones* in the mysteries of Mithras? And what did his status as *leo* mean to Jung?

The objects associated with the grade of *leo* depicted on the mosaic floor of the Mithraeum of Felicissimus at Ostia give us some clues: a fire shovel, a *sistrum* (a "sacred rattle" associated with Egypt and imported as part of the ritual instruments of the cult of Isis), and a thunderbolt. Fire is associated with the grade of *leo,* as it is with the astrological sign of Leo, which was Jung's sun sign. The thunderbolt was a symbol of Zeus, and in the classical world the constellation Leo was under the tutelage of Zeus.[45]

In the Hellenistic world, lions held a special status among animals. It was believed that they could be divided into two categories, as human beings with intelligence and moral acumen and as gods who could mete out divine retribution. Furthermore, lions were thought of as "fire-filled and as intimately associated with the sun," and their powerful fiery breath was a vehicle of divine punishment, for fire is a purifying agent. The initiate who attained the status of *leo,* therefore, assumed powers attributed to lions.

Therefore, the cluster of symbols associated with the status of *leo* mirrored those of lions: sun/fire/purity/mediation (between men and gods)/ the constellation Leo. Jung revealed his knowledge of this symbolic cluster in his amplification of the leonine qualities of the lion-headed god and a special Mithraic amphora in the 1925 seminars. And as we know from Jung's later work, these symbols form part of the transformation process in the alchemical opus as well.

In his December 1913 vision, Jung assumed the stance of the crucified Christ and then was transformed into the lion-headed god. Could these passages from his readings in archeology and mythology have provided him with the necessary elements that were cryptomnesically "condensed," as he put it, into his visionary "deification"? It certainly appears so.

But if we are to believe Jung and accept that there is a phylogenetic or collective unconscious from which these experiences actually originate, we face the problems that he would never attempt to resolve: cryptomnesia and the cultural diffusion of myths and symbols. Not once—ever—would Jung attempt to conclusively rule out these alternate hypotheses for the phyllogenetic or collective unconcious.

The mystery of deification

We do not know enough about the rituals of Mithraic initiation or their associated beliefs, so it is impossible to state conclusively that the culmination of the *Leonthica* was the transformation of the initiate into the *Deus Leontocephalus*. But it is clear from Jung's reading of Cumont and the archeological research he did in preparation for *Wandlungen* that he believed the process of "becoming-one-with-god" was the climax of the initiation process in the Mithraic mysteries. To Jung, this would mean becoming one with Mithras, or donning a lion's mask (as Cumont describes) and becoming one with the *Deus Leontocephalus*.

Jung believed, based on his reading of Cumont, that becoming a "participant" in the mysteries at the grade of *leo* conferred an eternal status on the individual. This may be conjectured from the specific form the lion-headed god took—a variant of Aion, the Hellenistic god of eternity.

In a series of lectures he gave in England in 1935, Jung gave his description of this deity:

> In the cult of Mithras there is a peculiar kind of god, the key god Aion, whose presence could not be explained. But I think it is quite understandable. He is represented with the winged body of a man and the head of a lion, and he is encoiled by a snake which rises up over his head. . . . He is Infinite Time

and Long Duration. He is the supreme god of the Mithraic hierarchy and creates and destroys all things. . . . He is a sun-god. Leo is the zodiacal sign where the sun dwells in summer, while the snake symbolizes the winter or wet time. So Aion, the lion-headed god with the snake round his body, again represents the union of opposites, light and dark, male and female, creation and destruction.

The god is represented as having his arms crossed and holding a key in each hand. He is the spiritual father of St. Peter, for he, too, holds the keys. The keys which Aion is holding are the keys to the past and future.[46]

As the scholar Howard Jackson has observed, the "crucial attributes" of the lion-headed god are "the serpent-entwined body, the wings, the clutched keys."[47] Jung's own deification experience did not include the wings or the clutched keys, but these aspects were part of the very first manifestation of the imaginal figure that evolved out of Elijah: Jung's guru, Philemon. In *MDR* Jung reports that at some point after December 1913, the figure of Philemon first appeared to him in a dream of "a winged being sailing across the sky." He was "an old man with the horns of a bull," perhaps indicating once again a Mithraic influence. "He held a bunch of four keys, one of which he clutched as if he were about to open a lock. He had the wings of a kingfisher with its characteristic colors."[48]

It is now clear that Jung's spirit guide Philemon appears to be based on elements generally associated with Aion, although in Jung's mind there seems to be a blending of Mithraic and Gnostic elements. By 1916 he began to link his self-identity and personal destiny with the Gnostic heresies and even took on the pseudonym (and literary voice) of the second-century Gnostic leader Basilides of Alexandria in an unusual treatise we shall consider in the next chapter.

Thus, the elements of mythological and archeological knowledge concerning Mithraism and Gnosticism that became important to Jung are condensed into Philemon, another symbol of the self for Jung, a transformed *imago dei* that became dominant in his life when he began to move from his fascination with the Mithraic mysteries, circa 1910–14, to Gnosticism, circa 1916. In the 1930s, Jung absorbed both into the grand symbolic system of alchemy.

"I have had experiences which are . . . 'ineffable,' 'secret' "

Until Jung's "Red Book" and his personal papers are put at the disposal of scholars, we will have no more information about what he really thought and felt about his initiation into the mysteries of Mithras. But confirmation—of sorts—that Jung did indeed believe in the reality of this experience can be found in a letter he wrote to Bernhard Baur-Celio on January 30, 1934.

Baur-Celio had written to Jung asking if he possessed any "secret knowledge" beyond what he had already written about. Jung sent him a highly provocative—and appropriately mysterious—response. It is a truly remarkable letter.

Jung admitted, "I have had experiences which are, so to speak, 'ineffable,' 'secret,' because they can never be told properly and because nobody can understand them (I don't know whether I have even approximately understood them myself)."[49] He acknowledged that these experiences were also "dangerous," because he would be called mad if he revealed such things. They are "catastrophic" because if Jung told them publicly, "the prejudices aroused by their telling might block other people's way to a living and wondrous mystery." They were "taboo" in the sense of the ancient mysteries and, lapsing into Greek, Jung claimed his experiences were a "sanctuary" protected by a "fear of the gods."

Jung then gave a hint of these experiences by citing a suggestive passage from Goethe's *Faust, Part 2* (act 5, last scene).

> The deepest cave gives shelter
> Lions in silence roam around
> Friendly and tame
> Protecting holy ground
> The sanctuary of love.

Then, in the familiar style of mystery-cult initiates from Lucius Apuleius to Julian the Apostate, Jung demurred: "And already too much has been said."

But in the remainder of the letter, Jung devalued the notion of simple belief in one's experience of the divine in favor of knowing the living reality of one's experience. And he directly tied an encounter with the unconscious to the promise of renewal in the ancient initiations: "the exploration of the unconscious has in fact and truth discovered the age-old, timeless *way of initiation*. . . . Now it is not merely my 'credo' but the greatest and most incisive experience of my life that this door [to the unconscious mind], a highly inconspicuous side-door on an unsuspicious-looking and easily overlooked footpath—narrow and indistinct because only a few have set foot on it—leads to the secret of transformation and renewal." Here, two decades after his original visions, Jung still interpreted them within a Mithraic framework.

Jung regarded his own visionary experiences as the path to redemption—"individuation" as he called it after 1916—that could be taught to others. Analysis became an initiatory process, a descent into the unconscious mind in order to spark a process of individual transformation through a direct encounter with the transcendental realm of the gods. Just as the Last Supper became the central event upon which the mystery of Communion in the Roman Catholic Mass was based, Jungian analysis became a ritualized reenactment of Jung's own inner drama, a story of heroic confrontation with the gods that is enshrined as the sacred myth of analytical psychology. For those who survived an encounter with the god or gods within, Jung promised rebirth as a true "individual," free from all the repressive mechanisms of conventional beliefs about family, society, and deity. The successful survivors of such pagan regeneration became reborn, spiritually superior "individuated" beings.

But there is much more that Jung isn't telling here. In the troubled times of the First World War when Jung forged the Jungian mysteries, they had a deeper significance for his core group of disciples, most of whom were Swiss by birth but German through the deeper bonds of blood and soil.

"The old Aryan deity"

The key to understanding the Jungian mysteries and their historical roots—at least as Jung perceived them—can be found in *Wandlungen und Symbole der Libido*. In *Wandlungen,* Jung followed Cumont (and Ernest Renan before him) in his wistful view that if historical events had gone a little differently, the Western world would be Mithraic today instead of Judeo-Christian. He makes reference to the cultural and spiritual war between "the two great antagonistic religions, Christianity on the one side, and Mithracism on the other."[50] To Jung, the grand solar, astronomical, and astrological symbolism of Mithraism indicate a form of nature worship that could not have been the more recent product of civilized human life. The mysteries of Mithras are nature worship "in the best sense of the word; while the primitive Christians exhibited throughout an antagonistic attitude to the beauties of the world."[51]

Jung's derisive attitude toward Christianity as a product of civilization is even more apparent in the following indictment: "In the past two thousand years Christianity has done its work and has erected barriers of repression, which protect us from the sight of our own 'sinfulness.' The elementary emotions of the libido have come to be unknown to us, for they are carried on in the unconscious; therefore, the belief which combats them has become hollow and empty. Let whoever does not believe that a mask covers our religion, obtain an impression for himself from the appearance of our modern churches, from which style and art have long since fled."[52]

Mithraism was far older than Christianity, which only arose in the first century C.E. With its solar symbolism and shamanistic deification rites in which initiates take on animal powers, it had direct ties to the original nature religion of all human beings.

Jung fully believed that the mysteries of Mithras were his direct experiential link to the ancient Aryans. Cumont referred to Mithras as "the old Aryan deity" who found new names and new faces in the religions of ancient India and Iran,[53] areas thought to be the homeland of the Aryans. It is probably for this reason that Jung found the Mithraic mysteries so meaningful, and why he placed a greater emphasis on this cult over the other, less Aryan, Hellenistic mysteries.

It is not surprising that between 1909 and 1914, Jung and his assistants (Honegger, Spielrein, Nelken, and Schneiter) found that the mythological elements in psychotic symptoms in patients were survivals from ancient Aryan cultures ranging from India, Iran, Greece, and Rome to the ancient Teutons. Other than the occasional biblical reference and solar symbolism, they never once found exclusively Semitic mythological symbols in these patients. This was consistent with the scientific research program of the Zurich School, since in order to prove the validity of the phylogenetic hypothesis, mythological symbols from Aryan sources should predominate among psychotic Germanic patients.

Jung interpreted the discoveries of the Zurich School in the following manner: Within each native European there was a living pre-Christian layer of the unconscious psyche that produced religious images from the Hellenistic pagan mystery cults or even the more archaic nature religions of the ancient Aryans. This phylogenetic unconscious does not produce purely Christian symbols but instead offers pagan images, such as that of the sun as god. If the sediment of two thousand years of Judeo-Christian culture could be disturbed (as in psychotic mental diseases with a physiological component, such as dementia praecox), then this Semitic "mask" might be removed, and the biologically true images of the original "god within" could be revealed: a natural god, perhaps a god of the sun or stars like Mithras, or matriarchal goddesses of the moon or blood, or phallic or chthonic gods from within Mother Earth.

It was precisely these images that dominated the ancient Hellenistic mysteries that most fascinated Jung: the mysteries of Mithras, the Eleusinian mysteries, the mysteries of Dionysus, the Great Mother, and Isis-

Osiris. Many of these images also overlap with the alleged mysteries of the ancient Teutons and perhaps even the Aryan *Urreligion*.[54] To Jung, the mystery cults of antiquity kept alive the ancient natural religion of human prehistory and were a corrective antidote to the poison of religions—like Judaism and Christianity—that had been forged by civilization.

Jung regarded Christianity as a Jewish religion that was cruelly imposed on the pagan peoples of Europe. Since Judaism was the product of an older and higher level of civilization than that of the European pagans, it had separated people from nature. The Aryans of Europe, especially the German peoples, had been civilized only a thousand years ago and were therefore closer to their ancestors and their *Urreligion* of the sun and the sky and sacred groves of trees. Semitic cultures, cut off from the primordial source of life, did not have mysteries in which a direct experience of the gods could be attained through initiation rituals. They were, therefore, cut off from the renewal and rebirth that such mysteries offered the Aryans. In his book on the Mithraic Liturgy, Albrecht Dieterich compares the central image of rebirth in ancient India, the mysteries of Isis, and other Aryan cultural contexts but notes that "the Jews do not have this image."[55] Only Aryans could receive the sacrament of redemption.

Jung often referred to the ancient mysteries as the "secret" or "hidden" or "underground" religions and their social organizations as the secret or hidden churches that kept alive the divine spark from the dawn of creation. This leads us to an obvious conclusion. When Jung became one with Aion in his visionary initiation experience, in his imagination he was not only becoming a full participant in the mysteries of Mithras; he was experiencing a direct initiation into the most ancient of the mysteries of his Aryan ancestors. His new science of psychoanalysis became the twentieth-century vehicle of those mysteries. Most important, as his initiation experience also entailed assuming the stance of the crucified Jesus as he metamorphosed into Aion, Jung thereby became the figure that fueled the fantasies of thousands of Volkish Germans and European and American anti-Semites at the turn of the century: the Aryan Christ.

The Aryan Christ

At first glance, it seems to be a paradox. An Aryan Christ? Isn't that a contradiction in terms? But for personal and cultural reasons—an affirming resonance of the inner with the outer—this symbol of paradoxical divinity made sense to Jung in ways that are difficult to understand today. As a magician, healer, and, most important, as a redeemer, the god-man Christ fascinated and repulsed Jung since childhood. But nonetheless, when Jung began to have fantasies of leading a movement to revitalize humanity spiritually, first through psychoanalysis and then with his own movement, the living presence of Christ in his ancestral soul proved to be an irresistible model. This was true even though Jung had fully accepted his new pagan self-identity by December 1913. In an age dominated by a widely accepted Volkish worldview, it is perfectly understandable that Jung's self-deification would take this form.

For many decades before Jung became conscious that he was the Aryan Christ for a new age, there had been a wide-ranging debate in German culture not only about the historical reality of Jesus of Nazareth, but about whether he was 100 percent Jewish. Fables of all sorts about non-Semitic tribes of Aryans being the original occupants of the Holy Land who may have transmitted their blood to Jesus, or of the true biological father of Jesus being a Roman centurion, circulated within Volkish circles.

Houston Stewart Chamberlain, a member of the inner circle at Bayreuth after Richard Wagner's death, was an internationally recognized proponent of these views at the turn of the century. His best-known work, the two-volume *Die Grundlagen des Neunzehnten Jahrhunderts* (The foundations of the nineteenth century) of 1899, was widely read and discussed. In it, Chamberlain argued that there are too many Indo-European, Indo-Iranian, or Aryan elements in the tenets of Christianity and in the personality of Jesus to believe that Christ or his ideas were in any way Jewish. Using philological and historical evidence, Chamberlain claimed it is a mistake to believe that only the Semitic races were in Galilee in the years before the birth of Jesus. He placed the "Hellenes" in the area at that time and argued that the population could not possibly have been entirely Semitic. And, he argued, given the Aryan characteristics of Jesus and his ideas and given that race is perhaps the most important determinant of personality, the modern view of Jesus should be revised. The biology of race should replace language and cultural history as determinants of ethnicity, especially that of Christ. In a characteristic passage, Chamberlain said:

> Yet it will not do simply to put race aside as a negligible quantity; still less will it do to proclaim anything directly false about race and to let such an historical lie crystallize into an indisputable dogma. Whoever makes the assertion that Christ was a Jew is either ignorant or insincere; ignorant when he confuses religion and race, insincere when he knows the history of Galilee and partly conceals, partly distorts the very entangled facts in favor of his religious prejudices or, it may be, to curry favor with the Jews. The probability that Christ was no Jew, that He had not a drop of genuinely Jewish blood in his veins is so great that it is almost equivalent to a certainty. To what race did He belong? This is a question that cannot be answered at all.[56]

But statements such as "Christ . . . became the God of the young, vigorous Indo-Europeans" leave little doubt that Chamberlain believed him to be a superior product of the Aryan race.[57] To be sure, many theologians objected to this revisionism, but such racialist philosophy was quite popular and was considered to be based on good science. Even Jung quotes from this work in a footnote in *Wandlungen und Symbole der Libido*.[58] Given Chamberlain's fame as a leading racialist thinker and anti-Semite, this citation must have leapt off the page at Freud and his Jewish colleagues. Indeed, most of Freud's statements that Jung was anti-Semitic started in 1912, the year the second part of *Wandlungen* appeared.

Richard Wagner tended to believe such stories about the Aryan racial elements of Jesus. His opera *Parsifal* is laden with images of the young knight Parsifal as a pagan Christ-figure and redeemer. Jung experienced the Wagnerian mysteries of *Parsifal* as a young man and they moved him deeply. The focus of the story is a holy order of knights whose duty is to guard the Holy Grail. This chalice filled with the blood of Christ was a potent Volkish symbol as the sacred container of pure Aryan blood. Spiritual redemption and renewal sprang from the mystical power of blood, which must be protected at all costs. When Parsifal arrives on the scene, all is not well in the community of Grail knights. The holy spear that lanced the body of Christ—and that therefore has tremendous healing properties—has been stolen by the evil magician Klingsor with the help of the seductress Kundry, who by her own account is Jewish. Amfortas, sovereign of the Grail kingdom, lies in perpetual agony from a wound that never heals, inflicted by Klingsor with the magic spear. The Grail is therefore unguarded and vulnerable to Klingsor. Parsifal, a stranger to the knights, stumbles into his role as hero, retrieves the spear, heals Amfortas with a touch of its tip, redeems the fallen Kundry through an act of love, and restores order to the kingdom. In the final act, accompanied by Wagner's "transformation music," Parsifal waves the Holy Grail over a congregation of the Teutonic Grail knights as everyone sings out the final mystical words of the drama, "Highest healing's wonder/Redemption to the Redeemer!"

Based on an entry in Cosima Wagner's diaries, many commentators have argued that this last line meant that Jesus, the Christian savior and god, himself needed to be redeemed from his Jewish origins.[59] Others dispute this. But undoubtedly, *Parsifal* is a Volkish epiphany and the highest dramatic expression of the longing for an Aryan Christ. And Bayreuth itself, the only place where one could see a full performance of *Parsifal* before 1913, was hailed by Volkish enthusiasts as the new mystery-cult site where the great Aryan mysteries would reach their full expression.[60]

Beliefs such as these were held by a great number of educated persons not only in German culture but in the entire Judeo-Christian world at the turn of the century. Yet even for persons who lapsed occasionally into anti-Semitism—like Jung and many German scholars and theologians—it was difficult simply to erase every trace of Christianity because of its Semitic origins. Instead, the myth of an Aryan Christ comforted those bourgeois members of the *Volk* who simply could not turn to the worship of the sun or retreat to the Teutoberg forest to make animal sacrifices to Wotan or Thor. As the historian George Mosse notes in his magisterial analysis of the Volkish movement, "another tendency of Volkish thought" was "to substitute the image of the Volk for the person and function of Christ."[61] Transpositions and substitutions that stretched the bounds of logic were presented as solutions for racially cleansing the body of Christ.

"Teach us the secret runes!"

Some Volkish scholars and their readers found their inspiration in a remarkable manuscript that had been written in Old Saxon around 830 C.E. but published for the first time in modern German in 1830. This untitled manuscript, which its publisher titled the *Heliand* (Savior), is the first rendering of the New Testament gospel into the language of the ancient Germans.[62] In this Saxon Gospel, Jesus is Germanized in his role as a chieftain of a group of warrior companions (the apostles). Since the author of this ninth-century text was attempting to speak directly to the hearts and minds of his Northern European contemporaries, who were still largely pagan, Jesus here takes on the familiar attributes of Wotan. Christ the chieftain is a magician, like Wotan, and knows the secrets of the runes. Also like Wotan, who had the ravens Nunin and Hugin (memory and mind) perched on his shoulders, Christ the chieftain often has a dove—a symbol of the Holy Spirit—on his.

Jung cultivated a special relationship to Wotan, whom he believed to be the true god of the Germanic peoples of Europe. Wotan came to him in a dream in the form of a wild huntsman as a sign he was taking the soul of Jung's mother with him to the Land of the Dead.[63] Wotan appeared in other guises as well throughout Jung's life. Eugen Bohler, who was on very intimate terms with Jung from 1955 onward, recalled that Jung "had several intuitions about death—of the death of his mother before the First World War and of the death of his wife. On both occasions there was Wotan, the German god who is said to dominate Northern Europe. He had a dream of Wotan riding in the sky. . . . Wotan is also a psychopompos, one who leads the souls of the dead, like Hermes." Bohler added, "Jung had several dreams with Wotan flowing, so to speak, beside him on the lake when he was at Bollingen."[64]

Perhaps Jung was right that Wotan was the living god of the German people. In Jung's own Switzerland, even to this day, double-beamed *Türstkreuze* (Wotan-crosses) still watch over the landscape in the hinterlands of the canton of Luzern, awaiting the return of Wotan's wild hunt for souls.[65]

In the Nineteenth Song of the *Heliand*, the mighty chieftain Himself, the Rescuer, the Son of the Ruler, the Guardian of the Land, the Chieftain of Mankind, was surrounded by his warrior companions on a mountain.[66] They eagerly awaited his instructions. He spoke to the twelve heroes, telling them of many wondrous things, but they wished to know more than words.

"*Gerihti us that geruni!*" one of the more intelligent men cried out. "Teach us the secret runes!"

The Powerful One said, "When you want to speak to the Ruling God, to address the most powerful of all kings, then say what I now teach you." The magic spell he taught them we know, in a different form, as the Lord's Prayer.

EIGHT

Zurich 1916:
Abraxas and the Return of the Pagan Gods

Sermo VII

Yet when night was come the Dead again approached with lamentable mien and said: "There is yet one matter we forgot to mention. Teach us about man!"

Man is a gateway, through which from the outer world of gods, daemons, and souls ye pass into the inner world; out of the greater into the smaller world. Small and transitory is man. Already is he behind you, and once again ye find yourselves in endless space, in the smaller one or innermost infinity. At immeasurable distance standeth one single Star in the zenith.

This is the one god of this one man. This is his world, his pleroma, his divinity.

In this world is man Abraxas, the creator and destroyer of his own world.

This Star is the god and the goal of man.

This is his one guiding god. In him goeth man to his rest. Toward him goeth the long journey of the soul after death. In him shineth forth as light all that man bringeth back from the greater world. To this one god man shall pray.

Prayer increaseth the light of the Star. It casteth a bridge over death. It prepareth life for the smaller world and assuageth the hopeless desires of the greater.

When the greater world waxeth cold, burneth the Star.

Between man and his one god there standeth nothing, so long as man can turn away his eyes from the flaming spectacle of Abraxas.

Man here, god there.

Weakness and nothingness here, there eternally creative power.

Here nothing but darkness and chilling moisture.

There wholly Sun.

> Whereupon the Dead were silent and ascended like the smoke above the herdsman's fire, who through the night kept watch over his flock.
> —Philemon, through the gateway known as C. G. Jung, Summer 1916[1]

In the spring of 1916, as the First World War raged outside the borders of Switzerland and Zurich recovered from its worst outbreak of influenza in recent memory, more than forty eager souls gathered around C. G. Jung to hear the logos, the word of the law. It was as if after a difficult ascent along an arduous and secret path, they found themselves at a precipice, at the edge of an old aeon, and could not quite yet comprehend the brilliant vista of the new age that lay before them.

Even then they knew they were to be the first of a new spiritual race of saviors. Even then they knew that the work they did on their own individual souls would bring all of humanity to a higher state of consciousness. Many were called but few were chosen for special redemption in Zurich, while brother rose against brother and Death rode triumphantly across Europe. "The great problems of humanity were never solved by general laws, but only through a regeneration of the attitudes of individuals," Jung wrote in December of 1916.[2] The spiritual rebirth of the human race would begin in Zurich with *them*.

Almost everyone in the room that day was civilized as Swiss and Christian—an accident of history, of time and place of birth—but German by culture, language, and the eternal bond of shared blood, landscape, and Fate. Their guide, their "New Light," the charismatic Doctor Jung, spoke to them in the language of their ancestors, in the sounds that resonated with memories deep within their collective soul, in the common German of their *Volk*. He spoke to them of things of the spirit, of the necessity of descents and self-deification and rebirth, of Holy Orders like theirs whose guiding symbols of transformation were the Holy Grail, the crucifix wound with roses, and the Tree of Life from which Wotan hung upside down in self-sacrifice so that he could learn the secrets of the runes.

Jung spoke slowly, deliberately, and with great solemnity. And with good reason. The year 1916 rewarded years of tremendous dreams and visions that pushed him to the brink of insanity and suicide. He had been practicing a highly dissociative trance-induction technique that enabled him to travel to the realm of the gods and to talk to entities such as Philemon, the spiritual guru who functioned as his spirit control in the way that Ivenes had served Helly Preiswerk. He had also established an ongoing dialogue with an inner feminine voice that he later called the anima. At times he would allow this female entity to take over his own vocal cords and would spend entire evenings in his study asking questions in his own voice and then answering himself in the falsetto of this entity whom he originally thought was one of the ancient female gods of matriarchal prehistory. Later, the anima became many things: his "soul," the voice of the eternal Feminine that Goethe spoke of in the last lines of *Faust;* the image of Persephone, who lived in the underworld "realm of the Mothers" (the unconscious) and was seen by initiates into the Eleusinian mysteries; the living symbol of the Wholly Other or of the unconscious itself; and the rejected feminine aspects of his own nature that he needed to integrate with his own one-sided, conscious male identity in order to achieve a state of wholeness through psychological hermaphroditism.

"Jung . . . could not submit to a personal God"

His former colleagues in the psychoanalytic movement were now his enemies. They cruelly spread rumors about him—many based on fact—and they wrote thinly veiled attacks on him in the guise of scientific papers. One, written by Ernest Jones in 1913, diagnosed him as suffering from a "colossal narcissism" because of his "god-complex."[3] Uncannily, Jones described that man with a god complex as having the belief that he is a god and as having "rebirth fantasies" and dreams of renewing the world. Such a man, claimed Jones, purposefully shrouded his personality with "a cloud of mystery" and was obsessed with "omnipotence phantasies." In addition, Jones said such men maintained an interest in religion to the point where it degenerated into mysticism, and that, being so godlike themselves, "they cannot suffer the existence of any other God." This was a hatchet job on Jung, but it contained elements of truth.

Alphonse Maeder knew this better than most. As a colleague and ally of Jung during the years of the psychoanalytic movement and during the early years of the Zurich School and the Psychological Club, Maeder was first attracted, then repulsed, by Jung's attitude toward religion. At the 1913 Munich conference both Maeder and Jung presented papers in which the "prospective" and goal-directed nature of the unconscious mind was stressed over the causal and reductive approach of the Viennese. This meant, in part, that the unconscious was thought to have a prophetic function, anticipating future developments in the personality. Operating under such assumptions, the analyst became a kind of prophet or clairvoyant who could tell the future of the patient. This places the analyst in a role similar to that of a spiritual adviser or guru, and psychoanalysis openly crosses the line into magic and religion. Yet this was precisely what attracted so many, including Maeder, to Jung in the first place.

But by the years of the First World War it became increasingly clear to those around him that while Jung may have been using the metaphors of Christian spirituality to convey psychological ideas, in reality he had a deep-seated hostility to the Christian way of life. "I think Jung had a very strong individuality which could not submit to a personal God," said Maeder. "I mean, a religiosity without this concrete factor was very, very serious and important for him. But in the Christian way of submission, it is different." Maeder said that "Even up to his last day he had a complex against the Church and her mission. He could never use the word 'Church' without swearing; it remained a real father complex."[4]

The consequences of Jung's Freudian and Christian apostasies were severe. The wild visions from within and the hurtful attacks from without began to take their toll. Jung became paranoid at times, emotionally labile, given to quick fits of anger and rage. His disciples, particularly his male associates, found him intolerant of their ideas and therefore intolerable. Many of his male colleagues broke from him. He kept a loaded pistol next to his bed and vowed to blow his brains out if he ever felt he had entirely lost his sanity. Toni Wolff helped him through this troubled time, and somehow he made it.

Jung spoke solemnly and carefully on that day in 1916, for he was speaking of his innermost experiences, the sacred rhythms of his soul. He revealed the path of initiation, self-deification, and recovery that he had trod, and he was now sharing his formula for regeneration with his disciples for the first time in a public forum. Jung did this, however, without any explicit reference to himself. He would not be ready to reveal his own self-deification experience in a public setting until 1925.

In private, however, within the safe container of his analytic sessions with his most trusted patients, Jung had no resistance to confessing the content of his visions. Sometimes he showed them his magical volume of illuminated manuscript pages that gave concrete form to his visions and dreams and that contained almost six hundred pages worth of his fantasies and conversations with Philemon and other discarnate entities. The "Red Book," as this pagan bible or transformation journal was later known, was begun in 1914 and completed in 1930. His patients could only stare in awe as Jung shared with them his book of life. This intimacy only strengthened their belief that Jung was indeed a holy man, a prophet for a new age, and that they were blessed to be in his presence.

Two early supporters of Jung who were there that day in 1916 were

Tina and Adolph Keller. Adolph was a pastor and an author of books that blended religious wisdom and psychoanalytic insights, and Tina was later a physician and psychotherapist. Her analysis with Jung had begun in 1915 and continued, on and off, for some time. Tina Keller was one of the privileged few who caught glimpses of the oracular side of Jung during her analytic sessions with him. "It was during the First World War, and Dr. Jung would occasionally allude to his overwhelming experiences," she recalled in a memoir written in 1968 for the C. G. Jung Biographical Archives Project.[5] "Once he mentioned that they had caused his hair to turn grey; another time he spoke of the relief he had felt when the outbreak of the war showed him that his visions of blood and destructions were precognitions and did not indicate the threat of psychosis, as he had feared." Such talk made a profound impression on the young woman who, by her own admission, was preoccupied with religious issues. "Whenever Dr. Jung spoke of these experiences I could feel his emotion. Coming to analysis at that time one entered a very special atmosphere."

Jung also shared with Tina the early paintings of his visions that would form the illuminated manuscript pages of his "Red Book." "Dr. Jung was of course gaining experience in those early years," she said. "What he said was tentative, and I believe he was often quite mistaken. He often spoke of himself and his own experience. Sometimes he would show a picture he was painting as illustration of a point he was making. One felt accepted into the very special atmosphere of the discovery of the inner world and of its mystery. No wonder the fascination he exerted."

Tina Keller's memories of those exciting times invoke the spirit of the circle around Jung and confirm the role of the First World War in the intensification of their feeling that they were special and part of a movement that might save the world from madness. "I was one of a group gathered around an explorer trying to penetrate life's mysteries," she recalled. "We were listening with eager anticipation. During the First World War, in the midst of the feeling of catastrophe, when cultural values were breaking down, when there was general consternation and dissillusionment, a small group around Dr. Jung participated in his vision of an inner world unfolding."

However, she added, "Many of us were later disappointed. The vision was too vast and leads into the future." The Kellers, Alphonse Maeder, Hans Trüb, and others eventually distanced themselves from Jung because they could not renounce their Christianity. They could not break with the faith of their families. They could not follow Jung into a neopagan promised land no matter how beautiful the realm of gods and goddesses and ancestors looked to them.

But others could.

In the spring of 1916, Jung was only forty years old, but already to many he was a wise old man. As a healer, his powers were, by all accounts, extraordinary. Jung did indeed bring light and life back into the souls of many who came in contact with him. As the guiding light of the Psychology Club, Jung was the incarnation of the spiritual principle of their sacred order. And he promised redemption to his redeemers.

"The struggle with the Dead and the descent into Hell are unavoidable"

The first words out of Jung's mouth at the 1916 meeting referred directly to his secret epiphany of December 1913, when he became the Aryan Christ.[6] "In the symbol of Christ lies an identification of the personality with the progressive tendency of the collective soul," Jung said. In 1916, the terms "collective soul" and "collective unconscious" were used interchangeably. Jung said the collective soul had "various aspects," both bad and good, both female and male. One is a regressive tendency, "represented by the Terrible Mother." The other "contains the symbols of redemption for suffering humanity" and is symbolized by Christ. Jung explained that both the human and divine are united in Christ, which is why Christ is the "God-man."

In an individual, especially one plagued by visions and dreams and overwhelmed by the inner mythological symbols shooting forth from the collective unconscious, Jung warned of the danger that "this identification of the personality with the collective unconscious manifests itself always in the phenomenon of self-deification." But this is the unavoidable first step to true individuation. "It is therefore a question of the overcoming of self-deification, which might also be compared with the Death of Christ, a death of the greatest agony." This overcoming of the grandiosity and inflated self-image that comes from experiencing the god within—indeed, from becoming a god oneself—is the second and most crucial step to surviving these awful trials.

Jung said that the "freeing of the personality" from the power of the unconscious is "one of the most painful tasks to be accomplished on the road to development to full individuality." But, by doing so, by trying to overcome one's new godlike state, there arises "a chaos, a darkness and a doubt of all that exists, and of all that may be." Indeed, Jung said, hell itself opens up. "This moment brings a feeling of great danger. One is quite conscious of standing before death."

But this separating of the individual personality from the collective soul "seems to disturb phylogenetically certain pictures or formations in the unconscious—a process which we still understand very little, but which needs the greatest care in treatment." And just what are these pictures or formations? In this public lecture, Jung was careful to stay away from what he really meant: transpersonal entities or gods like the ones he regularly met with in his own visions and in those experienced by many of his patients. For the most part, Jung stayed close to the mask that he used to cover up the true essence of the phenomena he described.

But then he said something tremendously interesting.

The process of personality transformation becomes a cosmic drama in which an individual struggles with the spirits of the Dead. But the patient/initiate also serves as a guide or psychopomp—like Hermes or Wotan—who can bring the Dead to eternal rest. In other words, Jung told his audience that the work they did on their individual souls in psychotherapeutic treatment would not only heal them and make them whole individuals, but in the process they would redeem their ancestors as well.

"The struggle with the Dead is terrible . . ." said Jung. "Here too the parallel with Christ continues. The struggle with the Dead and the descent into Hell are unavoidable. The Dead need much patience and the greatest care. Some must be brought to eternal rest, others have a message to bring us, for which we must prepare ourselves. The Dead need time for their highest fulfillment, only after full duty has been done to the Dead can man return slowly to his newly created personality. This new individuality thus contains all vital elements in a new constellation."

All around him Jung must have seen the astonished, enthralled faces of his people.

"In studying Christ's Descent into Hell I was surprised to find how closely the tradition coincides with human experience. This problem is therefore not new, it is a problem of general mankind, and for this reason probably too, symbolized through Christ." Jung no doubt studied Christ's descent into hell through his own visionary descents. (In this forum, in the presence of persons he may not have known very well, Jung was very careful to stick to Christian metaphors, giving himself the persona of a Christian.) Ancient mystery-cult initiations always involved a descent of sorts and an ordeal before the initiates saw or became a god themselves. Jung knew this from his own experience. It was no longer a matter of believing, it was a matter of *knowing,* but he wasn't about to let this out in public just yet. In Zurich in 1916, the success of Jung's social experiment was not assured. His next rival, his next Judas, could very well be in the Club. He had to be careful.

Jung said that he would attempt to "elucidate this problem more fully in a work on the Transcendental Function." He did indeed write such an essay in 1916, but it was not published until 1957, and then only in a small, privately printed booklet.[7] It is one of the most important essays Jung ever wrote, because in it he describes in great detail his method of analyzing dreams and his mediumistic psychotherapeutic techniques.

Most of that essay concerned itself with the technique Jung called active imagination—the suspension of the critical function of the conscious ego to allow images and feelings to arise from the unconscious mind. One's inner voice could also be found in this way, and like a medium one could speak to it and establish an ongoing dialogue with it, as it represented a higher intelligence in the unconscious mind that was not bound by time and space. Automatic writing, which Jung called "writing from the unconscious," became one of his characteristic prescriptions to his patients. Active imagination could also take the form of making drawings and painting, fashioning things with one's hands, or—like the dancers from Ascona—using body movement to express the messages coming from the Dead or other entities in the unconscious. The instinctual, archaic "man" could be freed through such techniques, and once a dialogue was established between the conscious and the unconscious minds, the transcendent function came into play. In current parlance, it was like mediumship or channeling. To Jung, the transcendent function was the process of integrating the unconscious contents with the conscious mind that would lead to the creation of a New Man, a spiritual *Übermensch,* who could then save the redeemable remainder of humanity. In 1916, Jung called this process of creating a spiritual *Übermensch* the "*Menschwerdung,*" becoming a complete human, or the "individuation process."

Conscious of the spiritual metaphors that would have the greatest impact on his Swiss-German audience, Jung turned to Wagner's *Parsifal*. But here, too, he referred back to his initiatory visions of wise old Elijah and the erotic Jewess Salome, transposed into the operatic characters of Gurnemanz (an old Grail knight) and Kundry (the Jewish temptress whom Parsifal redeems). Jung gave his audience the following example: "On Good Friday Parsifal comes back to the Gralsburg [the fortress in which the Grail knights live and protect the Holy Grail]. He is entirely in black, the symbol of death, and his visor is closed. The belief in being able to fulfill the work for which he has struggled for so long has deserted him, and it is Gurnemanz and Kundry, both very much changed, who freed him from his madness and show him the way to the Gralsburg."

Jung found the Gralsburg when he became the Aryan Christ. He was brought to that point by Elijah and Salome, but ultimately reached it on his own initiative, much as, at the climax of Wagner's opera, the Aryan Parsifal assumes the magical healing powers of Christ.

Only a chosen few disciples in the audience that day knew that Jung was referring to his own deification process with this example from *Parsifal*. Others, who would be uncomfortable with a rejection of their Protestant heritage (there were almost no Catholics in these early years of the club, few French, and no Jews), could only look upon him in admiration as he again resorted to Christian themes. This time he even drew the analogy between the members of the club and the apostles of Christ. "The Collective soul may be brought to constellation in a different way in every individual, but in principle all these manifestations are the same," said Jung. "When the Holy Ghost revealed Himself to the Apostles on Whitsuntide, the Apostles spoke in tongues, which means that each spoke in his own way, each had his own way of praising his own God, and yet all praised the same God." Hence, within the collectivity of the club, each could still be an individual working toward the same spiritual goals. All could be true apostles of the same master and yet each follow the master's path in her or his own way.

Jung's views of the utopian nature of such an analytical collectivity soon became clear: "Only after the overcoming of self-deification, only after the human being has been revealed to himself, and man recognizes the human being in mankind, can we speak of a real analytical collectivity—a collectivity which reaches out (extends) beyond type and sex." Only after the god within has been fully experienced through its manifestation in an individual can the limitations of personality type and gender be overcome. A community of such god-men would then manifest this transcendent functioning in a collective. Jung's followers would be the first to try this, something never before done in the history of humankind, and to then redeem it from the misunderstandings and even violence caused by the limitations of psychological type and sex. But Jung cautioned his flock that there was still much work to be done in their analytical collectivity before they could alter human destiny.

"But we have not yet come so far, we are on the way to the *Menschwerdung*. The recognition and the acceptance of the personal life's task leads to the *Menschwerdung*. The recognition that each has to fulfill his especial task, and to his own especial way, leads to the respect for the individual and his especial path," said Jung. "Only those who have been forced through their own individual laws to go their own ways, and thereby have come in conflict with the prevailing traditions, come to Analysis." By "prevailing traditions" Jung meant religious ones. Hence, analysis as Jung conceived it was a separate spiritual path that one could take only after rejecting the faith of one's birth.

Zurich 1916: Abraxas and the Return of the Pagan Gods

Near the end of his introductory remarks on his theory of spiritual transformation—he never uses the words "psychology" or "psychological" or "psychotherapy" but always the language of the spirit or of his mysteries—Jung listed his ideas for the principles of the new club. He said that the analytical collectivity should always have "respect for the individual and his individual purpose." The "original groups" of such a community of analyzed persons will pass through their own development, and there should be "perfect freedom to build an endless number of small groups." Difficulties, if they arise, "must be solved according to analytical principles." If difficulties persist, Jung said, "they must be brought before an analytical tribunal." One can only wonder if Jung was aware of how much this last remark recalled the institutions and inquisitions of the Roman Catholic Church.

Jung's closing remarks to his disciples were the most telling. Here, in undisguised language, was Jung's "guiding fiction" or group fantasy that would sustain them.[8] Here we do not find mention of the group's cultural activities or of its intellectual or psychological or medical aims. Instead we find the guiding fantasy of the holy order or secret society engaged in the redemptive work of the spirit. Here we find Jung reaching back to his grandfather, hence completing the spiritual arc between them, invoking the words of Goethe and the occult symbols of the Freemasons and the Rosicrucians. Here again are references to Wagner and to the Tree of Life—and we find a reference to the sun. Jung said:

> Nothing is new under the sun. That which I see ahead of us as an ideal analytical collectivity Goethe saw and speaks of in his *"Geheimnisse."* If it were not so long, I should be glad to read it to you now—it may not be familiar to you all.
>
> The poem was written in 1816 and no doubt was far ahead of its time. It describes a collectivity founded on the principle of the religious acceptance of the individual path, and the *Menschwerdung.* As a symbol this Cloister has a Cross wound with roses, symbol of the resurrected life—the Tannhäuser motif of the budding staff, the Chider, or the Tree of Life.
>
> The ancients say of the Tree of Life, "A Noble Tree planted with rare skill grows in the garden. Its roots reach down to the bottom of Hell—its crown touches the Throne of God, its wide spreading branches surround the Earth. The Tree stands in fullest beauty and is glorious in its foliage."
>
> This Tree is the expression of a collective function, created by Analysis and life.

The applause Jung received after this last line was well earned. In this very brief address he not only spelled out the path of individuation—a road that led to self-deification—but he also inspired his audience with the guiding fiction that they were fellow members of a mystical order on a quest for the creation of a new type of spiritually superior human being and for a new utopian society that would transcend type and sex.

The world-redeeming process had now officially begun. Patients became apostles. Analysis became initiation. Cures became secondary to conversions. Their formerly mundane and spiritually bankrupt lives took on cosmic dimensions. They were on the path.

Decknamen

These were precarious times for C. G. Jung. He was in danger of losing everything he had so carefully built up over the years. His adoption of polygamy threatened his marriage and family life. His decision to cut himself off from almost all external professional activities—his hospital job, his university lectureship, and his presidency of the psychoanalytic association—left him, by late 1914, with only his private practice and the most devoted of his followers. Would he still have them in five years? Ten? There was no guarantee that his decision to found his own movement of spiritual revitalization would lead to success.

But his heart told him he must assume the mantle that had been offered to him by fate. He had been initiated into the most ancient of mysteries and had become a god. The gods had shown him the mysteries of life and human history, visions of the future and of a New Man. He saw the absolute lies of Christian dogma and its belief in a single, unreachable god. He could redeem those biologically capable of rebirth—Aryans—by returning them to their natural pagan roots, to the archaic man still within. He could save the world. Having been blessed with the direct knowledge of the divine, who better than he to be the prophet of a new age?

But despite his disengagement from most professional activities, Jung knew he had to maintain at least a modicum of respectability. He was, after all, a physician, a world-renowned scientist, and a man who was increasingly identified as one who was offering a spiritual alternative to the atheistic Jewish science of Sigmund Freud. He continued to give occasional talks in such places as England, Scotland, and America to professional societies of physicians. Occasionally, he wrote papers that were printed in respected scientific journals. And, of course, he made sure to keep writing and publishing dense works of scholarship.

To make his spiritual movement a success, Jung had to adopt at least three false faces or masks. In his professional talks, his professional publications, and in his books (at least until the 1930s), he equivocated. He could not talk about the living mystery of the gods and of the ancestors in a public forum if he wanted to be taken seriously. To get around this problem, he constructed a confusing but somewhat poetic pseudoscientific vocabulary to cover up the true meaning of his experiences. Terms that he used in print and in lectures in 1916 such as "personal unconscious," "collective unconscious," and "persona" were in reality *Decknamen,* or cover names, that hid the true nature of the phenomena from outsiders. Jung here emulated alchemists, who developed an elaborate vocabulary of symbols and metaphors to hide actual chemical names and processes from competitors. Only those adepts initiated into the special code by the author of such works could then understand them.[9] To some degree, Jung reversed the function of cover names: he invented "scientific" terms to obfuscate the direct experiences of living mystery that he offered his initiates through analysis. This is the Jung of the *Collected Works* and of his many apologists who continue to insist that there is something legitimately scientific about Jung's ideas.

For those members of the initial core group surrounding him in 1916, there were two publications that provided them with the terms they could use in their conversations with outsiders. The first of these was a French translation of a talk given to the club in 1916 on "The Conception of the Unconscious" in which the terms "collective unconscious" and "personal unconscious" were used for the first time in print.[10] In this publication, the German transcript of which must have been available to the club members, Jung talks repeatedly and openly about the deification process and about the wonderfully mystical experience he could promise those who underwent his brand of treatment. Jung tempted the spiritually hungry with statements such as "The wealth of the possibilities of the collective psyche is both confusing and dazzling. The dissolution of the persona results in the release of phantasy, which apparently is nothing else but the functioning of the collective psyche. This release bring materials into consciousness of whose existence we had no suspicion before. A rich mine of mythological thought and feeling is revealed."[11] Who wouldn't be curious about such things?

In early 1917, his little volume entitled *Die Psychologie der unbewussten Prozesse* (The psychology of unconscious processes) became a textbook of sorts for those in Jung's circle.[12] It is the first published statement of the theory and methods of treatment that we still recognize as Jungian. Appropriately, the cover design for the original edition shows a chalice—the Holy Grail—with a large blazing sun positioned just above it.

In these publications and lectures Jung was careful to always speak and write in code. The Land of the Dead, the eternal realm of the gods, indeed the whole divine realm of the Hellenistic world, became the collective unconscious. The mortal shell that hides the god within us is the persona, or mask of false individuality. The gods themselves, including otherworldy entities such as Elijah, Salome, and Philemon, were given the name "dominants" of the collective or suprapersonal unconscious. When introducing this term for the first time, Jung even wrote that "These dominants are the Ruling Powers, the Gods."[13] Jung said the dominants (in 1919, the "archetypes") are a fact of "psychological reality," which itself is a *Deckname*—still very much used by Jungians today—for direct mystical experience of the spirit world or of the divine. All of this makes up Jung's first mask.

In a more familiar setting, such as his lecture to the Psychological Club, Jung was not afraid to make pointed allusions to metaphors of the spiritual. Particularly after 1930 or so, he was less afraid to speak publicly in the language of the spirit, but he was not very self-disclosing, and he stuck close to Christian metaphors to hide the pagan undertow of his stream of thought. This was his second mask.

In intimate settings—such as an analytic session—he could, on occasion, be quite explicit about the *mysteria* that awaited his patients if they continued along the path of initiation that would bring them a new experience of the gods. Still, even in these intimate moments of self-disclosure, Jung was still very much in his role as a religious prophet and leader of a charismatic cult of individuals looking up to him for guidance. This was his third mask.

These three levels of persona, these three faces of Jung, hid further mystical experiences from everyone except, perhaps, one person: Toni Wolff. How far Jung had gone down the path of the pagan only she knew. Jung still needed to use familiar Christian metaphors to wean away from Christianity those who earnestly sought rebirth. At times he turned to the confusing heretical Christians that we call the Gnostics. And he even taught Gnostic heresies to the Dead.

The year 1916 not only brought a return of the pagan gods to the dreams and relationships, to the sexuality and spirituality of the pilgrims who flocked to his consulting room, it brought dead Christian knights to Jung's doorstep. And they were angry.

"We have come back from Jerusalem where we found not what we sought"

The story Aniela Jaffé relates in Jung's voice in *MDR* is one of the most unforgettable in the book.[14] On a Sunday afternoon in the summer of 1916,

Jung's doorbell began ringing "frantically." Everyone in the house looked out the window but no one was seen. Jung himself was sitting near the doorbell, "and not only heard it but saw it moving." The place was haunted!

"The atmosphere was thick, believe me!" he said. "Then I knew something had to happen. The whole house was filled as if there was a crowd present, crammed full of spirits. They were packed up right to the door, and the air was so thick it was impossible to breathe. As for myself, I was all a-quiver with the question: 'For God's sake, what in the world is this?' Then they cried out in chorus, 'We have come back from Jerusalem where we found not what we sought.' "

For the next three nights, "compelled from within to formulate and express what might have been said by Philemon," Jung wrote his famous "Seven Sermons to the Dead."

"Seven Sermons" is written in an oracular style, under the pseudonym of a famous Hellenistic Gnostic by the name of Basilides of Alexandria, a second-century Christian who was eventually branded a heretic. Although none of the original writings of the Basilidean Christians have survived, images of Abraxas, one of their most important deities, can be found on magical medallions and stones. Abraxas was a powerful rooster-headed god with snakes for legs and who brandished a whip. Sometimes, however, Abraxas is seen with the head of a lion. Abraxas was thought to be the master of the hundreds of other gods who are his slaves and was therefore the supreme god of this planet—the demiurge—in which all contradictory forces and oppositional deities were contained.

The Dead came to Jung's house for help because they "found not what they sought" in Jerusalem, the promised land of salvation. These spirits are Christian Crusaders who realized only after death that no redemption awaited them in the Holy Land. They felt cheated out of their immortality. They had been deceived by a false religion.

Jung preached to them in the form of seven sermons. By the end of the seventh, he had converted these disaffected Christians to his own pagan philosophy and to Abraxas, a god both good and evil. Abraxas is a terrible, hidden god that humans cannot directly perceive. Abraxas is behind the sun and the night. Abraxas is the creator and destroyer of world, truth and evil, light and darkness. Abraxas is "the hermaphrodite of the earliest beginning." Abraxas is the operation of all the gods and devils, and is "the world, its becoming and passing." There is no deity more powerful.

In the seventh sermon, Jung tells the knights that they were mistaken to seek salvation outside of themselves by journeying to Jerusalem. Instead, the real secret of rebirth can only be found in the "innermost infinity." If they would only look inward they would see at a distance on the inner horizon a "single Star in the zenith." The inner star is the "one guiding god" and the "goal of man." Invoking familiar pagan beliefs, Jung tells the howling Christians that after death the soul does not go to the Christian promised land but toward God as the sun or the star within. With this revelation of the pagan path of redemption, the Dead become silent and vanish up into the night sky to find their eternal rest.

The idea that the god within is experienced as the sun or a star on the inner horizon is one of the most central ideas of Jung's teachings during these early years. Indeed, in 1916, Jung himself drew and painted an image that he later interpreted as a representation of his personality.[15] It is a series of concentric circles within a larger one. Weird gods and daemons crawl about its various levels. What is most significant, however, is that at its core—like the magma at the center of the earth—is a fiery sun.

From 1918 on, he called these images "mandalas." The Sanskrit word *mandala* means "circle" and is thought to refer to the sun. For the rest of his life, Jung continually pointed to the Indian (Aryan) mandala as the best symbolic representation of wholeness or completeness in an individual or as the supreme God in which all opposites are contained.

In the seventh sermon are Jung's final words to the Dead, in which he instructs them about mankind. The seventh sermon is an interpretation of the mandala that Jung painted in 1916. With it, we see the inner pantheon of gods and daemons that Jung experienced within himself. We see that the sun or a star is at the very core of his being, the supreme god hidden behind all the others.

At the very bottom of the sun circle of Jung's soul, on the outermost circle, we see the demiurge, the *dominus mundi* or lord of the physical world. He is Abraxas, and the rays of the sun shine forth as a halo around his head. He is Abraxas the *Leontocephalus,* the lion-headed variant of the Gnostic god.

PART THREE

Acts of the Apostles

There were many whose hearts told them that they should begin to tell the secret runes, the Word of God, the famous feats that the powerful Christ accomplished in words and in deed among human beings.

There were many of the wise who wanted to praise the teachings of Christ, the holy Word of God, and wanted to write a bright-shining book with their own hands, telling how the sons of men should carry out His commands.

—The *Heliand,* song 1, circa 830 C.E.

(*preceding page*) Fidus, frontispiece to Otto Borngräber, *König Friedwahn: Germanisches Trauerspiel*, 1905. Here is the Aryan Christ worshiped by a female disciple.

NINE

Fanny Bowditch Katz—
"Analysis Is Religion"

In the beginning, just like the celebrants in the ancient cults of Dionysus, it was mostly women who came to Jung from afar to celebrate in his mysteries. Beset by spiritual longing, shut out of any positions of authority or power in the Judeo-Christian faiths, enraptured by decades of spiritualist séances and Theosophical texts, many foreign women left their homes and set up residence in Switzerland so that they could be near Carl Gustav Jung. Jung was their "new light," their spiritual adviser and prophet, the Swiss physician and scientist who nonetheless also was a master of occult wisdom and magical practice. They came to Jung to heal themselves and learn to heal others through visionary contact with a transcendent realm of gods and goddesses. Two of them—both Americans from wealthy families—lived near Jung for many years before returning home to confront terrible problems in their respective marriages. These were marital problems exacerbated by Jung himself. A third—an unmarried English physician who was a self-made success story—remained in her native land and eventually escaped Jung's gravitational pull only when she found a new exotic wise man to follow.

All three women—Fanny Bowditch Katz, Edith Rockefeller McCormick, and Constance Long—found themselves in the first group of apostles around Jung at the same time. This was a very critical time in the establishment of Jung's analytical psychology and his cult, and therefore these three women exerted a long-lasting influence on his subsequent international movement and his place in history.

Let us begin with the story of the woman who has left us the most complete record—indeed the earliest surviving record—of what psychotherapy was like in the hands of Jung in the years immediately following his break with Freud.

The troubled soul of Fanny Bowditch

In the chill Boston winter of 1911, after a catastrophic bout with Parkinson's disease, Henry Pickering Bowditch died in his seventy-first year. He had enjoyed a long and distinguished career at Harvard Medical School as an experimental physiologist. His good friend William James, the philosopher and psychologist, had died the year before. Working in Bowditch's state-of-the-art laboratory inspired James to set up the very first experimental psychology laboratory in America at Harvard in the mid-1870s. Even after James had grown bored with experimental work and returned to philosophy, the two men remained close friends and shared many unconventional interests.

One of these was spiritualism and the whole range of parapsychological phenomena associated with it. Over several decades they studied "extraordinary mental states," as James termed them, and associated phenomena such as automatic writing and drawing, trance-induced multiple personalities, and waking hallucinations of the living and of the dead.

Mostly they studied mediums during spiritualist séances. James and Bowditch attended many spiritualist séances together over the course of the twenty-five years that followed their formation of the American Society for Psychical Research. In gaslit homes in Cambridge and on Beacon Hill these two old friends often spent evenings in the presence of women who seemed to go into deep trances and who spoke with the low, sometimes eerie, more often comical, voices of the Dead. They remained skeptical, yet their common bond was a fascination with transcendental issues, with matters of the spirit.

Harvard professors of philosophy and medicine, psychical researchers and their spooky mediums, conversations late into the night about the Big Issues in life and life after death informed the environment in which Fanny Pickering Bowditch, Henry's daughter, began her unusual life.

Fanny had always been intensely shy. She always appeared hesitant, afraid of life, unsure of herself. She felt vulnerable, sensitive to the looks and words of others, and was not very interested in intellectual matters in any focused way. Depressive episodes were not uncommon with her. At times, however, she could be quite a willful, even spiteful child. As the daughter of a famous professor and scientist much was demanded of her, and the life of social events and ritualized afternoon teas with the elite pained her. She tried to hide in the background as much as possible, but her cloak of invisibility did not work. She was not beautiful, and she knew it. She attracted few suitors, no husband. Life was routine, empty, and only to be endured, not enjoyed. By 1905 it was clear that Parkinson's disease was weakening Dr. Bowditch's heart. There was no treatment, and, still living at home, Fanny nursed her father through the last few painful years of his life. When he died, Fanny went into a depression so severe that suicide was her only comforting thought. Although grief-stricken herself, her mother, Selma, perceived the danger to her daughter's life and turned to a distant cousin of Fanny's for help.

"Cousin Jim," as Fanny called him, was none other than James Jackson Putnam of Harvard Medical School, a man still regarded as the American father of neurology, who by 1909 was one of the strongest promoters in America of psychoanalysis.[1] Putnam's prestige in the scientific and medical worlds helped to make Freud credible to American physicians. In the autumn of 1909, both Freud and Jung spent considerable time with Putnam. (After Freud and Jung parted company in 1913, Putnam remained closer to the circle around Freud until his own death in 1918.)

After talking with Fanny and realizing the depth of her disturbance, Putnam recommended that she go to Switzerland for extensive psychoanalytic treatment with Jung. Fanny's mother approved wholeheartedly. The prospect terrified Fanny, but she realized at some level that it was time to try out a new life: almost thirty-eight, unmarried, obsessively suicidal, there was nowhere else to go but oblivion. Switzerland was clearly the better alternative. At some point in early 1912, Fanny Bowditch arrived in Zurich and almost immediately began treatment with Dr. Jung.

"Your daughter . . . has to go through a ripening process of her character"

In Zurich, Fanny found friends and felt alive again. After a difficult period of adjustment she eventually settled into a new identity as a member of a community united by a shared belief system and a sense that the work they did together would one day bring the spiritual salvation of the world.

In February of that year, Jung and Franz Riklin set up a new organization made up of analysts and patients called the Society for Psychoanalytic Endeavors. Going further than the Viennese circle around Freud, this new organization sponsored lectures and classes on the application of psychoanalysis to culture as a interpretive worldview. Everyone who participated was united by their shared experience in psychoanalytic treatment, which had taught them a new language for describing their lives—a secret vocabulary that was sexual, clinical, liberating.

When Fanny began her sessions she was struggling with German. To facilitate her treatment, Jung did what he usually did with his patients from America and Great Britain: after an initial diagnosis, he referred her to his assistant and colleague, Maria Moltzer, for concurrent treatment. Moltzer was a Dutch nurse who entered Jung's circle in Zurich as early as 1910. She was the primary translator of Jung's Fordham lectures, and for many years was the only fluent English-speaking analyst in his circle. Moltzer was the daughter of the owner of the famous Bols distillery in the Netherlands, and she became a nurse to protest the abuse of alcohol. Jung's first mention of her is in a letter to Freud dated September 8, 1910, in which he claims that she and another of his female disciples, Martha Boddinghaus, are in "a loving jealousy over me."[2] She attended the Weimar conference in September 1911, but in the famous picture of the participants she sits in the front row to the left of most of the rest of the Zurich School. Her image is slightly blurred, but she looks intense, perhaps severe, with her dark hair pulled back.

In his initial diagnosis of Fanny, Jung revealed his view of psychotherapy as a ripening or maturational process in which the individual personality organically "grows" during the course of therapy, like plants or crystals in the natural world. And it is clear that Jung saw Fanny suffering from a stunted development of her personality. Jung wrote Fanny's mother, Selma, that Fanny must "go through a ripening process of her character until her personality has achieved complete independence."[3] Otherwise, he warned, she would never regain her health. Although this process may have seemed mysterious, he assured Selma that he could help her daughter.

But by later in 1912, something had gone seriously wrong in Fanny's analysis. Paradoxical feelings arose, making her feel anxious, ambivalent, confused, raw, exposed. Feelings of desperately needing approval from Jung and Moltzer were mixed in with a panic-driven impulse to flee from them and their perceived assaults on her—especially from Jung. Fanny had never felt more vulnerable then she did with these strange but fascinating people who were eroding her old sense of self. In need of advice, she wrote to her cousin Jim and poured out her heart to him.

Jung was in New York City in September to deliver the Fordham lectures and to see colleagues and patients in other American cities, and he then reassured Putnam that Fanny's treatment was proceeding well, uninfluenced by the splits forming in the psychoanalytic movement. In his response of October 12, Putnam told Fanny: "I suspect that Dr. Jung's very masterful ways may affect some of his patients more strongly than he realizes himself, and you must not get dependent on him or hesitate to form critical judgments of him in your mind. I went out to New York to meet him a few days ago . . . and also had a few words with him about you which made me feel sure that you are on the right track."

Putnam had enough experience with psychoanalytic treatment to recognize the psychological dynamics of the situation. Fanny was reacting to the early stages of therapy in a very characteristic way. The transference was beginning to set in and she was resisting. He knew that Fanny had been too cloistered all her life and that this was the first time she had ever really challenged herself. She had wanted to leave after a similar crisis in June, but Putnam convinced her then, too, that she should stay. It was too soon to quit. The alternative was too grim to contemplate, and they both knew it. On December 1, Putnam sent Fanny the following advice:

> I think perhaps you take the analysis with Dr. Jung and Schwester M. all too seriously, and feel yourself far too much of a fly on sticking paper. After all, they are only humans with limitations and failings, like you and me, and you are not obliged to see any more to the analysis than just what you do see. I wish I could talk with you about it and see what is in your mind.
>
> Perhaps you find *your need* of the kind of aid that Zurich has to offer too strongly and really need, now, more striking out intellectually and socially, for yourself. It is a fault in Dr. Jung (*entre nous*) that he is too self-assertive and I suspect that he is lacking in some needful kinds of imagination, that he is, indeed, a strong but vain person, who might and does do much good but might also tend to crush a patient. He is to be learned from but not followed too implicitly.

Putnam puts his finger on an aspect of Jung's personality that Jung himself became aware of in later years. Jung told more than one of his disciples that he had an unusual effect on people, that they were either "inflated by my presence or entirely crushed."[4] How revealing it is that Putnam uses the same verb to describe the harmful effects of Jung's personality on others.

At the end of his letter to her, Putnam offered Fanny some personal philosophy of his own: "Life is or should be an affair of each person, each one of us, getting in touch with the elemental forces of the universe (which is, throughout, a *personal* universe) [ ] more dignity and power at their full measure, cultivating sympathy and insight but refusing to be played tricks on by an infantile love of protection.* I'm not sure what you *know* enough of yourself—but [you] need to feel your own oats more (excuse the colloquial expression), not in an aggressive sense but in a big sense."

In accordance with the wishes of her cousin, she remained in treatment. Under the guidance of Jung and Moltzer, she still had much to learn as she struggled with analysis in 1912 and 1913.

At about this time, Jung's increasingly estranged colleagues in the psychoanalytic movement were speculating about the true nature of the relationship between Jung and Moltzer. Ernest Jones told Freud, on December 26, that Jung "broke loose furiously" in a letter to him, "proclaiming that he was not neurotic at all, having passed through a [psychoanalytic] treatment (with the Moltzer? I suppose, you may imagine what the treatment was)."[5] Three days earlier, on December 23, Freud had written to Ferenczi: "[Jung] is behaving like a florid fool and the brutal fellow that he is. The master who analyzed him could only have been Fraulein Moltzer, and he is so foolish as to be proud of this work of a woman with whom he is having an affair. She is probably the one who got him worked up immediately upon his return to Zurich."[6] Although Toni Wolff is most likely the woman who was exciting Jung in late 1912, the gossip about an affair with Moltzer even reached later generations of Jung's disciples. Jolande Jacobi said in an interview for the C. G. Jung Biographical Archives Project, "I heard from others, about the time before he [Jung] met Toni Wolff, that he had a love affair there in the Burghölzli with a girl—what was her name—Moltzer."[7] However, as this is gossip that was more than two decades old by the time Jacobi heard it, this "girl" was most likely Sabina Spielrein.

Was Jung having an affair with Maria Moltzer? Did he submit to a formal psychoanalysis conducted by her? Until historians have access to Jung's personal papers for this period in his life, or until Moltzer's personal papers surface, we cannot answer these questions. However, given Freud's assertion that it could only have been Moltzer who analyzed Jung, clearly he regarded her as the most capable analyst in Zurich to do so.

One of the most admirable aspects of Jung's therapeutic philosophy during this time was his emphasis on the intellectual education of his patients. This was especially valuable for the women who entered his orbit without

---

*For this chapter and the three that follow, whenever a passage in a letter or diary is illegible I have indicated it with [ ]. All translations from the German are mine.

any formal education in psychology, psychoanalysis, or the history of religion and comparative mythology. Jung regularly held seminars for the broader community of the Zurich School, and many patients attended, including Fanny. As Jung's life and interests changed, so did the material he presented in the classroom. By December 1912, he knew he was no longer a Christian and was actively seeking a new myth for himself and for humanity in the polytheism of pagan antiquity. The seminars that Fanny attended reflected this shift toward a more overt religious orientation. For example, the first seminar Fanny attended, in May 1912, was on "Psychoanalysis." Her notebook for this class reveals it to have been a fairly straightforward explanation of the basic tenets of psychoanalysis, illustrated with a great amount of material from his word-association studies and from case histories. Dream interpretation was also explained through clinical material. There were few overtly religious references in the flow of ideas. But by the summer of 1913, when Jung taught another introductory course on psychoanalysis, psychoanalytic concepts were blended with remarks on the history of religion and even alchemy. Presaging Jung's later interest in alchemy, Fanny jotted down the following condensation of Jung's remarks in her notebook: "Alchemie—die Geheimnis des Wiedergeburt zu finden" ("Alchemy—to find the secret of rebirth"). This is the earliest evidence of Jung's spiritual and redemptive interpretation of alchemy.

As the religious elements of analytical psychology became more pronounced during 1913, Fanny's fascination with her experience in Zurich increased proportionally. Everyone was trying to decipher their favorite mythological passages in *Wandlungen und Symbole der Libido*. Could these marvelous, though frightening, experiences of gods and goddesses and the scintillating power of the sun-libido-God one day be *hers*? Fanny, like others, longed for confirmation of a transcendent realm but also remained afraid of actually experiencing it. The vitality and brilliant intellect emanating from Jung seemed to give everyone hope that they, too, could be such interesting people one day. Maybe it *was* possible to survive such an ordeal. . . .

And yet, despite Jung's continual references to God and to things spiritual, his views confused everyone, including Fanny. Modern life created a crisis of meaning, a religious crisis, that must be counteracted with religion. Jung, as a parson's son and healer, seemed to be the right person to deepen their Christian faith and to breathe life back into their hopes for an afterlife and salvation. For many years Jung did this, but as he adopted a form of polytheistic paganism as his own personal myth, he found it increasingly difficult to hide behind Christian metaphors to get his therapeutic points across to his colleagues and patients who had not—yet—strayed from their monotheism. Knowing the time was not right to reveal his new pagan worldview, he confused—indeed deliberately misled—his flock.

Prophetic dreams

In January 1913, Selma Bowditch wrote to Jung to ask when her daughter would be returning home. With visions in mind of the popular story of Svengali and his hypnotic slave, the virtuous maiden Trilby, some relatives of American patients began to wonder what spell kept their female kin in Zurich. Jung assured Selma that Fanny had made great progress, so much so that he could soon "discharge" her from treatment. However, Jung insisted that it was Fanny herself who did not yet want to leave Zurich.

Fanny may not have been entirely happy in Zurich, but she was decidedly ambivalent about returning home. It was in Boston, after all, that she had watched her father die and where she had wanted to kill herself. She followed Jung's advice and looked for portents of the future in her dreams. The unconscious was to function as a higher intelligence, the oracle who would see into the future and let her know when the time was propitious. Jung and Alphonse Maeder had been teaching their patients how to use this "prospective" function of dreams to make decisions about their daily lives. Jung went one step further and insisted that some dreams were prophetic. Just as the old prophets of the Bible interpreted their dreams as messages from the future or from God, so could we. Fanny had been keeping Putnam informed of developments in Zurich, and they had begun to alarm him. On September 2, 1913, in a letter to Ernest Jones, he mentioned his concern over Jung's "prophetic dreams" and the discrepancy between his professed scientific theory and actual mystical practice with his patients. Fanny's identity is disguised here as that of "a former patient":

> They [Jung colleagues] would seem to say that Jung is devoting much more attention to "reality"; but I should like to know *practically* whether this is true. Jung's feelings about the prophetic dream seem to be positive with him. He has been treating a former patient of mine for the past year, and utilized her dreams as a means of deciding whether she ought to return to America for a visit. This seems queer, and the more so that during his absence just a little later, she analyzed her own dreams, and came to the conclusion that a different meaning was to be asserted in this respect!![8]

Apparently, Jung had been urging Fanny not to return to America, but during a hiatus from her analysis with him she decided otherwise.

In the late autumn of 1913, after her seminars were over, Fanny finally went home to Boston. She had been away almost a year and a half and returned a much more mature woman. But she had been having a difficult time. Jung had been aggressive, confrontational in her analysis. She sought out her cousin Jim's protection, but Putnam was reluctant to take her side even though he was beginning to have serious doubts about Jung. Still believing that Fanny was going through the usual transference resistances, he avoided saying anything that would damage her therapeutic process. And sensing his unwillingness, Fanny didn't tell him the full story of her treatment.

What Fanny didn't reveal was that in her sessions Jung had repeatedly called her a liar and a coward to her face. No one had ever spoken to her like that before and she resented it. But she was nevertheless aware of Putnam's high regard for Jung and set sail once more from America in late September 1913 and arrived in Zurich in mid-October. She immediately saw Jung and repeated all the private conversations she had with Putnam. Jung must have been horrified when Fanny related all the negative impressions of him she had transmitted to Putnam. The world-renowned Harvard neurologist was an important colleague whom Jung could not afford to lose to Freud's camp at this uncertain time. Freud, Jones, and Ferenczi were all courting Putnam as well, and the letters that passed between the three of them in November and December 1913 were filled with references to Putnam, his attitudes toward Jung, and whether or not Putnam was in the Freudian camp. They even passed Putnam's letters to Jones between them without Putnam's knowledge. They needed him and they knew it.

In November 1913, Jung was still nominally president of the International Psychoanalytic Association, but he and his Swiss colleagues knew a formal schism was in the offing. (Freud and Jung had broken off correspondence in January of that year.) The allegiance of James Jackson Putnam would be critical in determining whether Freudian or Jungian psychoanalysis would dominate the world, particularly in all-important America. Jung had the advantage because he had Putnam's relative in his pocket—or so he thought. Fanny Bowditch now became a critically important pawn in a larger political game for the future of psychoanalysis and Jung's own career. Jung realized that he could not let Fanny stray from him with the damaging attitudes that she now seemed to harbor. Therefore, he convinced Fanny that it was *she* who had been mistaken, it was she who had transgressed against *him*. This brought her back into the fold of the Zurich School. Then she sent a remarkable confession to Putnam on November 18, 1913:

Since leaving America now six weeks ago, I've thought of you very many times and have wanted to write, but the time has not seemed propitious as things have not been going as well as I hoped they might.

Very soon after sailing the reaction set in and all the old feelings of unreality, the depression and the haunting thoughts of suicide returned in full force so that I felt in no condition to write. I wanted to wait until I had seen Dr. Jung and had a chance to talk America and my problems there over with him.

Now I have been with him a month and I have told him a good deal about my conversations with you and my various experiences.

He has helped me to see things in their true light, to understand how although at the time unconsciously I misrepresented him to you and how faithless I have been to him, so now it is only fair toward you and toward him to write to you and show you my dishonesty.

Cousin Jim, I know that you will believe me when I tell you that I did not realize what I was doing—but my not realizing was inexcusable after a year and a half of analysis.

I should have understood as I do now that in telling you of the crisis of last June, I was not, as I imagined telling you of it in order to show you my worst and what Dr. Jung has had to contend with in analyzing me, but in reality in order to win from you sympathy and understanding for my wounded feelings—instead of honestly acknowledging my fault, taking the blame myself and facing the situation, I put all the blame on him, attributing it all to his having laughed at me; but I said nothing of the many hours of analysis, which through my dishonesty and unreasonableness I had made more than difficult for Dr. Jung—this side of it did not occur to me.

He tells me now that he purposely allowed the crisis to come as he knew that only in some such way could he make any impression on me—also, that he did not drive me back into it as I told you, but that some such demonstration would have come with *any* analyst, as even with Sister Moltzer, who is so wonderfully tactful my behavior was often so childish and incomprehensible that analysis was almost impossible.

In resenting his laughing, in fact in telling you that it would take years for me to recover from the shocks and suffering of analysis, I only showed the pitiable smallness of my mind; that nursing my wounded feelings is more important to me than overcoming my faults and profiting by analysis.

You see, Cousin Jim, while I was in America I was conscious of the strongest resistance toward Dr. Jung and instead of analyzing them and understanding them simply as feelings of revenge, I was not honest enough for this, and allowed myself to be faithless to him.

I've realized during these last few days more than ever before how deep-rooted my dishonesty is—Dr. Jung emphasized again lately that I am untrue, fake and dishonest and he has even used the word *liar*. He says I am particularly clever in erasing the truth, in misrepresenting things in order to shine at the expense of others, and it is with the deepest shame and humiliation that I must admit the absolute truth of all this. I am fearfully dishonest, Cousin Jim, I have lied in analysis both unconsciously and consciously; I have deceived Dr. Jung and sister and now you too—O Cousin Jim I've been dishonest all my life because I am too much of a coward to do anything else.

Dr. Jung says he is willing to go on with me if I care to come to him, but he has no more interest in my case—he says his only motive in taking me back is his duty to humanity.

You can see by this how desperate my situation is—it *is* desperate—but the feeling that at last you know me as I really am, that I've had the courage to tell you the fearful truth will be a help in going on, and I mean to go on at all costs—finishing analysis means more to me than my life—far more. And I'm ready to sacrifice anything and everything for it. You see, I've never yet known truth or perfect honesty. Dr. Jung says, and I know how true it is, that I must lose my life to find it—during these last days I've been down to the depths as never before and surely soon the uplift must come; the wonderful feeling of "Wiedergeburt" ["rebirth"] which keen suffering and a struggle for a higher life bring.

I am, and always shall be, full of gratitude to Dr. Jung for handling me with such absolute sincerity and seriousness—in my afterlife I may understand even more than I do now what it has done for me.

I can't write yet on the question you and I discussed so freely together as I haven't yet talked it over sufficiently with Dr. Jung, but here too I have given you wrong impressions and misrepresented him. I shall write and explain as soon as I can—but Cousin Jim I am full of the bitterest regrets concerning my visit to America; I made *many* mistakes for which I can never forgive myself, and at present my mind is in chaos and often on the verge of despair.

I can't forgive myself for having made misunderstandings between you and Dr. Jung and I shall not rest until I've been able to straighten these out; and *what* an impression I must have made on you! When I think of my conversations now, they seem impossible and horrible—you see how it was, Cousin Jim, don't you? My one idea was not to be a coward, because the word "Feigling" ["coward"] which I had heard so often in analysis has burned so deep into my soul, and my one idea was to harm myself and have courage—I thought then that I knew myself—but now I see how utterly mistaken I was.

It all makes me desperately unhappy. I shall read this to Dr. Jung before sending it to you to avoid all further misunderstandings.

With many thanks for all you did for me, all your interest and sympathy.

Fanny's remarkable letter tells us many things about the way Jung's brand of therapy took on a spiritualizing trend in 1913. Analysis leads one to a rebirth, the *Wiedergeburt,* just as the eighteenth-century Pietists and the ancient mystery cults promised. Fanny uses the metaphor of a descent or a *katabasis* when she says she has "been down to the depths as never before." Also akin to the ancient mystery cults, which promised initiates a better life after death, Fanny, too, sees her treatment with Dr. Jung as preparation for the afterlife. He agrees to continue treatment with her now not for her sake, but for the sake of "his duty to humanity."

A few days after Fanny showed the above letter to Jung, he instructed her to write again to Putnam to report the latest development in her analysis: her overpowering, almost oceanic, feelings of love for him. In just a month since returning from America, she swung from feeling crushed by Jung to feeling elevated, ecstatic, indeed inflated with divine love for her master. On November 23, Fanny wrote the following addendum and sent the two-part missive in the same envelope:

> Dr. Jung has heard this letter and says he considers it all true but he wants me to add more to tell you of my latest experiences, so I'll have to tax your patience still further—I'm so sorry.
>
> You see this letter was written during the [ ] that I voluntarily stayed away from analysis as I needed to come to myself and understand. Only after days of struggle and conflict could I bring myself to realize how *strongly* dishonest I really am; I was continually making excuses for myself and trying to erase the painful truth.
>
> Writing to you, to Sister, and going to Dr. Riklin who is analyzing my young friend Frl. Herzel and telling him of it, because I feared my influence might be bad on her, all helped me to reach a deeper insight, but in spite of it all I was harassed by the feeling that I couldn't love myself as I knew I must. I couldn't understand it and was in very great distress; all the time I had the strongest resistances and hatred for Dr. Jung with fantasies of shooting and stabbing him and there were moments when I thought seriously of stopping analysis with him and going to Dr. Riklin. It would have been fearful to me to have had to do this but I was in a desperate state of mind and it seemed the only possibility. Cousin Jim, it was *ghastly,* and it was only with the greatest effort that I can force myself to think of it and write to you. I had the blackest thoughts and suspicions of Dr. Jung and one day a sudden great fear of him which was quite new to me and I was continually being haunted by the thoughts of my experiences in America. I was sleeping badly and twice during that time I screamed so loudly in my sleep that I waked Miss [Sarah B.] Baker in the next room through closed doors.
>
> Then came last Thursday evening and on Friday I was to see Dr. Jung again. I was trying desperately hard to make order out of chaos and I felt vaguely that beside acknowledging my dishonesty I must make still another sacrifice, a greater one than I had ever made before—that only then could I love myself. But yet I couldn't find it and I had all sorts of extreme ideas, quite fanatical many of them.

Then, Cousin Jim, that evening as I was going to bed the truth suddenly came to me. I saw that it was my *pride* that I had to surrender, that in spite of my surrender to Dr. Jung in the beginning of analysis I had yet never really yielded my pride—and this was to be my sacrifice. It all came over me then that instead of hating Dr. Jung I felt a deep and overpowering love for him; that my fear of him had been a distorted love, and that for the first time in my life I was capable of a disinterested love, because I could love him without either his friendship or his respect and my sacrifice was to be in telling him so.

I've *never* found anything harder than writing you of this, but Dr. Jung wants you to know of it, so I am trying to put my feelings aside.

Having the truth come to me so suddenly was a very wonderful experience—overwhelming and indescribable and I wanted to pray—this had come to me only very seldom in my life but I found I had reached that for which I had been longing and struggling all my life.

That night I called out again in my sleep but this time not in distress—Miss Baker was woken by hearing me shouting out, "Oh, I am *so* glad, I really am," and then followed two great sighs of relief—she heard this through closed doors but I knew nothing of it.

Dr. Jung has shown me both my pride has been keeping me from reaching that which I've needed all my life, and that being capable of a disinterested love is the first step toward an understanding of religion. Oh, and Cousin Jim, I see now how very much I have misunderstood Dr. Jung, how much bigger and finer he is than I in my smallness have been able to understand.

It's all very overwhelming and I can't say that just now I feel hopeful of ever being well, the confusion and distress are too great, but I *have* taken a step in being able to show my soul to Dr. Jung as it really is and I firmly believe that in time I can overcome my faults even though they are so fearfully serious. Oh, I hope *you* believe so too!

I've read all this to Dr. Jung and he says it is right. . . . I *am* sending it gladly, Cousin Jim, and I am ready to take the consequences whatever they may be. Do write to me—it's fearfully hard to have to wait too long.

I've had to copy it all over as the original was not fit to send.

When Putnam read these letters he was appalled at Jung's actions and concerned for Fanny's psychological independence and safety. In the course of a few weeks, Jung had led her to an eroticized religious conversion and made her less sure of herself than ever. Putnam recognized the cultlike nature of Fanny's new worship of Jung. He also saw the danger in Jung's control over her communications to him. Although he couldn't say this to Fanny in his response if Jung might read it, some of his psychoanalyst colleagues in America were claiming, in the wake of his split with Freud, that Jung was insane.

On December 10, Putnam composed a lengthy response to Fanny.

On the left margin of his emotional letter Putnam scrawled, "I cannot write without constraint unless I feel sure it is for you alone." Whether Fanny showed this letter to Jung or not is unknown, but Putnam's outrage and concern are apparent.

> I have just read your letter and am naturally a good deal stirred up by it. . . .
>
> I should not want you to show this letter to Dr. Jung, or even tell him about it (simply for fear of concealing misunderstandings), so that if you feel that you ought positively to do that, *please leave it unread.* Do not be afraid, however, that anything you said to me gave any false impression of Dr. Jung. I understand it all.
>
> The main thing that I want to say is that I believe your present reaction of abnegation and self-reproach to be excessive and therefore unwise and injurious. Let it be true, ten times over, that you were activated by a feeling of revenge towards Dr. Jung, and that underneath the revenge there was love.
>
> Nevertheless, although—if all this is true, as may well be—you should see this, it should be seen and reacted to in calmness and with intelligent scrutiny, not in the way of self-abasement. The self-abasement reaction is "too easy" and becomes in its turn a sort of self-indulgence, like asceticism. You have, at your best, a fine mind and sound character, as was evident last summer, and you owe it to yourself to preserve a self-respect which should override and outlive even the discovery in yourself of more or less falseness.
>
> Who is not false? Not one of us, not Dr. Jung either. Doubtless we can aid each other, but it is as the blind *helping* the blind, by giving a feeble but new bit of insight. I have no doubt that Dr. Jung is consciously trying to help you but I cannot understand his saying that he has lost interest in your case, just because you admitted that you had had a feeling of revenge and acted on it. He must know (and indeed I have heard him say as much), as everybody knows who is engaged in this work, that such feelings are extremely common. Doubtless they should be gotten rid of, but not at the cost of a loss of self-respect.
>
> We should live by *our best,* and when we find that we are not doing so, we should look at ourselves critically but calmly, and quietly readjust our course.
>
> I remember that Dr. Freud pointed out to me, in the very first of our few conferences at Zurich, that I was a murderer! Think of that. But did he mean, or did I suppose he meant, that I was to go and jump overboard, or give myself up to the hangman? Not a bit of it. I was to be healthier-minded from then-on, and happier, and better able to stop being a murderer. Of course you understand that your suicidal tendencies or thoughts are (at least *in part,* which is as far as we can go) a kind of self-indulgent, and again, *excessive* attempt to find a short cut to some sort of stability and content.

But there are no short cuts and no excessive reactions of these sorts—most excepting your present reaction of humiliation, religious frenzy, or love which you call disinterested,—that fill the bill of good sense and helpful change of heart. You cannot and should not change the dear Fanny Bowditch whom we all love, into any other sort of creature whatever, except through a process of slow, intelligent, and quiet growth and—although I say this without wishing it to be taken too much to heart—I cannot but suspect that you are suffering in part from the influence of Dr. J.'s personality and [a] tendency to be excessive in a too personal way of taking things. Perhaps I am wrong, but there will be no harm in realizing that he is also no god but a blind man trying to lead the blind, and that you are as much at liberty to criticize him as he is to criticize you. . . .

Putnam's reminder that Jung was no god is chillingly ironic when we consider that during this same week, Jung began to experience a series of religious visions that culminated in his initiation into the mysteries of Mithras and his own self-deification. By the time Fanny received this letter, her analyst had become the Aryan Christ.

How much did she learn of this in the months that followed? How did these mystical revelations to Jung change the style of her treatment in the months that followed this crisis?

One clue as to how Jung dealt with Fanny's powerful erotic transference and religious frenzy can be found in a letter from Ernest Jones to Sigmund Freud on July 27, 1914: "You may be interested to learn the latest method of dealing with the Übertragung [transference]. The patient overcomes it by learning that she is not really in love with the analyst but that she is for the first time struggling to comprehend a Universal Idea (with capitals) in Plato's sense; after she had done this, then what seems to be Übertragung may remain."[9] Ferenczi learned of this a few days later and said to Freud (July 31, 1914): "The *Platonic idea* as a transference substrate is precious. Jung seems also to have used the word *imago* in a quite incorporeal way."[10]

Tina Keller, who was in analysis with Jung in 1915, described how Jung dealt with her "love" for him in the manner described by Jones:

> Dr. Jung never spoke of "transference" but obliged me to face the fact that I was "in love." It would have been easier to use a technical term. Dr. Jung's theory was that I was "in love" with some quality (or archetype) which he represented, and had touched in my psyche. If and in the measure that I would be able to realize this quality or this unknown element in myself, then I would be free of him as a person. He was convinced of the meaning of such a manifestation, and he said that what I brought was such an openness that

he owed me some spiritual value that would fertilize my psyche and my "individuation" would be a "spiritual child."[11]

Keller, who experienced difficulties with her husband, Adolph, because of her analysis, didn't buy this seductive promise of spiritual insemination. "This sounded good," she said. "He sincerely meant it, but it did not prove true." Jung's heterodox religious therapy could not win Tina away from Christianity or her husband. "All through this terrible period, when my husband was sad and angry, and I was unhappy, I still knew that I had married the 'right' man."[12] (The Kellers and Alphonse Maeder eventually broke with Jung and the Psychological Club and renewed their Christian faith through the Oxford Movement.)

What Fanny may have been struggling to comprehend was that she had been seized or possessed by a "god," to use Jung's private pagan metaphor, or had been overtaken by an *Urbild* (primordial image) from the phylogenetic unconscious. If all "projections" require a "hook," then Fanny's projections onto Jung did indeed have a basis in reality—at least Jung's personal reality. Fanny was not really in love with C. G. Jung the man. She was in love with C. G. Jung the god. At least this is how the thinking would have gone. And since everyone had the potential to become one with the god within, techniques that allowed this internal divine essence to speak for itself moved to the forefront of Jung's method of psychotherapy.

Given the traumatic crisis in her relationship with Jung in November and December 1913, and given her cousin Jim's strong advice to look more critically at Jung, it is probable that in 1914 Maria Moltzer became Fanny's primary analyst. By February 1915 we find the first evidence that Jung and his circle were urging their patients to draw and paint their dreams and fantasies. Although Fanny left behind a small collection of drawings, few of them are dated and none seems to be from 1915. On February 15, 1915, Fanny typed up her own psychological interpretation of a series of drawings she presented to Moltzer. Though the drawings themselves have not survived, from her own brief analysis of them we can see that the spiritualizing trend in Jungian treatment had finally prevailed and that references to Wagner's *Parsifal* and to Mozart's Masonic mystery opera, *Die Zauberflöte,* provide the anchors for interpretation.

"My drawings containing the very archaic and the very high," Fanny wrote as she free-associated from her artwork. "I must learn to understand them and how each of them can be lived. Certain archaic tendencies and certain spiritual aspirations too low or too high to be lived (as in the Zauberflote). To recognize the Kundry element in one. The possibility of developing from the very low to the very high. Of the value and importance of recognizing one's archaic tendencies, as part of oneself—loving them as being a part of one's soul." Fanny mentions St. Francis of Assisi "speaking lovingly to a wolf" and talking to birds. "A new idea in the unconscious shows itself at first in the conscious as something quite commonplace, banal,—then becomes spiritualized."

This indeed, in a nutshell, is how Jung revised personal memories and "infantile complexes": no inner experience, no memory or mental image, was simply personal ("banal"), but in reality collective or transcendent at its natural core. Fanny's jottings of her associations allow us to date them within the historical context of the development of Jung's thought. They are the earliest evidence that Jung took his former psychophysiological theory of the mind based on personal complexes—which he had established experimentally with the word-association studies—and elevated it to a transcendental plane. It was no longer those nettlesome complexes that made us forget things or say and do evil things we would not normally do; instead, our behavior was shaped by "primordial ideas" or "dominants" or "gods" or "archetypes." Once again, Jung found the universal in the particular, the sacred in the mundane.

In 1915, extraversion and introversion were the only two psychological types in his theory, and they roughly included the patterns that Jung would later call, respectively, the feeling type and the thinking type. These concepts referred to the direction of the flow of the libido in a person (extraverts project themselves outward, introverts toward the inner, subjective world). With the help of Toni Wolff, by 1916 he added the notion of intuition. Through a long and blunt discussion of the type problem in a series of letters with Hans Schmid, Jung came to the conclusion that there were the two "functions," of which everyone had one to a greater or lesser degree, and four types in two bipolar pairs: thinking-feeling and sensation-intuition.

During these early years of analytical psychology, a major point of distinction between the Vienna School and the Zurich School was the latter's emphasis on personality types. Fanny Bowditch was almost a textbook case of an introverted type. Maria Moltzer was another. As Fanny and she would discover, their lives paralleled in many other respects as well.

Beginning in late 1914, Jung was called up regularly for several months of duty per year in the medical corps. Whatever had happened between them regarding the continuation of her analysis, Fanny now saw less of Jung. His analysis of Fanny came to a standstill for another reason. Possibly due to his mishandling of Fanny Bowditch's treatment, Jung lost Putnam's support, although Jung still admired him very much. By 1915,

Putnam had allied himself firmly with Freud and his movement. Beginning in a February 22, 1915, note in which he sketched two hands clasped in friendship, Putnam now addressed Freud as "Dear Friend" in letters. Freud, delighted with the new intimacy, reciprocated with the same salutations. Hence, even though she was already at some remove in Moltzer's care, Jung no longer needed Fanny.

Fanny Bowditch continued her analysis with Moltzer and blossomed in ways that she had never dreamed possible. In 1915, a charming young psychiatrist from the Netherlands arrived and was in treatment with Jung and Alphonse Maeder. His name was Johann Rudolf Katz, and Fanny fell in love with him. Within a year or so they married. By late 1917 they settled in Amsterdam, where Katz practiced as a psychiatrist and an analyst.

Their courtship began in the spring of 1916. In May, Katz gave Fanny nine red roses bound with a golden ribbon. She had been around Jungians long enough to understand the sexual significance of the color of these flowers. They were a temptation, a challenge, and a confirmation that her life was about to change. As a forty-two-year-old virgin, Fanny's departure from maidenhood, from the protective container of a psychological world ruled by the mother-daughter dynamic, was long overdue. In the Jungian language of her circle, her individuation had been frozen by a transference to the principle of the Great Mother Goddess, and therefore as an adult she still remained a child. Here, now, was a man who offered the opportunity to bring her to full womanhood. But first there must be a sacrifice: the death of the maiden role in which she had been hiding.

Sacrificing her virginity to Wotan

On June 2, 1916, Fanny typed out a "fantasy" that she then acted out in real life. In it, she sounded very much like the café denizens of Schwabing described by Fanny zu Reventlow in her invocation of the great pagan cults of Mother Earth, the Great Mother Goddess, Volkish symbols of the sun, and the Tree of Life, the mighty oak. In a diary entry for August 29, 1917, she referred to "reading my Club fantasy to the Club," and this document may have been the basis of her short presentation. Such presentations were testimonials of a sort, giving witness to the healing powers of Jungian analysis. She wrote:

> The thought came to me that in breaking the transference which meant the tearing asunder of the bonds which had held me all my life,—the bonds

which had kept me bound to the great mother principle as a child is bound to the mother, I must use all the strength of my personality, give all I have,—and above all, make it beautiful. Then came a fantasy which needed to be lived,—and that afternoon I lived out in reality the expression of the great change now taking place within.

In the vase upon my table still stood three red roses,—the last of nine that had meant a great deal to me having deep symbolic value not yet fully understood,—their charm perhaps enhanced by the mystery of their meaning. The three faded red roses, now symbols of death, I bound together with the golden ribbon which had held them when they came to me fresh and beautiful. I took a trowel with me, and . . . I went out into the woods. Never have those woods seemed more beautiful, or more responsive to my mood,—one of nature's greatest gifts to man, the spirit of "Waldeinsamkeit" permeated my whole being and I felt consoled and uplifted. . . .

I was looking for an oak tree, the symbol of enduring strength, and although all others were plentiful, an oak tree seemed impossible to find. And so I wandered in my solitude, eagerly searching,—never finding,—but all the while feeling certain that somewhere in that fine forest *must* stand the tree which would mean to me more than all the rest,—the one tree which from now on was to be the guardian of my roses and a symbol of new strength, of a new life, born out of sacrifice and death.

Eventually Fanny found her oak tree, or as she put it, "Fate willed it that I should find my oak." She placed her roses within a cavity in the trunk on some "cool earth." With her copy of the poems of Walt Whitman beside her, Fanny then waxed Romantic in her description of inner bliss as she knelt in supplication to the mighty oak, that sacred symbol of Wotan, to which she had offered, in exchange for protection, the greatest of sacrifices: her immortal soul.

And as I knelt there filled with these solemn thoughts of death and life,—of love and sacrifice,—a sunbeam caught my eye. . . . All day the sky a dull dark grey had been, but now as if to give me all my heart desired, the sun shone forth, and in that moment came to me the meaning of the nine! All elements were here,—below me Mother Earth, symbol of the great mother principle and giver of our life,—beside me here the brook where flows loving water,—symbol of eternal change and motion,—of ever flowing thought,—around me everywhere, and all pervading, the element of air, symbol of the spirit, of the mind,—the part of us that calls on God, and striving ever upward realizes the Divine. And shining through the clouds, the great and living sun, symbol of the godly power and of might, life giver and destroyer of all life.

And here was I,—one human being and alone in this great nature,—one human being, small, and very much alone,—yet conscious now of something vast within, something that vibrates with all nature, that strives, and falls, and strives again,—that lives and must live,—and living is a part of God.

Her memoir ends with the statement, "A sprig of oak leaves now stands in the vase upon my table."

Fanny Bowditch, like most Americans and many of the British who came for treatment by Jung, had very little education in mythology, and everything they learned about it came through the filter of Jung and his disciples. We can only speculate as to why she reenacted a Volkish fantasy about the ritual sacrifices to Wotan made by the ancient Germans. In her mind, she was offering the sacrifice of her virginity in return for protection from the Tree of Life for living out her sexuality and furthering her individuation. Sacrificial offerings to oak trees, which were sacred to Wotan, are thought to be the basis of our contemporary custom of placing ornaments on Christmas trees. Fanny would have been largely oblivious to the deeper Volkish nuances that made her sacrifice to the oak such a pregnant pagan act.

Jung, however, modeled the scripts or guiding fictions through which his disciples enacted their self-sacrificial encounters with God or the gods. Fanny's way of concretizing or acting out fantasies of making sacrifices must have had special meaning for Jung and those around him. It was a means of reaching back to old pagan cults for new religious possibilities. And although Fanny probably didn't understand the full Volkish twist of this philosophy, she did begin to understand that Christianity had its limitations. It had kept her sexually "repressed" and afraid of the natural world and of life itself. Analysis would redeem her from her old faith and offer her rebirth into a new existence.

Fanny—like most of Jung's clueless American and British disciples—may not have been aware of the culture-specific nature of the Volkish neo-paganism that Jung was imparting, but James Putnam certainly saw its dangers and attempted to warn Fanny of them. In an undated note apparently written as an afterthought to a more critical exchange, Putnam said:

> Do you not think that you have been too excessively and too intensely under the influence of a small group of self-assertive people with many fixed ideas (new to you and overwhelming) to be able to form a fair judgment as to their value? May it not be a case of exchanging old prejudices for new prejudices, an old glamour for a new glamour?
>
> It seems to me that you may feel quite differently about the whole matter when you have exchanged again your German spectacles for your New England spectacles and German friends and traditions for your New England friends and traditions.

One should not be bullied into believing it is *necessarily* cowardice that determines one's course. It may be and it may not and usually both are partly true. The fear of cowardice is itself a cowardice—or may be such.

Putnam criticized here one of the techniques by which social cohesiveness was enforced by Jung and his analysts: the insistence that the patients did not know themselves and were afraid to do so. What's more, the greatest sin of all was that they were "afraid of the Unconscious." To be a coward meant one was not receptive to the informed interpretations of the analysts. Given Jung's syncretism of German mysticism, Hellenistic paganism, and Gnosticism with his brand of treatment, it is no wonder that so many patients from foreign cultures and Christian backgrounds had strong resistance to adopting his worldview. The weaker ones, such as Fanny, eventually submitted to the constant attack on their old religious beliefs and values and allowed their old persona or conscious self-identity to be replaced with a new one as a member of a wonderful new spiritual movement led by the charismatic Jung.

By the time Fanny enacted her pagan sacrifice to Wotan after four years in Zurich she had, consciously or not, fallen under the spell of the analysts. Despite his blunt warning, even Putnam couldn't pull her out of it.

Abraxas 1916: "Analysis is a therapy, and a religion"

In her diary from the summer of 1916, Fanny wrote, on Saturday, July 1, "Analysis is a therapy, and a religion— [   ] a going back of Christianity." Fanny is now fully conscious of the fact that she is in a religious movement led by Dr. Jung, and that it is based on a return to pagan spirituality as a method of redemption or rebirth. The Aryanized Christianity of *Parsifal* appears again and again in her diaries, indicating that these Wagnerian and Volkish motifs were part of the "common Greek" (koine) spoken by initiates into the Jungian subculture and its *mysteria*.

Through Fanny's notes we can witness the birth of Jung's new religion. We find in them instruction in a new polytheistic cosmology and an appeal to make sacrifices to the old pagan gods once more. And we share Fanny's confusion as she is introduced to Abraxas.

Fanny's language in the early pages of her June 1916 diary echoes that of Hermann Hesse's analysis, which began at the very same time. She wrote the following disjointed (and often illegible) notes of her sessions with Moltzer:

[ ] it comes from "das innere Erlebnis" ["the inner experience"] that convey to one that *this* creed only, This is the way life is to be lived; [ ] insight into the deepest meaning of life—seeing the Path before one [ ] or the Path one *must* go, or be guilty of the unpardonable sin—sinning against one's higher self. This "innere Erlebnis" reached through religion—analysis *is* religion. The Logos an abstract thought which cannot be expressed in a word—logos—and needs to be *lived,* not only thought—thus being lived it becomes "das Fleisch gewordene Word" ["the Word made flesh"]—[ ]—Christ.

We are all Christ when we free our life through das innere Erlebnis—*live it*—but it carried with it an [ ] responsibility. We *cannot* live our life as he did—but we can live in his spirit which means each living *according to his own inner spirit, his highest* [ ].

In speaking of god she [Moltzer] spoke of Dr. Jung's conception of *"Abraxas"*—the Urlibido, which she also accepts [ ]. The Abraxas is the great cosmic force behind each God (the god seen by seeing the *devil* [in God?])—Abraxas—a monotheistic conception—*the acceptance.* Very difficult to understand and have remembered little. I think she said the dualistic conception in the [ ], *light and* darkness, day and night, good and bad, etc.

Thus, monotheism must have come with a much later development when the function of thought existed, also [ ] is an intellectual conception, and may here come from the recognition of the one power greater than oneself in the child to the father attitude.

To accept the idea of the many God—

Abraxas made brief appearances throughout the 1916 diary in many tangential comments by Fanny. She jotted down the phrase "Abraxas regression" and the equation "Abraxas-love-hate." In an entry most likely made in July, Fanny wrote, "Abraxas—valuable to me—this Parsifal episode."

We should remember that in the summer of 1916, Jung converted those deceased Christian crusaders to his neopagan cosmology and revealed the truth about Abraxas to them in his "Seven Sermons to the Dead." It seems that Jung could not help but share his knowledge of the terrible lion-headed god Abraxes with his disciples, who immediately injected this new revelation into their patients.

With the therapeutic and spiritual success she experienced with Moltzer, and with the very real possibility of a true loving relationship with Katz, by the autumn of 1916, Fanny no longer felt so erotically bound to Jung. In fact, he was beginning to seem quite human to her. And then, one evening at a meeting of the Psychological Club, something quite awful happened that forced many, including Fanny, to reassess their feelings about Jung.

Tina Keller remembers being repulsed by Jung in social situations "because Dr. Jung could be so sarcastic" and because "he made fun of people in an unfeeling way."[13] "From the beginning I had been shocked at the way Dr. Jung could speak about people, and I also heard the complaints of some who had been in contact with him, but had turned away disillusioned," Keller said. "There were conflicts in the Psychological Club and some very valuable members left. I clung to the aspect of Dr. Jung that I had experienced in my psychological sessions with him, but I avoided going to any of the social gatherings, where Dr. Jung could be vulgar and repel me."[14] Keller also could not tolerate the attitude of those Club members who hung on Jung's every word and seemed to overlook his darker side.

Perhaps it was the night of the first big banquet of the Club in the autumn of 1916. Alphonse Maeder gave a talk after dinner concerning his view of "the leading function of a medical doctor, contrary to psychoanalysis, where the unconscious is brought up by the doctor who also analyzes." Maeder later recalled that he "used the word 'leader' and 'leading function.' Jung made very sharp remarks about this" in front of the Club members. It resulted in a violent spectacle, one Fanny may have witnessed: "Once there was a terrible quarrel between us: He said something unbelievable to me! He said, 'Here, blood will flow!' It was really . . . but first I have to tell why he said that. I had said to him that, 'You really have lied here!' I said that in front of the Club; it was really horrible; it was terrible! He was not always particular about everything. He was furious; he left the room. I followed him and then he said, 'Here, blood will flow!' "[15]

The sight of Jung threatening physical violence to one of his most trusted colleagues must have been quite an eye-opener. Whether it was this particular event or not, Fanny witnessed *something* one evening at the Club that shattered her godlike image of Jung. Immediately after the event, she wrote to Jung requesting to see him to work out her feelings analytically. Jung responded—negatively. "I am glad to know how you felt about Saturday," Jung said in a note to Fanny dated October 16, 1916, but he urged her to analyze her resistances to him with Miss Moltzer. Jung did not want to deal personally with Fanny's issues.

Still troubled, she wrote to him the next day, making sure that her letter passed the approval of Moltzer:

> I have received your letter, and I feel that I must write again to explain why I asked you to let me work this question out with you. A long time ago you said to me, that if a patient left Analysis with feelings of bitterness and resentment toward you, you knew there must be something wrong with his Analysis,—that remark of yours has come often to my mind of late, and it has seemed to me important for me to get back again, if possible, that good rapport which I had with you in [the] past, but which should now be won on a much more mature basis.

At that time I was still so much in unreality, and in such confusion that the real conditions of life could mean but little to me, and the transference I gave you was based almost solely on sexual excitation,—then finally came the evening at the Club, of which I spoke on Saturday, on which occasion my eyes were opened to the reality of things and I saw you in a new light,—for the first time, in the grip of your own complexes, and I realized then, and subsequently, in talking the matter over, under what stress the Club had been formed, and what a lack of harmony existed even among the Zurich analysts.

These things *must* reflect on the psychology of the patients Dr. Jung, and make it all harder for them to find the harmony within themselves,—for which reason it seems to be of utmost importance that such resistances as mine should be brought to headquarters, and worked out fully, even if very painful to both Analyst and patient. I cannot look at it as simply "a fact," but rather as a situation which ought to be worked out with all sincerity and honesty, recognizing the elements of right and wrong on both sides. And it is just because you and Frl. Moltzer represent symbolically the different values which I must bring into harmony within myself, that I feel so strongly the importance of working out this piece of my development,—my Analysis could never be complete without it.

I have read this letter to Frl. Moltzer, and am sending it to you with her consent.

Jung's response of October 22 promised her the meeting that she requested, but only after he returned from military duty at the beginning of December. He once again placed the blame on her for not achieving an inner harmony and claimed that it might be good for her to "devalue" him so that she could withdraw her projections from him and work on her own individuality. Jung said that he knew she needed to "see clearly." "But," he wrote, "your vision can only become clear if you look into your own heart."[16]

How did Fanny's encounter with Dr. Jung make out? There is a gap in our historical evidence. The rest is silence....

"I had *accepted the blasphemy*"

The year 1917 brought Fanny into a deeper connection with her creative self through the painting and drawing of her fantasies. For the first time, tiny drawings of her fantasies and dialogues with her fantasy figures appear in her journal.

Her notebook for 1917 begins in February. Her references to Abraxas begin to recede. But for the first time she used language that is recognizably Jungian: "shadow," "persona," "individuation," "transcendent function," and the "collective psyche." We learn that Maria Moltzer began to confide to Fanny about her own troubled personal life and relationship with Jung. Moltzer shared not only her own drawings with her patient but her own "Bible," modeled on Jung's illuminated "Red Book."

On the very first page Fanny wrote: "My [ ] fantasies [ ] the state of being is a point [ ] the reaching of the beginning of things, i.e.,—the creation of the Personal God—the alpha and the omega—and all and everything—my drawing is embryonic, as it should be, it is the embryo of this God—my own consciousness of religion—bringing with it the four degrees." She was witnessing, through her own drawings and fantasies, the evolution of her inner self as the god within, and it was a product of the religious nature of Jungian analysis.

On May 4, Fanny sketched three panels in her diary that seem to be the three-step transformation of a vision she had of an unusual man. In the first panel he is sitting high up on a pedestal, legs crossed in a meditative posture, head and upper torso bent forward in prayer. In the second panel he is lying in a bed and something with large batlike wings hovers over him. In the third panel he is standing, dressed in robes, and a halo of flames outlines his entire body. Above him, something with wings seems to be clutching an object. Her notes for her analytic session suggest that Moltzer was teaching her to talk to this little figure, to bring him to life. Jung referred to such representation of the Masculine in female patients as the animus, which is the Latin word for "spirit." In men, the Feminine counterpart was the anima, or "soul." To engage in a dialogue with these entities, Jung believed, was to contact the innermost core of life itself. This technique of active imagination clearly resembled magical procedures for animating statuettes for divinatory purposes in the Hellenistic world. Fanny described her attempt to master such magic and receive instruction from her inner voice:

> Still in my deep introversion and very tense. Was feeling as if [ ] I could only stay with her half an hour.
> [three sketches]
> She says I must keep very quiet, do only what is necessary in order to not lose my contact with life and wait—try to make the man speak again.
> He seems to represent my intellect [ ] intellect entirely expressed by my neurosis. The woman [ ] of feeling, of the soul.—Both are symbols of what I have lost in life.

In a later entry in May, Fanny said she must continue her commitment "to life and to religion—not only intellect, not science, but wherein initiation also plays a part." Below this statement she made a drawing of two crisscrossed wavy lines—like old images of radio waves—that intersect a large thick cross in the middle of the image. In the center of this cross is a circle, which an arrow indicates should be red. There are circles on other sides of the cross, and it is possible that the three circles symbolize the three psychological types that existed in Jung's theory in 1917. It is not clear which circle represents which function. The letters "M.M." are in the lefthand corner, indicating this chart was inspired by Maria Moltzer. Below it Fanny wrote: *"Science stands to Art as Art stands to Life.* Here are the functions united in the Logos. The red circle in the center is the symbol of life, of blood, of fire—it has [ ] fire, sacrifice, it is the very essence of life."

Here again we see the sun as a central symbol of divinity among Jung's disciples, with life, blood, and sun fused together as core representations of the god within. Wagnerian elements will pop up in Fanny's associations to her imagery, and in the entry for May 26 she mentioned the Grail, Lohengrin, and so on. In other passages she mentioned gold rings and Alberich. But in this entry we find Fanny believing that she is participating in the creation of a new religion by working on her psyche and that she should use her own visions as the revelatory basis of a new bright-shining book, a new Bible. Fanny wrote: "I had *accepted the blasphemy* which means I had given up my old conception of religion and am creating a new. It is only blasphemous from the old point of view. This found in the beginning of my Bible!"

Accepting the blasphemy may have been an ideal for Fanny as an individual, but trying to form a cohesive bond with a mate who also felt compelled to follow the unique call of his own path only led to disappointment.

"I should do for R. what she is doing for Dr. J.!"

Fanny's relationship with Johann Rudolph Katz was showing signs of strain. They had married, but they were having serious problems. Fanny was afraid of him, afraid to totally give her heart to him and for some very good reasons: he could not—would not—give up his "polygamous tendencies."

On July 16, she spoke of her "transference" to "Dr. Katz" and devoted considerable space trying to analyze her attraction to him. After her analytic session with Moltzer, Fanny wrote: "Had a long talk with her about R. [Katz] which was difficult for her and for me. His complete lack of understanding of her, and not being honest with himself—not accepting his transferences, etc.—and realizing that he wanted to live his polygamous tendency, and projecting everything onto others. He has suffered too little and is not finding himself. All this is not *the* Dr. Katz, his main object is [ ]—we need religious spirit."

Moltzer helped her put her personal relationship with Katz into a grander, more cosmic perspective. The personal problems of two individuals didn't amount to a hill of beans; it was their greater role in the evolving consciousness of humanity that counted. Moltzer reassured Fanny that the analytic work was refining her soul and making her one of the chosen who were going to bring about a change in consciousness for the whole human race:

> [ ] developing thereby my subjective life and finding my soul—that the relation means finding my adaptation to collectivity—and this I do with R.— it cannot be done alone—finding my relation to him I find it to collectivity—this is the overcoming of the hero, too.
>
> She spoke very beautifully of this new attitude to life—of some going further than others—some reaching the goal—others getting as far that they can see what will be done by the next generation—whether we live to see it matters less than the spirit be kept alive.

But Fanny was realistic—and somewhat prophetic—about her future with Katz. "In Rudy's and my relationship I have a very hard piece of life ahead of us," she wrote, adding later, "His polygamous tendencies must be very strong to cause such a conflict." Moltzer, who, as we shall soon see, was dealing with a very similar situation, told Fanny " 'there is another way,' that is the fulfilling of the progressive tendency in religion, and no longer polygamy." Although to the many women in Jung's circle replacing male polygamous instincts with religion may have seemed the ideal solution for everyone's problems, in practice things didn't work out quite that way. Not with Jung as Katz's analyst.

After this long talk with her analyst, Fanny was hopeful again. She was on the path. "I am at the beginning of my individuation," she confided to her diary, "gaining my inner life."

Fanny saw Moltzer on both Monday, July 30, and Tuesday, July 31. The entries for these sessions are among the most dramatic in her diaries. Before her first session with Moltzer, Fanny wrote to herself, "I *must* also force myself to talk with her of my deepest feelings." Fanny's confrontation with Katz over his polygamous instincts activated a complex in Moltzer (to use their language). Fanny's situation hit too close to home. The man whose polygamous tendencies were causing Maria Moltzer such grief was her master, C. G. Jung.

At first, Moltzer aggrandized Jung and her relationship to him, making it seem as if the two of them were a new Adam and Eve who were going to bring about the spiritual redemption of the world. It was heady stuff for Fanny to hear from a woman she idolized.

> Of this hour it's hard to write—I had perfect rapport and stayed 1¾ hours with her—at the end of the time I felt lifted with another woman and almost as if I had been in a divine presence. She spoke wonderfully, as if inspired, and I saw more clearly than ever before *what* she is working for—*what* her struggle with Dr. Jung means. How wonderfully she spoke of the work that she and Dr. Jung were to do together, for which they are only the instruments [ ] in the great universe, of our duty to life, of the subjection of self for the benefit of all—all these feeling are coming to me now as if never before. She spoke of the great struggle going on in the world, the great agony, which is the collective expression of the individual struggle.

Fanny then quoted from a letter from her cousin James Putnam: " 'To be able to stand alone and give our best strength to the community—that is the great aim and hard enough to reach.' "

Her next session with Moltzer was equally powerful, but for entirely different reasons. Here Moltzer disclosed their parallel difficulties with the polygamous men in their lives:

> The next day we talked for almost an hour, an hour in the dining room . . . Shall I soon forget it? She spoke of going to Chateau d'Or to see Dr. J. [at his Army post] of his injustice to her [ ] on one side he is fine and on the other almost a charlatan playing to the gallery.
>
> His attitude toward their differences is the attitude of the intellectual man—the historical man—and she feels Rudy would be much the same—and this shocked me—as I felt that was a [ ] which Dr. J. lacks.
>
> Then she said—and oh how she said it—with that wonderful far away look in her eyes, that she felt that forces here may run deep [and that] there could be an affinity between her and me—that it is meant that I should do for R. what she is doing for Dr. J.! This explains to her the meaning of my giving her such a valuable thing as the little ivory figure. She [ ] feels that R. has great value which *I* can bring out—and she spoke of overcoming the personal in order to do this—she certainly has with Dr. Jung!
>
> May I live up to her expectations!

"Everyone must write his Bible"

Fanny was entering the last stages of her analysis. She had learned to record her dreams and write down her associations to them. She had learned the power of painting and drawing the images that came to her when she was awake and asleep. She now felt comfortable talking to the images that she drew in her diary and reporting the dialogues she was having with her inner voice. Katz was learning to do the same. Fanny had learned that there was a personal god growing within her, a higher intelligence that she could communicate with through her drawings and automatic writing, and that the technical term for this communication was the "transcendent function."

She had learned to think in terms of types and compensation and had accepted Jung's dictum that the most unpardonable of all sins was to be too one-sided, to not live life to its fullest even if others consider your actions evil. She herself was too introverted, too feeling, and had needed to develop her intellect during her years in Zurich. Katz was her opposite in many ways: intellectual, a man of the world, more extraverted then she. She needed him in order to function well in the greater world outside the incestuous circle around Jung. Katz needed her, or so Moltzer told her, to be his "inspiratrice," to ripen him and bring him to full consciousness for the betterment of mankind. She also accepted that there were many gods in the one and that this one god was Abraxas, who was both good and evil.

With the help of Maria Moltzer, she had learned to construct and read her astrological horoscope. Astrology was an important aspect of Jungian therapy from its earliest days. Clues to understanding the logos, one's fate, could be discerned by reading horoscopic charts properly. By 1920, Jung introduced the *I Ching* to his disciples as the divinatory method of choice, saying the gods spoke to humans through such devices.

On August 17, 1917, Moltzer provided Fanny with a progress report of their work together:

> She spoke of the great difference still between my conscious and my unconscious—the latter being so rich while there is still so little in the conscious—herein I have gone right against my horoscope which indicates much material in the conscious—that is because I have developed my intellect. At times she has thought I had a man's intellect—to develop my thoughts, I must go further and further with my drawings. *Stick to it* and finally light will come, and this will be far more valuable to me than my horoscope's been—it is the direct [ ] out of [ ] unconscious.
>
> Everyone must write his Bible and in working out [ ]. I shall find my adaptation to R.—when on the Path one had a wonderful sense of peace.
>
> If my horoscope had been written out with greater understanding of the trans.[cendent] function nothing would have been said of my becoming ill through my projections—I need not become ill if I find the middle way.

Of her [Moltzer's] book, her Bible—pictures and each with writing—which I must also do.

For the analytic session of August 20, 1917, Fanny showed Moltzer some drawings she had made that contained images of the blazing sun. Moltzer's interpretation gives us a glimpse into the formulaic Jungian method of that period in which all such images were thought to be representations of the god within bursting out from the most archaic levels of the unconscious and into the patient's artwork. And as in the prevailing Aryan solar mysticism (such as in the illustrations of Fidus), the great principles of the Masculine and the Feminine are united within the sun as God: "The [ ] God of Life from which the Masculine and Feminine principles arise—particularly from the collective libido, becoming individualized in the unconscious, thus rising as a flame, [ ] God of thought, spirit—fire, the destroyer, as much as purifies. *Agni—the Fire God.* The thoughts are brought forth through the agony of sacrifice."

Although her individuation was progressing smoothly on the spiritual front, on the physical plane her marriage was in trouble. "It appears that I have unconsciously [ ] in my marriage difficulties," Fanny recorded in her diary on August 29. She wondered if certain patterns she was living out with Katz were "an escape from my inner development." Moltzer attempted to reassure Fanny that day by sharing her views on why it takes women so long to individuate through analysis:

Some patients can be cured in a short time, in an hour, a few months, etc. Other women in whom a new function has to be created through which they are to give new values to [ ] *must* take years—the function has to *grow.* She feels that it may take several years [ ] before I have found everything there is in me—such a development *can* take 6–8, even 10 years. If I neglect this inner life I can never be satisfied. I will become bitter and others will do the work I should have done. *I have been mistaking my regression tendency for life, and I lack faith and religion. My great danger is an escape into extraversion. Nothing could be plainer than the words of these I make, and it is quite clear where my path lies. There is absolute need of taking time to myself and developing my inner life.* [Her emphasis.]

She [Moltzer] spoke of Art, real Art, being the experience of Religion.

September 1917 was the last time Fanny met with Moltzer for formal therapy sessions. They had known each other for more than five years. It was time for Fanny to go along her own path. But first she needed to truly begin her own Bible. "I *must* write a book, just for myself—[ ] giving my life line and illustrated by my drawings," Fanny wrote on September 1.

Moltzer "feels I am very near the end of my work with her, although it may take another several years before I understand everything."

As they approached the end of their association, Fanny experienced an intense vision—a descent into the underworld—that resembled those of both Jung and Hesse. Not all the details of the visionary descent into a grotto are in the diary, but Fanny's associations are. We can only guess whether Fanny experienced this *katabasis* on her own, or if she was led to the underworld through a guided-imagery exercise by her analyst. "I was right," Fanny excitedly wrote on September 11, "my experience in the grotto *was* the realization of the Logos, the ice was the symbol of death, and in the Temple of the Holy Grail *Kundry dies*—What is Kundry to me?" To her, "Kundry is the undifferentiated libido—example of 'Treib' in the collective sense—belongs to the earth, the animal."

On September 14, Fanny Bowditch Katz made her last diary entry. Her visionary descent into a grotto brought her to the climax of her analysis: a realization of the sacred logos. The grotto became the Temple of the Holy Grail, and the Grail was the logos. Within the Temple of the Holy Grail was a hermaphrodite—an important symbol in the analyses of others in Jung's circle. "In the grotto," Fanny wrote, "instead of realizing my visions and fantasies, I tried to understand the intellectual significance of the hermaphrodite.

"The Logos [ ]. The Logos is a religious experience."

And with that, the Ur-Bible of Fanny Bowditch Katz comes to a close.

"Everyone has his own mysteries"

Finished with their analyses, Rudy and Fanny Katz left Zurich in the autumn of 1917 and moved to Amsterdam. Rudy resumed his psychiatric practice and Fanny continued with her own program of educational development. Fanny remained a member of the Psychological Club and shows up on its roster for February 1918, as does Maria Moltzer. Moltzer remained in Zurich, analyzing many of the English-speaking patients that Jung himself did not want to see any longer. Her patients over the years included many whose names will become familiar to us: Edith Rockefeller McCormick, Harold F. McCormick, their daughter Muriel McCormick, Beatrice Hinkle, and Constance Long.

Fanny found the cessation of her analysis difficult to bear. She continued to make drawings and sent them to Moltzer for an analytic interpretation. She also may have sent Moltzer the German text (still surviving) of a "homunculus" vision in which she descended down to the "realm of the Mothers," as Faust did in Goethe's epic. In Fanny's vision, however, she regressed further and further back through evolutionary history until she became the "tiniest embryo, only a cell, round and small" and suddenly "came the memory of an experience under an anesthetic which I had never spoken about with Dr. Jung."[17]

In November 1917, Fanny had written a letter to Moltzer about some visions, wondering if she was experiencing the transcendental function. Moltzer wrote back, "Through your introversion you came again in contact with the Divine, and in connection with this you realised, the transcendental funktion as the funktion by which the divine is expressed in a human form. So the transcendental funktion is the 'Mittler' between God and Mankind." With this helpful definition of the transcendental function we now know that this was another cover name that Jung invented for the process of self-deification.

Not long after Fanny's arrival in Amsterdam she received word that her mother had died. Both Jung and Moltzer sent brief notes of condolence in the first weeks of March 1918. All of the old feelings of depression and suicide that she thought she had eliminated through five years of analysis came back. In addition, she felt terribly guilty for not having returned to America since 1913 to see her mother. She immediately wrote to Moltzer, pouring out all of her sorrows. She sent her latest drawings, which were all gray and black. Moltzer wrote back on April 14. In contrast with her original note expressing sorrow, this one is not exactly the most empathetic letter ever written. Her response demonstrates to what extent even normal grief reactions were depersonalized and then elevated to a cosmic plane by those following Jung's lead.

> I am not astonished that it was after your Mother's death that your symptoms came on, although they have not exactly to do with it. Your Mother's death can probably mean but the death of the past, the death of your youth and your childhood.... In this moment the religious problem must come up again and now for the need of a continuity, for it is only with a religious attitude toward life that you can really conquer the difficulties of life. Although living together we are by the fact of our different personalities alone and it is only by acceptance of this loneliness and of our own qualities, that we are able to accept life. Although we have all a participation to the general subconsciousness, the picture of it is again so different and bound by individual values, that everyone has his own mysteries.
>
> I think you have come to the moment where I scarcely can help you anymore. *You* only can understand what the last picture means and it is only from your own subconscious that you can get the explanation.

As for her guilt over not seeing her mother because of the fascination that the Jung cult held for her, Moltzer says, "I think too that you ought not to be so sorry of not having seen your Mother anymore, for she would never have understood you, be sure of it."

Fanny kept in touch with her spiritual adviser and sent drawings to her from time to time. In July of 1918, Fanny heard that Moltzer had resigned from the Psychological Club. Wanting to know more, she sent her a letter and a cheerful picture. Moltzer was joyous in her reply, referring to the picture as "radiant," and saying that "radiance is the first manifestation of the infinite that we can conceive." Furthermore, Moltzer said, referring to Abraxas, "I too think that God and the Devil are two manifestations of the same principle," and that "one necessitates the other." "We must learn to value the devil again. The Christian religion expelled him. He asks for his rights again."

Moltzer confirmed that she was "working hard" and that "Yes, I resigned from the club."

> I could not live any longer in that atmosphere. I am glad I did. I think, that in time, when the Club really shall have become something, the club shall be thankful I did. My resignation has its silent effects. Silent, for it seems that it belongs to my path, that I openly don't get the recognition or the appreciation for what I do for the development of the whole analytic movement. I always work in the dark, and alone. This is fate and must be accepted. If the psychological steps I take work for the good of others, I must be contented and live in peace and so I am.

Rudy

Fanny's marriage to Rudy Katz proved difficult. Using Jung's relationship with Toni Wolff as his model, Rudy began a relationship with a woman much younger than his wife. Older than him, inexperienced in love and life, and still struggling with her own self-worth and confidence, Fanny let him. She did, however, make her resentment known in social situations. Maria Moltzer witnessed this when she saw them in January 1920 in Brussels and wrote Fanny immediately afterward. She advised Fanny to accept this new form of marriage for a new age. Abandoning her crusade to convince Jung and others that polygamous tendencies should be transmuted into religious fervor, Moltzer finally accepted the Schwabing-Ascona model of Otto Gross. Telling Fanny she was "looking at all the difficulties you have had with your husband from too narrow an angle," Moltzer placed the blame on Fanny and instructed her on the greater cosmic meaning in her personal situation. She wrote:

> Your difficulties have been great; that is true but. . . . You did not leave—you have asked a younger woman to live with your husband. So you have brought difficulties to yourself by yourself. When that is so revenge in this moment [ ] but revenge would not be fair play. . . .
>
> [With regard to Fanny's marriage she] had to go along the road of sacrifice—a path—is what the [ ] biological woman had to make sacrifice after sacrifice to acquire at last a new form of life and a new basis of marriage. A form we needed in our own times.

Moltzer then made reference to a book that Rudy had constructed of his drawings, paintings, and automatic writings that expressed the voice of his soul. He apparently showed this book, his Bible, to both Fanny and her analyst before their marriage proceeded with Moltzer's blessing.

> I think—you have to do what your husband had to do—you have to write a book and receive a dream in which the path is shown by which the new form of marriage is to be required.
>
> Now, you cannot write this book unless you have accepted marriage on a new basis. [ ] that you have not yet found the new form of marriage. [ ] I thought: when your husband would accept his "sacrifice" and the text of his drawings—where it is so clearly said.

Apparently, Rudy promised in his book to sacrifice his polygamous tendencies if the marriage with Fanny proceeded. Ultimately, as Jung found, it was not a sacrifice that allowed him to also follow the inner voice that urged him on to individuation. Perhaps Rudy simply followed Jung's counsel against the "unpardonable sin" of one-sidedness.

In the spring of 1925, Maria Moltzer sent Rudy three letters in which she tried to convince him to change his life. Moltzer told him he must choose between his work and his inclination to have extramarital affairs. She pulled no punches: Moltzer told Rudy that his infidelities put him in great danger and, furthermore, could lead him to insanity.

Other than one letter to Fanny in 1934 in which she said, "I want to see your drawings. . . . Your drawings are a part of your world," Maria Moltzer's trail ends here. Except for speculations about her possible affair with C. G. Jung, her name never appears in the history books. Most Jungians have never heard of her. She has been forgotten even by her own tribe.

Rudy died in 1938, ending a stormy marriage punctuated by many separations and renewals of vows to stay on the path.

Fanny spent her last years in Durham, New Hampshire, surrounded by her mandala paintings and other drawings. She went to Quaker meetings and saved newspaper clippings about Jung. Her friends called her "the Duchess of Durham." She died in 1967, at age ninety-three.

Only she would know if she remained on the path or not. But many people said that she often talked about those wild years in Zurich with Jung and his crew as the best she ever had.

TEN

Edith Rockefeller McCormick—The Rockefeller Psychoanalyst

Without her, he might never have succeeded. With her, he became known to the entire world. Yet despite her own celebrity, few know of the fateful collaboration of the Rockefeller psychoanalyst and C. G. Jung.

Edith Rockefeller McCormick is a mystery to her own family even today. She was the troubled daughter of John D. Rockefeller, whose personal fortune during the First World War was thought to comprise about 2 percent of the gross national product of the United States.

In 1913, Edith arrived in Zurich for treatment with Jung. The path that she undertook with Jung led her away from the responsibilities of marriage and motherhood and into a magical realm of gods and astrology and spiritualism. After 1913, Edith became a stranger to her father and siblings and even to her own husband and children. Indeed, Jung encouraged this separation from her old life and her compensatory integration into his community of disciples. Edith became an analyst in the Jungian mode, a magical healer who interpreted the dreams of her patients and pointed out the divine elements in their artistic productions.

Jung's magical world must have been tremendously attractive to Edith at that time. She had suffered the loss of two children and had withdrawn emotionally from her husband and from her surviving children, still quite young. She needed help and found it in Zurich. She came alive for the first time. Her former life, her former country, could not compare with the opportunity to participate in the salvation of the world and the birthing of a new god.

Edith Rockefeller McCormick remained in Zurich until 1921.

Misfortune among the fortunate

Of all the children of John D. Rockefeller, Edith always seemed the most unhappy. She was an intellectual by nature but as a woman and socialite at the turn of the century found few opportunities to satisfy her interests. She had few friends and rarely joined in the Rockefeller family activities unless her presence was required. She preferred being alone. She did not reveal her emotions, often seemed distant and taciturn, and carried herself with the superior attitude of someone critical and generally displeased. Rarely did she risk a smile or dispense compliments or make small talk, and her unwillingness or inability to extend herself often threw others off guard or left them cold. Perhaps all of this was a cover for her overpowering fears of external reality, fears that exploded into severe agoraphobia in her mid-thirties. These personality traits were most like her father's.

Naturally, she married a man who was her complete opposite. Harold Fowler McCormick was born with a first-class temperament and a second-rate intellect. He was a peacemaker, a placater, a surface skimmer. He thrived in a world of country clubs and racquetball tournaments, yachting competitions and philanthropic galas. He glided through Princeton University and received his A.B. there in 1895. He was being groomed to be the heir to his father's fortune and to command the empire that the International Harvester Company would become. This was a suitable track for Harold, for he was loyal, trustworthy, and eager to please. His polished social graces and buoyant superficiality made him the quintessential American business executive. Everyone liked Harold McCormick.

His father was Cyrus Hall McCormick (1809–84), the inventor of the McCormick reaper, which revolutionized harvesting. Cyrus was a brooding, unapproachable man. Born into near poverty, he developed a hard shell that aided his acquisition of fame and fortune. He died when Harold was twelve years old. Harold's mother, Nancy (Nettie) Fowler McCormick was deeply religious and an obsessively intrusive and overbearing mother. Of her five children, two were insane: her daughter Mary Virginia and her son Stanley. Harold and his sister Anita—another strong personality—spent much of their adulthoods preoccupied with the medical care of their younger siblings. Harold's older brother Cyrus generally removed himself from such concerns. Harold led the family negotiations and continually made peace among his relatives and between the warring teams of physicians called in to treat his sister and brother. Stanley McCormick, in fact, was treated by many of the most famous psychiatrists in the world, and the records of his treatment make him arguably the most fascinating case history of the twentieth century.[1]

The newspapers, savvy to the unspoken business deal about to take place, shouted with glee when Harold and Edith announced their engagement. They called Edith "the Princess of Standard Oil," and Harold "the Prince of International Harvester." Harold and Edith were both twenty-three when they were married on November 26, 1895. She was described as a "demure little blonde, with a high forehead, grey eyes, and a mass of ringlets under her hat."[2] It was a quiet affair, a private ceremony in a parlor of the Buckingham Hotel in Manhattan. Harold had graduated from Princeton that May and had already been provided a position in his father's company. By 1898 he was a vice president, and in 1918 he became the president of International Harvester. Educated by private tutors, Edith had freely followed her own interests. Her first actual job would be as a psychoanalyst during the First World War. Harold became close to Edith's father, and throughout the rest of his life—even after he and Edith were divorced—he wrote regularly to John D. Rockefeller and addressed him as "Father." Edith, for her part, had little in common with Harold's parents and avoided them whenever possible.

Edith had an analytical mind; Harold's tended toward synthesis and operated through the filter of feelings. Focused rational thought was foreign to him. He read newspapers, not books. Edith swam, skated, rode a horse and bicycle, but largely preferred to stay indoors, reading and studying. Harold could never play enough tennis and racquetball. No wonder he and Edith soon realized they had a difficult time communicating with one another. Edith's inwardness was reinforced by their inability to connect.

Their first child was nonetheless born in 1897. John D. Rockefeller McCormick was the apple of his grandfather's eye, but in 1901 he died from scarlet fever. Other children followed. Harold Fowler McCormick, Jr.—called Fowler—was born in 1898 and followed by three sisters: Muriel in 1902, Editha in 1903, and Mathilde in 1905. Editha's death a year after her birth propelled Edith into a depression from which she could not recover. She felt absolutely nothing most of the time, but seemed anxious—"nervous," Harold called it—and had difficulty sleeping. She was up at night and slept during the day. Maids and governesses filled the void as she struggled with her moods. She was afraid to venture far from their mansion on Lake Shore Drive in Chicago, a massive gray stone house with a conical tower that Edith herself had nicknamed "the bastion." Harold's generally sunny disposition did much to counteract the harmful effects of Edith's slow decline on their children, but they always regarded her as somewhat of a stranger.

Edith had been quite active in Chicago's social life prior to her son's death, but became less so afterward. As the primary benefactor of the Chicago Opera, Edith would don her $2 million pearl necklace and host brief dinners for her select guests just before the opening of each new opera, each course timed perfectly by a jeweled clock beside her plate. But Edith could not maintain her position as Chicago's premier hostess. Between 1905 and 1907, she suffered from tuberculosis of the kidney, which eventually went into remission after numerous rest cures. In 1911, she planned a cotillion, but suddenly and inexplicably recalled all 120 invitations. Rumors spread quickly about her bizarre behavior. Many speculated that she was suffering a nervous breakdown. The gossip was very close to the truth.

Harold soon realized that she was in need of professional medical attention. His experience with managing the care of his insane siblings helped him search for physicians for Edith, but she was stubborn and often refused his suggestions for treatment. The few she did try—mainly at resorts for wealthy neurasthenics—did not make much of a difference.

One of the remedies that Harold insisted upon was a trip through Hungary (primarily Transylvania) in July and August of 1910.[3] The excursion would be part pleasure, part business, as Harold scouted sites for a new factory. Edith finally agreed, traveling by automobile across Europe. She found the traveling exhausting, and wanted to be back home in "the bastion." Upon her return to America, Edith passed straight through New York and directly on to Chicago, missing her own mother's birthday celebrations at the original Rockefeller mansion in Cleveland. As usual, Harold was left to smooth over any misunderstandings caused by Edith's asocial behavior. "Dear Father," Harold wrote to John D. Rockefeller on September 22, 1911, "It is a matter of deep regret that I was unable to be present at mother's celebration and more of a regret that Edith was not able to be present. Please be assured, and it is almost unnecessary for me to say so, that Edith was deeply sorry that she could not come on to Cleveland. She is now taking a rest at [their home at] 1000 Lake Shore Drive, isolating herself from everybody and spending from five to eight hours a day out in the air and I think this will do her more good than anything else at the present time if she will only keep it up long enough."[4]

Refusing to give up on Edith, Harold began making inquiries among his extended family. The most promising referral came from Medill, Harold's cousin from the branch of the McCormick family that owned and operated the *Chicago Tribune*. Medill spoke highly of a Swiss psychiatrist who had treated him for depression and alcoholism: C. G. Jung.

Medill had first approached Jung in Zurich in late 1908.[5] Impressed with the new treatment known as psychoanalysis, during the first week of July 1909 he attempted unsuccessfully to have a consultation with Freud. When Jung was in New York that September he spent many hours with Medill, at one point advising him, as we have seen, to become polygamous to save his sanity and his soul. The rich American was quite a catch for the fledgling psychoanalytic movement, and Jung and Freud were delighted with this trophy of their international success.

And Jung was soon reeling in an even bigger catch for psychoanalysis and for himself, a daughter of the man many considered to be the richest in the Western world: Edith.

As 1912 began, Edith had not emerged from seclusion after returning from the Hungarian trip two years earlier. But Harold was hopeful. "Edith is doing well in her determination to gut out a good many varied occupations, and she certainly is getting her life down to one of more natural easement."[6]

At some fateful point during the late spring of 1912, though, Edith learned of the legendary healing powers of C. G. Jung. The fantasy of going to Zurich to be treated by him began to take on an almost obsessive quality. She hoped Switzerland would be the promised land of her salvation. Without even meeting him, Edith began to think of Jung as her only savior.

But Harold wanted to try at least one more cure in America. He accompanied Edith to Ellenville, New York, for "a trial of treatment" at the clinic of a Dr. Foord. He reported on the situation to his mother. "Edith does not give herself up to the treatment as yet, but I think is gaining in her confidence, or indifference; that is she is doing a little more gracefully what she is asked to do." Edith was a difficult, noncompliant patient. "I shall stay here until such time as the doctor can form an opinion as to what he thinks he can do if Edith will cooperate."[7]

But Harold was well aware that Edith might never give her American physician a fighting chance. Her heart and soul already were in Zurich. And Harold was dead set against it.

> For one who is ill or needs treatment, I think this place is fine. For one who is well, it is the slowest place in the world. I like Dr. Foord ever so much, and I think he can do wonders for Edith. But she finds it very hard indeed to submit to what is wanted. Just exactly as you put it in your letter. What she may have in mind is that after a trial here, it shall be pronounced a failure and that then we will all take a steamer, say 1st of August or thereabouts, and trot over

to Switzerland. That in its entirety I do not stand for. If anybody goes over it shall be Edith and me alone. I don't think it right or fair to dislodge you all after you are comfortably settled.

I believe Edith now thinks that if she could toss this all over, that then she could get to Zurich. She disregards the fact that Jung would be absent for all the time until the last two or three weeks of our stay over there. If I had the courage to say or if it was right to say that the European trip is cancelled for this summer I believe it would be a great help in deciding Edith to stay here.[8]

While in Ellenville, Harold received a letter from Woodrow Wilson, then governor of New Jersey, who with the help of William Jennings Bryan had just become the Democratic nominee for president. "I feel sure he would make a safe and sane president," Harold wrote his father-in-law, and he passed along Wilson's personal missive requesting Harold's support.[9] (Medill was a friend of Wilson's opponents, President William H. Taft and Teddy Roosevelt.) Sailing to Europe to see Jung would remove Harold from the arena during a critical part of the campaign.

Edith finally submitted herself to Dr. Foord's treatment, and Harold felt confident enough to return to Chicago. Foord recognized the severity of Edith's phobias—particularly her agoraphobia—and recommended some commonsense measures to help her overcome their disabling effects. Edith then sent her mother-in-law the following telegram: "Can you send me your automobile and chauffeur without Harold's knowing it. The doctor wants me to begin to learn to get away from the house without fear. Edith."[10] Foord was soon discarded like so many of her previous physicians.

Three days after Edith sent that telegram, on September 7, 1912, C. G. Jung set sail for New York City. Edith's life was about to change forever.

Edith meets Dr. Jung

Edith had Jung on her mind, but so did Harold's mother and sister, though for an entirely different reason: Stanley. Nettie McCormick was staying at the Plaza Hotel in order to ask Jung to go to Santa Barbara, California, and assess the condition of her son. He suffered from the catatonic type of dementia praecox and was so unmanageable that he had been tied up with bed sheets since 1906. Jung wrote to Nettie on October 8, 1912, that he would be able to see Stanley McCormick in California "at the end of October."[11]

Upon receiving this information, Nettie returned to Chicago and contacted her daughter Anita McCormick Blaine in upstate New York. Would she agree to meet with Jung and discuss Stanley? "In the question of seeing Jung for S. my province would not be different from yours," Anita informed her mother. "What you should do is take the question to Dr. Favill [Stanley's primary physician]. I could not do otherwise."[12] But three days later, Harold begged Anita in a telegram to meet Jung. "Why don't you run down to New York and have a talk with Jung. . . . You would be able to form first impressions and he would give you his experiences and ideas. Believe your time would be well spent."[13] Stanley was not on his mind, but Edith. And Edith, still in Ellenville, emerged from her shell and for once took the initiative.

Edith invited Jung to the Rockefeller estate in Pocantico Hills for a visit and for some preliminary consultations. Unsubstantiated legend has it that Edith insisted that Jung move to America with his family and become her personal physician. She allegedly offered to buy a house for him and his family and pay him handsomely. Jung refused and instead insisted that Edith come to Zurich for long-term analysis with him. She agreed.

After Jung returned home in the first week of November, he sent Maria Moltzer to America to conduct a preliminary analysis of Edith. Moltzer probably left Zurich in December 1912 or January 1913. On February 2, 1913, Sigmund Freud wrote to Sandor Ferenczi, "Jung's letter [to Ferenczi] sounds somewhat elegiac; perhaps his Egeria has already left him. She should go to America to bring Rockefeller's daughter to Zurich."[14] Freud, suspecting that Jung was having an affair with his female assistant, refers to her as Egeria, a nymph in Roman mythology who was the lover of and adviser to the legendary king Numa Pompilius and who was the power behind the throne.

Perhaps this was a compromise that Jung negotiated with Edith. Moltzer was the only analyst completely loyal to him who spoke English fluently. In late 1912, Jung was still not clear about the loyalties of many in his circle, including the only American analyst who could have treated Edith—the New York psychoanalyst Beatrice Hinkle. Although she was really the only Jungian practicing in America at the time, Hinkle had eclectic tendencies. Furthermore, she was too independent. Moltzer was the better bait to keep Edith hooked until he could treat her himself.

Whether it was Dr. Foord's health spa, Dr. Jung's visit, or a trial of psychoanalysis with Maria Moltzer, Edith began to improve by the end of 1912 and gingerly reentered Chicago social life. She and Harold put their energies into a grand "coming-out" party for Edith to be held in Chicago at the end of January 1913.

1913

In the first week of February 1913 Edith left Chicago—probably with Maria Moltzer—and soon arrived in New York to spend the next several weeks preparing for her voyage to Switzerland. Moltzer was back in Zurich by the first week in March. Within just days of her arrival, Jung was on an ocean liner to New York. Moltzer's analysis had been a failure. Jung would bring Edith back to Zurich himself.

This new turn of events made Edith the subject of gossip between Sigmund Freud and his allies. "Jung has gone to America again for five weeks, to see a Rockefeller woman, so they say," Freud wrote to Ferenczi on March 7, 1913.[15] Ferenczi responded by flattering Freud and insulting Jung: "I would rather have granted you the summons to the Rockefellers," Ferenczi wrote on March 9. "Still—the Americans don't deserve better."[16]

After almost three weeks of daily analytic sessions with Jung in New York, Edith enjoyed the same attention aboard their ocean liner. Edith, her two children, Fowler's tutor, and Muriel's governess all settled into a large suite of rooms in the luxurious Hotel Baur au Lac along Lake Zurich. Edith would live, study, teach, and psychoanalyze in these same rooms until the autumn of 1921.

Like Fanny Bowditch, Edith was most likely encouraged by Jung to sit in on his didactic seminars on psychoanalysis in the summer of 1913, as well as the seminar on the history of religion given by Professor Irené Hausheer. This was most likely the first time that Edith received any formal instruction in these subjects. Given her hunger for intellectual stimulation, she would have found these classes a welcome change from her life as a bored and agoraphobic socialite in Chicago.

In June and July, Fowler, his tutor, and his best friend were traveling in Italy. He returned to Zurich by the end of July and found that he did not care very much for the place. "Dear Grandfather," he wrote to John D. Rockefeller on August 10, 1913, "This is a very queer place. It has rained here this summer almost incessantly and some very peculiar weather phenomenons happen.... Zurich has many other peculiarities which are not worth mentioning."[17] It is clear from the many letters that survive that Fowler and Rockefeller had a very special bond, one not lost on Jung. He knew very well that this was the great Rockefeller's favorite grandchild. Jung always treated Fowler with special kindness that could only make his own son, Franz, quite jealous. His gradual adoption of Fowler was so successful that Fowler came to believe he was in the presence of a god.

In the years following the Second World War, Fowler became one of Jung's best friends. In an interview for the C. G. Jung Biographical Archives Project, Fowler confessed, "He was for me in my youth a 'father figure,' . . . of an intensely strong nature. In a sense the word 'father figure' is too mild a term because one would call it more of a 'God figure.' "[18]

But in September 1913, not yet attached to Jung, Fowler set sail for America. He was not to see his mother or Jung again for two years.

In late October, Harold and Mathilde arrived in Zurich. Harold hoped that it would be a short stay and that Edith would return with him. Edith had then been in analysis with Jung for more than six months. Relatives on both sides of the family had been sending regular requests to Edith concerning her return. What could possibly be keeping Harold's family in Europe for so long?

The family was indeed settling in: Edith was working daily with Jung; Muriel was in "German school" and receiving private lessons; Mathilde, who suffered from frequent colds and struggled with maintaining her weight, would soon be in the Sanatorium Schweizerhof Davos-Platz for physical "upbuilding" and intellectual development. "It is very nice to be together," Edith wrote in a letter to Nettie, "and I am appreciating these days very much."[19]

As Christmas approached, Harold realized that Edith was not coming home any time soon. He had originally planned to bring Muriel back with him, but decided against it. She was an impulsive and headstrong child, quick to anger and seemingly in continual warfare with her parents, tutors, and governess. Harold decided it would be best to leave her in the structured environment of the German school and with her mother.

On December 9, 1913, Harold poured out his troubles to his mother:

> Of course, I am greatly disappointed in one way, not to be back for Christmas. But, of course, it would not be the same if Edith were not there. Her pleasure still uncertain, but I have decided at *her insistence* to leave on the 20th by the Campania. . . . Edith wanted me to stay here longer, as her plans are uncertain, and she may not come over this winter. . . . So I was easily drawn to stay here. On the other hand she said the *20th and no longer.* So the plan is really hers.
>
> I will stop off a day to see Edith's family and report to them. . . . Edith is continuing to improve, and she is doing better and more each day. Today she went one and one-half hours out on the train and back, making a journey of three hours. Believe me, it does not come easily.[20]

Unknown to either Edith or Harold, Jung began the series of visionary descents into the Land of the Dead on December 12—just three days after Harold's letter to his mother—that culminated in his self-deification as the Aryan Christ.

Neopagan Switzerland: "Totimo, Suzy Perrottet, Katja Wulff, Maja Lederer, Betty Baaron Samoa, Rudolf von Laban, Ascona, 1914," by Johann Adam Meisenbach. Not only did a number of these dancers frequent the Dadaist Cabaret Voltaire in Zurich in February and March of 1916 (at the same time that Edith Rockefeller McCormick helped Jung found the Psychological Club), but several later established relations with Jung or his disciples.

Third Psychoanalytic Congress in Weimar, September 21–22, 1911. Sitting: Lou-Andreas Salomé, Beatrice Hinkle, Emma Jung, M. Von Stack, Toni Wolff, Martha Boddinghaus, Franz Riklin. Standing just to Riklin's right is Ernest Jones. Carl Jung is to the left, with his hands resting on the back of Emma's chair, and Sigmund Freud (bearded) stands to his right.

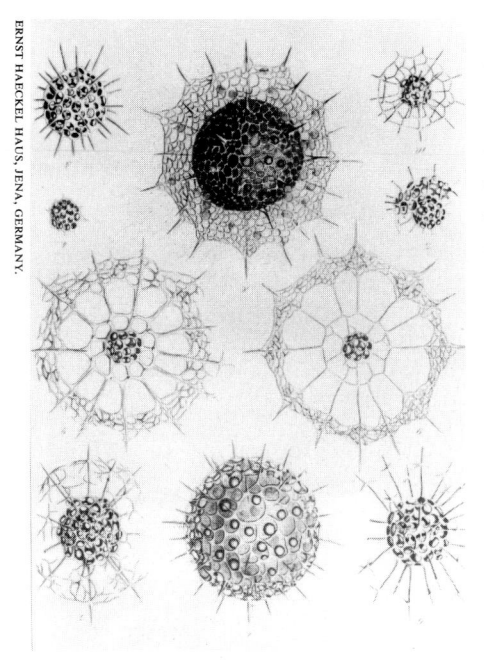

Ernst Haeckel, "Radiolaria," from his 1862 monograph of that name. Radiolaria are microorganisms that can be seen only with a microscope. In a dream, the teenage Jung saw a radiolarian three feet in diameter. This led him to study medicine and the natural sciences rather than become a philologist or archeologist.

Ernst Haeckel, the Romantic scientist as artist, in Rapallo, Italy, on his seventieth birthday, 1904.

Ernst Haeckel and Isadora Duncan in front of the Festspielhaus in Bayreuth, Germany, 1904. This photo—never before published—was taken at their first meeting. Just a few hours later, they sat in the Wagner family's private box and viewed a performance of *Parsifal*. The fusion of bohemians and scientists at the turn of the century was inspired by Haeckel pantheism.

A rare photograph of Otto Gross (bearded, arms crossed). It is not known who the other men are, or where or when this photograph was taken. It was Gross who convinced Jung of the revitalizing powers of polygamy.

Fidus, "Sexualreligion," 1897. This illustration for Maximilian Ferdinand's volumes of Aryan mysticism shows an early representation of androgynous wholeness. The image of a Janus-faced male/female is what Jung would later call the "animus/anima," united in the symbol of the "self," the Aryan sun wheel, or mandala, as the supreme symbol of wholeness or God.

Fidus, cover illustration for a Theosophical journal, 1910. The Edenic imagery of the snake and the female would be echoed in a vision Jung had of his deification in December 1913.

Stationery from the Hotel Baur au Lac in Zurich, c. 1915. Although she came to Switzerland to have Jung cure her agoraphobia, Edith Rockefeller McCormick lived in a suite in this hotel from 1913 until 1921 and rarely ventured out. After she'd spent more than two million dollars (in today's currency) to found his Psychological Club, Jung allowed her to become an analyst. All her patients came to see her at the hotel, so she never had to leave her rooms.

Edith Rockefeller McCormick, February 1917.

Edith Rockefeller McCormick, flanked by her two daughters, Muriel (left) and Mathilde (right), in her suite at the Hotel Baur au Lac, February 1917.

The last portrait ever taken of the McCormick family. Seated: Muriel and Edith. Standing: Mathilde, Fowler, and Harold Fowler McCormick. Only little Mathilde was not in analysis with Jung or Maria Moltzer.

Maria Moltzer at the psychoanalytic conference in Weimar, September 1911.

Fanny Bowditch Katz, photographed in Munich, c. 1925.

COURTESY OF THE COUNTWAY LIBRARY OF MEDICINE, HARVARD MEDICAL SCHOOL, BOSTON.

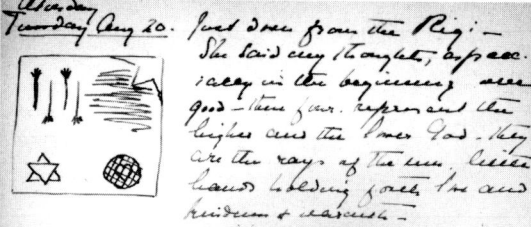

Tuesday Aug 20. Just down from the Rigi —
She said my thoughts, especi-
ally in the beginning were
good — then four represent the
higher and the lower God. They
are the rays of the sun, little
hands holding forth fire and
hindrance + narcissi —

The symbol of life from which the
masculine and feminine
principles arise — from which
pours forth the collective
Libido, becoming individualized
in the unconscious, then rising
as a flame, symbol of thought, spirit —
fire the destroyer, as well as purifier. Agni
the fire God. The thoughts are brought forth
through the agony of sacrifice.

Friday Aug 24. It appears that I am unconsciously allowing my interest in my marriage
difficulties and going about with R. to my
relations to be an escape from my inner development — when there is a great stra[in]

to life and to religion — not only intellectual science, but wherein in intuition also plays
a part.
M.M.

Science stands to Art as Art stands to Life.

Here are the functions united in the Logos.
the red circle in the centre is the symbol of
life, of blood, of fire — it has passed through
fire, sacrifice, it is the very essence of
life —

Friday May 18.
Rudolf's snake pictures
(in his book). Said his fantasies of wandering to his people — very Club fantasy,
which he says is very important for working out my death — which is strong in me —
if freely worked out it can be very valuable,
if not and it controls me, very harmful
to my development.
I was in a very humorous state of mind —
everything seemed a joke & I left early!!

Three pages from the analysis diary of Fanny Bowditch Katz.

A page from the diary of Constance Long, showing a drawing she made on August 31, 1920, in Sennen Cove, Cornwall, England, the site of a seminar and personal analysis by Jung.

BEATRICE HINKLE, *THE RE-CREATING OF THE INDIVIDUAL*, 1923.

A symbol direct from Jung's "archaic unconscious"? Or from the "personal unconscious" of the patient who drew it? Beatrice Hinkle mistakenly thought the former. It is obviously the famous sun worshiper image of the "Lichtgebet," by the German artist Fidus.

ANNUESTA
of
WISDOM'S CONTRIBUTION

OCTOBER
II

COURTESY OF THE COUNTWAY LIBRARY OF MEDICINE, HARVARD MEDICAL SCHOOL, BOSTON.

RITUAL

COURTESY OF THE COUNTWAY LIBRARY OF MEDICINE, HARVARD MEDICAL SCHOOL, BOSTON.

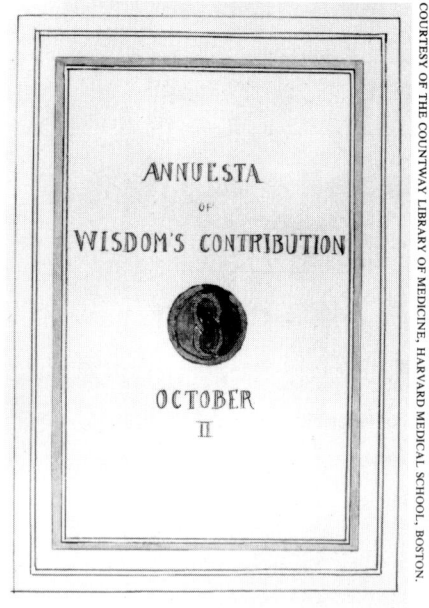

1. Wona reads Tribute to Carl G. Jung followed by Collection of Wise Sayings.

2. Mansol reads Collection of Longer Excerpts from large Notebook.

[They consider in each case the application of the truth to their own life.]

3. Music. Bach Fugue.

4. Wona reads from the Notebook brief descriptions of every book important to their life that she has read or reread since 1944.

5. Mansol does the same.

6. Wona and Mansol drink Toasts to the Authors of these sayings, excerpts and books.

COURTESY OF THE COUNTWAY LIBRARY OF MEDICINE, HARVARD MEDICAL SCHOOL, BOSTON.

TRIBUTE

We give homage to the Old Man for his great conception — Animus-Anima, which started us in righteous understanding along our path; for his teaching that the erotic problem in our civilization had never been faced and that its solution was the highest quest for the spirit; for his knowledge that in the transforming power of the Trances lay the seeds of creative development; for his wisdom which warned us of, and thereby helped to protect us from, the many difficulties to be encountered along the path; for his view that for man to create woman, and woman to create man was a great, courageous and most important adventure.

As Jung's patients in Zurich in the 1920s, Harvard psychologist Henry A. Murray and his mistress, Christiana Morgan, learned to induce visionary trance states and created their own neopagan cosmology. After finding and illustrating their own "Tower" in Massachusetts, Murray and Morgan practiced sexual magic and other rituals in honor of Jung. These four illuminated pages from a ritual "bible" created by Morgan are probably from the 1940s.

Jung at Harvard University, 1936. The man with the goatee is his disciple Ernest Harms.

On his return to the States, Harold dashed off a letter to John D. Rockefeller describing not only Jung's form of educational treatment for his community of patients, but also his own favorable impressions of the Swiss doctor. Indeed, Harold seems to have had quite a powerful therapeutic experience with Jung, and he viewed not only his wife but himself and his marriage in an entirely new light. For the first time in any of his correspondence Harold employed spiritual and mystical metaphors to describe Jung's methods. After assuring Rockefeller that Edith had "well-founded" reasons for remaining in Zurich and that she expressed a "relative unhappiness at feeling that her work demanded that she stay abroad," Harold had these remarkable things to say:

> Suffice it for the moment, please, to say that she *has made, is making* and *will make* great progress, and that she does not rest content in any other thought than that of a completed *treatment.* That word, by the way, seems almost profane, in her case because it is more of a *study* much more than anything connected with medicine, or hygiene, and instead of being simply fed *improvement,* she very largely makes her own mental recipes. . . . In a word Edith is becoming very *real* and *true to herself,* and is seeking and I'm sure will succeed, to find *her path.* Those words would form the *text.* The analysis would be along many directions.
>
> At any rate, she is in absolutely safe and trustworthy hands, for no finer man ever breathed than Dr. Jung. He has an intense admiration for Edith and yet recognizes that she is the toughest problem he ever had to deal with. At first he was doubtful of success and questioned what he would find. Now he sees a wonderful personality to engage his thoughts and his very best and most contentious efforts. He sees it is much worthwhile! . . .
>
> My time was most wonderfully well spent. It was not fun, it was very tiresome—in the sense of fatiguing—but mine was only a little of what Edith has to endure—but she knows what the reward is and will be and she sees the *light*—after passing through ever so much of deep and almost impenetrable darkness.
>
> I know you will not prejudge what I say—and perhaps I have ventured too far—and yet there is no mystery—only the situation is so unusual—I almost have to pinch myself to know that it really does exist.
>
> Edith has much of beautiful things to do in this world, she sees it, she knows it, and she is bound to realize their accomplishment. It was a Godsend that she met Dr. Jung, and that *her family stood back of her in her resolve* and that she felt this assurance.[21]

Edith, like Fanny Bowditch, Maria Moltzer, and many, many others before her, was now on the path. It was only a matter of time before Harold and Fowler would join her.

1914

For her father's birthday on May 2, twelve-year-old Muriel sent Harold a gardening tool as a present with a note: "For my dear Daddy, wishing him a very happy birthday, From his affectionate and loving daughter, Muriel." Harold wrote back thanking her for "the lovely little birthday present." "The trowel was simply fine," he wrote on May 9, "and I am keeping it on my desk. It was sweet of you to think of me, and I appreciate it as a peace offering from my lovely little daughter."[22]

Harold was here referring to the problems in their relationship caused by Muriel's mercurial—indeed, volatile—personality. Muriel told her father in a letter on July 13 that she and her governess, Mlle. Beley, had great "quarrels." As a remedy, Edith had insisted that her daughter undergo psychoanalysis as well. "My work with Miss Moltzer is getting along finely," Muriel told her father in the same letter.[23]

As we know from the case of Fanny Bowditch, Jung first began to incorporate his idea of a transcendent realm of primordial images (archetypes) into his practice in early 1914. His female patients fell in love with him not for who he was as a man but for his underlying godlikeness. Although spiritual metaphors and an interest in the occult had always attracted certain types of patients, in the early months of 1914 he became more explicit about his view of analysis as a spiritual path. The unconscious now became not only a place, but a "greater personality" or guardian spirit of sorts, an oracle that could be consulted to foretell the future if one learned the secret techniques of Jung's methods. Everyone now had a special spiritual fate or destiny to fulfill. No one believed this more than Edith.

She now took it upon herself to proselytize any and all who would listen. For far too many years she had lived in uncertainty and with the self-image of a weak and ill victim of circumstances. Now she began to take on the voice and advisory role of a prophetess. She began with her father, who was suffering through the prolonged, eventually fatal illness of his wife Laura.

"We all have our problems to face—this is living," Edith told John D. on June 25, 1914, in one of her characteristically short letters. "And I feel that you will rise above the things that are difficult for us now, and realize that we must all fulfill our greater Destiny. The great Divine guardian Spirit cannot do things wrong."[24] From this point until the day she died, this was the new, mediumistic voice of Edith Rockefeller McCormick.

Missing his family, Harold finally made plans to return to Europe with Fowler. However, he chose August 1, 1914, as his tentative date of arrival. With the outbreak of war, Harold had to cancel his plans. Fowler returned to Groton for the fall term. And Edith, although making great progress in her studies and in her treatment with Jung, now feared leaving the neutral sanctuary of Switzerland.

Anticipating the worst, Harold sent over a courier to deliver gold to Edith and to report on the conditions in Zurich. He included a letter, begging her to contact him. The sudden outbreak of war in Europe redirected Harold's attention to company business as well. The general manager of International Harvester, Alexander Legge, issued a confidential memo to all its division managers and department heads on August 29, 1914, urging caution: "Obviously, the only position for us to take is one of absolute neutrality, with the hope that the struggle may be over soon. We must realize that the Company is International in fact as well as in name, that we have property interests in practically all of the countries involved in the difficulty, and among our employees and stockholders there are representatives of all the nations involved in the struggle."[25] The war threatened not only Harold's family, but his livelihood.

Despite his business and the dangers, he got to Genoa on September 18. When he arrived in Zurich, he found that Edith was no longer in analysis with Jung but instead had embarked on her own intensive educational program with a series of private tutors. "Edith is doing wonderfully well and you will be delighted when you see her and will feel the time well spent," Harold wrote to Rockefeller on October 3. "She occupies herself all day long.... She studies astronomy, biology and history, and music. She does not go to see Dr. Jung anymore. Physically, I think she is fine."[26] Muriel is "doing well although she finds it hard to control herself." To his mother, Harold reported, "The war is very sad. Yesterday I went with two Swiss acquaintances to the frontier and felt the breath of battle. All the Swiss soldiers are guarding their frontier."[27] Jung would soon be among them.

Switzerland seemed to all to be the calm eye of the storm, and the only visible sign that anything was amiss was the large number of refugees huddled near the main train station on the Bahnofsplatz. On October 20, Harold sent the following description of their life in Zurich in one of his weekly letters to his mother:

> [Edith's] face is almost entirely clear and her step is springy and she walks with her arms free and swinging. She notices all the things of nature and dresses simply and in very artistic taste suitable to her makeup. In the morning we usually take a walk before lunch and in the afternoon also. Then in the evening we sit around the Hotel or go to some moving picture show.... Mathilde goes through a regular course of treatment each day and could be discharged by November.... One day goes much like another here and the war news absorbs the attention directed towards the outer world.[28]

What Harold didn't tell his mother or his father-in-law was that now he, too, was in analysis with Jung. As the weeks passed, he decided to stay in Zurich and complete his own course of treatment and began to make preparations accordingly. On October 28, Harold broke what he knew would be unwelcome news to his mother: "I don't know when we will be coming back. I am proposing to remain here with Edith until she is ready—and I do not propose to have the false alarms of last year."[29]

As his analysis progressed, Harold seemed to come under Jung's spell. Harold wrote his mother on November 28, "Dr. Jung grows on me all the time. You must know him sometime and I hope he will come to America sometime to make us a visit. He would interest you with the many and profound things he knows."[30]

On Christmas Eve, Harold, Edith, Muriel, and Mathilde exchanged gifts and sent their love through telegrams to Fowler, who was spending time with his grandfather at Pocantico Hills. They were pleased that Edith seemed to finally be happy—or as happy as she ever became. Living in a foreign country still made everything seem somewhat unreal, somewhat tentative, since they all knew that at any moment Edith could change her mind and want to return to Chicago. Even the war seemed unreal to them.

Within a few months, the war would have the psychological effect of hermetically sealing many foreigners in Switzerland, and C. G. Jung would seem to many to be the only savior of a world gone mad.

1915

Edith was no longer in analysis with Jung, but she still very much believed in him. At first she did not like some of his orders—such as washing the floors of her giant suite of rooms herself on her hands and knees, an activity that was supposed to help her learn humility. But she stuck with him and found new dimensions to their relationship that soon made her feel more like a colleague than a patient.

Although by now she read German quite well and spoke it passably, Edith saw how poor Harold struggled to understand Jung's writings. She wanted to share her transformative experience with her husband and with all those she left back home in America. To bring this about, Edith donated generous sums of money for the translation of his works into English. In 1916, Beatrice Hinkle's retitled translation of *Wandlungen, Psychology of the Unconscious,* appeared in New York and Jung's *Collected Papers on Analytical Psychology* was published in London. In 1918 the massive volume of Jung's word-association studies appeared in an English translation by M. D. Eder.

Rockefeller money introduced Jung to the English-speaking world and helped bring him the worldwide fame he has today. In the 1940s, Mary Mellon, with her husband, financier Paul Mellon, provided the funds for the translation of all the German works and retranslation of most of Jung's previous publications into English.[31] The Rockefellers, the McCormicks, and the Mellons were three of America's wealthiest families, and we can only wonder whether Jung would still be so popular today if he had not attracted and converted their women to his *mysteria*. Without their financial backing his works might still be in German and therefore inaccessible to much of the world.

The long-awaited wedding of Cyrus McCormick, Harold's older brother, had been scheduled for February 1915, and Nettie wanted the entire family, including Edith, Harold, and their children, present. In mid-January, however, Edith informed Harold that she would be unable to go. After some ambivalence, Harold decided to go alone. His visit would have been very short if Edith's mother, Laura Rockefeller, had not died while Harold was there. After seeing his son and visiting his grieving father-in-law in Pocantico Hills, Harold left New York on March 16 for Marseille.

The weather was cold and wet for almost the entire first two weeks of his return to Zurich. On April 14, 1915, he wrote his mother that Muriel was about to graduate from her German school and would then enter a boarding school outside Zurich. "This will get her out of the hotel, which is a bad place for her, and we can visit her on Sundays." Harold then tacked on an addition:

> Dr. and Mrs. Jung come this evening to dinner. . . . Edith has only seen Dr. Jung once while I was away and that was the morning before I arrived, when they went over some corrections Edith was making in the English proofs of some of Dr. Jung's writings. Edith is improving every day and now is almost independent of Dr. Jung's treatment. She is now once more almost entirely in contact with the world, from which she has so much withdrawn. She is working right along every day and learning "her path."

But in a scrawled note below his name, he admitted for the first time that something had been very wrong in Edith's understanding of herself as a mother. "She has improved greatly as to attitude towards the children, but still has some things to realize and carry out in this direction yet."[32] After years of abdicating the care of her own children to governesses and boarding schools, she no longer knew how to relate to them.

On that same day, Edith wrote a letter of encouragement to her father, fearing that the first letter she sent him after her mother's death did not reach him "on account of the war considerations." "I know that you are adapting yourself to this new life and fulfilling your own individual Destiny," Edith said. "We cannot mourn for the beautiful spirit which has gone beyond us, for we know that it is living on and developing. I am only sorry that my work is not yet finished here so that I could be nearer to you now."[33]

On May 7, 1915, 1,198 men, women, and children—including 128 Americans—lost their lives when the Germans torpedoed the British liner *Lusitania*. Harold knew someone on that doomed ship, a man by the name of Herbert Stone. "Everyone here speaks of the *Lusitania* with hushed voice," he wrote to his mother on May 31. "I cabled and wrote to Mary Stone. I am afraid Herbert was among those who could not swim and he surrendered any chance at the boats."[34]

Harold now realized the danger of crossing the ocean while the war still raged. The fear of leaving his family in the middle of a war zone helped him to overcome his remaining resistance to Jung. Rather than always having one foot in and one foot out of the magically unreal community of spiritual seekers around Jung, he now felt part of their mission. As others in analysis in Zurich found, the war seemed to heighten the social cohesiveness and group identity of the Jungians. Harold finally saw the need for the spiritual rebirth of the world and was certain that Jung was the man to bring it about. His conversion was complete.

In his letter to his mother, Harold discussed an article she had sent him about a young woman they both knew who had committed suicide. His high regard for the healing powers of Dr. Jung is evident, and he tells his mother he is postponing—once again—a return.

> As to Miss Farwell, it is indescribably sad. At once on reading the article my thoughts formed just two words "Dr. Jung." There is not the slightest doubt he could have saved her—saved a life and handed it back to the world in more beauty and usefulness than before. Spirits tired and worn and distracted are brightened and refreshed under his care and safe keeping. . . . I have decided as I cabled you to postpone my sailing which I had thought of as May 29th. I did this myself of my own account without regard to Edith. She was prepared that I should go but *I* wanted to stay here longer because there were some points with Dr. Jung I wanted to clear up.[35]

Despite Harold's reluctance to leave Switzerland, under Jung's care he began to believe in the inevitability of fate and, paradoxically, worried less about the safety of his family. "This place is so tranquil, you would never know any war was going on," he said to his mother on June 3, 1915. Oddly heedless of the *Lusitania* disaster, he assured her, "One can always leave without much difficulty."[36] Ocean liners still operated, although with great uncertainty, and Fowler set sail from New York on the *St. Paul* on June 19 with the hope "eventually . . . to turn up in Zurich, there to join my long-lost family."[37] He arrived safely in Zurich on July 1.

Harold wrote to his mother on July 9, assuring her that Fowler made the trip without incident. He informed her that, "This morning Fowler went with me to Küsnacht, both on bicycles, and then he left me at Dr. Jung's gate."[38] Harold's sessions with Dr. Jung assumed a greater importance in his life and he wanted everyone in his family to benefit from analysis. On July 15, he wrote, "Muriel goes to Miss Moltzer twice a week. It's doing great good."[39] Now it was Fowler's turn.

Fowler McCormick remembered it near the end of his life:

> In 1915 . . . my mother said to me, "Fowler, this question of analytical psychology is a very important one. There are many most interesting developments in it. I think it is something that you should know something about." Following that thought she arranged through Dr. Jung for me to spend two or three hours a week with Dr. Franz Riklin. . . . I was intensely interested in the subjects which Riklin spoke about and I read extensively in the works of Freud, Nietzsche, Schopenhauer. . . . I was fascinated by the conception of the ability to find meaning in dreams and the marvelous work of Freud in exposing his theories and giving the cases as he did. . . . In Nietzsche I read in a beginning way, not as much as I did on my next trip to Zurich.[40]

With the entire family now in Zurich, John D. Rockefeller finally became incensed that Harold and Edith were "banqueting" their days away and placing the entire family—including Fowler, his favorite—in jeopardy in the middle of a war. On June 18, Harold wrote a very strong (for him) letter to his father-in-law and attempted to explain the allure of analytical psychology and Jung.

> This is not a tabernacle of joy, but a shrine to which seekers only address themselves, and it is in this spirit that I have again postponed my sailing and that Edith still finds herself held. With both of us, every day counts. This is not a place (the school of Zurich) which encourages remaining here beyond the right or the normal time, but the whole question is one of degree at best, for no one who is really interested in analytical psychology and finds it of help ever drops it, because if it is one thing,—it is to be lived, and the more one studies the more one is prepared to live on its basis. So one must strike out again in life else it (analytical psychology) defeats its own purpose. The fundamental idea of it is to teach one, one's self—and this is not always easy, and still worse difficult, owing to conscious resistances, to follow one's path

when it has been laid out by one's own self.... I remained here purely on my own account, to finish up some work.[41]

In the last week of August 1915, Harold had an experience that convinced him more than ever of Jung's magical power.

Harold went on a "walking trip" with Jung through Switzerland and in the increased level of intimacy realized how "false" or "unreal" he was in comparison with Jung, whom he glowingly describes as a "real" or "natural" man. On August 31, he wrote a report of his experiences with Jung, Emma, and Toni Wolff that allows us to see not only how deeply involved Harold had become with Jung, but also the sorts of ideas about personality types and relationships Jung was then teaching his patients. It is a document of unparalleled insight.

> Dr. Jung told me he was going on a ten days vacation and knowing this would throw me out of the sittings, meanwhile and having for a long while wanted to get off this way with him, I wondered if I might go. He said certainly in the latter part of his trip, but at first he wanted a few days for solitude and meditation. So later Mrs. Jung and a Miss Wolff (an analitiker) who has been analyzed by him joined him and later I did.... The companions charming, so real and true to themselves. [ ] and flexible, Dr. Jung is as nearly perfect to my mind as a man can be.
>
> Naturally I was at first a little fearful how I would get on with such an analysed party. But it went beautifully, because the spirit, and my understanding were there. There were only two or three times when things went for a little while wrong—"resistances" or "repressions" on my part but these were easily cleared up by talking out. It was a rare chance. Naturally Dr. Jung and I were each studying the other. I was making notes of his attitude and method to apply it to my own case. He was sizing me up to see how I was compared to those professional times when he usually saw me. I told him yesterday I was delighted to see the *natural way* he acted and he said "of course." Then I told him I was sure that Edith in her [ ] way was a little too *inflexible* still. And he said "yes" as for me he said I was much more balanced than formerly, so much so that he remarked to his wife that it was now hard to discern from my actions whether I was "extravert" or "introvert." But still my great need yet is to cultivate on my own part an intimate knowledge of myself—to like to be *with* myself. Then other matters, when I learn to develop my "thinking" side, will take their natural and proper course, for my "feeling" side is plenty if not a little too much developed already. So on the whole the trip was profitable—every minute of it. Once when I made some remark which pleased him, Dr. Jung said, "Mr. McCormick you're all right"—which was a good deal for him to say and only had a general reference—here being plenty for me yet to do,—but I *know* very well I am stronger in many ways, and yet I

don't think the difference will be jarring, but rather the contrary. But this has yet to be seen. I know I am deeply grateful for what I have achieved and aside from its wonderful help in connection with and relation to Edith, it is for me a great thing in itself. I have, I know, opened up for myself a field of opportunity, and now it is for me to take ahold of it. . . .

I only wish Edith had been with us. But we had to do as he thinks best, and if Edith cannot or does not want to take such trips it is not for me always to stay back. There must be for the greatest peace and contentment a large amount of independence. This makes each more to the other not as long as there is an underlying *value* for each other, and this is something not to *assume* just because we are married, but to work for and strive for, and the more we are in a common work, the more we are together in thought and purpose. But there still is left room for individuality and separate interests and in following these we each bring to the other new thoughts and ideas and a freshness of things to talk about, and it gives us a *zest* which the reverse *suppresses,* leaving the desire still there but unsatisfied. This makes resistances and we project these on this basis into other things which in turn creates an entirely false situation and friction suppressed or unspoken issues—it's bound to.[42]

As Harold's involvement with the Jungian subculture of Zurich deepened that autumn, his letters to his mother and to John D. became more explicit about his and his daughter Muriel's experiences with analysis. His mother had been quite concerned about Muriel's entry into puberty and recommended a prominent book for her son to read on adolescence. Harold responded, "Oh yes, I know Stanley Hall's book. I have read it some years ago." He then added: "[Muriel] just had her first menstruation about a month ago. You may believe we are watchful and we love her dearly, and Dr. Jung and Miss Moltzer are master minds on the subject and even now Muriel goes to Miss Moltzer and talks out all her 'repressions' or a good many of them at any rate."[43] Later, Harold said often that Muriel's problematic personality reminded him of his insane sister Virginia. On the same day, Harold also wrote to Rockefeller in response to some queries that he had put forth:

Of Dr. Jung, it seems a trite thing to say, but I do most sincerely say that I am surprised how little I have known myself heretofore or how little I have cared for the society and acquaintance and intimacy of myself. I am told there is a wealth of opportunity in this direction, without in any way increasing self-adulation. Some people know themselves instinctively, others never do. It never occurred to me to compare the society of myself with that of others. I sought the latter consciously while unconsciously wanting to be more with myself, and here was a battle. Now I am learning a little the new way, and I am trying to learn to *think,* for I have always had a superabundance of "feelings"—With Edith it is just exactly the other way....

For the past week I have had the rare chance of being with Dr. Jung and his wife and a Miss Wolff. He is surely a *great man,* and a most genuine one, and spiritual.[44]

Harold was clearly finding his work with Jung beneficial. He wrote his mother, "If I were not impressed with the benefit of it for all time I should not have invested one year in analysis."[45] Harold was now exercising his new intellectual muscles; in this letter he also included a definition from Immanuel Kant of what is "right" for an individual. In a later letter he told Nettie he was reading "the translation of the writings of an old Chinese philosopher (B.C. 625), Lao-dze," and provided extensive quotes.[46]

The walking trip with Jung seems to have made Harold more comfortable with the idea of leaving Edith behind. He planned to sail on October 15 "with or without her," as he told his mother.[47] (Fowler left Zurich on the seventh of September.) But although Harold seemed to be improving, Edith was having a slower time of it. While some persons found analysis useful, Harold told his mother that "in Edith's case it is life itself." Although Edith's dreams seemed to be telling her that she should return to Chicago, her agoraphobia was still quite disabling. For almost a year she had not left the grounds of the Hotel.

> I wonder if I am betraying confidence in telling you just between us that Edith told me yesterday she had a dream in which she saw you coming into the parlor smiling, and she was much pleased. It was the first of its kind. She now is commencing to transfer her *desire* to Chicago which is a fine sign. It is an awakening as from a long dream. She now is commencing to travel. I started with her on her first try, the first in 11 months. We bought two tickers to Winterthur 35 minutes away *first stop.* Just before the train started she got out—could not do it. She was so disappointed. I could have cried. We then took a local and went 20 minutes up the Lake [ ]. Then she went and slept at a small hotel in Küsnacht unknown to Dr. Jung (with Emmy). She has twice done this since at other small towns, and so she will feel her way. She is indomitable in tenacity. *That* has carried her through. Tonight she is off again. I plan to sail Oct. 15th. She is trying to get ready to go too.[48]

Harold reserved his most detailed descriptions of analysis and its effects for his father-in-law. Harold badly wanted him to understand and approve of his new analytic insights, and he went to great lengths to describe in layman's terms what he had learned from Jung. The most revealing letter—of October 31—is also the longest: almost two thousand words. In it, Harold attempted to give concrete examples along with his definitions of Jung's concepts of "projection," "transference," "introversion," "extraversion," "thinking type," "feeling type," and the necessity for the balance between the conscious and the unconscious minds.

Harold's letter was in response to one from Rockefeller in which he expressed his concern that analysis was a form of "propaganda" and that Harold and Edith were caught up in a religious cult of sorts. Rockefeller was a Baptist and was unsettled by the hints of a non-Christian religious frenzy that Harold as well as Edith now seemed to exhibit. He had looked to Harold as his eccentric daughter's caretaker, but he now joined Nettie McCormick in his concern that Harold's talk of adopting a new "religious attitude to life" did not bode well for the future.

Taken as a whole, Harold's letter to Rockefeller is a remarkable summary of Jung's philosophy in 1915—a virtually unknown period in Jung's development that preceded his later and more familiar theories of psychological types, the collective unconscious, and archetypes. It also shows the extent to which Jung was promoting a totalizing religious philosophy and himself as its prophet. Harold was, in a sense, "witnessing" to his father-in-law in this letter. Here are some significant excerpts:

> I thank you for your reference to analysis and the work I am doing here. It is so strictly personal, it is hard to talk much about it, much less to write, and in a few experiences I have had I can see that this effort in either direction can be overdone and the object misunderstood. For a "visionary spirit" is the last in the world to have as to gaining converts or exercising any propaganda, but when one is interested to hear its principles of method can be outlined. But even to impart these is hard because so much of it has to be felt not in the way of "faith," but in the way of "need." And if one is studying it and feels its help the human tendency is to want everyone to have it and to know of it. . . .
>
> Well, anyway, "analytical psychology" is still in its infancy as a science, as a means for an end, as a method to obtain an attitude, and it is little known; and among those who know—generally among those who know only *somewhat* of it where it is as such sometimes misunderstood—it is not always believed in. Like anything new it has to "win its spurs," and that takes time, but the truth always prevails in the long run—"truth, a property of certain of our ideas in agreement with reality"—and I believe there is truth in "analytical psychology" and that in the course of time this will be recognized.
>
> I have a simple little thought that "analysis" is good for everyone but necessary (in the sense of *helpful*) in proportion as one is not at one with himself. This last is mostly emphasized among those who are very *neurotic*. For a businessman it is *good;* for a poor tired soul, worn out by mental struggle with the world or himself, it is more needed.
>
> To me it has two general aspects, one a scientific aspect: that is the knowledge and observance of certain laws of life, of human nature, etc.; and the other is metaphysical or spiritual. . . . In the case of the tired soul the

"religious attitude"—entirely different in precept from "religion" but of the same character, would appeal the more strongly.... The whole work itself is the development of an *attitude* towards life and things, and this attitude when *found* directs one's daily life in almost everything.... I don't mean everyone is *worthless* without analysis, I only mean that there is much in analysis which would *help* everyone is my belief and from what I have seen and realized or experienced....

I believe that without analysis few bring such situations before their minds for *contemplation* and *action*.... But there is to my mind a difference between doing this in a hap-hazard way or doing this systematically and intelligently and here is where analysis comes in as showing a *"method"* or a *"process"* towards the attainment of an *"attitude"* which *directs,* by uncovering and bringing to light the true inward situation from the *unconscious* into the "sunlight of consciousness" where the problems may be dealt with as *real, known,* propositions and factors rather than by indefinite hazy "un-get-at-able" longings or discontentments.... The knowledge of these problems, plus the knowledge of one's self, plus the action to harmonize and balance constitutes the state of mind called an *"attitude,"* and the recognition of this attitude constitutes "being at one with one's self."... Another way of putting this same thing is to say that when the conscious *and unconscious* are in balance "one is at one with one's self."...

Dr. Jung believes there is an *unconscious* part of our mind as distinguished from the *conscious,* and that the unconscious mind is very powerful but usually is not fully *recognized* and is *submerged* by the conscious but not dominated by it, and it (the unconscious) goes on working.... The conscious represents the self in the more *unreal way*. The unconscious in the more *real way*. Dr. Jung believes that through the interpretation of dreams which in themselves are symbolic, we arrive at a knowledge of the speech of the unconscious; also through the "association word method" so much used now in criminology; also through "reveries" when the conscious mind is in repose... and also through the "blocking" or "stumbling" process when a person says one thing while consciously meaning to say another. Now most Psychologists do not agree with Dr. Jung, or the truth or value of the interpretation of dreams, or in the unconscious being a separate proposition from the conscious. They believe it is *all conscious* simply of one degree or another of varying intensity, and that dreams are vagaries, and of no value to use.

Following a discussion of the importance of "self-esteem," Harold tried to explain Jung's notion of the two psychological types with reference to Edith and himself. Harold's remarks attest to the utility of these particular conceptual innovations, which are perhaps Jung's greatest practical contributions to psychology:

There are two types which stand out, for example, the one the "Introvert" (Edith's type), who *"thinks"* and the other is the "Extravert" (my type) who *"feels."* The "Introvert" is of the old, so-called "Stoic type"; he lives much within himself; he is apt to deny the existence of all not possessed in the mind; he draws and absorbs from the world; there is a sharp line between himself and the world. The "Extravert" feels, does, acts, lives in and is a part of the world; he gives out constantly; he runs dry; there is no sharp line between himself and the world, his own personality is relatively lost; he is of the old "sympathetic" type. Now neither extreme is *good;* a balance is better, but how? Well, the Introvert should develop his *feeling* and the Extravert his *thinking*. The conscious manifestation of the Introvert being the "ability" to think, he should develop his unconscious which contains his latent feelings, and vice versa the Extravert, should develop his unconscious which is along the line of bringing out his thoughts. . . . So in analysis the idea on this point is that each shall understand the other on one hand, and each shall develop his particular weak side to a more even balance. So this work has naturally been of great help to Edith and me in each understanding the other, and in each helping to get to the other's standpoint.

Harold attempted to teach Rockefeller the unique language of analysis:

"[R]epressions" [meant that] we would not speak out and tell each other what we thought of one another but would keep silent and just *remember,* instead of bringing them out to the surface and having it out in talk and *forgetting* it. Too many "repressions" bring "resistances" and that means resentment or dislike, and that is bad. I had plenty of "resistance" piled up against Edith if, for example, she spoke to the cook about dinner out of my hearing I would become displeased and would start in to pick a quarrel with the *cook,* and the first I knew I would be angry at *her.* This is "projection." I would project on the *cook* (entirely harmless) my feelings really directed at Edith. Then "transference" is another general law where you get to be *over dependent* upon the other person (I have done a lot of this in my life). . . . I think all the above will give you a general idea of what we are driving at. Naturally Edith started in analysis as a *salvation* and it has wonderfully succeeded with her. I started because I was here, and for myself and for the benefit in understanding the language she was acquiring, and in this I have done well indeed. As I progressed I became deeply appreciative and engrossed. Of course you get hardly any idea from this letter of the depths and heights embraced within analysis.

Harold recommended that Rockefeller read an article on psychoanalysis by Max Eastman in the June/July 1915 issue of *Everybody's Magazine,* although he admitted it "only skims the surface."

There are few scientific writings as yet, and what papers there are mostly in German, but some are now being translated into English. Analysis holds that individual psychology exists, that each person is a problem to himself; that if a person does not find that he is at one with himself, that there *is* a way to learn; and finally that learning this if he follows the path indicated he will secure the result desired to a greater or lesser extent according to circumstances, of patience, of submission, degree of need felt, etc. It is wonderful how the days and time pass. You cannot imagine how this happens.[49]

United in their newly adopted psychological and metaphysical belief system, Harold and Edith attempted to convert John D. and other members of their family to Jung's ideas. In 1915, Jung assigned many of his disciples and patients readings in Nietzsche, particularly the posthumous compilation of notes and diary entries and other previously unpublished material that his sister put together in the book entitled *The Will to Power*. Harold and Edith were so taken with it that they sent a copy to John D. as a Christmas gift. Rockefeller and Nietzsche mixed like oil and water. "Dear Edith and Harold," Rockefeller wrote on January 26, "I am just in receipt of your Christmas greetings, and the book, entitled 'The Will to Power' volume one, for which I send many thanks. I am sure the book will prove very interesting reading, though it may be far beyond me. I keep to a simple philosophy and almost primitive ideas of living. These seem to be best for my physical and mental composition, and am keeping very busy, although I may not be keeping up with the bandwagon."[50]

Harold was quick to pick up on his father-in-law's discomfort at the implication that he needed any improvement, especially the sort they were engaging in. Harold tried to smooth over any misunderstandings by buttering him up. On February 16, 1916, Harold wrote:

> We are glad you received the book "The Will to Power" vol. 1—It was not sent with any idea of being a guide, for you possess the title as few experience. It came to you more as iron to a magnet. It was thought a glance might be a pleasing collaboration. It cites the theory, you exemplify the practice. Others who are not so favored as you, or who have not developed the faculty, can I am sure get much good from it—using discretion and discernment of course. Like many who have new paths, "Nietzsche" was radical. Edith and I both feel and think you *are* unusually "at one with yourself." . . . Yours has been a life of pure intuitive psychology. For others this must be acquired and many may never get it.[51]

Once again, Christmas found the family united in Zurich, but without Fowler, who spent the day with his grandfather in Pocantico Hills. In an undated December 1915 letter to his grandmother, the lives of Harold and Edith are seen through the sad child they left behind in America.

> I, too, am deeply disappointed that the entire family is not to-day on this side of the ocean, but I am confident that there is some good reason for this not

being the case. And I can well understand Mother's feeling about coming back.... [She] is very happy in the surroundings and atmosphere of Zurich. She comes and goes and does what she wants, there is ample opportunity and time for study and she has few or no duties imposed upon her.

Father is divided by his desire to be over here with the business and his friends and family, and his desire to be with Mother. It certainly would simplify matters if Mother could come over. She imagines things worse over here and more difficult than they really are.

Don't worry about me![52]

For Edith and Harold, the only solution was to introduce Fowler to the wisdom of Jung. If only he could see the light—as they had with Jung's help—he would understand the present situation and not feel abandoned. Harold began sending books and long letters explaining analytical psychology, which Fowler showed to his grandmother when he stayed with her in Chicago. Realizing that she might lose her grandson to the weird spell Jung seemed to hold over the rest of her family, Nettie accused Harold of trying to convert his son to this unhealthy foreign philosophy. From the perspective of those left behind in America, adopting Jung's theories seemed the cause of the breakup of the family. On February 7, 1916, Harold sent her an equally sharp response. "I know how well-meaning your words are, but I am not trying to *influence* Fowler and I don't like others to."[53]

This would prove to be untrue.

1916

Harold and Edith were now zealots when it came to Jung and analytical psychology. And being Rockefellers and McCormicks, they knew they had the power to make Jung's influence felt in the world.

Both of them had attended the occasional lectures at the Psychological Club meetings that Jung had been holding in a private room of a local restaurant since 1913. The ambience, however, was not conducive to the free expression of ideas among intimates or the forging of stronger bonds between Club members. Given a lifetime spent in American country clubs, it was probably Harold who decided to buy a building to serve as a clubhouse for the analysts and patients. For Jung and analytical psychology to gain any respectability, it was clear to his American patrons that the Psychological Club needed a building for its lectures, seminars, and other social events and to lodge guests. Plans were made to buy or rent a building in Zurich and renovate it to resemble an American country club. It was up to Harold to find the right building and make all the arrangements. Borrowing heavily from a local bank by using her Rockefeller name as collateral, Edith paid for it.

The building that Harold found was in one of the most expensive districts in the city. With Harold's help, Edith borrowed enough money to establish a large reserve of funds to ensure the continued existence of the Club. She did this without consulting her father first, but she knew that he would always take care of her. Plans to secure the building were already in place by January 31, 1916, when Edith wrote to him to ask for more stocks in Standard Oil, pointing out that her "allowance" from him had remained the same since 1910. "As a woman of forty-three," Edith said, "I should like to have more money to help with. There are causes in which I am interested which are uplifting and of such importance to my development which I cannot help as I should like to because I have not the money. I hope that you will see that as a woman of earnestness of purpose and singleness of spirit I am worthy."[54]

Without waiting for a response, Edith and Harold rented and renovated the new building.

Due perhaps to the intensity of the war, Edith did not receive a response from her father until July. Of course, Rockefeller gave his daughter the money, but this time he wanted to know *exactly* how she was spending it. He wanted a detailed accounting from *her*—not her husband—of what she had been doing for so long in Zurich. He knew she was going to use the extra money for Jung's purposes, and he began to suspect that Jung was a charlatan who was only after the Rockefeller fortune. In her uncharacteristically long response to her father on July 20, 1916, Edith tried to explain herself. She revealed some startling new developments in Zurich.

For the first time we learn that Jung has now allowed Edith to be a practicing analyst. As she was still quite agoraphobic, her patients came to her suite at the hotel. Perhaps Jung felt that her generous patronage bought Edith the right to be an analyst if that's what she wanted, despite the severity of her many problems.

Edith wrote:

> I want to thank you for the letter you wrote to me . . . in answer to my letter asking if you would not give me some more money. I too am sorry that my work has taken me for such a long time away from you. . . .
>
> I'm getting healed myself and getting my nerves up. I am learning how I can help to heal other people who are struggling on with shattered nerves. It is a very difficult work, but it is a beautiful work. I have rented here a house and have founded a psychological club which gives the opportunity for those who are in analysis to come together. This is an important step forward in the collective development.

Except for small sums, my three large interests are the Memorial Institute for Infectious Diseases, the Chicago Opera Company, and Analysis. To the Institute I give $25,000.00 a year. To the Opera I give to the guarantee fund each year $12,000.00. To the Club I had to make the gift all at the same time, this was $120,000.00 Of this amount I had to borrow $80,000.00 at the Bank. But now I can begin paying this off next year. This work is unique in the history of mankind and its far reaching values are inestimable. For a cause such as this I would willingly make a bigger loan. The bankers are very nice with me and I expect no difficulties in paying off my debt in time. You would be interested to hear more of this work, and I shall be glad to tell you much about it when I come back.[55]

These sums would be generous in current dollars, let alone in 1916. Jung's movement was clearly the overwhelming recipient of Edith's largesse. In 1997 dollars, the money Edith donated to the Jungian cause would be close to $2 million. And this is in addition to paying for the translations of Jung's works into English.

Edith's language in her letters suggests that from the very start she and everyone else involved with Jung saw their work as religious in nature and that their small group in Zurich would be the first of many other such groups to eventually spread across the planet. The Zurich School would be the vanguard of a new movement that would bring a spiritual rebirth to the world. If Jung's movement was indeed "unique in the history of mankind," then the founding of the headquarters of the Psychological Club would be remembered as the moment that Jung and his disciples entered the history books. Edith was proud to be able to bring this about. Describing it later that year in her annual letter to her mother-in-law, Edith said: "I am enclosing a photograph of the Psychological Club which I founded and endowed on the 26th of January of this year. This house I have rented for two and a half years. It makes a center for analyzed people where we can be in pension, or come in for meals, or come for the evenings for lectures, discussions and study, all of which teaches collectivity. Any new movement has a slow growth, but this assures a lasting quality."[56]

Sigmund Freud was quite jealous. "[The Rev. Oskar] Pfister writes that Rockefeller's daughter presented Jung with a gift of 360,000 francs for the construction of a casino, analytic institute, etc.," he complained to Sandor Ferenczi on April 29, 1916. "So Swiss ethics have finally made their sought-after contact with American money. I think not without bitterness about the pitiful situations of the members of our Associations, our difficulties with the Verlag [publishing house], etc. Now Jung is supposedly talking about me again with 'veneration.' I replied to Pfister that this turnaround finds no resonance with me."[57]

Within a few years, however, the coffers of the Club were almost bare. Edith continued to borrow money from Swiss banks, and by March 1920 she would be over $800,000 in debt, which her father finally paid off for her. Unable to afford the lease and upkeep of the expensive building Harold had chosen, Edith bought the Psychological Club its own building on Gemeindestrasse, where it continues to operate today. John D. Rockefeller's money paid for all of this.

In his way, Harold, too, was trying to be a force of change in the world. Feeling more confident about his ability to think, in March, Harold wrote a long proposal for ending the war that he intended to be passed along to the leaders of the combative parties. His proposal—entitled "Cash Value of Ultimate Peace Terms"—was essentially a cost-benefit analysis of the situation. Using his new reasoning abilities, he constructed an argument based on the idea that war simply is too expensive. Harold believed that if everyone could only see his point, the war would come to a halt. He sent copies of his manuscript to the American ambassador to Switzerland and to President Wilson and other top officials. Harold received many polite responses, but nothing that indicated that anyone took him seriously. He circulated another proposal—"Via Pacis"—the following year, after the United States entered the war.[58] This time Harold got himself into hot water when he tried to send a copy directly to high-ranking German officials. The State and War Departments in Washington immediately sent an avalanche of cables to Harold and to the American ambassador to Switzerland to demand that Harold stop meddling in international affairs.

In May 1916, Fowler was accepted at Princeton University, and with his parents' permission he took off the year before college. Like Ernest Hemingway, Walt Disney, Dashiell Hammett, e. e. cummings, John Dos Passos, and hundreds of young men—mostly from elite New England prep schools and the Ivy League—Fowler signed on to be a member of the "Gentlemen Volunteers" of the first ambulance corps in France.[59] His enlistment was for three months beginning in July. Stationed in Paris, he repaired and reattached Model T Ford frames for the bodies of the ambulances. He certainly saw wounded soldiers, but never made it to the front.

On the first of October, he arrived in Zurich. After not seeing Fowler for more than a year, in which time Harold himself had learned to think psychologically through analysis, Harold immediately noticed certain qualities in his son he had never seen before. "Fowler reminds me so much of [his insane brother] Stanley I find myself often almost calling him by that name," Harold told his mother on October 18. Almost immediately, Fowler began analysis with Jung.

Now four members of the family—Edith, Harold, Muriel, and Fowler—

were deeply involved in analysis with Jung or Maria Moltzer. Only Mathilde seems to have escaped analysis, but she was once again in the sanitarium in Davos.

The Secret Church

Edith and Harold were in the audience when Jung gave his stirring inaugural talk to the Zurich Psychological Club. Edith explained to Harold the references Jung made in German about the Holy Grail and *Parsifal* and the Rosicrucians. Jung confirmed for them that they were members of a Holy Order like the Grail knights and that their new "religious attitude" and the work they did on themselves would ultimately redeem the entire world. At this point, Jung rarely mentioned in public that the religious attitude he was teaching them was a pagan one, antithetical to Judeo-Christian orthodoxies; he only remarked that this attitude was a "new" one.

But almost from the very beginning, there were serious problems in the Club. For the first time, the analysts and their patients all had frequent exposure to one another on a regular basis. Rather than promoting social cohesion, discord ruled. And no one was more disruptive to the harmony of the Club than Jung himself. A variety of factors may have been responsible for this. Jung's personal life was in turmoil as he tried to work out a polygamous ménage with Emma and Toni Wolff. His visions continued, and in the summer of 1916 his house was haunted by the dead Crusaders who had not found what they sought in Jerusalem.

The introduction of money and the international social status of the Rockefellers and the McCormicks into Jung's circle with the opening of the Club no doubt tempted many of his male colleagues to jockey for position and rank. They were astute enough to see that the gravy train had just pulled in, and they wanted to be on board. Some—such as Alphonse Maeder, Hans Trüb, Adolph Keller, and Hans Schmid—subtly attempted to dethrone Jung by challenging his authority. Jung was never one to tolerate criticism—especially in public—and his anger seeped out in sarcasm and insults.

Jung eventually won the power struggle by winning most of the female members of the Club to his side and by making it too unpleasant for too many male analysts to remain. The majority of analysts who allied themselves with Jung in these early days were female; they did not question his authority. Like Kundry, they existed only to serve their Parsifal. They wanted to continue to participate in the mystery of the Holy Grail that Jung promised them.

Harold and Edith certainly witnessed Jung's darker side, but they always seemed to give him the benefit of a doubt. To use their terms, their transference to Jung made them too dependent upon him to allow contradictory information to intrude on their idealizations.

Yet on a Saturday evening at the club—probably the night of October 14—*something* happened that upset everyone. We know how upset Fanny Bowditch became when she saw Jung "in the grip of his complexes," and from a previously unpublished document that Harold McCormick was deeply troubled about the atmosphere of his beloved club as well.

Emma Jung, who was president of the executive committee of the club, saw how upset Harold was and asked him to submit a report that outlined the social problems of the club and proposed solutions. Harold worked for almost a month polishing two rough first drafts into a final version that he then formally submitted on November 13, 1916. As with his previous proposals for ending the war, writing this report allowed Harold to practice thinking. Without ever mentioning Jung or anyone else by name, Harold made the following observations about the disharmony and in so doing gives us insight into the "guiding fictions" of this unusual spiritual community and its insular, utopian mentality:

> The School of Zurich stands for a set of principles and a set of expediencies—a set of uncompromising attitudes and a set of flexible ones.
>
> The School stands, in the unfolding of its truths or beliefs, virtually against the world. There are too few at present in the School, and too many outside it to warrant any difference among those who espouse its cause. . . .
>
> The School of Zurich and the Psychology Club are in one way two separate propositions, but in another sense they are identical in interest at the present time, owing to the fact that the extent of the membership of the Club makes this collective body almost coincident with that of the School of Zurich itself,—the Club being an expression of the ideas of the School.
>
> Therefore what affects the Club affects the School and vice versa. . . .
>
> Differences of opinion and views, . . . are bound to percolate, if not to become transferred with increased velocity and intensity to the other. . . . Reference herein, it may be said, is made *not* to those differences of personal view wherein only the individual is affected, nor to those differences which apply to the individual versus the community in general, *but only* to those differences the adherence to which affects the solidarity of the movement surrounding the School of Zurich and the Club and their natural and normal advance and progress. . . . Towards the School and Club there is a more definite obligation, it is suggested, than towards society in general. . . .
>
> It might be said with a good deal of truth that the School of Zurich is on trial, insofar as its relation to the outcome of the Club enterprise is concerned, for if 60 people in analysis cannot get along together, what can be expected for the future among 600 or 6000.

To-day the Club stands as the Citadel of the School as a whole; it is the Visible Church; the Workshop of which the School is the Laboratory. Many of the principles of the School are or should be lived out at the Club, and the living out in the Club life of these principles is one test of their value. . . .

It is ventured that no Club could possibly start with more given difficult situations to meet and deal with than confront the Psychology Club at this time and considering the relatively short time of its life and the fact that it entered the field as a stranger to all precedents, it can be marvelled that it has done as well as has been the case. Review the conditions and the component parts: a club to be devoted to intellectual pursuits; to social pursuits; a pension; a town club; a place for collateral society meetings; and a habitat for persons in various stages of Analysis. In this club are to be members of different nationalities, of trained divergent temperamental and psychic make-ups, joining in the spirit of collectivity. Here congregate people of different mental calibre, of different "Bildung," and in different stages of analysis. Here come together the "analytiker" [the analyst] and the "analysand" [the patient] in fellowship. . . .

In addition to finding ourselves individually it would seem that another logical step might be finding our Collectivity with people who are in analysis, and some would take the view that this step is more difficult than with people who are unanalyzed. If this *is* true it would surely be for the very reasons which cause the present difficulties of our club life, and if again in turn this would be so, does it not show the more importance of getting at once to the seat of the trouble in a united way to work out this problem to a harmonious result. What is more undignified than the spectacle of orthodox religious circles fighting among themselves over "claimed-for" important questions, which to on-lookers or those desired to be convinced, seem often times trivial and unimportant. . . .

I believe that unconsciously there is too much of an atmosphere of rank observed in the Club, the mental rank, and the rank between "analytiker" and "analysand" on the one hand, and as between people in various stages of analysis on the other. If this difficulty does exist it surely does not emanate principally from those in the higher rank, but rather on account of "transference" and lack of assertiveness on the part of those less assured. Still granting this, the remedy may be sought by cooperation from both sides. A kind act tendered at a personal sacrifice is one development. Such a kind act tendered with a contented spirit might be a still further development, helpful to our Club-life welfare. The mantle of "caste" should be laid aside at the threshold of the Club and the Natural Simple Human Relation assumed in its real aspect.[60]

Harold's reference to the club as the "Visible Church" reveals that he had been reading the works of Arthur Edward Waite, particularly his 1909 book *The Hidden Church of the Holy Grail*. Waite proposes that there has been an underground mystical tradition, pre-Christian in origin, whose truths have emerged in a disguised form in Hellenistic mystery cults, Gnosticism, Freemasonry, Rosicrucianism, alchemy, and particularly in the many legends of the Holy Grail. He refers to formal religious doctrines and institutions throughout history as the "Visible Church," which shows its face to the world. The visible church, however, is a mask for what Waite calls the "Hidden Church of Sacramental Mystery" or, more commonly, "The Secret Church." In his last chapter, Waite revealed the existence of this underground spiritual tradition throughout history. The Secret Church "is behind the Visible Church," and has always been kept alive by a chosen few.[61] Its existence has been hidden by rumors and "many literatures," which are "veils."[62] A mystical union with God and a spiritual regeneration or rebirth are experienced by those who are initiated into its mysteries. The Secret Church is therefore not an external or material construction that exists in space and time, for as Waite says, "If I may attempt one further definition, as the synthesis of all my statements—echoing and reflecting all—I would describe the Secret Church as the integration of believers in the higher consciousness."[63]

In this final chapter we have all the elements of Jung's guiding fiction about the nature of his cult of followers in Zurich in 1916.[64] It was a fantasy that he would keep alive for them for the rest of his life. Together they were on a Grail quest and participated together in a mystery: the Secret Church. Jung used this metaphor quite often during these years, particularly in connection with the Mithraic mysteries, because Franz Cumont and other scholars thought that the secret underground mystery chambers in which the initiations took place were directly below actual visible churches where more formal rites were conducted.

Harold and Edith consciously believed that analysis with Jung was an initiation into this Secret Church, this Temple of the Holy Grail. Jung had told them it was.

This did not please John D. Rockefeller. He did not like the strange tone of Edith and Harold's letters. The "religious attitude" they both now espoused was unfamiliar to him. Despite all their talk of spirituality, it did not seem Christian to him, certainly not Baptist. In her annual letter to her father in 1916, Edith attempted to address tactfully these differences while letting him know that she and Harold had found their path together.

> As it [the year] nears its close, we look onward with hope, confidence and trust. We know not what is ahead for us, but we do know that we have our home, we have found our path, so that while we know the road may be a hard one it will have its beauties.
>
> You on your path have your philosophy and your religion which guide

you. I on my path have my philosophy and my religion which guide me. That they differ makes no harm because we have love which makes the bond between us.[65]

Edith and Harold's new religion was analysis. Indeed, their acquaintance Fanny Bowditch was making such a statement to her diary in these same last months of 1916.

The final years in Zurich: 1917–1921

On January 18, 1917, Harold wrote, "Dear Mamma, Days roll by and sometimes I find myself wondering what, if anything, I am doing and accomplishing." As for Edith, "[she] is getting on her real feet every day—had not been to Dr. Jung for a long while—and is really independent more and more in spirit and in letter and gentle and tolerant of others and submissive and respective of the views of others, keeping her own individuality and strength at the same time."[66]

The war now occupied more and more of Harold and Edith's attention. Together they sponsored charities to help prisoners of war, and Edith became the secret patron of Irish writer and expatriate James Joyce. She provided him an anonymous monthly stipend that he picked up at a local Zurich bank. When he found out who his patron was, he came to the hotel to thank her. There is no record of their meeting, but Joyce later said she cut off her support when he refused to go into analysis with Jung or one of his disciples.

Harold felt that his marriage to Edith was blossoming as never before. "I must tell you in a word how lovely Edith is developing," he wrote to his mother on September 25. "*You would not know her.* All the lovely softness of her old attitude is returning with no loss of strength or firmness, but it is all so beautifully balanced. It is a charm to be with her. . . . Her time is beautifully spent and profitable to herself and others."[67]

Edith spent her time teaching others about analysis and philosophy and seeing her own patients. "I am teaching six hours a day besides my own studies," she told her father in November.[68] A year later, she informed him "I am so happy in my work, and go on generally from day to day, seeing very few people outside of those who come to me for their work."[69] Her new occupation as a psychoanalyst proved to fit in nicely with her agoraphobia: She never had to worry about leaving the hotel except for walks or club functions.

"New patients are coming to me all the time," Edith told her father in

March 1919, "and I have had some fifty cases now. I hear in a year twelve thousand dreams. This work is very concentrated and very different,—but so intensely interesting. It is so beautiful to see life and joy come into the eyes of those who have come to me so hopeless and seemingly lost!"[70]

In May 1918, Harold McCormick finally returned to the United States. His business had been threatened by the war and by his prolonged absence. By the end of 1918 he became president of the International Harvester Company. His life was consumed with business. There was no more time to analyze his dreams or read books by Nietzsche or about the Holy Grail. The most immediate historical consequence of Harold's return to America is that the paper trail ends. Edith rarely wrote letters, and the few she did were never very informative. What she did with her patients for the last three years of her life in Zurich is still a mystery.

With his wife and most of his family in Switzerland, and with no "analyzed people" to talk to in America, Harold felt quite lonely. Used to talking out his problems in Zurich, he had no one to turn to in Chicago. In June 1919, Emma Jung sent Harold a short letter telling him that she had recently seen Edith, which was unusual. After Harold returned to America no one seemed to see Edith except her patients. On Sunday, June 29, 1919, while with his mother at their Lake Forest estate, Harold wrote a rambling, nostalgic, depressed letter in which he poured out all his concerns and misgivings. It came to eighteen pages.[71] He never sent it, but it reveals that Harold was finding it difficult to cope without his usual support system.

Nettie McCormick was glad to have her son home, but she could not understand why Edith kept her grandchildren in Switzerland. Nettie cut out a newspaper article very critical of psychoanalysis entitled "Paralysis by Analysis" and sent it to Harold in August 1919. The author of the piece argued that this new technique of psychoanalysis made people worse, not better, because the incessant focusing of attention on one's inner thoughts and problems weakened their free will and rendered them incapable of making decisions for themselves. Harold was not pleased. "Radicals and zealots in all new movements go to extremes," he wrote back a few days later, "and in 'Analysis' we who believe in it are prone to go to extremes and make our paths difficult." Harold insisted that he, for one, was not paralyzed by analysis but indeed quite the opposite. "All the above means that I believe in *action* and *decision,* and if there is one thing that Dr. Jung does in his life, it is to decide things quickly, but for others this comes more painfully and more slowly until they have reached a certain point." The charges made in the article, Harold told her, are "not supported by the teachings of the school of psychoanalysis in Zurich."[72] Harold sent Nettie's letter and a copy of the article to Edith, Toni Wolff, Fowler, and Beatrice Hinkle. Hinkle told him not to expect too much from his mother. "You see," she wrote on September 26, "it is practically impossible for another person, no matter what their relation and how close the bond—indeed the closer the bond usually the more difficult, to understand what analysis really means to those of us who have experienced and thereby gained our knowledge."[73]

In the last week of September, a young woman by the name of Ganna Walska called on Harold while he was in New York City. She was young, vivacious, Polish, and claimed to have sung opera with Caruso in Cuba. Harold contacted the Chicago Opera Company and asked them to give her an audition. A friendship ensued. Harold was captivated by her.

To sort out his feelings, Harold went to Washington, D.C., in the first week of March 1920 to visit his cousin Medill McCormick, now a United States senator. The two men traded books by Freud and Jung, and Medill reminded him of Zurich and the lessons about life—and polygamy—Jung had taught them. He reminded Harold of the dangers of being too one-sided and of not heeding the primal call of life. On Senate stationery, Medill urged him to pursue "Your rediscovery of the joie de vivre."[74]

Harold's sexual affair with Ganna Walska began.

Meanwhile, in Zurich, Edith had formed an intimate bond of some sort with one of her Swiss patients, a gold digger and former gardener named Edwin Krenn. Younger than Edith, he claimed to have promise as an architect. Edith believed him and took him under her wing, convinced she could liberate his genius.

Mathilde and Muriel wrote anxious letters to their father, begging him to come to Zurich immediately. Harold put off his trip until late September 1920 and then only stayed for a month. Ganna Walska had become the most important person in his life. Harold told his father-in-law that he wanted to divorce Edith. In September 1921, Edith arrived in New York accompanied by Edwin Krenn. She went immediately to Pocantico Hills to meet with her older brother, John D. Rockefeller, Jr. But the word was not good: The Rockefeller men sided with Harold. The divorce went through in record time.

Edith did not see her father on this trip, and had not seen him since 1912. She never would again. On December 28, 1921, the marriage between the princess of Standard Oil and the prince of International Harvester was officially over. In August 1922, Harold married Ganna Walska in Paris. They were divorced in 1931. Harold married once more in his life, a brief but happy union with Adah Wilson from 1938 until his death in 1941.

Both daughters were soon married as well, as was Fowler. In 1931 he wed Mrs. Anne Urquhart ("Fifi") Stillman, who was nineteen years his senior, with four children from her previous marriage. She was the mother of one of Fowler's classmates at Princeton. He and Fifi never had children of their own. Fowler maintained his friendship with Jung and became one of his favorite traveling companions in the last forty years of Jung's life. When Jung came to America in 1925 he took an automobile trip to see the Grand Canyon and visit the Taos Indians in New Mexico. On this trip Jung taught Fowler how to use the divinatory device known as the *I Ching* and revealed that Toni Wolff had been his mistress for at least a decade.

Fowler McCormick rose through the ranks of his father's company and became chairman of the board in 1946. However, he was "asked" to resign in 1951 by the board. During this palace coup, he consulted the *I Ching* and kept detailed records of the advice of the oracle. In 1960, during one of his many summertime visits to Jung, he had his astrology chart done by Gret Bauman, Jung's daughter. Fowler died at seventy-five in Palm Desert, California, in January 1974.

As for Edith, soon after her arrival in America she returned to her "bastion" at 1000 Lake Shore Drive and emerged only to go on strolls through the grove of trees on her property, which she called the "bosky." She lived with her servants and Edwin Krenn. She continued to contribute to philanthropic organizations in Chicago and somehow built up a small private practice. She also held occasional séances and interpreted her patients' astrology charts. Her belief in reincarnation grew. After reading of the discovery of the tomb of King Tut, Edith began to tell her intimates that she was the reincarnation of Tutankhamen's child bride, the Princess Anknesenpaaten.

After she left Zurich, Edith's Swiss chauffeur sold his story to the *Schweizer Illustrierten*, a popular magazine that often ran celebrity gossip. It depicted Edith in a very unflattering light. "Her chauffeur liked to tell scandals about her," remembered Herman Müller, Jung's own chauffeur and gardener.[75] The story was reprinted many times over the years, including shortly after Edith's death.

In 1930, Edith had a mastectomy after a cancerous growth was discovered on one of her breasts. Two years later the cancer had spread to her liver. By then, almost broke, Edith had moved to a suite of rooms in the Drake Hotel in Chicago and waited to die. Her children all came to be near her, and even Harold made repeated visits. She died on August 25, 1932.

Harold, Fowler, John D. Rockefeller, Jr., and Edwin Krenn were among the pallbearers at her funeral. Harold, ever the feeling type, was sensitive to Krenn's intimacy with Edith and made sure he was included, even over the protests of Edith's brother. There is good reason to suspect that Harold and his brother-in-law immediately burned all her diaries and personal papers relating to her analysis. There was no need for further scandal.

From Switzerland, telegrams and letters poured in from Adolph Keller, then the president of the Zurich Psychological Club, Hans Trüb, and from other former acquaintances in the club. Harold received a touching four-page handwritten letter of sympathy from Emma Jung. "Hers seems a tragic fate . . . I feel great pity for her," she wrote, acknowledging that the period the McCormicks spent in Zurich marked an important period in her life.[76] Emma invited Harold to Küsnacht and mentioned that she and Jung had been vacationing at the Tower, where Jung remained after she'd left. What Emma did not mention to Harold was that Jung was not in the Tower alone.

And from the Tower the following one-line telegram had arrived for Harold from Edith's ex-analyst: "Thanks and warm sympathy for old times sake. Toni Wolff Dr Jung."[77]

ELEVEN

The Passion of Constance Long

Without a doubt, Constance Long was the most intellectually gifted of all the disciples who came to Jung after his break with Freud in January 1913. Her essays on dream interpretation, psychological types, the psychology of women, and child psychology all reveal a discriminating and independent mind that, unlike Jung's, tended toward analysis and not synthesis.[1] She always saw right to the heart of any theoretical matter. She was naturally attracted to highly detailed, hierarchical, and complex models of human experience, the more complex the better.

Unlike Fanny Bowditch Katz and Edith Rockefeller McCormick, she never spent more than two months in the rarefied atmosphere of the Jungian colony. As a result, she remained her own person and maintained an independent professional career, something those who remained in Switzerland found difficult to do. Still, Constance Long was one of Jung's first and most committed disciples in England.

At least until a new light captured her eye.

Like others who followed the Jungian path of analysis, Long recorded her struggles along the path in a book of colored paintings and drawings of images from her dreams and visions. She rarely encountered Jung in person, however, nor did her transformations take place in his domain. He was a burning star on her horizon for most of the years she devoted to him, maintaining the flame at a distance, sending spiritually inspiring letters to her. His words were magical, a healing balm, a ray of hope in a fallen world. He explicitly offered gnosis—true mystical knowledge—and promised to lead her to the home of the soul, which he insisted could only be reached through the call of one's blood and one's soil. And he promised spiritual insemination so that she could become pregnant with the spirit and give birth to the divine child-god who would save humanity.

But then something happened to change Constance Long's mind about Jung. Her diary reveals a story that has never been told and allows us to see, through her eyes, her painful transformation from believer to apostate.

Overcomings

Constance Ellen Long was born into a large family near Reading, England, in 1870. She was a petite woman, quick, birdlike, delicate. Throughout her childhood, she always seemed too thin and too prone to illness. But she was intellectually curious and alive and overcame her physical limitations to excel scholastically. After leaving school she worked as an art teacher in the School of Science and Art in South Kensington. Long was always a quietly religious person, inward, a compassionate woman whose one goal in life was, like Kundry's, "to serve." The British Empire had expanded deep into Africa during her youth and, like many young women and men, she dreamed of a career as a missionary to help those who could not help themselves. Around the age of twenty-three, she decided that the best way to do this would be as a medical missionary. And so, with her excellent academic record and obvious drive, she was immediately accepted into the London School of Medicine for Women.

In 1896, she earned both her L.S.A. (licensed surgical assistant) and medical degrees, but she was turned down for foreign missionary work because of her lack of physical vigor. In a career move typical for female physicians, Long became a resident medical officer in a maternity home. She later secured a post as resident medical officer at an orphanage in Hawkhurst, Kent. Here, Long finally found the confidence in herself as a novice physician that she had hoped for.

A sudden diphtheria outbreak in Hawkhurst threatened to kill dozens of people. Among the children she cared for there were forty cases within the first few days of the epidemic. Given the state of medical knowledge and the lack of antibiotics and vaccines, there was a good chance that all of the children would die within the week. As a recent medical-school graduate and a voracious reader of medical journals, Long knew of a new experimental "antitoxin" that was just coming into general use. She immediately ordered a large supply of the drug and began administering it as rapidly as she could. She did not lose a single child.

That the public perceived her as a hero helped her set up her own practice as a general practitioner. Long built up a highly successful practice in Crouch End, primarily among women and their children. She was a surgical clinical assistant at various hospitals and, for two years in a row, was president of the Association of Registered Medical Women. In the first decade of the twentieth century, Constance Long was one of the most prominent physicians in the British Empire. She became known as an effective instructor in courses on first aid, home nursing, and child care. But soon enough she developed an interest in psychotherapy that eventually turned into an obsession with psychoanalysis.

In 1913, she met C. G. Jung.

The new age

On October 30, 1913, under the stewardship of the Welshman Ernest Jones, the London Psycho-Analytic Society was formed with nine members; Constance Long was one of them. Jones had recently returned from several years of itinerant training in psychoanalysis at the hands of C. G. Jung, Otto Gross, Sandor Ferenczi, and Sigmund Freud. Freud was initially put off by Jones's fanatical attitude toward psychoanalysis and by the additional fact that he was not Jewish. "He is a Celt and consequently not quite acceptable to us," Freud wrote to Karl Abraham on May 3, 1908, but optimistically viewed this as a sign that "psychoanalysis escaped the danger of becoming a Jewish national affair."[2] But Jones won over the Viennese, perfecting his German and siding with them against Jung and his Swiss contingent. Convinced of Jones's loyalty after the breakdown of his personal relations with Jung, Freud anointed him to spread the gospel of psychoanalysis throughout the British Empire.

Jones didn't realize that his job was made easier by a feeling of cultural liberation in England; certain members of the cultural elite had already expressed an interest in psychoanalysis. With the death of Kind Edward VII in 1910, A. R. Orage, the creator and editor of *The New Age,* the premiere literary and cultural journal of the period, proclaimed that the new age had indeed arrived. "The last genuine link with the Victorian age has been broken with the death of King Edward VII," who was "spiritually the mere executor of Queen Victoria," Orage wrote in May 1910.[3]

The editions of *The New Age* that appeared between 1911 and 1914 reflect the changing interests of the London intelligentsia. Orage had been an ardent non-Marxist socialist and had written books on Nietzsche, but in the pages of *The New Age* Nietzsche was dethroned in favor of the vitalistic philosophy of Henri Bergson. Russian culture, particularly its music, ballet, and occultism, was of great interest. And, beginning in 1912 with what was probably the first discussion of the work of Sigmund Freud in a popular English journal, psychoanalysis became an increasingly important focus of discussion.

The first of Freud's books to be published in England, *The Interpretation of Dreams,* appeared in 1913. However, according to a publisher's note, circulation of A. A. Brill's translation was limited to "Members of the Medical, Scholastic, Legal and Clerical professions." As a physician, Constance Long may have been among the select few to have access to the book. (M. D. Eder's translation, *On Dreams,* was published for the general public the following year.)[4]

We do not know when Constance Long first became attracted to Jung and his ideas. He was in London in August 1913 to deliver papers on analytical psychology to the Psycho-Medical Society (of which Long was a member) and at the Seventeenth International Congress of Medicine. In his lecture to the Psycho-Medical Society on August 5, he spoke a great deal about the techniques of dream interpretation and the "metaphysical need" of human beings. He told his audience that psychological health depended on the adoption of a "religious or philosophical attitude," which is necessary if human beings are to "do creative work for the benefit of a future age" and, if necessary, to "sacrifice themselves for the welfare of the species."[5] Motivated by her religious longing to devote herself to humanitarian causes (as Maria Moltzer did with temperance work), Long could not help but be seduced by the hints Jung dropped of his vision of analytical psychology as a mission of world redemption.

"Constance Long, a virgin of 40"

In November 1913, Constance Long went to Zurich. Her friends David and Edith Eder had both had analytic sessions with Jung and spoke highly of his methods. These were the days when Jung began to flirt openly with the promise of spiritual rebirth that analysis could bring. In public, though, he stuck close to familiar Christian metaphors and avoided pagan ones. Outside of German-speaking Europe, he even avoided his usual allusions to Wagner and *Parsifal.* For those like Long who had been attracted to psychoanalysis as a method of healing sick souls, Jung seemed to be dispensing all the right metaphors of renewal and rebirth and in the right measure. He didn't scare anyone off with hints of neopaganism. Jung was struggling at that time with the difficult case of Fanny Bowditch and trying to prevent James Jackson Putnam from defecting to the Freudian camp. Like Fanny and Edith Rockefeller McCormick, Constance Long saw Jung as he approached his apotheosis.

On November 19, Ernest Jones wrote Freud about Long's trip. "It is a pity, this member of yours is going to Z[urich] for analysis," Freud lamented in his response. "He will be lost to you."[6] Jones wrote back, "Our member who goes to Jung is a woman, Constance Long, a virgin of 40, hence in any case not too hopeful."[7]

Whether Long was a virgin is unknown, but it is true that throughout her life she felt bottled up, incapable of really relaxing enough to feel the full flowering of love for another person except in the most abstract form. She never married. As she became more involved in the propagation of Jung's ideas, she met women with whom she could establish close friendships. During her visits to Switzerland she met Beatrice Hinkle, who became quite dear to Long in the last eight years of her life.[8] By 1915, Hinkle had lost one husband to death and one to divorce and had raised two children on her own. One of them, Consuela, was on the periphery of Jungian circles in Europe in the 1920s. Even though Long was a few years older, Hinkle was more experienced in matters of love and sex and related to her as an older sister and protector.

It is no wonder they became such good friends. In many ways their extraordinary, pioneering professional careers paralleled one another. Beatrice Moses was born in San Francisco and married that city's assistant district attorney, Walter Scot Hinkle, in 1892. Following in the footsteps of her father, Dr. B. Frederick Moses, she became the first female graduate of the Cooper (now Stanford) Medical School in 1899. Her husband died earlier that year, and she faced the prospect of supporting their two children. She was offered the position of San Francisco city physician and was the first female public-health doctor in the United States. Her interest in the psychology of suggestion and psychotherapy was awakened during the California bubonic-plague epidemic of 1899 to 1903, when she noticed the great variability of psychological responses to the same infection. In 1905, she moved to New York City, where, with Charles Dana, she established one of the first medical psychotherapy clinics in the United States, at the Cornell Medical College. She studied yoga, hypnotism, and books on psychoanalysis and went to Switzerland in 1911 for analysis with Jung. Her initial analysis still had strong Freudian elements, but she was attracted to his spiritual attitude toward life and the marked similarity between Henri Bergson's élan vital and Jung's new, broader, vitalistic concept of the libido.[9] She spent time with Jung intermittently until 1915, after which she went her own way intellectually and professionally.

Socialized into the Jungian worldview before the heady days of 1916, neither Hinkle nor Long developed the extreme one-sided mystical element in their professional work that Jung and his other apostles seemed to nurture. "The crippling kind of mysticism leads man away from earth to regions of the imagination," Long said in one essay, "whereupon common life loses its interest and intensity." For responsible physicians and thinking persons, the more reliable path seemed to be "enlightened mysticism" that "leads us to develop the precious faculties lying dormant in the unconscious, and to enrich our mundane existence by using those psychic powers of visions and perception which carry the profound conviction that the 'kingdom of heaven is within.'"[10] While appreciating Jung's recognition of the value of spirituality and a religious attitude in a mentally healthy life, neither of them believed they were forming a new pagan religion to replace Judeo-Christian orthodoxies quite as Maria Moltzer did, for example.

In January and early February 1914, Long returned to Switzerland for five weeks of analysis with Jung, which she told Ernest Jones she "greatly enjoyed."[11] Jung made England his most frequent foreign destination in the years following his break with Freud, and for a week in late July 1914 he stayed at Long's home in London. Jung was fighting a colonial war with Freud and he didn't want to lose the British empire. He also knew that England was his gateway to America. His books published in England would eventually make it to America and vice versa. He hoped analytical psychology would prevail over psychoanalysis in the English-speaking world.

Long saw as her mission the introduction of Jungian ideas into America and the British Empire. During Jung's 1914 visit, plans were finalized for Long to supervise the translation of a representative selection of Jung's clinical papers and bring them out in book form. With David Eder's translation of Freud's *On Dreams* arousing public interest, Long and others wanted to do the same for Jung. At that time, Beatrice Hinkle was busily translating Jung's 1912 *Wandlungen und Symbole der Libido* into English. By the beginning of 1916 it appeared in America under the title *Psychology of the Unconscious*.[12] With the help of the Eders and Dora Hecht, Long completed *Collected Papers on Analytical Psychology*, and, backed by Edith Rockefeller McCormick's money, it was in print by February 1916.[13]

In August 1914, war had broken out. Other than a few of her talks that were published, we have no real knowledge of Long's activities during the war years, but we do know that the war convinced her more than ever that the world needed Jung and his ideas. For her, he offered hope for the salvation of humanity. When the war was finally over, she and Jung's disciples would lead others into a new, higher, more exalted state of consciousness. Only those chosen few whose insights had been given to them personally by Jung would be able to do this. She was one of them. And she wanted to do as much as she could to bring about this great spiritual awakening.

In the preface to *Collected Papers on Analytical Psychology*, she wrote:

> Those who read this book with the attention it requires, will find they gain an impression of many new truths. It is issued . . . at a time when much we had valued and held sacred is in the melting-pot. But we believe that out of the crucible, new forms will arise. The study of Psycho-Analysis produces something of the effect of a war in the psyche; indeed we need to make conscious this war in the inner things if we would be delivered in the future from the war in the external world, either in the form of individual or international neurosis. In the pain and the upheaval, one recognizes the birth-pangs of a newer, and let us hope, truer thought, and more natural adaptations. We need a new philosophy of life to take the place of that which has perished in the general cataclysm, and it is because I see in the analytical psychology which grows out of a scientific study of the Unconscious, the germs of a new construction, that I have gathered the following essays together.[14]

The diary

Jung did not return to England until July 1919, after he had been released from the yearly interruptions of military service. Despite the war, these had been his most intellectually fertile years. By 1919 he had developed the structure of his final theory of personality types with its two attitudes (extraversion and introversion) and its four functions (thinking, feeling, sensation, intuition). He had invented the terms "collective unconscious," "persona," "shadow," "anima," and "animus." Like Jung's type theory, the latter three concepts would be mentioned in print in later years only as "archetypes." The previous year, while on military duty, Jung drew a mandala every day and realized that it was a symbol of wholeness, completeness, of God as the sun. Later it was thought of as the archetype of archetypes, the image of the grand container of all the gods, the symbol of the microcosm (the whole, individuated personality) that mirrors the macrocosm (God). In

1928, he referred to this god within as the self (following theological form, many Jungians still capitalize "self" to indicate divinity).

Constance Long's diary documents that all these terms were already in use by Jung by the summer of 1919.[15] Perplexingly, one month before Jung's arrival in London, Long made detailed references to his new, more complex theory of personality types and tried to grasp its internal structure with compasslike graphs and other illustrations. She had clearly received instruction in Jung's new theory before his arrival, but where and from whom? She does not say.

The initials MKB appear throughout the diary from the first pages until the last. Many references to MKB identify this person as female. For most of the diary, MKB shares Long's heart only with Jung. Who MKB may have been remains a mystery. There are many with the initials "MB" in Long's circle of friends (including Dr. Mary Bell, who analyzed along Jungian lines), but none whose middle initial begins with K. Connie Long seems to have been in love with MKB.

In June 1919, Long confessed, "MKB's anger with me because 'You cannot accept anything or any authority but J.' " Was she referring to Jung here? It is not clear.

One clue to MKB's identity is that she wrote, or was writing, a book. Long had a dream of three books and attempted the following analysis of its elements:

AJ's paper   Jung's book
MKB book   My own
          Jealousy

12.6.19 Dream [ ] Two books—his—MKB—and a third book = mine. My last paper. The conflict I have over writing . . .

Health. Introverted feeling. Depreciation.

Introverted feeling was an element of Jung's new psychological typology. Two pages later, Long returned to the theme of MKB and her own difficulty in writing. "Perhaps," Long said, "some of my resistance to MKB's book lies in the fact that I want to write a book, but I am not sure that I have a single original idea."

Long seems to have kept a separate dream book in which she more fully elaborated her dreams, keeping her diary for association and personal references. Her entries suggest she was working analytically with someone in June 1919 who had training in Jung's new theories and was now imparting them to her. The evidence suggests it was not Jung himself, but it was clearly someone who was close to him and the goings-on in his circle in Switzerland.

On several pages Long made tiny mandala drawings over the crease at the top of two adjoining leaves. Who taught her this? Below the mandala and an odd sketch of two rectangular beams intersecting, she wrote, mysteriously, what seem to be abbreviated interpretations by someone else: "The soul the family demand the [ ] things the past. Doing something for the soul. You might work with tools. When you handle the tools, you might attract the family spirit." Whatever is going on here, there are certainly references that invoke images of ancestors and the idea that the ancestors form the collective soul, to put it in Jung's terms during this period.

On the pages between the entries for June 12 and 16 are pencil sketches of a circle bisected vertically with a line. The left side of the diagram, beyond the circle, represents "external reality" and the corresponding left interior of the circle has a symbol for "female" and is labeled "persona." In Jungian terms, the persona is a mask—literally—that the conscious ego wears as its personal identity. As a woman, Long's ego identity is female. To the right of the circle is the abbreviation "Int. Obj. Unc." for the "internal objects" of the "unconscious mind." In accordance with Jungian theory, it is represented by the opposite sex, the "not-I," which for her is male. There is a corresponding symbol for male commonly used in medical shorthand. The right half of the circle—the opposite of the persona—is labeled "soul." Inside this right, unconscious half of Long's personality, are four strange symbols. The uppermost is labeled the "Upper Hermaphroditic God" and the lower the "Lower Hermaphroditic God." The elements of the picture are designated 1 for persona, 2 for soul, 3 for upper hermaphroditic god, and 4 for lower hermaphroditic god. Taken as a whole, this illustration is a representation of the individual human personality in its conscious and unconscious components.

Just what Jung and his disciples meant by the upper and lower hermaphroditic gods of the unconscious is anyone's guess. The last entries of Fanny Bowditch Katz's diaries were concerned with her descent into a "grotto" and a hermaphrodite who appears there. Here the hermaphrodite appears as a concern of Constance Long. It may have represented psychological wholeness or completeness as a counterpart to the fact that even humans have contrabiological elements. It is a symbol that Jung found again and again in alchemical texts when studying them in the late 1920s.

Long was clearly receiving instruction here. And the next lesson was on how to become a god.

On the page facing the graph of Jung's notion of the psyche, Long wrote: "When one is adapted to the unconscious by the pain of opposites—

and is god-like. Miss Moltzer is at 3 and 4. The hermaph above and the hermaphrodite below. It is only permitted to the god or gods to be hermaph. You need to be female."

It appears that Long may have viewed Moltzer as godlike, as a synthesis of the upper and lower hermaphroditic gods in her unconscious. Long, however, must remain simply female. The cross on which one may suffer the "pain of opposites" is also sketched on this same page:

```
                    coldness
                    intuition
                       N



death
sexuality    W                   E    [ ] madness
rebirth                               thinking



                       S
                    passion
```

No explanation of this compass chart of the soul appears in the diary.

Other references indicate that Long was struggling to learn the new theory and its practical application. Her entries for June 16 are a bit more legible and reveal, once again, the religious nature of Jung's practice of psychotherapy and a Volkish fascination with ancestral tendencies in the soul:

16.6.19 [ ] about the friend in the soul. If [ ] be the friend and the soul. The soul is to the unc. [unconscious] what the persona is to the consc. [conscious mind]. When you identify with the soul you project because it is uncon. We always project the unc. contents.

16.6 19 The dream of June 5. It is an attitude of devotion. She cuts herself off from the world to worship the god. [ ] The family tendencies have much to do with the soul. The only tool I want to handle is the pen—this I use to write—[ ] etc. and don't keep enough libido to myself. My attempt at unc. last night was "dead wrong." It was far too conscious—when it had to do with repression.

This entry is accompanied by one of her signature drawings of a tree that has human-like and animal-like faces emerging out of its bark. She named the drawing on this page "Tree spirit," and wrote beneath it, "The rain—the rain—the rain. [ ] The spirit falls. The spirit that part of the Col

Unc [collective unconscious] that feels alive to con [consciousness]—I should not be [ ] the spirit become 'word' logos."

A woman emerges from these fragments, a woman who is trying very, very hard to understand herself and her place in life, an introverted woman with health concerns who fears that she isn't good enough to write anything original. She is a woman who seeks love but does not receive it, turning her libido instead toward pursuing the promise of a better life that Jung offered to all his disciples.

The day the archetypes were born

In 1917, Constance Long brought out a second edition of *Collected Papers on Analytical Psychology*. For the first time, the anthology included the essay written by Jung in 1916 but published in German in 1917 in which he introduced the "dominants" as the "gods" of the unconscious.[16] By July 1919, when Jung was once again in England, these gods would become the archetypes.

Long was with Jung when the term "archetype" was introduced to the world. By this point she and the other Jungian-oriented analysts no longer participated in the London Psycho-Analytic Society with Ernest Jones and his cronies. (David Eder was the exception.) The Jungians were on their own, but without an official society. Jung favored Long's friend (and, possibly, occasional analyst) Maurice Nicoll as the leader of the British group. However, it was Helton Godwin ("Peter") Baynes who became Jung's first official assistant and heir apparent.[17] Baynes was a big, blustery extravert who was fond of sports and wives (he had at least four of the latter within the time he knew Jung). He had served as a medical officer during the First World War in the Balkans and in India. Jung liked him immensely and took him under his wing in Zurich. After a while, once Baynes learned enough German, he adopted Jung's physical gestures and mannerisms of speech.

Jung gave three lectures in London that July. He delivered "On the Problem of Psychogenesis" to the Royal Society of Medicine, "The Psychological Foundation of a Belief in Spirits" to the Society for Psychical Research, and, the most historic of the three, "Instinct and the Unconscious" for a symposium on instinct and the unconscious.[18] During the last of these lectures Jung introduced the term "archetype."

Constance Long was in the audience and made notes of Jung's remarks during the discussion that followed. Although it isn't clear from the published versions of Jung's lectures, his off-the-cuff remarks reveal that he thought of the archetypes as combining the prophetic or prospective function of the unconscious mind, its precognitive function, with "racial memories." Here is Long's summary of Jung's remarks: "12.7.19 The Symposium discussion: The coll.[ective] unc.[onscious] is a psychological state; it is that which is unconscious in everybody. On the one side there is the [ ] of racial memories, on the other side images preparing our psychological future. I am sure 'time' and 'space' depend on archetypes. All our concepts are mythological images. All our impulses are instincts."

"Experience—fun—vanity—'the opportunity' "

The experience of the First World War challenged women in ways that had been unthinkable before August 1914. Women were thrust into societal roles traditionally reserved for men. Conventional notions of masculine and feminine no longer held in many areas of life. After the war, in 1919, female physicians—many of them in the forefront of the women's movement—convened a six-week conference to share experiences and propose solutions to some of the pervasive problems created by the war.

From September 15 until October 24, 1919, the International Conference of Women Physicians was held at the headquarters of the YWCA in New York City. Every woman physician in the United States and Canada was invited, as well as about thirty women from foreign countries. Only three physicians were invited from England. Constance Long was one of them.

When Long was invited, she didn't know whether to go and decided to analyze her dreams and mental imagery to see what her unconscious mind told her about the future. She relied on the prophetic function of her dreams, just as Fanny Bowditch had in 1913 to decide whether she should visit America or not. In her diary for August 16, 1919, Long wrote:

> I'm dubious about N. York—
> *Things against*—hot weather—noise—expensive—exhaustion
> *For*—experience—fun—vanity—"the opportunity"
> The desired unc.[onscious] material was as follows:
> *Hypnagogic: Putting up a frieze rail in one of my small rooms* (Gordon Square) *it was too high. A little man sits on a narrow shelf* opposite at same height as *frieze rail* and looks at it critically.
> *Dream: There was a beaten track into some ripe corn (a small very prolific field) and something that paid for the corn—and had to be carried to the other side.*

The conference was a major event in the history of the women's movement in the early twentieth century. And, as we shall see, it also proved to be a defining moment for the future of the Jungian movement in the United States. The conference and its dozens of programs were divided into three general topic areas: "The Woman Physician and the Health of Women," "The Presentation of the Practical Program for Meeting the Needs of Girls in the Light of a Better Understanding of Their Emotional Life," and "The Present Social Conditions and Their Effect on Health and Personality." It was in this final section that one lecture by Constance Long and two by Beatrice Hinkle were given.

Both Hinkle and Long found Jung's theory of psychological types to be one of his most valuable contributions to the world. His insight that human beings had problems relating to one another because they saw the world differently depending on their types—introverted or extraverted— became a major point of departure for their work. Both women were also intrigued by the idea that men had a female component to their psychology—the anima—and women had a male component—the animus. Both women proposed that psychological hermaphroditism or androgyny, the integration of one's contrabiological psychological components, was the true goal of psychotherapy. Not only would an inner wholeness or completeness result in the individual, but—in the best of all possible worlds—the relationship between the sexes would improve. As both Hinkle and Long were women who excelled in a man's world, they certainly recognized the so-called masculine components in their own psyches (intellect, ambition, drive, and so on) and wanted to help other women be aware of them as well.

Beatrice Hinkle gave lectures on "Personality and Will in Light of the New Psychology" and on "Arbitrary Use of the Terms Masculine and Feminine." Constance Long delivered a lecture on what we now know was a very relevant personal topic: "Sex as a Basis of Character." It was an eloquently argued and compassionately constructed explanation of the universal presence of autoerotism in its various forms and of the essential bisexual nature of all human beings. Above all, it is a plea for an empathetic understanding of the nature of homosexual love.

She began by making a case for the important and unrecognized role that the unconscious mind plays in everyday actions. Her next step in outlining the basis of human character was to address the "bi-sexuality or hermaphroditic character of the human being." "There is no excessively masculine man or exclusively feminine woman," Long explained. "Each bears traces of the other sex, not only physiologically, but psychologically. The importance of this well-known fact is not sufficiently realised."[19] "In mature life," each sex does under certain conditions display what are somewhat arbitrarily distinguished as qualities belonging to the opposite sex. Under war conditions this capacity is an asset of extraordinary value."[20] Libido is freed up from neurotic constraints, and there is more zest "for the performance of each other's relegated task."

Facing an audience of women who as physicians had confronted the destructive effects of war firsthand, Long then invoked the horrors all of them had seen, as well as the unforeseen positive effects of the war:

> The European War has had the effect of separating men and women and massing together those of one sex. It has produced tremendous emotional problems of every sort. It has torn youthful civilians from home and normal conditions of life, and placed them under conditions where the ordinary moral notions are entirely reversed. Living through months of segregation as in camps, barracks, on ships, and on expeditions, is not a new thing, but it is accentuated by being experienced on such a huge scale. We have already a few obvious legacies from these cataclysmic times. There is a mass of venereal disease, a great outbreak of hysteria and other psychoneuroses among men, and not least there is a shortage of some ten million men in Europe. At such times homo-sexuality is bound to make its appearance as a problem for humanity.
>
> Something else has been happening. Women have been obliged willy-nilly to do men's work in engine yards, in munitions factories, on the land—in every field in fact of industrial and professional life. Something male in a woman's psychology has been called for, and we have seen there is a latent sex-element which enables her to respond. . . .
>
> If homo-sexuality crops up at such a time, as my foregoing remarks show, its existence is not new. Perhaps the necessity to accept and consider it as one of the problems of our times is new. Franker discussion of all sex problems has made it possible to consider it here today. . . .
>
> The homo-sexual tendency may become "fixed," because in the absence of personal effort and development, it is the easiest sexual expression life offers to a given individual. It arises as we have seen out of unnatural conditions such as the segregation of the sexes,—or out of the economic difficulties in the way of marriage. Among women, whose numbers considerably surpass those of men, there is an arithmetical reason for it in the impossibility of marriage. . . .
>
> My experience as a physician leads me to believe that the emotional problems of the married are no more or less severe than those of the unmarried, and that both men and women have much the same sexual problems, and are in a similar relation to them. Friendship, which we all like to think is untroubled by sex, is often wrecked upon it, and that most often where the sex element remains unconscious.[21]

At this conference Long met three women—two American and one English—who were to be the founding mothers of the Jungian movement in the United States. Although Beatrice Hinkle had been the first of Jung's analysands to practice in New York and did much to help found an Analytical Psychology Club there, she was no proselytizer for Jung, and she was so different from the others that she kept her distance from them. She taught at Cornell Medical College and operated her own private sanitarium in Connecticut. Her adaptation to the demands of external reality proved to be better than that of the others. For another, Hinkle was heterosexual.

The first of the Americans that Long met was Kristine Mann, who was brought up in a Swedenborgian household with a keen belief in spiritualism. Before becoming a physician, she had taught English at Vassar College. At Vassar she befriended one of her pupils, Eleanor Bertine, the second member of the group. Bertine became a physician and an activist for women's rights. After the 1919 conference, Bertine accompanied Long back to England to undergo analysis with her, but Long became gravely ill, and she urged Bertine to go on to Zurich. The third member was a native of Shropshire, England. Mary Esther Harding was an internist who turned to a career as a Jungian psychoanalyst. She went to Zurich in 1922.

At home again in London in late October, Long was immediately taken ill with intestinal pain. Nevertheless, she visited friends, including Joan Corrie, another disciple of Jung.[22] After a good start, she was suddenly doubled over with pain and had to be placed in a bed. "J C took me in an ambulance." Upon reaching the hospital she lay perfectly still, and this seemed to help keep the pain away. She was fearful and anxious. The problem turned out to be gallstones that had to be removed surgically. She was back in her home on November 8, answering her mail and regaining her strength.

"The child is a new god, actually born in many individuals, but they don't know it"

Recuperating, Long was visited frequently by her friends, including Joan Corrie. Like Long, Corrie was unmarried and enjoyed directing her energy to various causes. Long probably introduced her to Jung. During the first week of January 1920, Corrie brought Long a letter that Jung had sent her. Still weak from her surgery, Long was so taken with it that she transcribed it into her own diary. Corrie had sent Jung some dreams to analyze and had expressed regret that she had canceled her plans to go to Zurich to undergo treatment. Jung attempted to cheer her up and inspire her to continue the work on her soul where she was.

According to Long, Jung's remarkable letter was filled with spiritualized eroticism and more than just a touch of Gnostic philosophy. It gave Long hope to go on with life. According to her, Jung wrote the following:

> The center of oneself is not necessarily conscious ego. It is something much greater.
>
> [Jung then addresses Corrie's cancellation of her trip to Zurich]
>
> You have the necessary thing: the god is living in you. But you need more introversion (2nd dream) in order to perceive his voice. It is one small voice of a little child, yet powerful and full of wisdom. The child comes out of nowhere, it has not existed before until it has been generated out of one everywhere, where it has been hidden as a dismembered and dispersed god. This child in its infinite smallness is your individuality, and with practice, it is a god—smaller than small yet greater than great. The primordial creator of the world, the blind creative libido, becomes transformed in man through individuation and out of this process which is like pregnancy, arises the divine child, a reborn god, no longer more dispersed into the millions of creatures but being one and this individual, and at the same time all individuals, the same in you as in me.
>
> Dr. L[ong] has a little book: VII Sermones Ad Mortuous. There you find the description of the creator dispersed into his creatures, and in the very last sermon you find the beginning of individuation, out of which, the divine child arises.
>
> Please do not speak of these things to other people. It could do harm to the child. The child is fate and *amor fati* [the love of fate] and guidance and necessity and peace and fulfillment (Isa[iah]. 9.6). But don't allow yourself to be dispersed into people and opinions and discussions. The child is a new god, actually born in many individuals, but they don't know it. He is a "spiritual" god. A spirit in many people, yet one and the same everywhere. Keep in your [ ] and you will experience these qualities.

This letter is unlike any other by Jung ever published. He is attempting to initiate a disciple into his own *mysteria* and even swears her to secrecy. This letter is the first on record in which Jung gives an interpretation of his "Seven Sermons to the Dead." The "blind creative libido" is, of course, Abraxas.[23]

If there was ever any doubt that Jung was quite self-consciously the charismatic leader of his own mystery cult, this private letter to his disciple should dispel it. Jung considered himself a heresiarch of the first order, a redeemer who offered redemption to others so that they, too, could be involved in the grand work of bringing to life the new god that was trapped within everyone, waiting to be released.

This letter also demonstrates the many levels of Jung, the many masks he wore depending on his degree of intimacy with his correspondent. In these early years he never dared deliver a lecture using the language he employed in this letter. In his writings, he began to sound like this only in his books on alchemy. Peter Baynes, who became Jung's mouthpiece in England in 1923, gave a "public" interpretation of Jung's Gnostic heresy without the explicit proselytizing in which Jung indulged in private. There is no mention of a collective participation in the creation or redemption of a new god or of its sparks buried in each individual.[24]

Long was now forty-nine years old, ill, and often alone. She needed her spiritual beliefs more than ever. She ached for rejuvenation, for rebirth. Despite her anger at Jung for we don't know what, his beautiful letter erased all bad feelings. She felt the rush of religious conversion once again. Below where she copied Jung's letter in her diary, she wrote: "The letter began by saying he has to participate in a scientific work of great importance for my country—the enterprise has to remain secret for a long time. It is so important I could not hesitate for a moment to sacrifice my practice and devote myself to the new task. Our times are so confused and so full of [ ] possibilities that everyone in his place must devote himself to the upbuilding of social health."

If, in fact, Jung did write that he was engaged in a secret project of great importance for England, it could only have been his personal goal of converting as many of the British as possible to the cultivation of the new god. He had recognized his own divinity as the Aryan Christ and he wanted to redeem other Aryans as well. Despite the war, most Germans considered the English to be racially similar, true keepers of the Aryan flame.

But one thing is clear. Jung here was also using Volkish ideas about liberating the German god within so as to make one powerful race of spiritually superior human beings. Such imagery blends easily with his corruption of some of the ideas of the Hellenistic Gnostics about the divine essence being trapped in matter, and that to release the god a process of redemption must take place. Once the dispersed divine essence is released, it can rejoin itself and achieve a primordial unity.

Jung's genius for syncretism hid the elements of his worldview that emerged out of his German blood and soil. During this period, Jung used the metaphors of the Gnostics but fused them with frequent references to the importance of one's "blood" (race) and the ancestral soul made up of one's ancestors in the Land of the Dead.

With the participation of the collective, the god of the *Volk* awakes.

"I lack my love, my love I lack"

Long's recent reminder of her own mortality and her renewed enthusiasm for Jung provided her with a new direction. To show her appreciation to Jung, and to bring him back to England as soon as possible, she organized a private seminar in the autumn of 1920 to be attended only by an intimate few. She wanted to experience the Jung who spoke so directly to her heart in the wonderful spiritual messages he sent to her and Joan Corrie. She wanted to get beyond the professorial mask that Jung had shown in his previous public presentation in London. In preparation, she began her struggle with German in the privately printed edition (1916) of "Seven Sermons to the Dead." She so desperately wanted to understand.

Her renewed enthusiasm for Jung may have snowballed into her obsessive feeling that she was in love with him. It happened with all of his female disciples sooner or later, as he often told them at the beginning of their treatment. But, alas, this was unrequited love. In a poem written at the time, the object of her affection is clearly male—the first time this appears in her diary. If MKB—the usual focus of her passion—is in fact male, this love poem is the only evidence of it. Perhaps another way to read her poem is as an expression of her unrequited love for her master, Jung, whom she shares with her local intimate, MKB. But whoever "he" may be in this poem, Long felt that he underestimated the depth of her soul. The introverted, reserved, cool, and detached mask of the self-possessed thinker falls away to reveal the passion of Constance Long:

> *A Day in Woods—letter for MKB*
> ....
> I lack my love, my love I lack
> And voice of bird, and flash of blue
> And stir of trees in sunswept air
> Within my chilled heart spread despair!
> ....
> He does not really seem to care
> Although he creaks and groans like doors.
> He feeds on a different kind of dole
> Which comes from his superior soul.
> For mine "a little thing" it is
> And "little things" have "little pain"
> The worst thing is he thinks he knows
> The depth and height of all my woes
> What care I for any man
> To live alone is all my plan.

At last, in late September, Jung arrived at the Sennen Cove Hotel in Cornwall with his wife, Emma. The seminar began on September 24. There were twelve participants in all, including Jung and Emma, Hinkle and Long, Esther Harding and Eleanor Bertine, Peter Baynes and Maurice Nicoll. We can guess that Joan Corrie may have been there, and perhaps James Young, a physician, and Dr. Mary Bell, Harding's analyst. This would account for eleven of the twelve. The identity of the twelfth participant is still a mystery.

No detailed notes of the program exist, not even in Long's diaries. It is clear that she had analytic sessions with Jung, in one instance bringing him a dream she had had weeks before his arrival. This was a dream of September 2 that contained something, some symbol perhaps, that Jung said was "Abraxas." The focus of the seminar was to be the text of a book called *Authentic Dreams of Peter Blobbs,* but it is clear that they were to do much more. Indeed, the Holy Grail and *Parsifal* seem to have been the focus of discussion at this convocation of the Secret Church. Long records only the following schedule:

24 Sept	Talk on Parsifal by Mrs Jung
28th	Seminar and analysis of dream of worm in the head
pm	Talk on Parsifal symbolism

Oddly, given her reconversion to discipleship, very little about Jung appears in her comments. Her focus was strictly on her dreams and her association to them, and she relied on either Emma or C. G. Jung for help. The influence of the Swiss Germans is apparent in the nature of the associations Long gave to her dreams while she was in Sennen Cove. On October 3, she recorded a "phantasy" that involved a "gold ring—symbol of transcendent function." Here again Wagnerian elements were used by Jung to get across the main points of his new religious outlook. The gold ring is of course the "Ring of the Nibelungs" that is the focus of the quest by Nibelungs, mortals, and gods in Wagner's four-part Ring Cycle of operas. Long's notes to her dreams and fantasy material that follow refer again to "Abraxas," the "transcendent function," "Philemon," the Egyptian idea of the "Ka soul" and even Zarathustra. Above all, however, there are many references to the animus, and it is apparent that Long was trying to understand this concept as it applied to herself, speaking at one point of "analysis of the animus."

She and Hinkle shared practical information relating to their psychotherapy practices. Hinkle brought a copy of her standard interview form that she filled out during the first session with every new patient. Long copied it into her diary as "Dr. Hinkle's Form." Interestingly, not only is heredity a consideration (standard for that time), but Hinkle included a space for an assessment of psychological type.

Somewhere, somehow, Long had become acquainted with Rudy and Fanny Katz. On the sixth of December, they visited her on their return after several months in America. She admired Rudy and maintained a correspondence with him. Sometimes she would bare her soul to him in her letters, and he would give her advice, often, ironically, about love.

"Tremendous death phantasies overcome me"

Nineteen twenty-one became a year of disillusionment and conflict for Long.

After spending time with Jung in Cornwall, she again saw how human he was. She was losing her faith in him. A cryptic note in April hints at the story: "That was also the M.K.B. prob[lem]!," she wrote. "It was dreamt at Cornwall, just after C.G. J. had turned her down—where I was most completely enraged and outraged (July 4.19)." Apparently, Jung had rejected MKB in 1919, and whatever the issue was, it resurfaced again in the spring of 1921.

In the autumn of 1921, Long met a man whom she believed to be a genuine sage, a new light, a true rival to Jung. Even more appealing, he lived in London. Suddenly, being the disciple of a distant master no longer seemed to be worth the effort.

Introduced to the Russian mystic P. D. Ouspensky by friends, she began to attend his classes and became increasingly intrigued with his spiritual lessons. No more fumbling around with associations to her dreams to find out the meaning of her life. She now had an elaborate new metaphysical system to analyze, and she felt a spark within herself that she had not felt with Jung. She knew she was going to have to sacrifice Jung for her new spiritual teacher, but she was ambivalent, confused. Caught in the middle, she tried to keep her attachments to both, but this only made her more miserable. Jung caught wind of her imminent defection and tried to woo her back. This only made everything worse.

By December 1921, after months of agonizing over her separation from Jung and her proportionally decreasing sense of self-worth, Long made the following entry in her diary:

> 30th XII.21. The weeks since November 5th have been full of illness and conflict. Tremendous death phantasies overcome me, and still do so in the

still night. There is something psychically wrong. A real drastic case of [ ] as follows—Two disillusionments in MKB and CGJ. I doubt if I have allowed the bitterness of these with the realisation that love as an inner value is from [ ].

When anywhere do I love—"love is consideration"—Generally speaking that operates partially—care of objects—but no answering warmth within, and often the [ ] crass disregard of objects.

Katz writes from Zollikon [Switzerland] that the missing word is "love." He wonders how he could think [ ] was played out—and regards it as "just begun." This is one that is my own [ ] too. The new orientation includes self-love. Now though profoundly selfish I have little of that. The very selfishness prevents me from loving myself. I feed my body, I clothe it, but do I *love* my *self*? . . .

I am more of a failure than my neurotic patients. I *am* neurotic.

This entry marks the true transition point in her life. She had become, as she realizes, an apostate. And worse, she was so dissociated from herself—even after eight years of following Jung and his promises of rebirth—that she had forgotten who she was.

Soon she found help. She soon made diary entries such as "All men are asleep" and "Must practice self-remembering." These were the teachings of her new master, Ouspensky, and his guru, the Armenian George Ivanovitch Gurdjieff.

"Foreign gods are a sweet poison"

P. D. Ouspensky's ideas of the "fourth dimension" of reality and other of his Theosophical and occultist notions were hot topics of conversation in the years before the First World War, and Russian expatriates brought these and other occultist philosophies from the East. They gained a certain currency in Schwabing and Ascona, and even in the cabarets and cafés of Zurich. Ouspensky's major works were translated into German and, after the war, into English, making him known to a select group of spiritual seekers before he set foot in London.

A. R. Orage, the editor of *The New Age,* had met Ouspensky before the war. During the war and the Russian Revolution, Ouspensky had occasionally contributed reports from inside Russia to *The New Age.* No friend of the Bolsheviks, he waited out the revolution in the territory held by the Whites until at Orage's suggestion he came to London in August 1921.

Orage was quite taken with Ouspensky's elaborate metaphysical system, which to a large degree had roots in Gurdjieff's teachings. The signature idea of these two men is that we are all "asleep," that we do not know ourselves, and that we must adopt certain practices and learn detailed occult knowledge in order to wake up, as if reality is a dream state from which we are always trying to awaken. The focus of the disciples who followed Ouspensky and Gurdjieff was something called, generally, "self-remembering." This is a gross simplification of their metaphysics, but it is enough to help us understand Constance Long's diary.[25]

Just after the war, Orage organized a psychoanalysis study group to come up with a new form of treatment that was neither Freudian nor Jungian. By 1921, this group focused on methods of psychosynthesis to find better ways to integrate the human personality rather than break it down into parts as traditional Freudian psychoanalysis did. Although several of the group's members were more Jungian than Freudian, they had never become wholehearted disciples of Jung. The known participants in the group were David Eder, Maurice Nicoll, James Young, and occasionally Havelock Ellis. It is very likely that Constance Long was an intermittent participant in this group, as several of her friends were in it and its ideals were congruent with her interests. However, there is no indication in her diary or in her published work that the ideas took hold.

In the beginning of October, Orage sent word that a "new light" may have arrived in London to show the group the way to psychosynthesis. The group for the first meeting comprised Ouspensky, Lady Rothermere, James Young, J. M. Alcock, David Eder, Maurice Nicoll, J. D. Beresford (a novelist), and Clifford Sharp (an editor and journalist). Throughout the next two years there were occasional visits from T. S. Eliot and Herbert Read, a poet who later became one of the editors of the *Collected Works of C. G. Jung*.[26]

Although the histories of this group never mention her, we now know that very soon after Ouspensky began his teachings, Connie Long became one of the most devoted of participants. In the back cover of her diary, she wrote the names and addresses of Ouspensky, Nicoll, and Orage. She clearly had contact with them.

Ouspensky was a large man with almost albino-blond hair. He spoke English with a Slavic accent (part of his mystique, no doubt), and his keen intelligence and vast knowledge of occult lore—details and formulas and charts and mathematical mysticism—were expressed to an awestruck audience.

When Long stopped writing down her dreams that autumn, she filled her diary with the teachings of Ouspensky. They were intellectually satisfying in a way that the fuzziness of Jungian psychology was not. In her diary are charts, diagrams, and tables of various sorts that Ouspensky dispensed.

Her diary even includes her enneagram, a mandala-like construction of her metaphysical being that is still a popular tool in Ouspensky-Gurdjieffian circles.

Since Long, Nicoll, and Young were among the original admirers of Jung who had not broken from him, the usurpation of their affections by another wise man shocked Jung when he heard about it, and he immediately took steps to try to put a stop to it. Jung had carefully cultivated this core group of professional physicians so as not to lose them to Freud. They were the concrete evidence that analytical psychology could prevail over Freud's psychoanalysis in England. The thought that he could lose them all to a Russian guru horrified him. If they left him, he would be stuck with a handful of mediocre physicians—such as the playboy Peter Baynes—or laypersons who were strong supporters but who had no credentials of any distinction. We don't have the letters Jung sent Nicoll or Young, but whatever it was he said to them soon convinced them that Jung was no longer the light they were looking for. Something Jung said pushed these men away from him. By mid-1922 their break with him was irrevocable.

We do have the text of a letter that he sent Constance Long on December 17, 1921. She copied it into her diary, wedged in between elaborate explanations of Ouspensky's metaphysics. The letter needs no explanation. Long's notes from it begin with a warning from Jung that "programmed teaching" is a "great danger." And then he goes directly to the heart of what he is all about:

> Gnosis should be an experience of your own life, a plant grown on your own tree. Foreign gods are a sweet poison, but the vegetable gods you have raised in your own garden are nourishing. They are perhaps less beautiful, but they have [ ].
>
> You shall not make totems of foreign trees [ ] No one shall keep you else you trespass your limits; but blessed be the place where we meet the beginning of our limitations. Beyond one's frontiers there is nothing but illusion and misery, because there you arrive in a country of the wrong ancestor spirits and the wrong charms.
>
> No teacher shall teach you else you should become weak, but your soul gives you the right medicine.
>
> You should be strong within your country. You have good strong trees and plenty of rich fields, and good water.
>
> Why do you look for foreign teachings? They are poisons, they did not come out of your blood. You should be on your own feet, and you have your own rich earth below them. Why should you listen to the word of a man who is off his own soil? Who is also off his own feet? Truth is a tree with roots. It is not words. Truth only grows in your own garden, nowhere else.

Only feeble men eat the food of a stranger. But your people need a strong man, one who gets his truth in his own roots and out of his own blood. That is good for the people, and only that . . . I appeal to your own natural strength. You would lose your [   ] in people if you adopt strange charms. If you refuse help then your gods come to your help. There is still too much Christianity in that seeking a helper or a teacher somewhere. Everything must be earned.

Jung's German spirituality was never more apparent: his references to the rootedness of one's spirituality, of the fact that one's spirituality must come from one's blood, and the appeal to stay within the boundaries of one's mystical landscape. In a 1918 essay, "Über das Unbewusste" (translated as "The Role of the Unconscious"), Jung used "rootedness" to argue that the psychoanalysis of Freud and Alfred Adler could apply only to Jews.[27] Jung argued that Germans would find Jewish psychoanalysis unsatisfying. Analytical psychology is therefore an Aryan science and form of spiritual psychotherapy that can truly assist only those of Aryan blood. Whereas Jung considered the English an extension of Germanic blood, his tolerance did not extend to Slavs such as Ouspensky. The English were Aryans, they could be redeemed with his methods. Slavs, although originally Aryan, had too much Asian blood mixed in; they would have a difficult time. Jews could not be redeemed.

Although every foreigner who came into contact with Jung received a heavy dose of Volkish mysticism, few understood its uniquely German context. Fanny Bowditch Katz didn't. And certainly Connie Long in England didn't either. Most people today trying to make sense out of Jung don't get it either because they are rarely informed about the pervasiveness of Volkish ideas in German culture before 1933. To understand the hidden layers of meaning in Jung's appeal to Long, the following statement by historian George Mosse may shed light:

The term rooted was constantly invoked by Volkish thinkers—and with good reason. Such rootedness conveyed the sense of man's correspondence with the landscape through his soul and thus with the Volk, which embodied the life spirit of the cosmos. It provided the essential link in the Volkish chain of being. Moreover, rural rootedness served as a contrast to urban dislocation, or what was termed "uprootedness." It also furnished a convenient criterion for excluding foreigners from the Volk and the virtues of rootedness. In addition, the concept of rootedness provided a standard for measuring man's completeness and his inner worth. Accordingly, having no roots stigmatized a person as being deprived of the life force and thus lacking a properly functioning soul. Rootlessness condemned the whole man, whereas rootedness signified membership in the Volk which rendered man his humanity.[28]

Jung's Volkish appeal to his British disciples to remain within the racial boundaries of their spirituality came in the spring of 1922 with the arrival of Gurdjieff. Everyone recognized the charismatic man with the piercing black eyes, thick black mustache, and shaven head topped by an astrakhan cap as the true master. Gurdjieff stayed until September, when he moved to France and set up his own commune.

Connie Long, too, was taken with this new master. Her diary was soon filled front and back with his teachings. She didn't care about Jung anymore. And neither did the others.

By April 1922 Jung realized there had been a schism in London and that he was the big loser. Long recorded in her diary the following note: "Ap[ril] 20. Baynes to Joan [Corrie]. 'But my dear J., the separatist movement has taken place. The O.[uspensky] point of view is not only different, it is altogether destructive of any scientific approach to psychological problems. You cannot turn to O.[uspensky] as a hobby or as a secret cult while you are admittedly and professionally practicing Jung's analytical psychology.' "

By the end of 1922 both Nicoll and Young were living with Gurdjieff in his commune in France.

The Jung cult lost this early battle, but it won many others as the twentieth century rolled along. Long did not live to see them. In December 1922, in her early fifties and still weakened from her operation three years earlier, Long settled in for a long visit in Hinkle's home. In the early weeks of 1923 she came down with a bad case of influenza. Soon it developed into pneumonia. She died in New York on February 16, 1923.

PART FOUR

Revelations

(*preceding page*) Fidus, "Sonnenwanderer" ("Sun Wanderers"), 1908.

TWELVE

From Volkish Prophet to Wise Old Man

Even as Jung attracted more and more American and British disciples after the First World War, he became further entrenched in his Volkish worldview. The Swiss Germans and the expatriate Germans in Zurich had always understood the coded metaphors of racialism and Aryan mysticism that he synthesized with the ideas and practices of the great pagan religious attitude of the Hellenistic world. For them, Jung only confirmed the historical continuity of the spiritual genius of the Aryan race from the *Urreligion* of all original humans who worshiped the sun and the stars, a golden thread of secret traditions that connected the Iranians and the Indians, the mystery cults of the Greeks and the Romans, the Gnostics and the alchemists, the Freemasons and the Rosicrucians, the German natural philosophers and finally them, the analyzed disciples of Jung. They understood the Volkish Jung when he spoke of the need for one's spirituality to be rooted in one's blood and soil, to not follow the sweet poisons of foreign gods, to bring forth the god within so that together they could reach a critical mass that would unleash the spiritual power of the *Volk*.

By this argument, the Jews had been civilized for at least two thousand years before Christian missionaries mutilated the spiritual life of the ancient Germans in the ninth century C.E., but this very civilization cut them off from spiritual redemption. In German culture at the turn of the century, to say the Jews were civilized meant that they were tainted with degeneracy. In Jung's commonly held opinion, the rootlessness of the wandering Jews and their millennia-long separation from the spiritual beauties of nature made them biologically and psychologically different from Aryans. After all, there was no evidence of Jewish mystery cults in the Hellenistic period, and there is no promise of rebirth or regeneration or redemption in Judaism. As a result, for many years Jung did not allow persons of Jewish descent to penetrate his inner circle or to practice in his name. He referred such patients to Sigmund Freud or other Jewish psychoanalysts. Jung's analytical psychology was a path of redemption for those of Aryan heredity only. (Paradoxically—although consistent with Jung's oppositional streak toward higher authorities—it wasn't until the rise of National Socialism that Jung began inviting Jewish physicians to practice in his name.)

Jung taught his American and British disciples that these were universal ideas. Ignorant of German culture and history, and often ignorant of the language, they willingly believed him, and they still do. In the decades that followed, his disciples have taken this cluster of uniquely German ideas and transmitted them around the world with absolutely no awareness of their origin in a specific historical context. Disengaged from their historical roots, Jung's ideas and their racialist and Aryanist mysticism have taken on lives of their own. As sociologist Heinz Gess has argued, these ideas are echoed not only in National Socialism and in fascist philosophy in general, but also in modern occultist and New Age thought.[1]

In a May 26, 1923, letter to Oskar Schmitz, a writer and pupil of Jung's who introduced Count Hermann Keyserling to Jung's work in 1922, Jung referred to Christianity—a Semitic religion—as a "foreign growth" that was cruelly grafted onto the "Germanic tribes" of old. In this letter, Jung counted himself as a member of those tribes. "Like Wotan's oaks," he lamented, "the gods were felled and a wholly incongruous Christianity, born of monotheism on a much higher cultural level, was grafted onto the stumps. The Germanic man is still suffering from this mutilation." Jung told Schmitz that he had been working on a solution to this problem for years: "We must dig down to the primitive in us, for only out of the conflict between civilized man and the Germanic barbarian will there come what we need: a new experience of God."[2] Jung wrote this letter to Schmitz to urge him and his colleagues in Keyserling's "School of Wisdom" to stay away from a full immersion in Asian spiritual practices such as yoga because they were not rooted in the Aryan tradition. This letter is strikingly similar to the letters redolent with Volkish philosophy that Jung sent to Joan Corrie and Constance Long.

How such ideas penetrated the work of Jung's foreign disciples can be seen in a book by Beatrice Hinkle. Hinkle had not really been a part of the Jungian scene in Zurich since 1915, but she saw Jung at the Sennen Cove seminar and had kept abreast of his ideas of the collective unconscious and its gods, the archetypes. She fully believed in an inherited racial or archaic layer of the unconscious mind that could occasionally be discerned in the dreams or psychotic symptoms of her patients. And, just as Jung taught her, the archaic layers of the unconscious burst forth in the patient's artistic productions. Since our ancestors worshiped the sun, the deepest layers of the unconscious produced religious symbols of a solar nature. In her 1923 book, *The Re-Creating of the Individual*, Hinkle reproduced two illustrations that support this point. One is "the unconscious drawing of a modern man who never before had made an attempt to draw."[3] The second is from a female patient and is, in Hinkle's words, "equally archaic." What is remarkable about both of them is that they depict "archaic sun worship." In both drawings there is a single individual, seen from the rear, facing the sun with arms outstretched in a Y-shaped posture of supplication to a glowing orb on the horizon. Although Hinkle believed that this was conclusive evidence that she had struck the deepest and most impersonal layers of the collective unconscious in her patients, her patients were merely reproducing the famous—and seemingly ubiquitous—images of the Aryan *Lichtgebet* (Prayer to the light) by Fidus. Like her master, Hinkle made the common mistake of discounting her patients' personal "hidden memories" and leapt prematurely to a cosmic interpretation of psychological material.

A major component of Jung's way of thinking was the belief that the soil upon which one trod, soil soaked with the blood of the generations who had previously lived there, could shape not only one's soul but also one's physical characteristics. This Lamarckian notion thrived in German science at the turn of the century and lives on in Jung's writings. In 1925, Jung gave a seminar to a group of his disciples in New York City in which he spoke of such things. According to the notes of Esther Harding, Jung "spoke on racial psychology and said many interesting things about the ancestors, how they seem to be in the land. As evidence of this, he spoke about the morphological changes in the skulls of people here in the U.S.A. and in Australia."[4] Jung continued such a line of thought in Zurich in the spring of 1925, when he outlined the "geology of the personality" in a seminar on analytical psychology.[5] This seminar was the first time Jung revealed his inner visions and self-deification experience in public. His self-disclosures helped to fan the flames of a cult of personality that persists even today.

"There is no question about the fact he is the prophet"

Among the most important of the American disciples who entered Jung's orbit in 1925 and 1926 were Christiana Morgan and Henry Murray. In the 1930s and 1940s, the two were lovers and collaborators at Harvard, where they created the psychological projective test known as the "Thematic Apperception Test," or TAT, which is still in use.

Jung was captivated by Morgan, a highly intelligent and artistically gifted woman who was, like Fanny Bowditch Katz, a daughter of Boston Brahmins. She was also a master of Jung's visionary-trance techniques, the magical procedure known as active imagination. Morgan not only left behind diaries of her 1925 and 1926 analysis, but she later constructed perhaps the most beautiful of all the "bright-shining books" or "bibles" left behind by Jung's apostles.

The very first painting in her leather-bound illuminated manuscript of visions is that of a five-pointed star with a blazing sun at its core. "Be still and know that I am God," Morgan inscribed beneath this Volkish image of divinity, the god within as the sun or a star. Jung had constructed a similar image of his inner self in his 1916 mandala painting containing the lion-headed god Abraxas. Later, when Morgan and Murray constructed their own "Tower" in Massachusetts complete with murals depicting their pantheon of personal gods, the supreme god was called Hola, a golden sun symbol that was painted on the ceiling of their sacred space. Morgan kept a red notebook with the title "The Gods and Their Representation in the House," to record the meaning and personal significance of each deity that they created.[6]

In her analysis diaries we find not only that Jung continued to communicate his intention to be the leader of a new religious movement to redeem the world—a "new order," he called it—but that this spiritual rebirth was clearly rooted in the German Romantic natural philosophy and Volkish beliefs that were so meaningful to him. In her 1925 notebook, Morgan inserted this typed copy of a letter she sent to Murray:

> And now I want to write to you about Jung, although to tell you what I think of him seems peculiarly difficult. As you said, he has indeed the true fire. . . .
>
> It is wonderful his quiet rejection of the Christian attitude. (Rejection isn't quite the right word—rather his passing beyond it). . . .
>
> To me his significance is this:
>
> He seems definitely to have achieved a new attitude. He is honestly attempting a new way. There is no question about the fact he is the prophet. . . .
>
> He says, "There are some situations on which you are on untrodden

sands. No footstep has been there ahead of yours. You are beginning the way of a new order. If you are weak you will side with society and say, 'Yes, I too believe as you believe.' If you are strong you will seek out the new way. You may succeed, you may fail, but you will have dealt with life. You will have struggled for the new reality."[7]

Once, after a dream in which Morgan knelt to Christ but then left him to follow an American Indian and a bull, Jung told her, "Christ is a great figure and we all do him homage—but he no longer holds life for us. I have often thought I would like to accept Christ and the Catholic Church for its great beauty but I soon realize it would mean an atrophy of myself in a beautiful form—that life would go by me."[8]

In her diary entries for June and July of 1926, she recorded her dreams in red ink and then below them, in black, she jotted down Jung's associations to them during her analytic sessions. On the evening of June 9, 1926, after a "Dionysian evening," Morgan dreamed of two nursemaids, one of whom said to her, "Well, you must be a Jew because you have two Jewish fathers." Although not herself Jewish, Morgan had a brief but meaningful affair with Chaim Weizmann a few years before meeting Henry Murray, and this formed the basis of Jung's interpretation. During her analytic session of June 11, 1926, Morgan noted the following remarks by Jung:

> Servants are your inferior functions—or inferior self.... You are dealing with them as though infantile. The two Jewish fathers are Weizmann and Christ. The Jews enter our unconscious through a hole—the hole being the lack of any religion for our animal nature—our nature-forming selves. The Jews have domesticated their instincts—they are not savage as ours are—so your inferior animal self says—you are Jewish—you have given up nature—the return to earth—the source of life.[9]

Later, during a session on June 25, 1926, Jung told Morgan, "Sexuality is the sine qua non of spirituality—one only exists through the other."[10] Acting on this advice to Morgan, and inspired by Jung's revelation of his relationship with Toni Wolff to Henry Murray, the two Americans began an extramarital relationship that lasted decades. Polygamy released the archaic energies within them, for which they were eternally grateful to Jung. During the magical rituals they performed in their "Tower," Murray and Morgan paid special tribute to Jung for teaching them the "transformative power of the trances" and for his insights into the sexual nature of humankind, especially his concepts of anima and animus. Morgan kept illustrated records of their rituals.

When they were with Jung in the mid-1920s, Morgan and Murray consciously realized that they were witnessing the birth of a new polytheistic religion that offered the experience of mysteries in the form of visions of the pagan gods of antiquity. "Is he really Christian or not?" Murray asked himself shortly after arriving in Zurich. "When I first saw him in 1925, my impression was that he had gone completely outside of Christianity, and he was developing a kind of religion of the archetypes, you might say."[11] Analysis with Jung continued to be an initiation into mysteries, and others in Zurich in the late 1920s found this as well.

One such analysand was Ernest Harms. Harms had worked as a researcher for Jung from 1919 to 1922 and had had some analytic sessions with him. He left Zurich to pursue other interests, but then found himself back in Jung's circle in Zurich in 1929. "The picture around Jung had changed," Harms remembered later in life. "More and more I saw the psychological development, not only overcome what in earlier books was so strong—the pathological side—by the initiation side directed towards the healthy development of the psyche as regards to transformation in the sense of the old mysteries."[12] Secure in his position as a prophet and leader of a neopagan religious movement, a hierophant who presided over his own mysteries, Jung no longer felt the need to hide his agenda from others by couching his remarks about spirituality in Christian metaphors.

Jung soon saw no need to adhere to the demands of historical or factual truth. Myth became more important to him.

Intuition and feeling, not rational thought, became the basis of decision making. If a story helped bring someone closer to an emotional experience of transcendence or of the god within, it no longer mattered to Jung whether it was "true" historically. Only its magical effect of enhancing the belief of others in the transcendent reality of the gods and ancestors that he called the collective unconscious was important.

As he became more confident in his role as a prophet, Jung boldly altered historical facts at will.

The disappearance of J. J. Honegger from history

In 1931, Jung's book *Seelenprobleme der Gegenwart* appeared in print with his essay "Die Struktur der Seele."[13] In it, Jung made one of his many references to the case of an institutionalized psychotic patient, "E. Schwyzer," born in 1862, who had a delusion or hallucination that a large phallus hung from the sun and that the moving of this phallus back and forth created the wind. Jung first mentioned this patient in 1911, in part 1 of his *Wandlungen und Symbole der Libido*. Even as late as 1959, in a televised interview with the BBC, Jung pointed to this case as the one that convinced him of the reality of a collective unconscious.[14]

In 1911, Jung had identified the treating physician as Johann Jakob Honegger, his younger assistant. "Honegger discovered the following hallucination in an insane man (paranoid dement)," Jung then wrote.[15] Honegger unexpectedly committed suicide in the spring of 1911. But by 1930 he had been dead for almost twenty years, and with no living heirs to complain, Jung saw no reason why anyone would object if he removed J. J. Honegger from history and took credit for the case himself. And that is what he did.

From 1930 onward, Jung consciously altered significant dates connected with Schwyzer's case. Honegger began work under Jung's supervision at the Burghölzli Clinic in 1909. This would have been the earliest point at which Honegger could have collected the contents of his patient's psychotic symptoms. Jung later claimed that he himself collected this information from the patient in 1906.[16]

Why the change? Jung must have realized—far too late—that he had made a major error, and then lied to cover it up, surmising that no one would catch him or care very much in the years to come. The error concerns the remarkable claims that Jung made about the similarity of the solar phallus hallucination to a passage in the Greek Magical Papyri that was thought to be an authentic excerpt from the rituals enacted in the Mithraic mysteries. In the original 1911 report, Jung cautiously stated, "This strange hallucination remained unintelligible to us for a long time until I became acquainted with the Mithraic liturgy and its visions."[17] Jung then provided his readers with a quote from the Mithraic Liturgy that he took from a 1907 book by G.R.S. Mead entitled *A Mithraic Ritual,* which he cited as his own source for this ancient text.[18]

As the years rolled by, Jung recounted the story of "the Solar Phallus Man" (as he is called today) time and again and probably with embellishments that eventually found their way into his later writings. It was a magical story that convinced—and continues to convince—many people that there is undeniable evidence of the existence of a collective unconscious. As Jung would tell it, the sun-phallus material could not have been known to Schwyzer because (a) he had been institutionalized, (b) he was not a scholar, and (c) the Mithraic Liturgy had only appeared in print for the first time in 1910, a year after the material had been collected from the patient. From the 1930s onward, in print and in interviews, Jung claimed that the first time that the Mithraic Liturgy had appeared in print was in a 1910 book by Albrecht Dieterich entitled *Eine Mithrasliturgie.*[19] Jung had forgotten about Mead's book, and it in turn was based on the *first* edition of

Dieterich's *Eine Mithrasliturgie,* which appeared in 1903. A footnote by the editors of Jung's *Collected Works* admits that Jung later learned there was a 1903 first edition but covers up for him by adding, "The patient had, however, been committed some years before 1903."[20] This may be so, but it does not explain why Jung never retracted his "mistake" and why, to the end of his life, he insisted that the Mithraic Liturgy first appeared in print in 1910.

Moving the date of his encounter with Schwyzer back to 1906 allowed Jung to claim that he collected the material from the patient himself at least one year before Mead's 1907 book. Someone must have read either the book-length edition of *Wandlungen* (1912) or Beatrice Hinkle's translation and pointed out the discrepancy. Jung simply changed the facts to fit his story.

By covering up for him, the editors of Jung's *Collected Works* were attempting on his behalf to erase the argument that cryptomnesia (hidden personal memories) could be the source of the sun-phallus image. But thanks to the incredible publishing machine put into force by the Theosophical Publishing Society in the late 1880s, philosophies of the East and Western occult traditions had been distilled and disseminated to Western civilization.[21]

These Theosophical journals and books were ubiquitous in Western Europe and North America. Anyone could find them at newspaper kiosks or in bookstores or in libraries, especially the libraries of the local chapters of the Theosophical Society. Even an institutionalized mental patient could pick up a Theosophical journal and ingest an occultist interpretation of the latest scholarship on the Greek Magical Papyri (including the Mithraic Liturgy), the Hellenistic mystery cults, polytheistic Greco-Roman religion, Zoroastrianism, Buddhism, Jainism, Hinduism, Islam, Neoplatonism, Egyptian magic and religion, the New Testament gospels and apocrypha, the ideas of the Gnostics, Hermeticism, alchemy, Swedenborgianism, psychical research, astral projection, spiritualism, vegetarianism, and especially reincarnation—just to name a few. The likelihood that Honegger's patient—or anyone else with an interest in spirituality—could have come into contact with such publications is quite high. The myriad publications of the Theosophical Society provided more than enough material to fill any personal unconscious with the sort of mythological material that Jung and his associates claim was from a nonpersonal source.

Most of the patients who came to Jung after 1913 already had exposure to Theosophy, Anthroposophy, Swedenborgianism, spiritualism, or other nontraditional spiritual paths. They knew of Jung's emphasis on spirituality before making the long trip to Zurich. In this sense, one may argue that Jung collected all of his evidence for the impersonal collective unconscious from a very small and highly biased sample.

Jung knew this and, as with the case of the Solar Phallus Man, deliberately lied about it. I realize "lie" is a strong word, but I can think of no other that expresses the nature of Jung's actions. This is not a simple mistake or two, but a pattern of intentional alterations of facts. For example, in 1950 Jung published an enlarged and revised version of a lecture he gave at the Eranos conferences held in Ascona in 1933. In the new version, entitled "Zur Empirie des Individuationsprozesses" (translated in the *Collected Works* as "A Study in the Process of Individuation"), Jung documented the case of an unmarried female American patient whom he claims he treated in 1928 when she was fifty-five. Jung admitted that she was "cultured, and possessed a lively turn of mind." She also had an "exceptional father." Very little other personal information is provided about her. She came to Zurich and began the usual regime of drawing and painting her visions and dreams. The thrust of Jung's 1950 paper is his attempt to demonstrate the presence of Indian (Aryan) mandalas and other symbols that all have parallels in alchemical imagery. He assured his readers with his usual authoritative disclaimer that "all these ideas and inferences were naturally unknown to my patient" and that "there could be no question of my having unintentionally infected her with alchemical ideas."[22]

There are problems with this claim. First of all, there are dozens of accounts on record of Jung routinely showing his patients illustrations from books—including from his own "Red Book"—during their analytic sessions with him. Second, we know that this American patient was none other than Kristine Mann, who came to Jung well acquainted not only with his own writings but with the works of Emanuel Swedenborg and other occult ideas, including alchemy.[23] Again, as Jung advanced in years his disregard for historical truth or fact grew proportionally.

What would cause Jung to go down this path and to lie on the rare occasions he was challenged? Indisputably a genius who made significant contributions to the theory and practice of psychotherapy with his complex theory and some of his early ideas about psychological types, he seems to have been so convinced of the reality of a collective unconscious that he could even lie to protect the idea. For him, it was the alpha and the omega, the true source of all mystery and meaning. A patient's past history or personal problems were "baby work," as he called it, to be handled by his associates. Jung only wanted to have his belief in the collective unconscious continually reinforced by the visions and dreams of his patients. Truth be told, many claimed that this wild ride into mythological symbolism was indeed therapeutic. It helped make their individual, mundane lives seem much more interesting and even important on a cosmic level.

Jung's obsession with the collective unconscious—and the bending of facts that sometimes resulted from this—was obvious to many of those around him. Michael Fordham, since the 1930s the most prominent Jungian analyst in England, related a telling episode in a 1969 interview. He recalled that at a dinner party Emma Jung once publicly attacked her husband on this issue during a conversation about the dreams of children. " 'You know perfectly well that you are not interested in anybody unless they exhibit features of the collective unconscious,' " she said. This put Jung in his place. "He shut up after that," Fordham said.[24]

Others have been less diplomatic. John Layard, a British anthropologist who was trained by Jung in Zurich, recalled reading one of his richly illustrated case histories, that of a man who had alchemical symbolism in his dreams. Like most of Jung's patients, Layard believed Jung at first.

> He gave the impression there [in the published case history], and wanted to give the impression, that these things happened spontaneously without any nursing, so to speak—independent of any analytical or psychological relationship. This struck me as being very extraordinary, but I believed it until I found out afterwards that during the whole of that period the man in whom Jung found these forty archetypes was under analysis with [Jungian analyst] Erna Rosenbaum. This is part of Jung's falsification of data in support of the collective unconscious being independent of personal relationships.[25]

Gene Nameche, who conducted the interviews with Fordham and Layard and more than 140 other persons for the C. G. Jung Biographical Archives Project, confessed to one of his interviewees, "I am frequently appalled at the lack of historical information—that is personal historical information—in Jungian writing, including Jung."[26] With the exceptions of Fordham and Layard, few other interviewees seemed to share Nameche's concerns. For the overwhelming majority, Jung's ahistorical approach was their panacea. Jung enabled their escape from history—*personal* history—and into mystery. This was why they found their way to Jung in the first place. "I never felt, when I worked with him, that he neglected the historic," said Irene Champernowne, who began analysis with Jung in 1936.

> He merely helped one not to get bogged down with it. That what happened to you was not just your history—it was all these reverberations that your history set going in you. Oh, I have felt . . . as if I was lifted up out of a petty life into something quite with dignity and spiritual possibilities. The petty

problems, which didn't feel petty in one's history, were against the great background of collective history or of life as a whole, of God, if you like. That of course is the main thing I owe to him. He put me back into relation to my religious life—which had become meaningless.[27]

But in the political climate of German Europe in the 1930s, Jung's lack of historical consciousness and his preference for a belief in the possibilities of myth over fact-based reasoning led him into treacherous waters.

"For a short time he believed in the possibilities of Nazism"

Perhaps the most painful issue confronting both Jungians and non-Jungians alike is Jung's alleged involvement with National Socialism. Gene Nameche, to his credit, specifically asked almost all of his interviewees who knew Jung in the 1930s and 1940s about his attitudes toward Jews and National Socialism and his possible involvement with the Nazis. The vast majority of his disciples absolve him of this. Others equivocate. The truth is no doubt somewhere in between.

Jung's Volkish worldview and his love of pagan symbolism and myth made the National Socialist movement in Germany attractive to him at first. The National Socialists constructed their ideology out of the elements of German Volkish thought that had been popular for several generations among the educated middle classes. They borrowed their solar symbolism from occultism and Aryan mysticism. The National Socialist flag contains a white solar disk or mandala at its center, in which is set another solar symbol: the *Hakenkreutz* or swastika, a symbol of eternal recurrence and regenerative power. The sun was a potent natural symbol and National Socialist rhetoric was often laced with references that link the power of the sun to the *Volk*.[28] Runic symbols were also borrowed by the National Socialists to signify various political and military organizations.

Jung was always interested in the spiritual regeneration of the Aryan race. He sought ways to reach the "archaic man" or "German barbarian" within the members of his tribe. Like Houston Stewart Chamberlain, he considered the English to be racially closest to the Germans, Swiss, and Austrians. Jung had little interest in politics per se. He may have been a Volkish German and perhaps anti-Semitic, but there is no evidence that he was ever a Nazi.

This is not to say he opposed the Nazis, either. Wilhelm Bitter, the founder of the Stuttgart Institute for Psychotherapy, who was in analysis with Jung in the 1930s, captured the paradoxical attitudes and behavior of

Jung during the Nazi period. "It's so easy for the Freudians, and not only the Jewish, to say Jung was a Nazi, an anti-Semite," Bitter said to Nameche in September 1970. "This statement is wrong. But for a short time he believed in the possibilities of Nazism, and favored it. He spoke of Jewish psychology, but not in an anti-Semitic sense. His best pupils are Jewish—Erich Neumann, Gerhard Adler . . . and Jacobi are all Jewish pupils." Earlier, Bitter had indicated that in 1933 and 1934 there was great sympathy for the Nazis in Jung's circle. Intrigued, Nameche pushed further.

INT: You did say here that Jung and some of his pupils became Nazis in 1934. Would you say it so strongly?
WB: 1933, yes.
INT: That *he* became a Nazi?
WB: Jung? Not a Nazi in the strict sense.

As Bitter took pains to point out, Jung was interested primarily in the spiritual revitalization of the German peoples. "He thought of rebirth, rebirth in the good sense," said Bitter.[29] Like Bitter, many others were of the opinion that Jung's fatal flaw was that he tended to "psychologize" everything and disregard the dangers of the political developments in Germany. After almost twenty years of being relatively ignored by the German media, suddenly in 1933, 1934, and 1935 Jung enjoyed a popularity north of the Swiss border that was unprecedented. He was courted by German scholars as never before. He gave seminars in Berlin and lectured in other German cities. According to Jolande Jacobi, one of his closest disciples from the thirties on, "His idea [about the Nazi movement] was that chaos gives birth to good or to something valuable. So in the German movement he saw a chaotic (we could say) pre-condition for the birth of a new world." In response to a letter to him expressing her concerns about the dangers of Nazism, Jacobi said, "He answered me: 'Keep your eyes open. You can't reject the evil because the evil is the bringer of light.' Lucifer means light-bringer. He was convinced of this, you see. That shows that he didn't see and didn't understand the outer world. For him this [the Nazi movement] was an inner happening which had to be accepted as a psychological pre-condition for rebirth."[30]

In the spring of 1936, Jung's famous essay on Wotan appeared.[31] As Jung often claimed later in life, it was indeed the first time he expressed concern about the excesses of the Germans. However, at the same time, Jung confirmed his belief that Germany was possessed by Wotan, the true god of the German peoples, and that the only problem was that far too many of them were unconscious of this fact. Their unconsciousness of the reemergence of this pagan god in the twentieth century led to their "possession," he said. If only they would become conscious of their god, then the Germans would find their way to a true spiritual rebirth. Again, Jung simply psychologizes the political problem.

On the issue of anti-Semitism, Jacobi herself presents conflicting opinions. On the one hand, she defends Jung against such charges, citing her long friendship with him and the innocence of his Volkish ideas about the differences between the civilized Jews and the barbarian Germans. "You know your ancestors were already doctors and Rabbis and scientific persons six thousand years ago and my ancestors were running around naked with the skins of animals a thousand years ago in the German woods," he once told her. On the other hand, Jacobi admitted that his opinions were sometimes crude. "But he also said one day . . . 'You know, I would never like to have children from a person who has Jewish blood.' "[32]

In the early years of the Nazi era, Jung at times expressed himself in ways that were consistent with anti-Semitic rhetoric, particularly when in the presence of non-Jewish people. On his way to meet Jung for the first time in 1933, Michael Fordham found himself in a third-class compartment with a Jewish man who told him he was leaving Germany because of the National Socialists.

> When I arrived in Zurich the next day and met Jung I . . . remarked about the Jew in the carriage coming out of Germany. To my astonishment this started Jung off and he went on and on and on. I was used to people talking like this for personal reasons so I just listened. He talked about the Jews at top speed for, I should think, three-quarters of an hour. What he said was very extensive but two points stood out in my memory. One was that he made a very strong point that Jews were different from other people and that they ought to be dressed up in different clothes because otherwise we mistook them for people like ourselves. I suppose he told me about their customs in the way he might usually do on other occasions. I think this difference of the Jews from others was the main point he made. . . . The second one . . . was . . . he asked me rhetorically what I thought the Jews were doing in the desert for forty years: eating sand? Of course they were, he said, feeding off other people's crops until they moved on.[33]

Other disciples reported similar attitudes of Jung during the early 1930s, but Cornelia Brunner remembered Jung being "terribly upset" the day that the synagogues burned in Germany. Prior to that time, according to her, Jung "was always working on this fact: Why are we so different? What is the difference [between Aryans and Jews]? In a way," she confessed, "we also were frightened of the Jews because they are so clever.

They are more clever than we are, and so they could take over. . . . We felt the difference—they are Mediterranean people with a much longer history and a much more developed intellect. We just think in another way. I have a lot of Jewish friends, by the way—very nice ones."[34]

Irene Champernowne alleged in her December 1969 interview with Gene Nameche that Jung actually encouraged anti-Jewish attitudes in his patients as a form of psychotherapeutic technique, a way of always being conscious of their "shadow":

> Well, he was very strong about the Jews. You know that there was a great problem, a great collective problem, . . . that we could all make the Jews our shadow because we were jealous of them and their position. And he also pointed out that they were such opportunists that you really had to be quite clear that you were being exploited if you felt you were, and stand firm else you would be caught in a pogrom. So he used to encourage negativity toward the Jews in us, if you see what I mean, insofar as he would say, "Well, you see what you feel about the Jews who use you."[35]

Champernowne, who then practiced in London, recounted the problems that the British Jungians had in maintaining the "British" flavor of their organizations when so many Jews flooded England in the 1930s. She discussed these tensions with Jung.

> [He] said, "If you have any feeling against Jewish people" (and of course we all had at this particular moment with them all swamping us and using us), "be clear. Keep it up. Don't let it go down. Because if you do you'll be caught in a pogrom." Well, this is a difficult thing. This is something that I think leaked out as a negative attitude to the Jews. And yet nobody helped the Jewish analysts more than Peter Baynes and Jung. . . . so I am quite sure he wasn't anti-Semitic in the sense of the word that some Jews have made out. But I think he felt that we must keep our shadow up, which was so easy to happen in any country where the Jews take possession like they did in Germany, and like they did to a certain extent and in certain circles in England.[36]

During the 1930s, many of the Swiss German members of the Psychological Club in Zurich were, like Jung, sympathetic to what was happening north of the border. "In the Club were some real Nazis," remembers Aline Valangin, the first wife of Dr. Vladimir Rosenbaum, who was one of Jung's disciples from the late 1910s until the mid-1930s, when the Psychological Club threw Rosenbaum out.[37] Another patient of Jung's who was in Zurich in the late 1930s, Mary Elliot, also remembered a similar Club atmosphere. "I think that in the beginning of the war quite a lot of the

Club people were pro-German." She does add, however, that "they were just uncomfortably pro-German. They were not even pro-Nazi, but they are very Germanic in this part of Switzerland."[38]

Whether one regards Jung as an anti-Semite, a Nazi, a Nazi sympathizer, or any combination thereof, the roots of the attitudes expressed during the Nazi era can be found in his Volkish utopianism and Aryanist mysticism, which predate the rise of Adolf Hitler and National Socialism in Germany. We must remember that these Volkish ideas had a vibrant cultural life of their own—often even independent of politics—in the years before the First World War. To be fair to Jung and to those who lived in German Europe at the turn of the century, we must remain sensitive to the specific cognitive categories of those times. It was an era in which biology and spirituality were fused into a potent amalgam and one in which the idea of an Aryan Christ appeared viable—indeed, preferable—to many. And it was only natural that they should look for his closest representative on Earth.

The Wise Old Man

Nineteen thirty-six was the pivotal year in the transformation of Jung's public image. He spoke at Harvard University during the college's three-hundredth anniversary. Although many were resistant to inviting Jung, Henry Murray, by then a famous Harvard psychologist, prevailed. Jung returned to America the following year to deliver the Terry Lectures on religion at Yale University. These two invitations to speak did more to solidify Jung's international image than anything that had happened to him in the previous twenty years.

In Zurich, Jung's community of disciples began to swell with physicians and spiritual seekers from England and America. These disciples began, and in many cases continue today, the sanitizing of Jung's image from a Germanic mystic or charlatan with anti-Semitic leanings to that of a wise old man. The Second World War and the Holocaust forced Jung to downplay his Volkish utopianism and Aryan mysticism because the international community now associated this cluster of ideas with Hitler and the Nazis. (This association persists today.) Sensitive to the anti-German sentiment in England and America, Jung began publicly referring to his Swiss nationality whenever possible in order to distinguish himself from the Germans. He also began using more and more of his research on alchemy to give the impression that there was still something Christian and monotheistic about his religious outlook. Alchemical texts are filled with references to the Bible and especially to Christ, and Jung made a point of emphasizing alchemical work as an act of spiritual redemption. Jung did not entirely drop his Volkish biases, however, for in several of his works on alchemy he equates the figure of the "spirit Mercurius" not only with Christ but with Wotan. Since no known alchemical texts make reference to Wotan or to the ancient pagan gods of the Germans, this appears to be subtle evidence of Jung's Aryanism and of the persistence of his worldview well into the 1940s and 1950s.

In Zurich, the level of adoration of Jung reached new heights among his apostles. "It was like a cult," remembered Liliane Frey, who had entered analysis with Jung in 1934 and remained one of his most loyal disciples for the next four decades.[39] Jane Wheelwright, an American analyst who trained with Jung in the 1930s also employed the word "cultism" to describe the atmosphere in Küsnacht and Zurich in the 1930s.[40] Jolande Jacobi remembered Jung writing "a furious letter" in response to her decision to convert to Catholicism after witnessing the last rites given to her Austrian fiancé. Jacobi said, "He answered: 'With me nobody has his place who is in the Church. There you have your confessor. I am for those people who are out of the Church.' " Jacobi offered this letter to Aniela Jaffé for publication with Jung's *Letters,* but she refused it "because it doesn't throw a good light on Jung." Jolande Jacobi's final assessment of Jung after spending four decades as an anointed disciple should not be forgotten: "He himself behaved as if his psychology was another religion."[41]

Anything which tries to go beyond intuitive acceptance, and presses deeper into the nature and substance of the Whole, is no longer religion, and when it tries to get itself accepted as religion, inevitably sinks to empty mythology.

—Friedrich Schleiermacher, "Lectures on Religion" (1799)

Acknowledgments

I wrote the bulk of this book between May and August 1996, but many institutions and individuals were helpful to me over the preceding years of my primary research on C. G. Jung and his movement.

I wish to thank Richard Wolfe of the Countway Library of Medicine, Harvard Medical School, for permission to reproduce photographs and quote from the following materials in the rare books and manuscripts collection: selections from the unpublished diaries and notebooks of Fanny Bowditch Katz, Constance Long, and Christiana Morgan; selections from the letters of Fanny Bowditch Katz, Maria Moltzer, James Jackson Putnam, and C. G. Jung in the Fanny Katz papers; and selections from the interviews in the C. G. Jung Biographical Archives.

Nina Murray generously gave me permission to read and quote from the restricted materials in the Henry A. Murray Papers in the Harvard University Archives.

Cynthia Knight, archivist at the McCormick–International Harvester Collection at the State Historical Society of Wisconsin in Madison, was extremely generous with her time and impressive in her knowledge of the materials in her archive. I wish to thank her and her institution for permission to quote from the papers of the McCormick family and for the 1917 family photographs of Edith Rockefeller McCormick, Harold Fowler McCormick, and their children.

The friendly staff of the Rockefeller Archive Center, Pocantico Hills, North Tarrytown, New York, kept their institution open just for me despite the problems created by one of the worst blizzards in the past century. In particular, Darwin Stapleton, the director of the center, and Tom Rosenbaum were extraordinarily generous to me and regularly made sure I had all the materials and soup that I needed. I thank that institution for permission to quote from the letters of the Rockefeller family.

The Kunsthaus Zurich in Switzerland kindly supplied me with photographs and provided me with permission to reproduce them here. Dr. Harald Szeemann graciously provided me with copies of every existing photo of Otto Gross, as well as photos of Hermann Hesse and Fidus. I could not use all of them here, but I will treasure my copies always.

Erika Krause and Olaf Breidbach of Ernst Haeckel Haus in Jena, Germany, have been extraordinarily kind to me over the course of my visits there to research the life of Ernst Haeckel. I thank Ernst Haeckel Haus for permission to reproduce the photos of Haeckel, Isadora Duncan, and Haeckel's drawings of radiolaria that appear in this book.

Martin Green has been my steadfast friend and continual inspiration for this project. He graciously shared unpublished material relating to Otto Gross that will appear in a biography of Gross that he is now finishing.

Steven Borack prepared all photographic material for me, often under tight deadlines, and for this I am very grateful.

Kurt Almqvist kindly supplied me with his copy of Jung's disturbing 1913 letter to Poul Bjerre from the Kungliga Biblioteket in Stockholm. I wish to thank Lars Holm for informing me of the existence of this letter.

My literary agent for this book, John Brockman, is to be given credit for its provocative title. I wish to thank him and Katinka Matson, also of Brockman, Inc., for their considerable efforts in making this book possible.

This book would have been far worse without the careful attention of my editor at Random House, Ann Godoff, and my editor at Macmillan (U.K.), Georgina Morley. The designers at Random House and Macmillan did a wonderful job, and I thank them all. Timothy Mennel copyedited the manuscript and suffered through the Yogi Berra syndrome of "déjà vu all over again."

Others who have clarified my thinking or inspired me in numerous ways during the course of this project are: Paul Bishop, Alan Elms, Frank Sulloway, Richard Webster, Frank McLynn, Steve Wasserstrom, Leonard George, Vivian Alie, David Ulansey, Katherine Ramsland, Nelson dos Reis, Lucia Maria Gonzales Barbosa, Leonardo Boff, Pam Donleavy, Elizabeth Knoll, Robert Richards, Ralph Raffio, Jim Pawlik, Wyatt Reed, and Stosh, Jerzy, and Ignaz.

Due to the international controversy provoked by my previous book, *The Jung Cult: Origins of a Charismatic Movement* (Princeton: Princeton University Press, 1994), I was privileged to lecture, discuss, and debate my research on Jung before audiences on three continents. I wish to thank the hosting institutions and audiences in the following cities: Stockholm, London, New York, Boston, Rio de Janeiro, São Paulo, Vancouver, and, of course, Cambridge, Massachusetts.

A week-long cyberseminar on Jung that I was invited to host in January 1997 survived some rather vigorous attempts by Jungian analysts in America, Canada, and England to organize a boycott against the efforts of Professor John Hollwitz of Creighton University (the sponsor of the JUNG-PSYC mailing list). I wish to thank Professor Hollwitz for standing firm in the face of bullying by some prominent Jungian analysts and for not posting their bizarrely false (indeed libelous) comments about me on the Internet. The lengths to which some Jungian analysts will go to prevent me from openly presenting my views to "Jungians" not only speaks volumes about their fear of having their traditional authority challenged but also demonstrates their incredibly bad manners. The Jung cult is alive and well, I'm afraid. Grow up, guys.

My parents, Richard and Betty Noll, and my sisters, Linda, Lori, Barbara, and

Beverley, all played a role in keeping me motivated to finish this project and get on with my fiction-writing career. Memories of my grandmother, Belle Marie (Tipinski) Adamczak, also sustained me.

This book is dedicated to Susan Naylor, who once again weathered my temporary bout with graphomania and who always reminds me of what is really important in life.

Richard Noll
Cambridge, Massachusetts
March 1997

Notes

Key to Abbreviations

Archives

CLM	Rare Books Department, Francis A. Countway Library of Medicine, Harvard Medical School, Boston, Massachusetts
HL	Houghton Library, Harvard University, Cambridge, Massachusetts
HUA	Harvard University Archives, Harvard University, Cambridge, Massachusetts
FBK	Fanny Bowditch Katz papers, CLM
JBA	C. G. Jung Biographical Archives, CLM
KB	Kungliga Biblioteket, Stockholm, Sweden
LC	Bollingen Archives, Library of Congress, Washington, D.C.
MIH	McCormick–International Harvester Corporation Collection, State Historical Society of Wisconsin, Madison, Wisconsin
RAC	Rockefeller Archive Center, Pocantico Hills, North Tarrytown, New York

Texts

CW	*The Collected Works of C. G. Jung,* ed. Herbert Read, Michael Fordham, and Gerhard Adler; exec. ed., William McGuire; trans. R.F.C. Hull and others (Princeton: Princeton University Press). 20 vols. and supplements, 1953–1992.
ETG	*Erinnerungen, Träume, Gedanken von C. G. Jung,* Aufgezeichnet und herausgegeben von Aniela Jaffé. Ninth special edition, 1995 (Solothurn and Düsseldorf: Walter-Verlag, 1971).
FJ	*The Freud/Jung Letters,* ed. William McGuire; trans. Ralph Manheim and R.F.C. Hull (London: Hogarth Press and Routledge and Kegan Paul, 1974).
GW	*Gesammelte Werke von C. G. Jung,* ed. Lilly Jung-Merkur, Marianne Niehus-Jung, Lena Hurwitz-Eisner, Franz Riklin, Elisabeth Rüf, and Leonie Zander (Olten and Freiburg im Breisgau, 1960–1983). 20 vols.
JC	Richard Noll, *The Jung Cult: Origins of a Charismatic Movement,* 2d printing, revised, with corrections (Princeton: Princeton University

Press, 1994). See also the further revised and corrected paperback edition, with a new introduction (New York: The Free Press, 1997).

JL   *C. G. Jung: Letters. Vol. 1: 1906–1950; Vol. 2: 1951–1961,* selected and ed. Gerhard Adler in collaboration with Aniela Jaffé; trans. R.F.C. Hull and Jane A. Pratt (Princeton: Princeton University Press, 1973, 1975).

MDR   *Memories, Dreams, Reflections,* by C. G. Jung, recorded and ed. Aniela Jaffé, trans. Richard and Clara Winston (New York: Pantheon, 1962).

Introduction

1. Vladimir Nabokov, *Speak, Memory: An Autobiography Revisited* (New York: Vintage, 1967 [1951]), 19.

2. Photographs of Jung's fantastic art nouveau paintings of his visions appear in two large-format picture books: Aniela Jaffé, ed., *C. G. Jung: Bild und Wort* (Olten, Switz.: Walter-Verlag, 1977), published in the United States as *C. G. Jung: Word and Image,* ed. Aniela Jaffé, trans. Krishna Winston (Princeton: Princeton University Press, 1979), and Gerhard Wehr, *An Illustrated Biography of C. G. Jung,* trans. Michael Kohn (Boston: Shambhala, 1989). See additional material in Aniela Jaffé, "The Creative Phases in Jung's Life," *Spring* (1972): 162–90. The German edition of Jung's "autobiography" includes a closing statement added to the "Red Book" by Jung in the autumn of 1959 (*ETG,* 387).

3. Repeated written requests for access to the Honegger papers sent to Zurich to the late C. A. Meier (to whom Jung gave the papers), to Franz Jung (Jung's only son), and to Beat Glaus, the director of the C. G. Jung Archives at the Eidgenossische Technische Hochschule Bibliothek in Zurich, all went unanswered—a story familiar to almost every scholar who has attempted to conduct biographical research on Jung. For a brief summary of what *might* be available, see Beat Glaus, "Autographen und Manuskripten zur ETH- und zur Wissenschaftsgeschichte: Aus den wissenschaftshistorischen Sammlung der ETH-Bibliothek Zurich," *Gesnerus* 39 (1982): 4437–42. My own unsuccessful attempts to gain access to the Honegger papers are summarized in the following newspaper articles: Jessica Marshall, "In the Name of the Father," *Lingua Franca,* May/June 1995, 15; Dinitia Smith, "Scholar Who Says Jung Lied Is at War with Descendants," *The New York Times,* June 3, 1995, A1, A9; *NY Times* Service, "Scholar Denied Access to Jung Papers: Did Psychoanalyst Fake Key Data?" *Chicago Tribune,* June 4, 1995; Ben Macintyre, "Harvard Scholar Says Jung Was Fraud," *The Times* (London), June 5, 1995, overseas news section; Hella Boschmann, " 'Lügner des Jahrhunderts' US-Forscher entlarvt C. G. Jung als Fälscher seiner eigenen Theorie," *Die Welt* (Hamburg), June 8, 1995; Domink Wichmann, "Dreiste Mogelpackung," *Süddeutsche Zeitung* (Munich), Aug. 26/27, 1995, V2/34; Martin Stingelin, "Mithras auf der Couch—Geheimnis der Erde: Das Unbewusste als antikes Mysterium," *Frankfurter Allgemeine Zeitung,* July 19, 1995, N5; Scott Heller,

"Flare-up over Jung: Dispute Involves an Author, a University Press, and a Psychoanalyst's Heirs," *Chronicle of Higher Education,* June 16, 1995, 10E, and my letter in response, "Controversy over Jung," *Chronicle of Higher Education,* Sept. 15, 1995, B6; Jose Luiz Silva, "Uma religiao moderna: Psicologo ataca ideia de inconsciente coletivo em 'O Culto de Jung,' " *Folha de São Paulo* (São Paulo, Brazil), May 26, 1996; and Claudio Figueiredo, "A velha nova era de Carl Gustav Jung," *Jornal de Brasil* (Rio de Janeiro), May 28, 1996. On August 7, 8, 9, 11, 14, and 15, 1995, the *Svenska Dagbladet* (Stockholm) published a wide-ranging analysis and discussion of my work in a series titled *"Jungkulten."* After I gave a series of lectures in Stockholm in October 1995, the following articles appeared in the *Svenska Dagbladet:* Peter Ostman, "Jungkult har blivit religion," Oct. 24, 1995; Kay Glans, "Under Strecket: Sokandet efter C G Jung i historien," Nov. 10, 1995; and Kay Glans, " 'Jungs teori en segligvad myt:' Den amerikanske idenhistorikern Richard Noll till frontalangrepp mot jungianismen," Nov. 11, 1995.

4. Alan Elms, "The Auntification of C. G. Jung," chap. 4 of his *Uncovering Lives: The Uneasy Alliance of Biography and Psychology* (New York: Oxford University Press, 1994), 51–70. There is a sad anecdote in this chapter concerning Aniela Jaffé, who had faithfully—and often selflessly—served Jung and his memory for decades. Although Jaffé had essentially written most of *MDR,* when Elms visited her in 1991 in her Zurich apartment, she told him that the Jung family "had repeatedly tried to deprive her of the title-page credit and the royalties she deserved for co-authoring the autobiography" (54).

5. Eugen Bohler interview, May 1970, JBA, 5.

6. Although my *JC* was an intellectual history written from the perspectives of the history of science and the history of medicine, it aroused the attention of people interested in Jung from a religious perspective and brought a response from the conservative Roman Catholic community in the United States. See the following articles in *The Wanderer* (a national Catholic weekly), all by Paul Likoudis: "The Jung Cult . . . The Church's Greatest Threat Since Julian the Apostate," Dec. 29, 1994, 1, 6; "Jung Replaces Jesus in Catholic Spirituality," Jan. 5, 1995, 1, 6; "Jungians Believe Traditional Catholics Impede 'Renewal,' " Jan. 5, 1995, 7.

7. R.F.C. Hull interview, May 25, 1971, JBA, 16–18.

1: The Inner Fatherland

1. On the origins of Philemon in Gnostic and Mithraic symbolism, see Richard Noll, "Jung the *Leontocephalus,*" *Spring* 53 (1993): 38–39.

2. On Philemon, see the chapter "Confrontation with the Unconscious," in *MDR*. All quotations here are from the English translation of *MDR.*

3. Ibid., 232.

4. Ibid., 35.

5. Ibid., 233.

6. Eyewitness accounts of the 1817 Wartburgfest can be found in Heinrich

Ferdinand Massmann, *Kurze und Wahrhaftige Beschreibung des grossen Burschenfestes auf der Wartburg bei Eisenach* (n.p., 1817), and in *Beschreibung des Festes auf der Wartburg, Ein Sendschreiben an die gutgesinnten* (n.p., 1818). See also the contextualization in George Mosse, *The Nationalization of the Masses: Political Symbolism and Mass Movements in Germany from the Napoleonic Wars through the Third Reich* (Ithaca, N.Y.: Cornell University Press, 1975), as well as the special volume of papers on the Wartburg festival in Klaus Malettke, ed., *Darstellungen und Quellen zur Geschichte der deutschen Einheitsbewegung im neunzehnten und zwanzigsten Jahrhundert*, vol. 14, *175 Jahre Wartburgfest 18. Oktober 1817–18. Oktober 1992. Studien zur politischen Bedeutung und zum Zeithintergrund der Wartburgfeier* (Heidelberg, 1992).

7. On the student societies, see Joachim Bauer, "Studentische Verbindungen zwischen Revolution und Restauration. Von den Landsmannschaften zur Burschenschaft," in Friedrich Stark, ed., *Evolution des Geistes: Jena um 1800. Natur und Kunst, Philosophie und Wissenschaft im Spannungsfeld der Geschichte* (Stuttgart: Kelin-Cotta, 1994).

8. Heinrich Heine, *Religion and Philosophy in Germany: A Fragment*, trans. John Snodgrass (London: Trubner, 1882).

9. This drawing by Ernst Fries, a landscape painter from Heidelberg, is in a private collection. A reproduction appears in Huldrych M. Koelbing, "Die Berufung Karl Gustav Jungs (1794–1864) nach Basel und ihre Vorgeschichte," *Gesnerus* 34 (1977): 321.

10. Schoenbrun's remarks and those by him that follow are from Friedrich Rintelen, "Zur Persönlichkeit Karl Gustav Jungs," *Gesnerus* 39 (1982): 237.

11. On Arndt, see Alfred Pundt, *Arndt and the Nationalist Awakening in Germany* (New York: Columbia University Press, 1935).

12. Carl Jung mentions his grandfather's baptismal certificate and black, red, and gold ribbon in a letter to Huldrych M. Koelbing dated October 27, 1954. See Koelbing, "Die Berufung Karl Gustav Jungs," 328.

13. A limited edition of selections from Karl Gustav's diary from 1849 to 1864 was published by his son Ernst Jung (*Aus dem Tagebüchern meines Vaters* [Basel, 1910]). References to Karl's earlier life experiences abound, but the story of his religious conversion and political activism is incomplete. Unlike the testimonies of the Pietists, the diary contains references to God on almost every page, yet Karl Jung does not appear to have been a particularly pious or introspective man. "He was," Friedrich Rintelen concluded, "too self-centered, too extraverted" ("Karl Gustav Jungs," 241).

14. On this complex religious movement I am indebted to the following: Gerhard Kaiser, *Pietismus und Patriotismus im Literarischen Deutschland: Ein Beitrag zum Problem der Saekularisation* (Wiesbaden: Franz Steiner Verlag, 1961), from which I borrowed the chapter title "Das innere Vaterland"; and Koppel Pinson, *Pietism as a Factor in the Rise of German Nationalism* (New York: Columbia University Press, 1934). A useful summary is also found in Liah Greenfeld, *Nationalism: Five Roads to Modernity* (Cambridge, Mass.: Harvard University

Press, 1993), 314–22. According to Greenfeld, the German Romantic movement is "a direct heir of Pietism" that "secularized central Pietist notions" (322).

15. On the psychological techniques of introversion or introspection in Pietist practice, see Kaiser, *Pietismus,* 11, 47; and Pinson, *Pietism,* 57, citing Schleiermacher's *Monologen:* "As often as I turn my gaze inward upon my inmost self, I am at once within the domain of eternity. I behold the spirit's action which no one can change and no time can destroy but which itself creates both world and time."

16. Pinson, *Pietism,* 52.

17. Nicholas Boyle, *Goethe: The Poet and the Age,* vol. 1, *The Poetry of Desire* (Oxford: Oxford University Press, 1991), 12–13.

18. See Kaiser, *Pietismus,* 40–57; also Jost Hermand, *Old Dreams of a New Reich: Volkish Utopias and National Socialism,* trans. Paul Levesque (Bloomington: Indiana University Press, 1992), 7, originally published as *Der alte Traum von neuen Reich: Völkische Utopien und Nationalsozialismus* (Frankfurt am Main: Athenaeum, 1988).

19. Cited in Pundt, *Arndt,* 166.

20. For a complete list of the books in Jung's library that survived with him until the end of his life (some doubtless disappeared over the years), see *C. G. Jung Bibliothek: Katalog* (Küsnacht-Zurich, 1967).

21. For a well-illustrated introduction to the man and his science career, see Douglas Botting, *Humboldt and the Cosmos* (New York: Harper and Row, 1973).

22. "Ich bin kein Deutscher meht." Cited in Rintelen, "Karl Gustav Jungs," 240.

23. A brief but useful history of Freemasonry in Switzerland published during Karl Jung's lifetime is Carl Ludwig von Haller, *Freymaurerey und ihr Einfluss in der Schweitz* (Schaffhausen: Hurter'sche Buchhandlung, 1840).

24. The fantasy of the pristine theologians (*prisci theologi*) is an essential element of all modern occultism. For the origins and Renaissance revival of this idea, see D. P. Walker, *The Ancient Theology: Studies in Christian Platonism from the Fifteenth to the Eighteenth Century* (London: Duckworth, 1972).

25. The best work on Rosicrucianism thus far remains Frances Yates, *The Rosicrucian Enlightenment* (London: Routledge and Kegan Paul, 1972).

26. Cited in Boyle, *Goethe: The Poet and the Age,* 1:274.

27. Ibid.

28. My reference text for *Die Geheimnisse: Ein Fragment* (1816) is J. W. von Goethe, *Goethes Werke,* vol. 2, *Gedichte und Epen,* 7th ed., with textual criticism and notes by Erich Trunz (Hamburg: Christian Weger Verlag, 1965), 271–81. The translations are my own. This poem has been an inspiration for occultist organizations and Volkish German secret societies.

29. The Rosicrucian ritual room or chapel was emulated at the Swiss cult site where Luc Jouret's Solar Temple members were found dead in October 1994. See Tom Post, "Suicide Cult," *Newsweek,* international edition, Oct. 17, 1994. On the similarities in symbolism and psychological dynamics between this group and

Jung's inner circle of disciples, see Richard Noll, "The Rose, the Cross, and the Analyst," *The New York Times*, Oct. 15, 1994, A19.

30. For the complete text, see *JC*, 250–54.

31. C. G. Jung, *Analytical Psychology: Notes of the Seminar Given in 1925*, ed. William McGuire (Princeton: Princeton University Press, 1989), 37, 82.

32. "Es stroemte wie ein Wunderbalsam in meine Seele" *MDR*, 60.

33. Letter to Max Rychner, Feb. 28, 1932, *JL* 1:89.

34. *MDR*, 60.

35. Ibid., 319.

36. Transcripts of unpublished interviews with Jung by Aniela Jaffé are in the Bollingen Foundation Archives at the Library of Congress in Washington, D.C., but quoting directly from them is not permitted.

37. *MDR*, 317.

38. This claim is made in several interviews in JBA.

2: Summoning the Spirits

1. This chapter of Jung's life remains largely uncharted due to a lack of access to primary-source material (namely, Jung's notes of the spiritualist séances and his own diaries). I have relied on the following secondary sources: Stephanie Zumstein-Preiswerk, *C. G. Jungs Medium: Die Geschichte der Helly Preiswerk* (Munich: Kindler Verlag, 1975); although submitted to Jung himself for correction during his lifetime, the discussion of Jung's spiritualist experiments in Henri Ellenberger, *The Discovery of the Unconscious* (New York: Basic Books, 1970), is historically inaccurate and is corrected by Ellenberger in his 1991 paper on the subject: "C. G. Jung and the Story of Hélène Preiswerk: A Critical Study with New Documents [1991]," in Mark Micale, ed., *Beyond the Unconscious: Essays of Henri F. Ellenberger in the History of Psychiatry* (Princeton: Princeton University Press, 1993); James Hillman, "Some Early Background to Jung's Ideas: Notes on *C. G. Jungs Medium* by Stephanie Zumstein-Preiswerk," *Spring* (1976): 123–36; Aniela Jaffé, "Parapsychology: Experience and Theory," in *From the Life and Work of C. G. Jung,* trans. R.F.C. Hull (New York: Harper Colophon, 1971), first published as *Aus Leben und Werkstatt von C. G. Jung: Parapsychologie, Alchemie, Nationalsozialismus, Erinnerungen aus den letzten Jahren* (Zurich: Rascher and Cie, 1968); and F. X. Charet, *Spiritualism and the Foundations of C. G. Jung's Psychology* (Albany: State University of New York Press, 1993). Jung's 1902 doctoral dissertation—his first publication—is the most extensive public statement by Jung concerning his spiritualist experiments, but, as Ellenberger has pointed out, it conflicts markedly with the account given by Zumstein-Preiswerk: "On the Psychology and Pathology of So-Called Occult Phenomena," *CW* 1. It was originally published as C. G. Jung, *Zur Psychologie und Pathologie sogennanter occulter Phänomene. Eine psychiatrische Studie* (Leipzig: Oswald Mutze, 1902). The first English translation, by M. D. Eder, appears in Constance

Long, ed., *Collected Papers on Analytical Psychology* (New York: Moffat, Yard; London: Bailliére, Tindall and Cox, 1916). Jung also discusses his experience with Hélène Preiswerk at the outset of a seminar given in English in 1925: C. G. Jung, *Analytical Psychology: Notes of the Seminar Given in 1925,* ed. William McGuire (Princeton: Princeton University Press, 1989). The story Jung tells in *MDR* (106–7) is obviously false and serves only to deflect any public perception that he had initiated or was deeply involved in séances.

2. Ellenberger, *Discovery,* 687.

3. C. G. Jung, "The Swiss Line in the European Spectrum [1928]," in *CW* 10. The original is C. G. Jung, "Die Bedeutung der schweitzerischen Linie im Spektrum Europas," *Neue Schweitzer Rundschau* (Zurich) 34 (1928): 1–11, 469–79.

4. See James Mearns, "Preiswerk, Samuel," in J. Julian, ed., *A Dictionary of Hymology.* (1907, reprint, New York: Dover, 1957), 2: 907–8; B. Pick, "Preiswerk, Samuel, Dr.," in John McClintock and James Strong, eds., *Cyclopedia of Biblical, Theological and Ecclesiastical Literature.* (New York: Harper and Brothers, 1879), 8: 505. On the history of the Preiswerk family through the centuries, including fifty genealogical tables, see Ernst Schopf-Preiswerk, *Die Basler Familie Preiswerk* (Basel: Verlag Friedrich Reinhard, 1952), which was updated with supplements in 1961 and 1979.

5. Aniela Jaffé, "Parapsychology," 2.

6. Zumstein-Preiswerk, *C. G. Jungs Medium,* 53. The following translations of passages concerning the earliest séances are all from this work, 53–58. All translations from this book are my own.

7. On these changes, see ibid., 59–65.

8. For an introduction to many of these figures, see Alan Gauld, *The Founders of Psychical Research* (New York: Schocken, 1968).

9. Johann C. F. Zoellner, *Transcendental Physics: An Account of Experimental Investigations, From the Scientific Treatises,* trans. Charles Carlton Massey (London: W. H. Harrison, 1880).

10. Immanuel Kant, *Dreams of a Spirit-Seer and Other Related Writings,* trans. John Manolesco (New York: Vantage, 1969), originally published in German in 1766.

11. Arthur Schopenhauer, "Essay on Spirit-Seeing and Everything Connected Therewith [1851]," in *Parega and Paralipomena: Short Philosophical Essays,* trans. E.F.J. Payne (Oxford: Clarendon Press, 1974), 1:282.

12. Ibid., 287.

13. Johann Heinrich Jung-Stilling, *Theorie der Geister-Kunde* (Nuremberg: Raw, 1808). This book appeared in English as *Theory of Pneumatology,* trans. Samuel Jackson (London: Longman, Rees, Orme, Brown, Breen and Longman, 1834).

14. Jung-Stilling, *Theory of Pneumatology,* 370–87.

15. Ibid., 371.

16. Ibid., 373.

17. Ibid., 225.

18. Justinius Kerner, *Die Seherin von Prevorst, Eroffnungen über das innere Leben des Menschen und über das hereinragen einer Geisterwelt in die unsere,* pt. 2 (Stuttgart: J. G. Cotta'scher, 1829). The first English edition is *The Seeress of Prevorst; being revelations concerning the inner life of Man, and the interdiffusion of a world of spirits in the one we inhabit,* trans. Mrs. Crowe (New York: Harper and Brothers, 1845).

19. Kerner, *Seeress,* 49.

20. Ibid., 20.

21. Ibid., 24.

22. Ibid., 26.

23. Ibid., 28.

24. Ibid., 119.

25. The publication later that year of *Die Seherin von Prevorst* aroused such interest that in 1831 Kerner founded a journal, *Blätter von Prevorst,* to publish similar reports of spiritualist and paranormal phenomena from around Europe. It was, perhaps, the first journal devoted specifically to parapsychology. Hermann Hesse compiled an anthology of selections from this early publication, published as *Blätter aus Prevorst: Eine Auswahl von Berichten über Magnetismus, Hellsehen, Geistererscheinungen aus dem Kreise Justinius Kerners und seiner Freunde* (Berlin: S. Fischer Verlag, 1926).

26. Zumstein-Preiswerk, *C. G. Jungs Medium,* 74.

27. C. G. Jung, *The Zofingia Lectures, CW* A, trans. Jan van Heurck (Princeton: Princeton University Press, 1983). Jung delivered five lectures to his fraternity between November 1896 and January 1899.

28. Camille Flammarion, *Astronomie populaire* (Paris: Marpon and Flammarion, 1881).

29. *MDR,* 104–6.

30. Jung, *Analytical Psychology,* 5–6.

31. On Jung's early adoption of "vitalism" and his merger of this concept with speculations on the independence of the human soul, see C. G. Jung, "Some Thoughts on Psychology [May 1897]," in *The Zofingia Lectures,* 31, 38–40.

32. Zumstein-Preiswerk, *C. G. Jungs Medium,* 100.

33. I strongly disagree here with Henri Ellenberger, who attributes Jung's later, more disingenuous public attitudes to the young medical student when he claims that Jung "understood fully that he was not dealing with the voice of the disembodied in these séances, but rather with projections of unconscious material, that is, with what he called 'psychological realities' " in Micale, *Beyond the Unconscious,* 304.

3: Hidden Memories

1. For a magical evocation of the Munich that Jung saw in 1900, see the short story by Thomas Mann, "Gladius Dei" (1902), of which there are many German

editions. The translation here is my own. Another version appears in Thomas Mann, *Stories of Three Decades,* trans. H. T. Lowe-Porter (New York: Alfred A. Knopf, 1936). On Munich cultural life at the turn of the century, see also Thomas E. Willey, "Thomas Mann's Munich," in Gerald Chapple and Hans Schulte, eds., *The Turn of the Century: German Literature and Art 1890–1915* (Bonn: Bouvier, 1981). On the relationship between Mann and Jung and on the influence of Jungian concepts on Mann, including a bibliography of the secondary literature, see Paul Bishop, " 'Literarische Beziehungen haben nie bestanden?' Thomas Mann and C. G. Jung," *Oxford German Studies* 23 (1994): 124–72.

2. Extensive information about Jung's foreign travels can be found in "Appendix IX. Travels" in the unpublished English typescript of *MDR* at CLM. Neither *ETG* nor the published version of *MDR* contain much of this information.

3. On the bohemian subculture and its haunts in Munich, see Dirk Heisserer, *Wo die Geister wandern: Eine Topographie der Schwabinger Boheme um 1900* (Munich: Eugen Diederichs Verlag, 1993); and Hermann Wilhelm, *Die Münchner Boheme: Von der Jahrhundertswende bis zum Ersten Weltkrieg* (Munich: Buchendorfer Verlag, 1993).

4. *MDR,* 111.

5. Information on Jung's reading of Nietzsche can be found in Paul Bishop, "Jung's Annotation of Nietzsche's Works: An Analysis," *Nietzsche-Studien: Internationales Jahrbuch für die Nietzsche-Forschung,* vol. 24 (Berlin: Walter de Gruyter, 1995).

6. On the Munich Secession, see Ekkehard Mai, "Akademie, Sezession und Avantgarde—München um 1900," in Thomas Zacharias, ed., *Die Münchener Kunstakademie zwischen Aufklärung und Romantik: Ein Beitrag zur Kunsttheorie und Kunstpolitik unter Max I. Joseph,* Miscellanea Bavarica Monacensia, no. 123, eds. Karl Bosl and Richard Bauer (Munich: Stadtarchiv München, 1984); and Maria Makela, *The Munich Secession: Art and Artists in Turn-of-the-Century Munich* (Princeton: Princeton University Press, 1990).

7. See Edwin Becker, *Franz von Stuck, 1863–1928: Eros and Pathos* (Amsterdam: Van Gogh Museum, 1995).

8. On the fin-de-siècle reinterpretation of religious imagery, see Friedrich Gross, *Jesus, Luther, und der Papst im Bilderkampf 1871 bis 1918, Zur Malereigeschichte der Kaiserzeit* (Marburg, 1989).

9. "Sometimes the snake creeps into the mouth, sometimes it bites the breast like Cleopatra's legendary asp, sometimes it comes in the role of the paradisical snake, or in the variations of Franz Stuck, whose pictures of snakes bear the significant titles 'Vice,' 'Sin,' 'Lust.' The mixture of lust and anxiety is expressed incomparably in the very atmosphere of these pictures, and far more brutally, indeed, than in Mörike's charming poem [*The Maiden's First Love Song*]." C. G. Jung, *Psychology of the Unconscious: A Study of the Transformations and Symbolisms of the Libido,* trans. Beatrice M. Hinkle (New York: Moffat, Yard, 1916), 10–11.

10. See *MDR,* 112–49.

11. Eugen Bleuler, "Die Prognose der Dementia Praecox—Schizophreniengruppe," *Allegemeine Zeitschrift für Psychiatrie* 65 (1908): 436–64; Eugen Bleuler, *Dementia Praecox oder die Gruppe der Schizophrenien* (Leipzig: Franz Deuticke, 1911). A translation of Bleuler's 1908 article can be found in J. Cutting and M. Shepherd, eds., *The Clinical Roots of the Schizophrenia Concept: Translations of Seminal European Contributions on Schizophrenia* (Cambridge: Cambridge University Press, 1987).

12. *MDR*, 112.

13. Richard W. Semon, *Die Mneme als erhaltendes Prinzip im Wechsel des organischen Geschehens* (Leipzig: Engelmann, 1904); Richard W. Semon, *Die mnemischen Empfindungen* (Leipzig: Englemann, 1909). On Semon's life and work, see the following: Daniel Schachter, *Stranger Behind the Engram* (Hillsdale, N.J.: Lawrence Erlbaum, 1982); and Daniel Schachter, J. E. Eich, and E. Tulving, "Richard Semon's Theory of Memory," *Journal of Verbal Learning and Verbal Behavior* 17 (1978): 721–43.

14. Ewald Hering, "Über das Gedächtniss als eine allgemeine Function der organisirten Materie," *Almanach der kaiserlicheneten Akademie der Wissenschaften* (Vienna) 20 (1870): 253–78.

15. See *CW* 2. See also William McGuire, "Jung's Complex Reactions (1907): Word Association Experiments Performed by Binswanger," *Spring* (1984): 1–34. For the intellectual background to the word-association studies, see Marielene Putscher, "Storung der Erinnerung: Die Assoziation in Neurologie (S. Freud) und Psychiatrie (C. G. Jung 1904/05)," in Gunter Mann and Rolf Winau, eds., *Medizin, Naturwissenschaft, Technik und das Zweite Kaiserreich. Studien zur Medizingeschichte des 19. Jahrhunderts,* vol. 8 (Göttingen: Vandenhoeck and Ruprecht, 1977).

16. For Bleuler's formal approval of Jung, see H. R. Wilhelm, "Carl Gustav Jung: Promotionsakten. Dokumente aus dem Staatsarchiv des Kantons Zürich," *Südhoffs Archiv zur Wissenschaftsgeschichte* 79 (1995), 231–33. For the history of the French dissociationist school of psychiatry, see Henri Ellenberger, *The Discovery of the Unconscious* (New York: Basic Books, 1970).

17. C. G. Jung, "On the Psychology and Pathology of So-Called Occult Phenomena [1902]," trans. M. D. Eder, in Constance Long, ed., *Collected Papers on Analytical Psychology* (New York: Moffat, Yard; London: Bailliére, Tindall and Cox, 1916), 69. I have consulted the copy of this work once owned by Johann Katz, a participant in Jung's circle in Zurich during the First World War.

18. Ibid., 69–70.

19. Théodore Flournoy, *Des Indes à la Planete Mars: Etude sur un cas de somnambulisme avec glossolalie* (Paris, 1899). The first English translation, abridged, was *From India to the Planet Mars: A Study of a Case of Somnambulism with Glossolalia,* trans. Daniel Vermilye (New York: Harper and Brothers, 1900). An anonymously translated German edition appeared in 1914.

20. See Robert Baker, *Hidden Memories: Voices and Visions from Within* (Buffalo: Prometheus Books, 1992); Elizabeth Loftus and Katherine Ketcham,

The Myth of Repressed Memory: False Memories and Allegations of Sexual Abuse (New York: St. Martin's, 1994); and Frederick Crews et al., *The Memory Wars: Freud's Legacy in Dispute* (New York: NYREV, 1995). Contemporary research on cryptomnesia by cognitive scientists is conducted as part of the study of the larger phenomenon of implicit memory. See Daniel Schacter, "Implicit Memory: History and Current Status," *Journal of Experimental Psychology: Learning, Memory and Cognition* 13 (1987): 501–18; Daniel Schacter, "Memory Distortion: History and Current Status," in D. L. Schacter, J. T. Coyle, C. D. Fischbach, M. M. Mesulam, and L. E. Sullivan, eds., *Memory Distortion: How Minds, Brains and Societies Reconstruct the Past* (Cambridge, Mass.: Harvard University Press, 1995); and Daniel Schacter, *Searching for Memory: The Brain, the Mind, and the Past* (New York: Basic Books, 1996).

21. On this issue, see Richard Noll, "Max Nordau's *Degeneration*, C. G. Jung's Taint," *Spring* 55 (1995): 67–79.

22. Henri Ellenberger reports the existence of three letters from Jung to Helly written between November 1902 and January 1903 that were discovered by Stephanie Zumstein-Preiswerk, although their present location is not indicated. See Henri Ellenberger, "C. G. Jung and the Story of Hélène Preiswerk: A Critical Study with New Documents [1991]," in Mark Micale, ed., *Beyond the Unconscious: Essays of Henri F. Ellenberger in the History of Psychiatry* (Princeton: Princeton University Press, 1993), 303.

23. Jung, "Cryptomnesia [1905]," *CW* 1.

24. Jung and Rhine met only once, in New York City in October 1937. See William Sloane, "Jung and Rhine: A Letter by William Sloane," in *Quadrant* 8 (Winter 1975): 73–78. On Rhine, see Denis Brian, *The Enchanted Voyager: The Life of J. B. Rhine* (Englewood Cliffs, N.J.: Prentice-Hall, 1982). On the history of psychical research and parapsychology, see Seymour Mauskopf and Michael McVaugh, *The Elusive Science: Origins of Experimental Psychical Research* (Baltimore: The Johns Hopkins University Press, 1980).

25. Jung, "Cryptomnesia."

4: Religion Can Only Be Replaced by Religion

1. *MDR*, 146–47.

2. For the text of this letter and a discussion, see Bernard Minder, "Jung an Freud 1905: Ein Bericht über Sabina Spielrein," *Gesnerus* 50 (1993): 113–20.

3. On the relationship of Nietzsche and Wagner, and on nineteenth-century conceptions of genius, see Carl Pletsch, *Young Nietzsche: Becoming a Genius* (New York: The Free Press, 1991).

4. *MDR*, 112–13.

5. Sander Gilman, "Sexology, Psychoanalysis and Degeneration: From a Theory of Race to a Race of Theory," in J. Edward Chamberlin and Sander

Gilman, eds., *Degeneration: The Dark Side of Progress* (New York: Columbia University Press, 1985), 89.

6. Emil Kraepelin, *Psychiatrie: Ein Lehrbuch für Studierende und Ärzte* (Leipzig: Verlag von Johann Ambrosius Barth, 1896).

7. Josef Breuer and Sigmund Freud, *Studien über Hysterie* (Leipzig and Vienna: Franz Deuticke, 1895). The English translation by James Strachey appears as *Studies on Hysteria* (New York: Basic Books, 1982).

8. This was published in an English translation by William Alanson White as *Wish-Fulfillment and Symbolism in Fairy Tales,* Nervous and Mental Disease Monograph Series, no. 21 (New York: Journal of Nervous and Mental Disease, 1915).

9. John B. Watson, "Content of a Course in Psychology for Medical Students," *Journal of the American Medical Association* (March 30, 1912), 916.

10. Robert S. Woodworth, letter to the editor, *The Nation* 103 (1916): 396.

11. Knight Dunlap, *Mysticism, Freudianism, and Scientific Psychology* (St. Louis: Mosby, 1920), 8.

12. See my *JC*.

13. Philip Rieff, *The Triumph of the Therapeutic: Uses of Faith after Freud* (New York: Harper and Row, 1966); Richard Webster, *Why Freud Was Wrong: Sin, Science, and Psychoanalysis* (New York: Basic Books, 1995).

14. Cited in Webster, *Why Freud,* 362.

15. Ibid., 355.

16. Ibid., 362–63.

17. Ibid., 355.

18. Georg Weisz, "Scientists and Sectarians: The Case of Psychoanalysis," *Journal of the History of the Behavioral Sciences* 11 (1975): 350–64.

19. Frank Sulloway, "Reassessing Freud's Case Histories: The Social Construction of Psychoanalysis," *Isis* 82 (1991): 245–75.

20. Rodney Stark and William Sims Bainbridge, *The Future of Religion: Secularization, Revival and Cult Formation* (Berkeley and Los Angeles: University of California Press, 1985), 185. The definition of what constitutes a "cult" varies slightly depending on the source. See, for example, William Sims Bainbridge and Rodney Stark, "Cult Formation: Three Compatible Models," *Sociological Analysis* 40 (1979): 283–95; Marc Galanter, *Cults: Faith, Healing and Coercion* (New York: Oxford University Press, 1989); and Bryan Wilson, *The Social Dimensions of Sectarianism: Sects and New Religious Movements in Contemporary Society* (Oxford: Clarendon Press, 1990). On the related issue of how humans can be deliberately influenced by others (and why intelligence and education make little difference), see Robert Cialdini, *Influence: Science and Practice,* 3d ed. (New York: HarperCollins College Publishers, 1993).

21. Stark and Bainbridge, *Future of Religion,* 419.

22. *FJ,* 95.

23. John Kerr, *A Most Dangerous Method: The Story of Jung, Freud, and Sabina Spielrein* (New York: Alfred A. Knopf, 1993), 171.

24. Jolande Jacobi interview, December 1969, JBA, 42–43.

25. Eva Brabant, Ernst Falzeder, and Patricia Giampieri-Deutsch, eds., *The Correspondence of Sigmund Freud and Sandor Ferenczi,* vol. 1, *1908–1914,* trans. Peter T. Hoffer (Cambridge, Mass.: Harvard University Press, 1993), 434.

26. Jolande Jacobi interview, JBA, 44–45.

27. Ibid., 45–46.

28. John Gedo, "Magna Est Vis Veritas Tuā et Prāvalebit," *The Annual of Psychoanalysis,* vol. 7 (New York: International Universities Press, 1979); Peter Homans, *Jung in Context: Modernity and the Making of a Psychology* (Chicago: The University of Chicago Press, 1979).

29. Kerr, *A Most Dangerous Method,* 296–318.

30. F. X. Charet, *Spiritualism and the Foundations of C. G. Jung's Psychology* (Albany, N.Y.: State University of New York Press, 1993), 171–230.

31. *FJ,* 294.

32. Ibid., 295.

33. Ibid., 296.

34. Ibid., 345.

5: Polygamy

1. *FJ,* 184.

2. The best single source on Gross is Michael Raub, *Opposition und Anpassung: Eine individualpsychologische Interpretation von Leben und Werk des frühen Psychoanalytikers Otto Gross* (Frankfurt am Main: Peter Lang, 1994). In English the best source is Jennifer Michaels, *Anarchy and Eros: Otto Gross' Impact on German Expressionist Writers* (New York: Peter Lang, 1983). Martin Green is almost single-handedly responsible for resurrecting Otto Gross from obscurity with his books *The von Richthofen Sisters: The Triumphant and the Tragic Modes of Love* (New York: Basic Books, 1974) and *Mountain of Truth: The Counterculture Begins, Ascona 1900–1920* (Hanover, N.H.: University Press of New England, 1986). Green is now completing the first full biography of Gross. On Gross's treatment by Jung and for his place in the psychoanalytic movement, see Emanuel Hurwitz, *Otto Gross: "Paradies"—Sucher zwischen Freud und Jung* (Zurich: Suhrkamp Verlag, 1979). New information on Gross also appears in Janet Byrne, *A Genius for Living: The Life of Frieda Lawrence* (New York: HarperCollins, 1995).

3. *FJ,* 126. On Gross's early psychiatric publications, see Michael Turnheim, "Otto Gross und die deutsche Psychiatrie," in his *Freud und der Rest. Aufsätze zur Geschichte der Psychoanalyse* (Vienna: Verlag Turia and Kant, 1994).

4. Ernest Jones, *Free Associations: Memories of a Psychoanalyst* (New York: Basic Books, 1959), 173–74.

5. For Gross's attitude toward degenerates and how to get rid of them (a colony in German Southwest Africa was one solution), see Hurwitz, *Otto Gross,* 35–48. Many of Gross's statements on degeneration appeared in the *Archiv für*

Kriminalanthropologie und Kriminalistik, which he founded, edited, and published in Leipzig from 1899 until his death in 1915. Gross devoted an entire chapter to Gypsies in his textbook, *Handbuch für Untersuchungsrichter* (Munich, 1893). In the third edition of this book (1898) he coined the term "criminalistics." For his handling of a case of suspected ritual murder of Christians by Jews, see Arthur Nussbaum, "The 'Ritual Murder' Trial of Polna," *Historia Judaica* 9 (1950): 57–74.

6. Waldemar Kämpffert, "The Crime-Master and How He Works," *McClure's* 43 (June 1914): 99–111, 144. For further biographical information, see Erich Doehring, "Hans Gross," *Neue Deutsche Biographie* 7 (1966): 139–41; and Roland Grassberger, "Hans Gross," *Journal of Criminal Law, Criminology and Police Science* 47 (1956–7): 397–405.

7. Hurwitz, *Otto Gross,* 45.

8. Otto Gross, *Compendium der Pharmaco-therapie für Polykliniker und junge Ärzte* (Leipzig, 1901); Otto Gross, "Zur Phyllogenese der Ethik," *Archiv für Kriminalanthropologie und Kriminalistik* 9 (1902): 100–103.

9. Hurwitz, *Otto Gross,* 137.

10. Ibid.

11. Otto Gross, *Das Freud'sche Ideogenitätsmoment und seine Bedeutung im manisch-depressiven Irrsein Kraepelins* (Leipzig: Vogel, 1907).

12. Richard Seewald, *Der Mann von gegenueber* (Munich: List, 1963), 138. See his discussion of the Café Stefanie, 137–43. See also the poem by Johannes Becher, "Café Stefanie 1912," in *Johannes R. Becher* (Berlin: Aufbau-Verlag, 1960), 2:227–28. A more detailed description of Gross and the bohemian circuit of Schwabing-Ascona appears in *JC,* 151–69.

13. Seewald, *Mann,* 140.

14. Leonhard Frank, *Links wo das Herz ist* (Munich: Nymphenburger Verlagshandlung, 1952), 49.

15. See the original and the English translation of Erich Mühsam's May 28, 1907, letter to Freud in Kurt Eissler, *Victor Tausk's Suicide* (New York: International Universities Press, 1983), 277–84. See also Erich Mühsam, *Tegebücher 1910–1924,* ed. Chris Hirte (Munich: DTV, 1994). His diaries and other papers are in the Maxim Gorki Institute in Moscow.

16. Jones, *Free Associations,* 173–74.

17. On the Asconan counterculture see Green, *Mountain of Truth;* Harald Szeeman, *Monte Verita—Berg der Wahrheit. Austellungskatalog* (Milan, 1978); and an early view by Erich Mühsam, *Ascona. Eine Broschuere* (Locarno: Verlag Birger Carlson, 1905; reprint, Zurich, 1979). A sociological analysis of the antibourgeois or nonbourgeois subcultures of Europe is provided by Helmut Kreuzer, *Die Boheme: Beiträge zu ihre Beschreibung* (Stuttgart: J. B. Metzlersche Verlagsbuchhandlung, 1968).

18. Max Brod, *Das grosse Wagnis* (Leipzig: Kurt Wolff, 1918).

19. Marianne Weber, *Max Weber: A Biography,* trans. Harry Zorn (New Brunswick, N.J.: Transaction, 1988), 380. The original edition is Marianne Weber, *Max*

Weber: Ein Lebensbild (Tübingen: Mohr, 1926). On this connection, see Nicholas Sombert, "Max Weber and Otto Gross: On the Relationship Between Science, Politics and Eros in Wilhelmine Germany," *History of Political Thought* 8 (1987): 131–52; Nicholas Sombert, "Gruppenbild mit zwei Damen: Zum Verhältnis von Wissenschaft, Politik und Eros im wilhelminischen Zeitalter," *Merkur* 30 (1976): 972–90; and Eduard Baumgarten, "Über Max Weber: Ein Brief an Nicholas Sombart," *Merkur* 31 (1977): 296–300.

20. See Green, *von Richthofen Sisters*.

21. Weber, *Max Weber*, 374.

22. Else von Richthofen, when literally on her deathbed, summoned Martin Green to Germany to give him the love letters, largely undated, between Otto Gross and Frieda. The originals are in the archives of Tufts University in Medford, Mass. See the translations by John Turner and Cornelia Rumpf-Worthen and Ruth Jenkins in the *D. H. Lawrence Review* 22 (Summer 1990). The letter quoted here appears on 188–89.

23. Weber, *Max Weber*, 375.

24. Selections from these letters are in Hurwitz, *Otto Gross*, 133–34.

25. *FJ*, 90.

26. R. Andrew Paskauskas, ed., *The Complete Correspondence of Sigmund Freud and Ernest Jones, 1908–1939* (Cambridge, Mass.: Harvard University Press, 1993), 1.

27. Wilhelm Stekel, *An Autobiography of Wilhelm Stekel: The Life Story of a Pioneer Psychoanalyst*, ed. Emil Gutheil (New York: Liveright, 1950), 122. See also Stekel's posthumous appreciation of Otto Gross, "In Memoriam," *Psyche and Eros* (New York: n.p., 1920), 49.

28. The original report of this interview—in Jung's own handwriting—and all of Otto Gross's clinical-progress notes were recovered from the archives of the Burghölzli in 1967 by an assistant physician, Emanuel Hurwitz. More than a decade later Hurwitz reproduced these documents in *Otto Gross*, after determining that Gross had no living descendants who would contest the publication of this very private information. I have checked Hurwitz against photocopies of the original Burghölzli documents. The report by Frieda Gross and its attached supplement are reproduced in Hurwitz, *Otto Gross*, 139–44. Translations are mine.

29. Hurwitz reproduces most of the regular progress notes by Jung and all of the relevant ones. I have freely translated using photocopies of the originals checked against ibid., 144–47.

30. *FJ*, 155.

31. Hurwitz's discovery of these documents surprised Manfred Bleuler, who had followed in his father's footsteps and was then clinical director of the Burghölzli. Here, in the handwriting of Jung, Freud, and Hans Gross, was evidence of a botched psychoanalytic treatment. Fearing even the slightest potential of a scandal, he immediately gathered the originals from Hurwitz. For many years Bleuler kept them locked in his private office.

32. Paskauskas, *Freud/Jones*, 3–4.

33. Sandor Ferenczi had a racialist interpretation of the prevalence of dementia praecox in Aryans such as Otto Gross and, as many psychoanalysts later claimed, Jung himself. In a letter to Freud dated July 15, 1915, Ferenczi said he remarked to a friend "how remarkable it was that Nordic writers . . . have such an excellent understanding of dementia praecox. I also said that it struck me that in the Zurich mental hospitals dementia praecox was so much more prevalent than in Hungarian ones. This illness is evidently the natural condition, as it were, of Nordic man, who has not yet completely overcome the last period of the Ice Age." Ernst Falzeder and Eva Brabant, eds., *The Correspondence of Sigmund Freud and Sandor Ferenczi,* vol. 2, *1914–1919,* trans. Peter Hoffer (Cambridge, Mass.: Harvard University Press, 1996), 67.

34. *FJ,* 153.

35. Ibid., 156.

36. On Bachofen, see Karl Meuli, "J. J. Bachofens Alterswerk," in Karl Meuli, *Gesammelte Schriften,* ed. Thomas Gelzer (Basel: Schwabe, 1975), 2: 1125–38. See also the discussion of Bachofen's influence on Jung in *JC,* 161–76.

37. Friedrich Engels, *The Origin of the Family, Private Property and the State,* trans. Evelyn Reed (New York: Pathfinder Press, 1972). This work was originally published in Zurich in 1884.

38. Jung first used the terms "introversion" and "extraversion" in public at the 1913 psychoanalytic congress in Munich. This speech was published in a French translation in a well-known psychological (not psychoanalytic) journal. See C. G. Jung, "Contribution à l'étude des types psychologiques," *Archives de Psychologie* (Geneva) 13 (December 1913): 289–99. It appears in translation in *CW* 6.

39. See, for example, John C. Loehlin, *Genes and Environment in Personality Development* (Newbury Park, Calif.: Sage, 1992), 9.

40. C. G. Jung, *Psychological Types, or, The Psychology of Individuation,* trans. H. Godwin Baynes (New York: Harcourt, Brace, 1923), 352–53. Jung discusses these ideas in the chapter on "The Type Problem in Psychology," 337–57. See also the translation in *CW* 6. The development of Jung's theory of psychological types is documented in his extensive correspondence with Hans Schmid-Guisan. See Hans Konrad, *Zur Entstehung von C. G. Jungs "Psychologischen Typen": Der Briefwechsel zwischen C. G. Jung und Hans Schmid-Guisan im Lichte ihrer Freundschaft* (Aarau, Switz.: Sauerlander, 1982).

41. Falzeder and Brabant, *Freud/Ferenczi,* 2: 261.

42. Aldo Carotenuto, *A Secret Symmetry: Sabina Spielrein Between Jung and Freud. The Untold Story of the Woman Who Changed the Early History of Psychoanalysis,* trans. Arno Pomerans, John Shepley, and Krishna Winston (New York: Pantheon, 1982), 107. For an expanded narrative of these relationships, see John Kerr, *A Most Dangerous Method: The Story of Jung, Freud, and Sabina Spielrein* (New York: Alfred A. Knopf, 1993). Spielrein's diaries for 1907 and 1908 were found later and appear in Mireille Cifali, "Extraits inedits d'un journal: De l'amour, de la mort et de la transformation," *Le Bloc-Notes de la Psychoanalyse* 3 (1983): 149–70.

43. The diaries of Sabina Spielrein between 1909 and 1912, her correspondence with Freud, and copies of some of her letters to Jung constituted the rest of the documents. There are also thirty-four letters from Jung to Spielrein. These papers were edited and published by Aldo Carotenuto in *Diario de una segreta simmetria* (Milan: Casa Editrice Astrolabio, 1980); The German edition, *Tagebuch einer heimlichen Symmetrie: Sabina Spielrein zwischen Jung und Freud* (Freiburg in Breisgau: Kore, 1896), contains some of Jung's letters to Spielrein. The English-language edition (Carotenuto, *Secret Symmetry*) does not.

44. This letter is reproduced in full, with commentary, by Bernard Minder, "Jung an Freud 1905: Ein Bericht über Sabina Spielrein," *Gesnerus* 50 (1993): 113–20. The translation here is mine. All of the Burghölzli documents pertaining to Spielrein's treatment have been reproduced, with photos of the original documents, in Bernard Minder, "Sabina Spielrein. Jungs Patientin am Burghölzli," *Luzifer-Amor. Zeitschrift zur Geschichte der Psychoanalyse* 7, no. 14 (1994): 55–127. This article produced most of Minder's 1992 doctoral dissertation for the medical faculty of the University of Bern. I would like to thank Minder, who is currently a staff psychiatrist at the Burghölzli, for generously sending me copies of all his publications.

45. *FJ*, 207.

46. Ibid., 289.

47. Different editions of Spielrein's work currently exist: Sabina Spielrein, *Samtliche Schriften* (Freiburg im Breisgau: Kore, 1987); and Sabina Spielrein, *Ausgewahlte Schriften* (Berlin: Brinkman and Bose, 1986). Her most famous work, an essay that reflects her deep involvement in Jung's mythological researches, is Sabina Spielrein, "Die Destruktion als Ursache des Werdens," *Jahrbuch für psychoanalytische und psychopathologische Forschungen* (1912) 4. This has been reprinted in Sabina Spielrein, *Die Destruktion als Ursache des Werdens,* ed. Gerd Kimmerle (Tübingen: Edition Diskord, 1986). An English translation by Kenneth McCormick appears as Sabina Spielrein, "Destruction as the Cause of Coming into Being," *Journal of Analytical Psychology* 39 (1994): 187–90.

48. In the spring of 1996, her relationships with Freud and Jung were the subject of a play performed off-Broadway in New York City entitled, simply, *Sabina.* Written by Willy Holtzman and directed by Melia Bensussen, it ran for several months at the Primary Stages theater.

49. *FJ*, 207–8.

50. Kristie Miller, "The Letters of C. G. Jung and Medill and Ruth McCormick," *Spring* 50 (1990): 21–22. For further background, see Kristie Miller, *Ruth Hanna McCormick: A Life in Politics* (Albuquerque: University of New Mexico Press, 1992).

51. Aline Valangin interview, Sept. 2, 1970, JBA, 4–5, 7.

52. Tina Keller, "Recollections of My Encounter with Dr. Jung," JBA, B12. Keller had originally been interviewed in 1968 but asked that the transcript be destroyed and her own memoirs put in its place.

53. Forrest Robinson, *Love's Story Told: A Life of Henry A. Murray* (Cam-

bridge, Mass.: Harvard University Press, 1992). This is the most reliable scholarly treatment of the relationship between Murray and Morgan.

54. Ritual manuals and detailed descriptions of a new personal mythology can be found in the personal papers of Christiana Morgan at CLM.

55. Susanne Trüb interview, Sept. 21, 24, 1970, JBA, 20, 29.

56. The whereabouts of Toni Wolff's diaries today remain a mystery, although they clearly existed in September 1970, when Susanne Trüb was interviewed for the C. G. Jung Biographical Archives Project.

57. Trüb interview, JBA, 73–74.

58. *FJ*, 440.

59. See the original transcripts in the LC.

60. Keller statement, JBA, D5.

61. John Layard interview, Dec. 17, 1969, JBA, 34.

62. This is according to Henry A. Murray, interview, 1970, JBA.

63. Trüb interview, JBA, 15–16.

64. Carl A. Meier interview, Sept. 11, 15, 22, 1970, JBA, 26–27.

65. Layard interview, Dec. 17, 1969, JBA, 59.

6: Sun Worship

1. *MDR*, 158–59.

2. C. G. Jung, *Analytical Psychology: Notes of the Seminar Given in 1925,* ed. William McGuire (Princeton: Princeton University Press, 1989), 23.

3. E. A. Bennett, *Meetings with Jung: Conversations Recorded During the Years 1946–1961* (Zurich: Daimon, 1985), 117–18.

4. *FJ*, 251–52.

5. Ibid., 258.

6. Ibid., 296.

7. Ibid., 308.

8. Ibid., 483–84.

9. Ibid., 269.

10. Ibid., 279.

11. C. G. Jung, *Über die Psychologie der Dementia praecox: Ein Versuch* (Halle: Carl Marhold, 1907). The first English edition was *The Psychology of Dementia Praecox,* trans. Frederick W. Peterson and A. A. Brill (New York: The Journal of Nervous and Mental Disease, 1909). It appears in *CW* 3.

12. Sabina Spielrein, "Über den psychologischen Inhalt eines Falls von Schizophrenie," *Jahrbuch für psychoanalytische und psychopathologische Forschungen* 3 (1912): 329–400; Jan Nelken, "Analytische Beobachten über Phantasien eines Schizophrenen," *Jahrbuch für psychoanalytische und psychopathologische Forschungen* 4 (1912): 504–62; and Carl Schneiter, "Archaische Elemente in den Wahnideen eines Paranoiden," in C. G. Jung, ed., *Psychologische Abhandlungen* (Leipzig: Franz Deuticke, 1914).

13. *Jahrbuch für psychoanalytische und psychopathologische Forschungen* 3 (1911): 120–227; 4 (1912): 162–464. C. G. Jung, *Wandlungen und Symbole der Libido: Beiträge zur Entwicklungsgeschichte des Denkens* (Leipzig: Franz Deuticke, 1912). The first English translation was C. G. Jung, *Psychology of the Unconscious: A Study of the Transformations and Symbolisms of the Libido,* trans. Beatrice M. Hinkle (New York: Moffat, Yard, 1916). This translation was reissued in 1991 as *CW* B. All English-language citations here are to the 1916 edition.

14. For a detailed analysis of *Wandlungen,* see *JC,* 109–37.

15. Frank Miller, "Some Instances of Unconscious Creative Imagination," *Journal of the American Society for Psychical Research* 1 (1907): 287–308. For photographs, see Sonu Shamdasani, "A Woman Called Frank," *Spring* 50 (1990): 26–56.

16. *MDR,* 85.

17. Ernst Haeckel, *Die Radiolarien (Rhizopoda radiaria): Eine Monograph* (Berlin: G. Reimer, 1862). Haeckel's best-known book, which contains a discussion of the phylogeny of psychology, is *Die Welträtzel: Gemeinverständliche Studien über Monistische Philosophie* (Bonn: E. Strauss, 1899), first translated as *The Riddle of the Universe,* trans. Joseph McCabe (New York: Harper and Brothers, 1900).

18. Jung *Psychology of the Unconscious,* 104.

19. Ibid., 96.

20. Ibid., 508.

21. Ibid., 501.

22. Eva Brabant, Ernst Falzeder, and Patrizia Giampieri-Deutsch, eds., *The Correspondence of Sigmund Freud and Sandor Ferenczi,* vol. 1, *1908–1914,* trans. Peter T. Hoffer (Cambridge, Mass.: Harvard University Press, 1992), 399.

23. Jung, *Psychology of the Unconscious,* 128.

24. See Leon Poliakov, *The Aryan Myth: A History of Racist and Nationalist Ideas in Europe,* trans. Edmund Howard (New York: Basic Books, 1974); Maurice Oleander, *The Languages of Paradise: Race, Religion and Philology in the Nineteenth Century* (Cambridge, Mass.: Harvard University Press, 1992); and J. P. Mallory, *In Search of the Indo-Europeans* (London: Thames and Hudson, 1989).

25. Suzanne Marchand, *Down from Olympus: Archaeology and Philhellenism in Germany, 1750–1970* (Princeton: Princeton University Press, 1996); Eliza Marian Butler, *The Tyranny of Greece Over Germany: A Study of the Influence Exercised by Greek Art and Poetry Over the Great German Writers of the Eighteenth, Nineteenth, and Twentieth Centuries* (Cambridge: Cambridge University Press, 1935); and Anthony La Vopa, "Specialists Against Specialization: Hellenism as Professional Ideology in German Classical Studies," in Geoffrey Cocks and Konrad Jarausch, eds., *German Professions, 1800–1950* (New York: Oxford University Press, 1990).

26. *MDR,* 29.

27. Ernest Jones, *Free Associations: Memoirs of a Psychoanalyst* (New York: Basic Books, 1959), 35.

28. Jung, *Analytical Psychology,* 25.

29. Richard Dorson, "The Eclipse of Solar Mythology," in Thomas Sebeok, ed., *Myth: A Symposium* (Bloomington: Indiana University Press, 1968).

30. Friedrich Max Müller, *India: What Can It Teach Us? A Course of Lectures Delivered before the University of Cambridge* (New York, 1883), 216.

31. F. Max Müller, *Lectures on the Science of Language, Delivered at the Royal Institution of Great Britain in February, March, April and May, 1868,* 2d series (New York: Scribner's, 1869), 520.

32. R. Andrew Paskauskas, ed., *The Complete Correspondence of Sigmund Freud and Ernest Jones, 1908–1939* (Cambridge, Mass.: Harvard University Press, 1993), 180.

33. Ibid., 182.

34. Brabant et al., *Freud/Ferenczi,* 1: 490–91.

35. Lou Andreas-Salomé, *The Freud Journal,* trans. Stanley Leavy (London: Quartet Books, 1987), 138.

36. *FJ,* 386.

37. Poul Bjerre, *The History and Practice of Psychoanalysis,* trans. Elizabeth Barrow (Boston: Richard Badger, 1916).

38. C. G. Jung to Poul Bjerre, Nov. 10, 1913. Poul Bjerre Papers, KB. I am indebted to Kurt Almqvist, who discovered this letter, and Lars Holm, who alerted me to its existence. Although it is clear that this batch of letters was consulted by the editors of the two volumes of Jung's collected letters (see *JL*), this letter is conspicuously absent there.

39. *FJ,* 550.

40. Jung to Bjerre, Nov. 10, 1913, KB.

41. *JC,* 75–108.

42. For background, see Jost Hermand, *Old Dreams of a New Reich: Volkish Utopias and National Socialism* (Bloomington: Indiana University Press, 1992); Richard Hamann and Jost Hermand, *Stillkunst um 1900* (Munich: Nymphenburger Verlagshandlung, 1973); Jost Hermand, "The Distorted Vision: Pre-Fascist Mythology at the Turn of the Century," in Walter Wetzels, ed., *Myth and Reason: A Symposium* (Austin: University of Texas Press, 1973); George Mosse, *The Crisis of German Ideology: Intellectual Origins of the Third Reich* (New York: Grosset and Dunlap, 1964); Nicholas Goodrick-Clarke, *The Occult Roots of Nazism: Secret Aryan Cults and Their Influence on Nazi Ideology* (New York: New York University Press, 1995); Peter Levenda, *Unholy Alliance: A History of Nazi Involvement with the Occult* (New York: Avon Books, 1995); Karlheinz Weissmann, *Schwarze Fahnen, Runenzeichen: Die Entwicklung der politischen Symbolik der deutschen Rechten zwishen 1890 und 1945* (Dusseldorf: Droste Verlag, 1991); Hermann Gilbhard, *Die Thule Gesellschaft: Vom okkulten Mummenschanz zum Hakenkreuz* (Munich: Kiessling Verlag, 1994); and Rene Freund,

Braune Magie? Okkultismus, New Age und Nationalsozialismus (Vienna: Picus Verlag, 1995).

43. On the transformation of nineteenth-century German cultural fantasies about the nature religion of the ancient Germans and on ancient German religion and the so-called mysteries of Odin/Woden/Wotan, see the following: Karl-Heinz Kohl, "Naturreligion: Zur Transformationsgeschichte eines Begriffs," in Richard Faber and Renate Schleiser, eds., *Die Restauration der Götter: Antike Religion und Neo-Paganismus* (Würzburg: Koenigshausen and Neumann, 1986). Also in this same volume see Ekkehard Hieronimus, "Von der Germanen-Forschung zum Germanen-Glauben: Zur Religionsgeschichte des Präfaschismus." In English, see the works of Hilda Ellis Davidson: "Germanic Religion," in C. Jouco Bleeker and George Widengred, eds., *Historia Religionum: Handbook for the History of Religions,* vol. 1 (Leiden: E. J. Brill, 1969); "The Germanic World," in Michael Loewe and Carmen Blacker, eds., *Divination and Oracles* (London: George Allen and Unwin, 1981); and *The Lost Beliefs of Northern Europe* (London: Routledge, 1993). Also useful are the chapters on "The Germanic Peoples" and "Late Germanic Religion" in Prudence Jones and Nigel Pennick, *A History of Pagan Europe* (London: Routledge, 1995).

44. Cited in Mosse, *Crisis of German Ideology,* 59.

45. "Sonnwendfest," *Der Monismus: Zeitschrift für einheitliche Weltanschauung und Kulturpolitik* 5 (1910): 126. For a representative Aryanist view on sun worship and the sun cults by one of Jung's contemporaries, see Leopold von Schroeder, *Arische Religion* (Leipzig: H. Haessel Verlag, 1916), vol. 2, which discusses the sun, sun gods, and the *Sonnenkult der Arier* and their sun and fire festivals. For a national socialist perspective on related festivals, see Jakob Wilhelm Hauer, *Fest und Feier aus deutscher Art* (Stuttgart: K. Gutbrod, 1936).

46. Paul Bramwell Means, *Things That Are Caesar's: The Genesis of the German Church Conflict* (New York: Round Table Press, 1935), 166.

47. "Eine geistige Bewegung, ein Niveau, eine Richtung, ein Protest, ein neuer Kult oder vielmehr der Versuch, aus uralten Kulten wieder neue religiöse Möglichkeiten zu gewinnen." Franziska zu Reventlow, *Von Paul zu Pedro/Herrn Dames Aufzeichnungen: Zwei Romanen,* ed. Else Reventlow (Frankfurt am Main: Verlag Ullstein, 1976), 128–29. On her life and work, see Richard Faber, *Franziska zu Reventlow und die Schwabinger Gegenkultur* (Vienna: Boehlau, 1993).

48. Reventlow, *Herrn Dames Aufzeichnungen,* 154.

49. On Fidus, see Janos Frecot, Johann Friedrich Geist, and Diethart Kerbs, *Fidus 1868–1948: Zur asthetischen Praxis bürgerlicher Fluchtbewegungen* (Munich: Rogner and Bernhard, 1972).

50. Von Werth sometimes wrote under the pseudonyms Maximilian Ferdinand and G. Herman. See Maximilian Ferdinand, *D.I.S. "Sexualreligion." Enthuellungen,* 3 vols, *Sexual-Mystik, Sexual Moral, Sexual-Magie, Bilderschmuck von Fidus.* (Leipzig: Wilhelm Friedrich, 1897); and Maximilian Ferdinand, *Wanidis. D.I.S. Die arische "Sexualreligion" als Volks-Veredelung in Zeugen, Leben,*

und Sterben. Bilder von Fidus. Mit einem Anhang über "Menschenzüchtung" von Carl du Prel. (Leipzig: Wilhelm Friedrich, 1897).

51. Aleister Crowley, *The Confessions of Aleister Crowley: An Autobiography,* eds. John Symonds and Kenneth Grant (New York: Bantam, 1969), 889.

7: The Mystery of Deification

1. Most of this chapter (as well as the portions of chapter 6 dealing with Max Müller's solar mythology and philology in general) is taken from two previous works of mine, one published and one almost published. The first of these is my article "Jung the *Leontocephalus*," which appeared in *Spring* 53 (1992). I wish to thank Charles Boer, the editor of *Spring,* for kindly giving permission to reproduce parts of it. The second source for this chapter is my introduction to my selections from Jung's work in the ill-fated anthology *Mysteria: Jung and the Mysteries,* which was to appear in print in the spring of 1995 but was canceled by my publisher due to objections by the Jung family. I wish to thank Princeton University Press for graciously reverting to me all legal rights to my essay.

Throughout this chapter, all citations from Jung's 1925 seminar on analytical psychology were checked against an archival copy of the original November 1925 multigraph compiled directly from written notes taken during the lectures by Cary F. de Angulo. I have altered the punctuation slightly to make the English a bit more readable, but the meaning of the text has not been changed. For the sake of convenience, I have provided the page numbers of the 1989 published version of the second edition (1939) of Cary de Angulo's notes. This version is C. G. Jung, *Analytical Psychology: Notes of the Seminar Given in 1925 by C. G. Jung,* ed. William McGuire (Princeton: Princeton University Press, 1989), hereafter in this chapter known as *AP*. The opening epigraph appears in *AP,* 97–98.

2. *MDR,* vii.
3. Ibid., 170–99.
4. Ibid., 181.
5. *AP,* 89.
6. *MDR,* 182.
7. *AP,* 95. Jung's deification experience, outlined in this lecture from June 8, 1925, can be found in *AP,* 95–99.
8. *AP,* 96.
9. Ibid., 98.
10. Ibid., 99.
11. Ibid., 92.
12. C. G. Jung, *Nietzsche's "Zarathustra": Notes of the Seminar Given in 1934–1939,* ed. James L. Jarrett, 2 vols. (Princeton: Princeton University Press, 1988), 1: 460–61.
13. See Friedrich Creuzer, *Symbolik und Mythologie der alten Völker, besonders der Griechen,* 4 vols. (Leipzig: Heyer and Leske, 1810–1812). On Creuzer,

see Arnoldo Momigliano, "Friedrich Creuzer and Greek Historiography," *Journal of the Wartburg and Courtald Institutes* 9 (1946): 152–63; A. Momigliano, "Ancient History and the Antiquarians," *Journal of the Wartburg and Courtald Institutes* 13 (1950): 285–318; Martin Donougho, "Hegel and Friedrich Creuzer: Or, Did Hegel Believe in Myth?" in David Kolb, ed., *New Perspectives on Hegel's Philosophy of Religion* (Albany: State University of New York Press, 1992). In German, see the discussion in Alfred Bäumler, "Einleitung," in *Der Mythus von Orient und Occident: Eine Metaphysik der Alten Welt, aus den Werken von J. J. Bachofen*, ed. Alfred Bäumler (Munich: C. H. Beck'sche Verlagsbuchhandlung, 1926). Bäumler's introductory essay provides a useful overview not only of the mythological researches of Creuzer, but also those of Goerres, Savigny, Grimm, K. O. Mueller, Ranke, and Bachofen, as well as the mythological and philosophical interests of the Romantic movement.

14. *FJ,* 258.

15. Jung owned and absorbed the following works by Dieterich: *Abraxas: Studien zer Religionsgeschichte des spätern Altertums* (Leipzig: B. G. Teubner, 1891); *Nekyia: Beiträge zur Erklärung derneuentdeckten Petrusapokalypse* (Leipzig: B. G. Teubner, 1905); *Mutter Erde: Ein Versuch über Volksreligion* (Leipzig: B. G. Teubner, 1905); and *Eine Mithrasliturgie* (Leipzig: B. G. Teubner, 1903).

16. Walter Burkert, *Ancient Mystery Cults* (Cambridge, Mass.: Harvard University Press, 1987), 1.

17. In his later alchemical writings, Jung did acknowledge the role that Reitzenstein played in drawing his attention to the similarities of Hermetic, Gnostic, and alchemical symbolism in such books as *Poimandres: Studien zur griechischaegyptische und früchristlischen Literatur* (Leipzig: B. G. Teubner, 1904) and *Die hellenistischen Mysterienreligionon nach ihren Grundgedanken und Wirkungen* (Leipzig: B. G. Teubner, 1910). See also the English translation by John Steely of the 1926 third edition of this latter work, *Hellenistic Mystery Religions: Their Basic Ideas and Significance* (Pittsburgh: Pickwick Press, 1978).

18. Franz Cumont, *Textes et monumentes figurés relatifs aux mystères de Mithra,* 2 vols. (Brussels: H. Lamertin, 1896, 1899). In *Wandlungen,* Jung refers to Franz Cumont, *Die Mysterien des Mithra: Ein Beitrag zur Religionsgeschichte der römischen Kaiserzeit,* trans. H. Gehrich (Leipzig: B. G. Teubner, 1903).

19. K.H.E. De Jong, *Das Antike Mysterienwesen in religionsgeschichtlicher, ethnologischer und psychologischer Beleuchtung* (Leiden, E. J. Brill, 1909).

20. Ibid., 269.

21. See A. J. Festugiere, *Personal Religion Among the Greeks* (Berkeley: University of California Press, 1954). Other useful sources on the ancient mysteries are Luther Martin, *Hellenistic Religions: An Introduction* (New York: Oxford University Press, 1987); Marvin Meyer, ed., *The Ancient Mysteries: A Sourcebook* (San Francisco: Harper and Row, 1987); Arthur Darby Nock, *Conversion: The Old and New in Religion from Alexander the Great to Augustine of Hippo* (London: Oxford University Press, 1933); and Walter Burkert, *Greek Religion,* trans. John Raffan (Cambridge, Mass.: Harvard University Press, 1985), which

originally appeared as *Griechische Religion der archaischen und klassischen Epoche* (Stuttgart: Verlag W. Kohlhammer, 1977). For an informative portrait of the pagan Hellenistic world of late antiquity, see Robin Lane Fox, *Pagans and Christians* (New York: Alfred A. Knopf, 1989).

22. Burkert, *Ancient Mystery Cults,* 11–12.

23. Ibid., 8.

24. The concept of a stage model of rites of initiation was first put forth to describe this form of ritual behavior by a contemporary of Jung, Arnold van Gennep, in his *Les rites de passage* (Paris: Nourry, 1908). See also especially Victor Turner, *The Ritual Process: Structure and Anti-Structure* (Ithaca, N.Y.: Cornell University Press, 1969). Also useful is Mircea Eliade, *Rites and Symbols of Initiation: The Mysteries of Birth and Rebirth* (New York: Harper Colophon, 1958).

25. Burkert, *Ancient Mystery Cults,* 3.

26. "It could be held that the quest for the mystery texts is essentially futile for more basic reasons: no Nag Hammadi library of mysteries will ever be discovered because it never existed, and there was not even a shipwreck as imagined by Cumont." Ibid., 69.

27. See *JC*, 69.

28. This is a slightly altered version of the translation of the passage by J. Gwen Griffiths, *Apuleius of Madauros: The Isis-Book* (*Metamorphoses Book XI*) (Leiden: E. J. Brill, 1975), 23.

29. Franz Cumont, *The Mysteries of Mithras,* trans. Thomas McCormick (New York: Open Court, 1903), 43.

30. Cumont's and Jung's view that certain features of the Mithraic ritual were incorporated into the rituals of the Christian church is treated more skeptically by scholars today. See J. P. Kane, "The Mithraic Cult Meal in Its Greek and Roman Environment," in J. Hinnells, ed., *Mithraic Studies,* vol. 2 (Manchester: Manchester University Press, 1975).

31. See David Ulansey, "The Mithraic Mysteries," *Scientific American* 261 (Dec. 1989): 130–35; "Mithras and the Hypercosmic Sun," in John Hinnells, ed., *Studies on Mithraism* (Rome: L'Erma di Bretschneider, 1996); and *The Origins of the Mithraic Mysteries* (New York: Oxford University Press, 1989). For additional perspectives on the Mithraic mysteries, see Roger Beck, *Planetary Gods and Planetary Orders in the Mysteries of Mithras* (Leiden: E. J. Brill, 1988); Roger Beck, "Mithraism Since Franz Cumont," *Aufsteig und Niedergang der römischen Welt,* vol. 2 (Berlin: Walter de Gruyter, 1984); R. L. Gordon, "Franz Cumont and the Doctrine of Mithraism," in J. Hinnells, ed., *Mithraic Studies,* vol. 1 (Manchester: Manchester University Press, 1971); R. L. Gordon, "Reality, Evocation and Boundary in the Mysteries of Mithras," *Journal of Mithraic Studies* 3 (1982): 19–99. The most comprehensive work in German is Reinhold Merkelbach, *Mithras: Ein persisch-römischer Mysterienkult* (Koenigstein: Verlag Anton Hain Meisenheim, 1984).

32. Ulansey, *Origins,* 103–12.

33. C. G. Jung, *Psychology of the Unconscious,* trans. Beatrice M. Hinkle (New York: Moffat, Yard, 1916), 222.

34. *FJ,* 326. In *Psychology of the Unconscious,* Jung wrote that "Julian the Apostate made the last, unsuccessful attempt to cause the triumph of Mithracism over Christianity," *Psychology of the Unconscious,* 498. In a letter to Freud of June 26, 1910, Jung seemed to ally himself with Julian when he wrote, "That is why Julian the Apostate attempted, meritoriously and with the utmost energy, to oppose the Christian mystery with that of Mithras (because of its favorable outcome)," *FJ,* 337.

35. Ulansey, *Origins,* 93.

36. Jung, *Psychology of the Unconscious,* 474.

37. *FJ,* 334. This quote is from an undated fragment from Freud to Jung, probably written and posted circa June 22, 1910.

38. Ibid., 337. This letter is dated June 26, 1910.

39. Ibid.

40. Ibid., 427.

41. Jung, *Psychology of the Unconscious,* 557.

42. Gordon, "Reality, Evocation and Boundary," 32.

43. Cumont, *The Mysteries of Mithras,* 155.

44. Jung, *Psychology of the Unconscious,* 494; C. G. Jung, *Mysterium Coniunctionis, CW* 14, par. 168.

45. Howard Jackson, "The Meaning and Function of the Leontocephaline in Roman Mithraism," *Numen* 32 (1985): 29.

46. C. G. Jung, "The Tavistock Lectures," *CW* 18.

47. Jackson, "Meaning and Function," 34.

48. *MDR,* 182–83.

49. *JL,* 1:40–41.

50. Jung, *Psychology of the Unconscious,* 78.

51. Ibid., 82–83.

52. Ibid., 80.

53. Cumont, *The Mysteries of Mithras,* 4.

54. For a view of the assumptions about the religion of the ancient Aryans by Jung's contemporaries, see the following: Leopold von Schroeder, *Arische Religion,* 2 vols. (Leipzig: Hässel Verlag, 1914, 1916); Hermann Brunnhofer, *Arische Urzeit, Forschungen auf dem Gebeite des Altexten Vorder- und Zentralasiens nebst Osteuropa* (Bern: A. Francke, 1910); Rudolph Otto, *Gotheit und Gottheiten der Arier* (Giesen: Alfred Topelmann Verlag, 1932); Jakob Wilhelm Hauer, *Das religiose Artbild der Indogermanen und die Grundtypen der indo-arischen Religion* (Stuttgart: W. Kohlhammer, 1937). See also Jung's extensive footnotes in *Wandlungen.*

55. Dieterich, *Eine Mithrasliturgie,* ix, 161. This view is echoed in what George Moose once called the bible of the Volkish movement, Houston Stewart Chamberlain, *The Foundations of the Nineteenth Century,* 2 vols., trans. John Lees (London: John Lane, 1911). In his discussion of "The Mythology of Inner

Experience," Chamberlain says that "the central idea in all Indo-Iranian religions" (and he includes his Aryanized view of Christianity) is "the longing for redemption, the hope of salvation; nor was this idea of redemption strange to the Hellenes; we find it in their mysteries." On the other hand, "this idea has always been and is still strange to Jews; it absolutely contradicts their whole conception of religion," 2:31.

56. Chamberlain, *Foundations*, 1:211–12. The original German edition is *Die Grundlagen des Neunzehnten Jahrhunderts*, 2 vols. (Munich: F. Bruckmann Verlag, 1899). For background on Chamberlain's life and work, see Geoffrey Field, *Evangelist of Race: The Germanic Vision of Houston Stewart Chamberlain* (New York: Columbia University Press, 1981). For an example of the high regard in which Chamberlain was held during the Third Reich, see Hugo Meyer, *Houston Stewart Chamberlain als völkischer Denker* (Munich: F. Bruckmann Verlag, 1939).

57. Chamberlain, *Foundations*, 1:200.

58. Jung, *Psychology of the Unconscious*, 499.

59. See the discussions of *Parsifal* in Peter Wapnewski, "The Operas as Literary Works," and Dieter Borchmeyer, "The Question of Anti-Semitism," in Ulrich Mueller and Peter Wapnewski, eds., *Wagner Handbook*, trans. ed. John Deathridge (Cambridge, Mass.: Harvard University Press, 1992). The original edition is *Richard-Wagner-Handbuch* (Stuttgart: Alfred Kröner Verlag, 1986).

60. See Leopold von Schroeder, *Die Vollendung des Arischen Mysteriums in Bayreuth* (Munich: J. F. Lehmann, 1911).

61. George Mosse, *The Crisis of Germany Ideology: Intellectual Origins of the Third Reich* (New York: Schocken, 1981 [1964]), 43.

62. See Felix Genzmer, *Heliand und die Bruchstücke der Genesis* (Stuttgart: Reclam, 1982), regarded as one of the best translations. For a nineteenth-century Volkish interpretation of the *Heliand*, see A.F.C. Vilmar, *Deutsche Altertürmer im Heliand als Einkleidung der evangelischen Geschichte* (Marburg: N. G. Elwert'sche Universitäts-Buchhandlung, 1845). In English, see the translation from the original Old Saxon by G. Ronald Murphy, S.J., *The Heliand: The Saxon Gospel* (New York: Oxford University Press, 1992). See also G. Ronald Murphy, S.J., *The Saxon Savior: The Transformation of the Gospel in the Ninth-Century Heliand* (New York: Oxford University Press, 1989).

63. *MDR*, 313–14.

64. Eugen Bohler interview, May 1970, JBA, 5, 10.

65. See the photo of a *Türstkreuze* and the accompanying article, "Wotans wilde Jagd: Archaische Nachtgespenster im Luzerner Hinterland," *Neue Zürcher Zeitung*, Dec. 12, 1995, 44.

66. Murphy, *The Heliand*, 54–55.

8: Zurich 1916: Abraxas and the Return of the Pagan Gods

1. C. G. Jung's *Septem Sermones ad Mortuous* (Seven sermons to the dead) did not appear in the first printings of *MDR* but did appear as an appendix in subsequent editions. I wish to thank Random House, Inc., and Pantheon Books, a division of Random House, for allowing me to reproduce Sermo VII in its entirety. The sermons appear as an appendix in all German editions of *ETG*. For a useful interpretation, see Stephan A. Hoeller, *The Gnostic Jung and the Seven Sermons to the Dead* (Wheaton, Ill.: The Theosophical Publishing House, 1982).

2. "Die grossen Probleme der Menschheit wurden noch nie durch allgemeine Gesetze, sondern immer nur durch die Erneuerung der Einstellung des Einzelnen gelöst." C. G. Jung, *Die Psychologie der unbewussten Prozesse: Ein Überblick über de moderne Theorie und Methode der analytischen Psychologie* (Zurich: Verlag von Rascher & Cie, 1917), 7. The first English translation appeared in C. G. Jung, *Collected Papers on Analytical Psychology,* 2d ed., ed. Constance Long (New York: Moffat, Yard, 1917) under the title, "The Psychology of Unconscious Processes," trans. Dora Hecht.

3. Ernest Jones, "Der Gottmensch-Komplex; der Glaube, Gott zu Sein, und die daraus folgenden Charaktermerkmale," *Internationale Zeitschrift für ärtzliche Psychoanalyse* 1 (1913): 313–29. An English translation, "The God Complex: The Belief That One Is God and the Resulting Character Traits," appears in Ernest Jones, *Essays in Applied Psychoanalysis,* vol. 2 (New York: International Universities Press, 1964).

4. Alphonse Maeder interview, Jan. 28, 1970, JBA, 18, 10.

5. Tina Keller interview manuscript, "Recollections of My Encounter with Dr. Jung," 1968, JBA, A2, B12, A5. Keller's statement is the best single source of information about Jung's psychotherapeutic techniques during these early years.

6. An untitled transcript of a translation of Jung's probable talk to the Psychology Club in 1916 is among the papers of Fanny Bowditch Katz at CLM. The typewritten copy contains corrections in an unknown hand, and these have been included in the portions of the text cited here. The references to the founding of a Club and to the paper on the "Transcendental Function" date this document to 1916 and make it highly probable that it is Jung who is speaking. In the upper right-hand corner of the first page "Frl. Moltzer" is handwritten, perhaps indicating that Maria Moltzer is the translator. By 1916, Moltzer had long established herself as Jung's most competent translator into English, and until further documentation appears that conclusively proves otherwise, I assume that this is a translation and not a document written by Jung himself in English. The full transcript of this document appears in *JC,* 250–54. Despite the fact that the Jung estate gave Princeton University Press permission in 1994 to print this "Lecture on Goethe" (as they called it), they have not provided proof that this is, indeed, a talk by C. G. Jung. It could very well be that this document is more Moltzer than Jung. Perhaps a German original will appear one day to settle the matter.

7. C. G. Jung, *The Transcendent Function,* trans. A. R. Pope (Zurich: The Students' Association, C. G. Jung Institute, 1957). This translation includes material that does not appear in the version of this essay in *CW* 8.

8. Jung used the term "guiding fictions" in his 1913 essay on psychological types. It echoes very similar concepts by Alfred Adler.

9. E. O. Lippman, *Entstehung und Ausbreitung der Alchemie,* vol. 1 (Berlin: Springer, 1919); and Julius Ruska and E. Wiedemann, "Beiträge zur Geschichte der Naturwissenschaften, LXVII: Alchemistische Decknamen," *Sitzungsberichte der physikalisch-medizinischen Sozietät in Erlangen* 5 (1923): 1–23, 6 (1924): 17–36. In his later work, Jung even attempted to Aryanize alchemy by claiming that the common figure of Mercurius was in fact also Wotan—a difficult argument to make, since no alchemical text exists that refers to Wotan or equates the two. For a useful critique of Jung's ahistorical and excessively psychological approach to alchemy, see Barbara Obrist, *Les débuts de l'imagerie alchemique (XIVe–XVe siècles)* (Paris: Le Sycomore, 1982).

10. See C. G. Jung, "The Conception of the Unconscious," in Long, *Collected Papers,* for the first English version. It first appeared in print in a French translation by M. Marsen from Jung's original German manuscript. See C. G. Jung, "La Structure de l'inconscient," *Archives de psychologie* (Geneva) 16 (1916): 152–79. See also *CW* 7 for a different English translation.

11. Jung, "Conception of the Unconscious," 458.

12. See n. 2, above. I have used the personal copy of Fanny Bowditch, who had it in her possession in Zurich in 1917.

13 "Diese Dominanten sind die Herrschenden, die Götter." Jung, *Die Psychologie der unbewussten Prozesse,* 117.

14. *MDR,* 189–91.

15. For a full-page color reproduction, see Aniela Jaffé, *C. G. Jung: Word and Image* (Princeton: Princeton University Press, 1979), 76.

9: Fanny Bowditch Katz—"Analysis Is Religion"

1. See Nathan Hale, ed., *James Jackson Putnam and Psychoanalysis: Letters Between Putnam and Sigmund Freud, Ernest Jones, William James, Sandor Ferenczi, and Morton Prince, 1877–1917* (Cambridge, Mass.: Harvard University Press, 1971).

2. *FJ,* 352.

3. This and other letters are in the papers of Fanny Bowditch Katz, CLM. In this chapter, I provide within the body of the text the dates of all letters that I cite from this collection. I have therefore not footnoted each letter as I quote from it. Cited letters include those from Fanny to Jung and James Jackson Putnam, from Jung and Putnam to Fanny, from Maria Moltzer to Fanny and Rudolf Katz, and from Jung to Selma Bowditch. Fanny's 1916 diary of her analysis consists of a group of pages beginning in June 1916 that are in a separate file from the 1916 notebook itself. There is also an analysis notebook from 1917. There are no page numbers in these notebooks, but I indicate the date of the entry from which mate-

rial is taken. There are also notebooks from 1912 and 1913 with class notes from seminars from Jung and Prof. Hausherr. These also do not have page numbers.

4. Reference to this remark appears in several JBA interviews.

5. R. Andrew Paskauskas, ed., *The Complete Correspondence of Sigmund Freud and Ernest Jones, 1908–1939* (Cambridge, Mass.: Harvard University Press, 1993), 186.

6. Eva Brabant, Ernst Falzeder, and Patrizia Giampieri-Deutsch, eds., *The Correspondence of Sigmund Freud and Sandor Ferenczi*, vol. 1, *1908–1914* (Cambridge, Mass.: Harvard University Press, 1992), 446.

7. Jolande Jacobi interview, JBA, 110.

8. Hale, *James Jackson Putnam and Psychoanalysis,* 33.

9. Paskauskas, *Freud/Jones,* 296.

10. Ernst Falzeder and Eva Brabant, eds. *The Correspondence of Sigmund Freud and Sandor Ferenczi*, vol. 2, *1914–1919,* trans. Peter Hoffer (Cambridge, Mass.: Harvard University Press, 1996), 10.

11. Tina Keller statement, 1968, JBA, B19.

12. Ibid.

13. Ibid., B3.

14. Ibid., D1.

15. Alphone Maeder interview, Jan. 28, 1970, JBA, 11.

16. "Ihr Blick klärt sich aber nur, wenn Sie in Ihr eignese Herz sehen."

17. "Dort wurde ich wie der kleinste Embryo, nur eine Celle, rund und klein,—sofort kam die Erinnerung an die Erfahrung in der Narkose worüber ich nie mit Dr. Jung gesprochen hatte." She did not elaborate on this experience.

10: Edith Rockefeller McCormick—The Rockefeller Psychoanalyst

1. Richard Noll, "Styles of Psychiatric Practice, 1906–1925: Clinical Evaluations of the Same Patient by James Jackson Putnam, Adolph Meyer, August Hoch, Emil Kraepelin, and Smith Ely Jelliffe," *History of Psychiatry,* forthcoming.

2. This description comes from her obituary, "End of a Princess," *Time,* Sept. 5, 1932, 12, a wry summation of Edith's eccentricities and the basis of some of the information that I relate here.

3. See Harold F. McCormick, "An Account of Our Hungarian Trip," probably written in 1913, in box 29 of the Harold F. McCormick Papers, Correspondence, Series 1F: 1892–1947 (and n.d.), 90 boxes, including 12 vols. MIH. Hereafter these papers are designated HFM Corr.

4. HFM to John D. Rockefeller, Sr. (hereafter JDR), Sept. 22, 1911, folder 248, box 32, family correspondence, Record Group (hereafter RG), Senior III 2A, Rockefeller Family Archives (hereafter RFA), RAC.

5. See Kristie Miller, "The Letters of C. G. Jung and Medill and Ruth McCormick," *Spring* 50 (1990): 1–25.

6. HFM to Nettie Fowler McCormick (hereafter NFM), HFM Corr., box 28, MIH.

7. HFM to NFM, July 12, 1912, NFM Corr. (incoming), box 127, MIH.

8. Ibid.

9. HFM to JDR, July 13, 1912, folder 248, box 32, family corr., RG Senior III 2A, RFA, RAC.

10. Edith Rockefeller McCormick (hereafter ERM) to NFM, Sept. 4, 1912, NFM Corr. (incoming), box 127, MIH.

11. C. G. Jung to NFM, Oct. 8, 1912, Stanley R. McCormick Papers, general correspondence, Series 1G: 1881–1931 (and n.d.), box 4, MIH.

12. Anita McCormick Blaine (hereafter AMB) to NFM, Oct. 11, 1912, NFM Corr. (incoming), box 125, MIH.

13. HFM to AMB, Oct. 14, 1912, NFM Corr. (incoming), box 127, MIH.

14. Eva Brabant, Ernst Falzeder, and Patrizia Giampieri-Deutsch, eds., *The Correspondence of Sigmund Freud and Sandor Ferenczi,* vol. 1, *1908–1914,* trans. Peter T. Hoffer (Cambridge, Mass.: Harvard University Press, 1992), 464.

15. Ibid., 473.

16. Ibid., 474.

17. Fowler McCormick (hereafter FM) to JDR, Aug. 10, 1913, folder 249, box 32, family corr., RG Senior III 2A, RFA, RAC.

18. FM interview, April 14, 1969, JBA, 7–8.

19. ERM to NFM, Nov. 22, 1913, NFM Corr. (incoming), box 131, MIH.

20. HFM to NFM, Dec. 9, 1913 (copy), folder 249, box 32, family corr., RG Senior III 2A, RFA, RAC.

21. HFM to JDR, Dec. 28, 1913, ibid.

22. HFM to Muriel McCormick, May 9, 1914, HFM Corr., box 29, MIH.

23. Muriel McCormick to HFM, July 13, 1914 (copy), NFM Corr. (incoming), box 137, MIH.

24. ERM to JDR, June 25, 1914, folder 249, box 32, family corr., RG Senior III 2A, RFA, RAC.

25. Alexander Legge, "Comments on European War," Aug. 29, 1914, HFM Corr., box 29, MIH.

26. HFM to JDR, Oct. 3, 1914, folder 249, box 32, family corr., RG Senior III 2A, RFA, RAC.

27. HFM to NFM, Oct. 12, 1914, NFM Corr. (incoming), box 137, MIH.

28. Ibid., Oct. 20, 1914.

29. Ibid., Oct. 28, 1914.

30. Ibid., Nov. 28, 1914.

31. For Paul Mellon's view of Jung, see Paul Mellon (with John Baskett), *Reflection in a Silver Spoon: A Memoir* (New York: William Morrow, 1992), chap. 9, "C. G. Jung, Zurich, and Bollingen Foundation," 157–82.

32. HFM to NFM, April 14, 1915, NFM Corr. (incoming), box 144, MIH.

33. ERM to JDR, April 14, 1915, folder 250, box 32, family corr., RG Senior III 2A, RFA, RAC.

34. HFM to NFM, May 31, 1915, NFM Corr. (incoming), box 144, MIH.

35. Ibid.

36. Ibid., June 3, 1915.

37. FM to NFM, June 18, 1915, in ibid.
38. HFM to NFM, July 9, 1915, in ibid.
39. Ibid., July 15, 1915.
40. FM interview, April 14, 1969, JBA, 3–4.
41. HFM to JDR, June 18, 1915, folder 250, box 32, family corr., RG Senior III 2A, RFA, RAC.
42. HFM to NFM, Aug. 31, 1915, NFM Corr. (incoming), box 144, MIH.
43. Ibid., Sept. 1, 1915.
44. HFM to JDR, Sept. 1, 1915, folder 250, box 32, family corr., RG Senior III 2A, RFA, RAC.
45. HFM to NFM, Sept. 14, 1915, NFM Corr. (incoming), box 144, MIH.
46. Ibid., Oct. 12, 1915.
47. Ibid., Sept. 6, 1915
48. Ibid., Sept. 14, 1915.
49. HFM to JDR, Oct. 31, 1915, folder 250, box 32, family corr., RG Senior III 2A, RFA, RAC. The article that Harold recommended is Max Eastman, "Exploring the Soul and Healing the Body," *Everybody's Magazine* 32 (June/July 1915): 741–50. This article did much to introduce Freud, Jung, and psychoanalysis to the lay public in America.
50. JDR to ERM and HFM, Jan. 26, 1916, folder 251 in ibid.
51. HFM to JDR, Feb. 16, 1916, in ibid.
52. FM to NFM, Dec. 1915, NFM Corr. (incoming), box 144, MIH.
53. HFM to NFM, Feb. 7, 1916, in ibid., box 152.
54. ERM to JDR, Jan. 31, 1916, folder 251, box 32, family corr., RG Senior III 2A, RFA, RAC.
55. Ibid., July 20, 1916.
56. ERM to NFM, Dec. 6, 1916, NFM Corr. (incoming), box 152, MIH.
57. Eva Brabant and Ernst Felzeder, eds., *The Correspondence of Sigmund Freud and Sandor Ferenczi*, vol. 2, *1914–1919*, trans. Peter Hoffer (Cambridge, Mass.: Harvard University Press, 1996), 126.
58. These two proposals can be found in multiple copies among Harold McCormick's papers at MIH.
59. For background, see Arlen J. Hansen, *Gentlemen Volunteers: The Story of the American Ambulance Drivers in the Great War, August 1914–September 1918* (New York: Arcade, 1996).
60. HFM, "The Welfare of the Psychology Club," McCormick Estates Papers, HFM, box 8, file 7. HFM's original foundation notes, handwritten MS., a first typed draft, and a final typed draft are included in this file.
61. Arthur Edward Waite, *The Hidden Church of the Holy Grail, Its Legends and Symbolism, Considered in Their Affinity with Certain Mysteries of Initiation and Other Traces of a Secret Tradition in Christian Times* (London: Rebman, 1909), 611. Many turn-of-the-century Theosophists saw the Grail legends related to the ancient Hellenistic mystery-cult traditions. See the selections from Waite and others in James Webb, ed., *A Quest Anthology* (New York: Arno, 1976).

62. Waite, *Hidden Church*, 632.

63. Ibid., 642.

64. In Germany at the turn of the century, the role of the Grail seeker was a common script through which spiritual seekers sought renewal, and Jung's cult can be counted among these Grail cults. See Jost Hermand, "Gralsmotiv um die Jahrhundertswende," *Deutsche Vierteljahrsschrift für Literaturwissenschaft und Geistesgeschichte* 36 (1962): 521–43.

65. ERM to JDR, Dec. 5, 1916, folder 251, box 32, family corr., RG Senior III 2A, RFA, RAC.

66. HFM to NFM, Jan. 18, 1917, NFM Corr. (incoming), box 158, MIH.

67. Ibid., Sept. 25, 1917.

68. ERM to JDR, Nov. 26, 1917, folder 252, box 33, family corr, RG Senior III 2A, RFA, RAC.

69. Ibid., Nov. 18, 1918.

70. Ibid., March 27, 1919, folder 253.

71. HFM to Emma Jung, June 29, 1919, NFM Corr. (incoming), box 168, MIH.

72. HFM to NFM, Aug. 12, 1919, HFM Corr., box 30, MIH.

73. Beatrice Hinkle to HFM, Sept. 26, 1919, NFM Corr. (incoming), box 166, MIH.

74. Medill McCormick to HFM, March 5, 1920, HFM Corr., box 31, MIH.

75. Hermann Mueller interview, May 4, 1970, JBA, 4.

76. Emma Jung to HFM, Sept. 1, 1932, HFM Corr., box 48, MIH.

77. Toni Wolff and C. G. Jung to HFM, Aug. 27, 1932, in ibid.

11: The Passion of Constance Long

1. Most of these are republished in Constance Long, *Collected Papers on the Psychology of Phantasy* (New York: Dodd, Mead, 1924).

2. H. C. Abraham and E. L. Freud, eds., *A Psycho-Analytic Dialogue: The Letters of Sigmund Freud and Karl Abraham, 1907–1926* (London: Hogarth Press, 1965), 34.

3. A. R. Orage, *The New Age* 7 (May 12, 1910): 26. See Philip Mairet, *A. R. Orage: A Memoir* (New Hyde Park, N.Y.: University Books, 1966); Louise Welch, *Orage with Gurdjieff in America* (Boston: Routledge and Kegan Paul, 1982); and Wallace Martin, *The New Age Under Osage: Chapters in English Cultural History* (Manchester: Manchester University Press, 1967).

4. Sigmund Freud, *On Dreams*, trans. M. D. Eder, from the 2d German edition, introduction by W. Leslie Mackenzie (New York: Rebman, 1914).

5. C. G. Jung, *Psycho-Analysis. A Paper Read Before the Psycho-Medical Society* (Cockermouth, U.K.: Psycho-Medical Society, 1913). This is reprinted from *Transactions of the Psycho-Medical Society* 4 (1913), pt. 2, and appeared in *CW* 4 under the title "General Aspects of Psychoanalysis."

6. R. Andrew Paskauskas, ed., *The Complete Correspondence of Sigmund Freud and Ernest Jones, 1908-1939* (Cambridge, Mass.: Harvard University Press, 1993), 242.

7. Ibid., 244.

8. On Beatrice Hinkle, see Nancy Hale, "Beatrice Moses Hinkle (Oct. 10, 1874–Feb. 28, 1953)," in John A. Garraty, ed., *Dictionary of American Biography. Supplement Five, 1951-1955* (New York: Charles Scribner's Sons, 1977), which includes a useful but incomplete listing of her publications. Hale also wrote a series of articles in the 1950s about a psychotherapist who resembled Hinkle. They were published as *Heaven and Hardpan Farm* (1957).

I hope that biographies of both Long and Hinkle will be written one day. For those interested, some of Hinkle's personal papers are in the Kristine Mann Library at the C. G. Jung Center in New York City and also in the Library of the C. G. Jung Institute in San Francisco. There are a few materials relating to Long in these collections. Hinkle's only book, which contains revisions of many of her writings up to that point, is Beatrice Hinkle, *The Re-Creating of the Individual: A Study of Psychological Types and Their Relation to Psychoanalysis* (New York: Harcourt, Brace, 1923). The dedication reads, "To the memory of my beloved friend Constance E. Long, M.D. this book is affectionately dedicated."

9. Beatrice Hinkle, "Jung's Libido Theory and the Bergsonian Philosophy," *New York Medical Journal,* May 30, 1914, 1080–86.

10. Long, *Psychology of Phantasy,* 126.

11. Ernest Jones to Sigmund Freud, Feb. 15, 1914, in Paskauskas, *Freud/Jones,* 288.

12. C. G. Jung, *Psychology of the Unconscious: A Study of the Transformations and Symbolisms of the Libido,* trans. Beatrice Hinkle (New York: Moffat, Yard, 1916).

13. C. G. Jung, *Collected Papers on Analytical Psychology,* ed. Constance Long (London: Bailliére, Tindall and Cox, 1916; 2d ed., 1917).

14. Ibid., vi.

15. The 1919–22 diary of Constance Long is in the CLM. The pages are not numbered, but significant entries are often dated. Where possible, I have given the entry date of each citation in the text. As there is so much material on Ouspensky and Gurdjieff in Long's diary, I am sure this will prove to be a useful primary source for those studying the early movement of these two men. I must confess I know next to nothing about the greater metaphysical systems of these men, and I beg the forgiveness of those who do know more than I.

16. See "The Psychology of the Unconscious Processes," in Jung, *Collected Papers on Analytical Psychology,* 2d ed., 426–36.

17. For personal information on H. G. Baynes, see Michael Fordham interview, Feb. 17, 1969, JBA.

18. These lectures were published as "On the Problem of Psychogenesis in Mental Disease," *CW* 3; "Instinct and the Unconscious," *CW* 8; and "The Psychological Foundation of a Belief in Spirits," *CW* 8.

19. Long, *Psychology of Phantasy*, 132.

20. Ibid., 26.

21. Ibid., 138, 141, 143.

22. In 1922, Corrie published "Personal Experience of the Night-Sea Journey Under the Sea," *British Journal of Psychology, Medical Section* 2 (1922) 303–12. The night-sea journey is one of Jung's metaphors for the terrifying encounter with the mythological contents of the unconscious, which is also likened to heroic myths about the sun. Corrie's paper is the first extensive use of the night-sea metaphor in print by one of Jung's disciples. She also published *ABC of Jung's Psychology* (London: Kegan Paul, 1927), a primer that was translated into German by Fanny Altherr-Rutishauser as *C. G. Jung's Psychologie im Abriss* (Zurich: Bascher, 1929).

23. Jung may have given Long a copy of "Seven Sermons to the Dead" when he saw her in July 1919, and they may have discussed it when he came to England again in September 1920, for it is in them that references to Abraxas appear in her journal. Until the appearance of original letters by Jung that correspond to the passages in Long's fantasy-laden diary, we must consider them a kind of "hearsay."

24. H. Godwin Baynes, "Translator's Preface," in C. G. Jung, *Psychological Types, or The Psychology of Individuation* (London: Kegan Paul, Trench, Trubner; New York: Harcourt, Brace, 1923), xx.

25. For historical background on Ouspensky and Gurdjieff, see James Webb, *The Occult Establishment* (La Salle, Ill.: Open Court, 1976); and Peter Washington, *Madame Blavatsky's Baboon: A History of the Mystics, Mediums, and Misfits Who Brought Spiritualism to America* (New York: Schocken, 1995).

26. Read was not impressed with Ouspensky. "After a trial run of a dozen lectures I turned away," he remembered. See James King, *The Last Modern: A Life of Herbert Read* (New York: St. Martin's, 1990), 73.

27. C. G. Jung, "Über das Unbewusste," *Schweizerland: Monatshefte für Schweizer Art und Arbeit* (Zurich) 4 (1918): 464–72, 548–58; *CW* 10.

28. George Mosse, *The Crisis of German Ideology: Intellectual Origins of the Third Reich* (New York: Schocken, 1981 [1964]), 16.

12: From Volkish Prophet to Wise Old Man

1. Heinz Gess, *Vom Faschismus zum Neuen Denken: C. G. Jung's Theorie im Wandel der Zeit* (Luneburg: zu Klampen, 1994).

2. *JL*, 1:39–40.

3. Beatrice Hinkle, *The Re-Creating of the Individual: A Study of Psychological Types and Their Relation to Psychoanalysis* (New York: Harcourt, Brace, 1923), 128–29. The two illustrations—figs. 5 and 6—appear between these two pages.

4. See "From Esther Harding's Notebooks: 1922–1925," in William McGuire and R.F.C. Hull, eds., *C. G. Jung Speaking: Interviews and Encounters* (Princeton: Princeton University Press, 1977).

5. See *JC*, 99–103.

6. Christiana Morgan, "The Gods and Their Representation in the House" (notebook), Christiana Morgan Papers, CLM.

7. Christiana Morgan, "Notebook. Zurich 1925," Christiana Morgan Materials: Letters and Personal Writings, 1910–1980, box 2, HUGFP 97.75, Henry A. Murray Papers, HUA.

8. Christiana Morgan, "Notebook. Dreams, Analysis, June 8, 1926 to October 20, 1926." Christiana Morgan Papers, CLM.

9. Ibid.

10. Ibid.

11. Henry A. Murray interview, November 1968, JBA, 56.

12. Ernest Harms interview, November 1968, JBA, 16–17.

13. C. G. Jung, *Seelenprobleme der Gegenwart* (Zurich: Rascher, 1931). This volume contains many of Jung's most Volkish essays.

14. See McGuire and Hull, *C. G. Jung Speaking*, 433–35.

15. C. G. Jung, *Psychology of the Unconscious: A Study of the Transformations and Symbolisms of the Libido,* trans. Beatrice M. Hinkle (New York: Moffat, Yard, 1916), 108–9. On Honegger, see Hans Walser, "An Early Psychoanalytical Tragedy: J. J. Honegger and the Beginnings of Training Analysis," *Spring* (1974):

16. For Jung's "revised" versions, see "The Structure of the Psyche" (1928/1931), in *CW* 8, para. 319; and especially "The Concept of the Collective Unconscious" (1936), *CW* 9, i, para. 105.

17. Jung, *Psychology of the Unconscious,* 109.

18. G.R.S. Mead, *A Mithraic Ritual* (London: Theosophical Publishing Society, 1907).

19. Albrecht Dieterich, *Eine Mithrasliturgie* (Leipzig: B. G. Teubner, 1903; 2d ed., Leipzig, 1910).

20. See *CW* 9, i, para. 105 n. 5.

21. For context, see Elizabeth Eisenstein, *The Printing Press as an Agent of Change,* 2 vols. (Cambridge: Cambridge University Press, 1979). The prevalence of Theosophical literature in the popular culture of Europe for almost three decades before Jung and his associates began amassing evidence for a collective unconscious at the Burghölzli provides a sufficient and plausible alternate hypothesis for the presence of mythological motifs and Gnostic/alchemical/Hermetic symbols in the dreams of twentieth-century individuals in Jung's Switzerland.

22. C. G. Jung, "A Study in the Process of Individuation," *CW* 9, i, para. 542.

23. On Kristine Mann, her Swedenborgian upbringing, and her exposure to alchemical ideas, see James Webb, *The Occult Establishment* (La Salle, Ill.: Open Court, 1976), 388–94.

24. Michael Fordham interview, Feb. 17, 1969, JBA, 21–22.

25. John Layard interview, Dec. 17, 1969, JBA, 67.

26. James Hillman interview, Jan. 1, 1970, JBA, 32.

27. Irene Champernowne interview, Dec. 19, 1969, JBA, 56.

28. According to Ernst Hanfstängl, one of Hitler's closest associates during his rise to power, "We got to talking about the Party flag, which he [Hitler] had taken great care to design himself. I told him I did not like the use of black for the swastika, which was a sun symbol and should be in red." Ernst Hanfstängl, *Hitler: The Missing Years* (New York: Arcade, 1994 [1957]). It was in Hanfstängl's house that Hitler hid after his 1923 Munich putsch. Coincidentally, just prior to the First World War, Hanfstängl was a personal assistant and lower-level manager for Harold McCormick and the International Harvester Company. Letters from Hanfstängl to McCormick can be found scattered among the papers in the HFM Corr. at MIH. See also Malcolm Quinn, *The Swastika: Constructing the Symbol* (London: Routledge, 1994).

29. Wilhelm Bitter interview, Sept. 10, 1970, JBA, 17.

30. Jolande Jacobi interview, Dec. 26, 1969, JBA, 53.

31. C. G. Jung, "Wotan," *Neue schweizer Rundshau* 3 (March 1936): 657–69. See also *CW* 10.

32. Jolande Jacobi interview, Dec. 23, 1969, JBA, 24.

33. Michael Fordham interview, Feb. 1969, JBA, 1–2.

34. Cornelia Brunner interview, Jan. 8, 1970, JBA, 26–27.

35. Irene Champernowne interview, Dec. 19, 1969, JBA, 58.

36. Ibid., 60.

37. Aline Valangin interview, Sept. 2, 1970, JBA, 13.

38. Mary Elliot interview, Dec. 1969, JBA, 22.

39. Lilane Frey interview, Dec. 1969, JBA, 4.

40. Jane Wheelwright interview, Dec. 1968, JBA, 15.

41. Jolande Jacobi interview, Dec. 23, 1969, JBA, 27–28.

Index

Page numbers in *italics* refer to illustrations.

Abraham, Karl, 59, 108, 238
Abraxas, 127, 161–62, 251, 254, 266, 318*n*
   F. B. Katz and, 185–86, 188, 193
active imagination, 24, 121, 137, 155, 266
Adler, Alfred, 57, 59, 259, 312*n*
Adler, Gerhard, 274
Africa, CGJ in, 96
Ahnenerbe, 4, 245
   see also collective unconscious; inner fatherland
Aion (*Deus Leontocephalus*), *iv*, 121, 123, 124, 138–39, 143
alchemy, 7, 14–15, 16, 130, 271
   CGJ's interest in, xiv, 131, 138, 139, 159, 171, 244, 277–78, 307*n*, 312*n*
Alcock, J. M., 257
Almqvist, Kurt, 304*n*
Also Sprach Zarathustra (Nietzsche), 51, 126
American Society of Psychical Research, 166
Amsterdam, 182, 195, 196
analytic psychology, 23, 120, 121, 148–60, 311*n*–12*n*
   collectivity of, 156, 157
   in England, 236, 239, 241–44, 246–47, 252–55, 258, 260, 276
   guiding fiction and, 157–58, 228, 230, 312*n*
   initiatory process in, 141
   intellectual education and, 170–71, 207, 209
   H. F. McCormick on allure of, 215–21
   Roman Catholicism compared with, 141, 157
   in United States, 206, 241, 248, 249–50, 265, 277
   women's attraction to, 165–66
   see also specific concepts and people
ancestor possession, 19–21
Ancient Mystery Cults (Burkert), 127, 129, 130
Andreae, Johann Valentin, 14
Andreas-Salomé, Lou, 57, 113

anima, 95, 118, 122, 156, 242, 248, 267
animal magnetism, 32–36, 51
animus, 95, 118, 242, 248, 254, 267
anti-Semitism, 108, 112, 114, 143, 145, 146, 259, 273–77
Antike Mysterienwesen in religionsgeschichtlicher, ethnologischer und psychologischer Beleuchtung, Das (De Jong), 128
anxiety, 47, 82, 84
Apollo, 86, 132
Apuleius, 131–32
archeology, 85, 127
   CGJ's interest in, 42, 43–44, 64, 100–103, 110, 125, 138
   of Mithraeums, 132, 136
archetypes, xiii, 3, 54, 95, 126, 160, 179, 181, 210, 242, 246–47
Archiv für Kriminalanthropologie und Kriminalistik, 297*n*–98*n*
Arminius, 10, 107
Arndt, Ernst Moritz, 8, 10–11, 115–16, 288*n*
art, 124, 133
   CGJ's interest in, 42, 44–45
   psychoanalytic interpretation of, 57–58
Aryan Christ, 143–46, 153, 155–56, *164*, 179, 208, 252, 277
Aryans, *iv*, xvi, 66, 107–16, 125, 141–47, 259, 263–64, 273–78, 309*n*–10*n*
   dementia praecox in, 300*n*
   sun worship of, *68*, 111–12, 114–18, 194, 263
Ascona, 75, 79, 84, 85, 86, 114, 117, 118–19, 155, 271, 298
astrology, 128, 130, 133, 135–36, 141
   in Jungian therapy, 193, 234
astronomy, 133, 134–35, 141
Austria-Hungary, 57, 59, 71–72, 88, 108
"Autobiographical Fragment" (von Humboldt), vii

Index

autobiographies, xi
   spiritual, 11, 30
   see also Memories, Dreams, Reflections
automatic writing, 155, 166

Baader, Franz von, 37
Bachofen, Johann Jakob, 85–86, 106, 126, 300*n*, 307*n*
Bailey, Ruth, 96–97
Bainbridge, William Sims, 61
Baldur, 116
Ball, Hugo, 74
Basel, 12–13, 100
Basel, University of, 7, 12, 29
Basilides of Alexandria, 139, 161
Bauman, Gret Jung, 69, 234
Bäumler, Alfred, 307*n*
Baur-Celio, Bernhard, 140
Bavaria, 13–14, 42–45, 114
Baynes, Helton Godwin (Peter), 246, 252, 254, 258, 260
Bayreuth, 144, 145
Becher, Johannes, 74
Bell, Mary, 243, 254
Bennett, E. A., 100
Beresford, J. D., 257
Bergson, Henri, 239, 241
Berlin, 8, 10, 11–12, 274
   O. Gross in, 79, 88, 89
Bertine, Eleanor, 250, 254
"Betender Knabe" (Fidus), *68*
Bible, personal, 189, 190, 192–95, 198, 266
Binet, Alfred, 30, 48
Bing, Henri, 74
biology, biological theories:
   evolutionary, 30, 46, 86, 102, 104–6, 108, 111
   as historical science, 105
   Lamarckian, 20, 46, 105, 108, 112, 265
   spirituality and, 19–20, 99, 277
Bitter, Wilhelm, 273–74
Bjerre, Poul Carl, 113–14
Blaine, Anita McCormick, 201, 205–6
Blätter von Prevorst, 292*n*
Blavatsky, Madame, 126, 127
Bleuler, Eugen, 45, 47, 51, 69, 77, 294*n*
   psychoanalysis and, 56, 57, 64
Bleuler, Manfred, 299*n*
Boddinghaus, Martha, 168
Boehme, Jakob, 30
Boer, Charles, 306*n*
bohemians, bohemian life, 72–77, 84, 85, 87, 96, 100, 298*n*
   O. Gross's arrest and, 88
   Wandlungen and, 104, 117, 118–19

Bohler, Eugen, xiv–xv, 146–47
Bollingen, Jung's Tower in, 3–4, 15, 96, 122–23, 235
Borngräber, Otto, *164*
bourgeoisie, bourgeois life, 69–76, 88, 100
   of CGJ, 69–70, 78, 87, 90, 96
Bowditch, Fanny, *see* Katz, Fanny Bowditch
Bowditch, Henry Pickering, 166, 167
Bowditch, Selma, 167, 168, 172, 196–97
Boyle, Nicholas, 10
Breuer, Josef, 56
Brill, A. A., 239
Brod, Max, 75, 88
Brunner, Cornelia, 275–76
Bruno, Giordano, 109
Bryan, William Jennings, 205
Burghölzli Psychiatric Clinic, 50, 53, 55–57, 69, 112, 299*n*
   O. Gross at, 70, 73, 77–84, 87, 89, 299*n*
   CGJ's resignation from, 101
   CGJ's start at, 31, 42, 45–47
   psychoanalysis and, 45, 56, 57, 81–84, 87, 89–90
   Spielrein's treatment at, 89–90, 301*n*
Burkert, Walter, 127, 129, 130

Café Stefanie, 74, 76, 298*n*
Campbell, Joseph, xvi
capitalism, progressive reaction against, 114–15
Carus, Carl Gustav, 30
"Cash Value of Ultimate Peace Terms" (H. F. McCormick), 226
Cerebrale Sekundärfunktion, Die (O. Gross), 88
C. G. Jung Biographical Archives Project, 62–63, 90, 152, 170, 208, 272, 302*n*
C. G. Jungs Medium (Zumstein-Preiswerk), 26
Chamberlain, Houston Stewart, 144–45, 273, 309*n*–10*n*
Champernowne, Irene, 272–73, 276
Charcot, J. M., 30
Charet, F. X., 64
Chicago, Ill., 202–7, 218, 223, 234–35
Christianity, 171–72, 239, 277–78
   mystery cults compared with, 130, 132, 133, 308*n*
   Stuck's paintings and, 44–45
   see also Judeo-Christian tradition; Protestants, Protestantism; Roman Catholicism, Roman Catholics
Chymische Hochzeit Christiani Rosencreutz (Andreae), 14
civilization, 102, 112, 115
   Jews and, 143, 263–64, 275
   repression and, 76, 78, 86

Index

clairvoyance, 25, 31–32, 35, 37, 51, 150
Collected Papers on Analytical Psychology (Jung), 212, 241, 242, 246
Collected Works (Jung), xii, xvi, 159, 270, 271
collective unconscious, xiii, 47, 54, 99–104, 121, 126, 159, 242, 246
   arguments in support of, 37, 265
   individuation and, 153–54
   CGJ's fact bending and, 271–72
   origin of theory of, 3, 100
   phylogeny and, 99, 101–6, 133, 138
   positive vs. negative sides of, 153
   Wolff and, 95, 96
complexes, 49, 81, 102, 181, 191
"Conception of the Unconscious, The" (Jung), 159–60, 312*n*
Confessio (pamphlet), 14
Congress for Neuro-Psychiatry (1907), 77–78
consciousness, 46, 48, 49, 220, 244
   active imagination and, 155
   change and, 100, 113
Corrie, Joan, 250, 253, 254, 260, 264, 318*n*
Cosmic Circle, 85
creativity, 50–51, 74–75, 86–87, 96, 104, 118, 188
Creuzer, Friedrich, 126–27, 306*n*–7*n*
Crews, Frederick, 58
Criminalistic Institute, 71
criminology, 47, 71–72, 297*n*–98*n*
Crookes, William, 31
cross, as symbol, 5, 6, 14–18, 149, 157
Crowley, Aleister, 119
cryptomnesia, 39, 41–52, 104, 125, 138, 265, 270, 292*n*–95*n*
"Cryptomnesia" (Jung), 50–51
cults, 64, 114, 117–19, 278, 296*n*
   psychoanalysis compared with, 58–61, 64–66, 99–100, 112–13, 150–51
cultural evolution, 85–86, 105, 106
Cumont, Franz, 127–28, 135, 141, 142, 230, 307*n*
   Christianity compared to mystery cults by, 130, 132, 133, 308*n*
   on Mithraic initiation process, 137, 138
Cusanus, Nicholas, 30

Dada movement, 74, 89
Dana, Charles, 240
Darwin, Charles, 30, 110–11
Darwinism, 104–5
Dead, the, 33, 125
   individuation and, 153–54
   CGJ's encounters and discussions with, xii, xiii, xvi, 3–4, 22–29, 34, 38–41, 154, 161–62

Seeress of Prevorst and, 35, 38
de Angulo, Cary F., 120, 306*n*
death, life after, xiii, 20, 31, 176
degeneracy, 264
   at Burghölzli, 45
   H. Gross's views on, 71–72, 75, 297*n*–98*n*
   hereditary, 45, 50, 55–56
De Jong, Karel Hendrik Eduard, 128
dementia praecox, 45, 56, 83, 84, 102, 103, 142, 205, 300*n*
Demeter, 86, 129
depression, 91, 204, 232
   of F. B. Katz, 167, 196
   of E. R. McCormick, 202–4
Des Indes à la planete Mars (From India to the Planet Mars) (Flournoy), 48–49, 294*n*
Deus Leontocephalus (Aion), *iv,* 121, 123, 124, 138–39, 143
Dialogues et fragments philosophiques (Renan), 107
diaries:
   of CGJ, xii, 123, 290*n*; *see also* "Red Book"
   of Emilie Jung, 25
   of Karl Gustav Jung, 288*n*
   of F. B. Katz, 182–86, 188–91, 193, 194–95, 244
   of Long, 237, 242–47, 250, 252–60, 317*n*, 318*n*
   of Spielrein, 300*n*–301*n*
   of C. Wagner, 145
   of Wolff, 93, 302*n*
Diederichs, Eugen, 116
Dieterich, Albrecht, 127, 143, 169, 307*n*
Dionysus, 43, 86, 106, 117
   mystery cult of, 126, 128, 129, 130, 142, 165
diphtheria, 237–38
dissociation, 34, 36, 47–48, 54, 94, 149
divorce, 92, 96, 202, 203, 233
dominants, 54, 95, 160, 181, 246
   see also archetypes
dreams, 32, 39, 111, 171, 220, 239, 272
   of CGJ, 20, 94, 99, 100, 101, 105, 122–25, 139, 146–47, 149, 151
   of Emilie Jung, 25
   of Kerner, 37–38
   of Long, 236, 243, 245, 250, 254, 255
   of Morgan, 266–67
   prophetic, 172
Dreams of a Spirit-Seer (Kant), 31
Drewerman, Eugen, xvi
Duke University, 51
Dunlap, Knight, 58
Dürer, Albrecht, 44

Eastman, Max, 221, 315*n*
Eckhardt, Meister, 20, 21, 30
Eder, Edith, 239, 241
Eder, M. David, 213, 239, 241, 246, 257
Edward VII, King of England, 238
ego, 49, 135, 155, 244
Eitington, Max, 78
Eleusinian mysteries, 86, 128, 129, 130, 142, 150
Elijah, 122, 123, 133, 134, 139, 155, 160
Eliot, T. S., 257
Ellenberger, Henri, 23, 290*n*, 292*n*, 295*n*
Ellenville, N.Y., 204–5, 206
Elliot, Mary, 276–77
Ellis, Havelock, 257
Elms, Alan, xiii, 287*n*
Empedocles, 30
Engels, Friedrich, 85, 300*n*
England, 9, 138–39, 250–60
　analytic psychology in, 236, 239, 241–44, 246–47, 252–55, 258, 260, 276
　psychoanalysis in, 236–41, 246, 257, 258
Enlightenment, Freemasonry and, 13, 14, 15
Eranos conference, 271
Eschenmayer, Adam Carl August von, 37
Essay on Spirit-Seeing (Schopenhauer), 32
eugenics, 115, 118
Everybody's Magazine, 221, 315*n*
evolution, 99, 125
　biological, 30, 46, 86, 102, 104–6, 108, 111
　cultural, 85–86, 105, 106
　O. Gross's views on, 72–73, 76, 84–86
extrasensory perception (ESP), 51
extraversion, 87–88, 181, 219, 220–21, 242, 248, 300*n*

fairy tales, psychoanalytic interpretation of, 57–58, 296*n*
false memory syndrome, 49
Fama (pamphlet), 14
Faust (Goethe), 16, 20, 140, 150, 196
Favill, Dr., 206
Fechner, Gustav, 30
feeling type, 181, 219, 221, 242
Feminine principle, 118, 150, 194
Ferenczi, Sandor, 59, 238
　Freud's correspondence with, 63, 88, 108, 109, 112–13, 170, 179, 206, 207, 225, 300*n*
　Putnam's correspondence with, 173
Fidus (Karl Höppner), 2, 68, 117–18, 164, 194, 262, 265, 305*n*
Fiechter, Ernst, 70
Flammarion, Camille, 39
Flournoy, Théodore, 23, 30, 48–49, 54, 104, 294*n*
Foord, Dr., 204, 205, 206

Fordham, Michael, 272, 275
France, 9, 32, 260
　CGJ in, 40, 42
　Karl Gustav Jung in, 12, 13
　in Napoleonic wars, 5, 6, 7, 14
Frank, Leonhard, 74, 88
free love, 76–77, 86–87
　see also polygamy; sexual liberation
Freemasons, Freemasonry, 5, 13–19, 66, 127, 130, 157, 289*n*
　see also Rosicrucians, Rosicrucianism
Freud, Sigmund, 23, 46, 53–66, 70, 100–103, 145, 215, 238, 239, 259, 264, 295*n*–97*n*, 315*n*
　Ferenczi's correspondence with, 63, 88, 108, 109, 112–13, 170, 179, 206, 207, 225, 300*n*
　O. Gross and, 71–81, 83, 84, 88
　Haeckel and, 105, 106
　Jones's correspondence with, 78, 83, 112, 170, 179, 240
　CGJ compared with, 41, 54, 64–66, 97, 99, 106, 135, 158
　CGJ's correspondence with, xii, 53, 62–66, 77–81, 83, 84, 89–91, 93–94, 101–2, 108, 113–14, 126, 134, 135, 309*n*
　CGJ as heir apparent of, 53–54, 65–66, 69, 108
　CGJ's "religious crush" on, 61–64
　CGJ's split with, 53–54, 66, 99, 107–9, 112–13, 135, 136, 166, 173, 177, 236, 238, 241
　E. R. McCormick and, 206, 207, 225
　M. McCormick and, 204
　Mithraism and, 133, 135–36
　Nietzsche compared with, 74, 76, 78, 79
　Putnam and, 167, 173, 182, 240
　sexual theory of, 54, 56, 99, 106, 109, 113, 136
Frey, Liliane, 278
Fries, Ernst, 288*n*
From India to the Planet Mars (*Des Indes à la planete Mars*) (Flournoy), 48–49, 294*n*

Gedo, John, 64
Geheimnisse, Die (Goethe), 17–18, 289*n*
genius, 21, 55, 71, 74, 79, 89, 295*n*
　of Goethe, 18, 20
　hidden memories and, 50–51
　of CGJ, 102–3, 271
"Gentlemen Volunteers," 226
George, Stefan, 43, 85
Germany, 5–16, 32, 214, 263–64
　Freemasonry in, 13–16
　Graecophilia in, 110, 303*n*
　Nazism in, xvi, 264, 273–77
　sun worship in, 114–17
　unification of, 115
　see also nationalism, German; *specific cities*

Index

Gess, Heinz, 264
Gilman, Sander, 55
"Gladius Dei" (Mann), 42, 292*n*–93*n*
Glaus, Beat, 286*n*
Gnostics, Gnosticism, xvi, 127, 130, 131, 160–62, 185, 251, 252, 307*n*
  Philemon and, 3–4, 139, 287*n*
God, 21
  CGJ's conception of, xiv–xv, 104, 106–7
  Pietism and, 9–11
"Gods and Their Representation in the House, The" (Morgan), 266
Goerres, Josef, 30, 37, 307*n*
Goethe, Johann Wolfgang von, 12, 16–21, 30, 38, 43, 105, 109, 110, 140, 150, 157, 196, 289*n*
  CGJ as reincarnation of, 18–21
  Karl Gustav Jung as illegitimate son of, 18, 19
Gordon, R. L., 137
Graf, Max, 59
Great Mother Goddess, 85, 86, 117, 129, 130, 142, 182, 183
Greece, ancient, 85–86, 142
  Germany and, 110, 303*n*
Greek Magical Papyri, 269, 270
Green, Martin, 299*n*
Greenfeld, Liah, 288*n*–89*n*
Gross, Frieda, 73, 77, 79–80, 82, 83, 88
Gross, Hans, 71–72, 73, 75, 77, 78, 88, 89, 297*n*–98*n*
Gross, Otto, 70–91, 97, 98, 117, 238, 297*n*–300*n*
  arrest of, 88
  at Burghölzli, 70, 73, 77–84, 87, 89, 299*n*
  death of, 79, 88, 89
  as drug addict, 71, 73, 78–81, 83, 88
  CGJ analyzed by, 83–84, 87
  CGJ's dislike of, 77, 78, 83
  CGJ's notes on, 79–83, 91, 299*n*
  polygamy and, 70, 76–79, 85–87, 89–91, 97, 99, 197, 299*n*
Gross, Peter, 77, 88
Gross-Cophta, Der (Goethe), 16
Grundlagen des Neunzehnten Jahrhunderts, Die (Chamberlain), 144–45
guiding fiction, 157–58, 228, 230, 312*n*
Gurdjieff, George Ivanovitch, 256–58, 260, 317*n*, 318*n*
Gypsies, 71–72, 298*n*

Haeckel, Ernst, 30, 46, 104–6, 109, 111, 116, 303*n*
Hall, Stanley, 217
Handbuch für Untersuchungsrichter (H. Gross), 298*n*
Hanfstängl, Ernst, 320*n*

Harding, Mary Esther, 250, 254, 265
Harms, Ernest, 268
Hartmann, Eduard von, 30
Harvard University, 166, 167, 277
Hauffe, Friedericke (Seeress of Prevorst), 35–39, 48
Hausheer, Irené, 207
Hecht, Dora, 241
Heidelberg, 7–8, 76, 83, 84
Heine, Heinrich, 5–6, 43
Helios, 132, 133
Hellenes, 144, 310*n*
Hennings, Emmy, 74
Heraclitus, 20, 30
Herder, J. G., 8, 115
hereditary degeneration, 45, 50, 55–56
Hering, Ewald, 46–47
Hermand, Jost, 115
hermaphrodites, hermaphroditism, 195, 244, 248
Hermes, 146, 154
Hermeticism, 15, 130, 307*n*
Herrn Dames Aufzeichnungen (Reventlow), 117
Herzensreligion, 9
Herzl, Theodor, 25
Hesse, Hermann, 9, 118, 185, 195, 292*n*
hetairism, 85, 106
Hidden Church of the Holy Grail, The (Waite), 229–30
hieros logos, 129
Hinkle, Consuela, 240
Hinkle, Walter Scot, 240
Hinkle-Eastwick, Beatrice, 94, 206, 232–33, 248, 250, 254–55, 265, 317*n*
  analysis of, 195
  background of, 240–41
  CGJ translated by, 212, 241, 270
  Long's friendship with, 240, 260
Hitler, Adolf, xvi, 116, 277
Holm, Lars, 304*n*
Holtzman, Willy, 301*n*
Holy Grail, 15, 116, 145, 149, 155, 159, 190, 195, 227, 230, 254, 315*n*, 316*n*
Holy Spirit, 9, 146, 156
Homans, Peter, 64
homosexuality, 62–63, 248, 249
Honegger, Johann Jakob, 102, 103, 127, 142, 269
  papers of, xii, 286*n*–87*n*
  suicide of, 63, 93, 269
Höppner, Karl, *see* Fidus
Hull, R.F.C., xvi
Humboldt, Alexander von, 12, 289*n*
Humboldt, Wilhelm von, vii
Hungary, 203, 313*n*

Hurwitz, Emanuel, 299n
"Hymn to King Helios" (Julian), 98, 109, 134
Hymn to the Mother of the Gods (Julian), 67
hypnosis, 30, 34, 128
hysteria, 25, 30, 45, 55, 56, 90, 128
   spiritualism and, 33, 34, 48, 50, 51

I Ching, 193, 234
Illuminati, 13, 15, 16, 19, 66
imagination, 104
   active, 24, 121, 137, 155, 266
India, 114, 142
individuation, xiii, 54, 64, 95, 122, 141, 153–54, 157, 180, 198
   of F. B. Katz, 182, 194
inner fatherland, 3–21, 41, 109, 129, 287n–90n
   ancestor possession and, 19–21
   Freemasonry and, 13–19, 289n
   Pietism and, 8–11, 19, 288n–89n
   Wartburgfest and, 5–7, 287n–88n
International Conference of Women Physicians (1919), 247–50
International Harvester Company, 201, 202, 211, 232, 234, 320n
International Order for Ethics and Culture, 64–65
International Psychoanalytic Association:
   CGJ as president of, 57, 158, 173
   conferences of, 57, 78–79, 93–94, 113, 114, 150–51, 168, 300n
Interpretation of Dreams, The (Freud), 53, 113, 239
introversion:
   Pietism and, 9, 289n
   as psychological type, 87–88, 110, 181, 219, 220–21, 242, 248, 251, 300n
intuition, xvi, 9, 115, 125, 131, 146, 181, 242
Iran, 114, 126, 142
Isis, 127, 128, 129, 131–32, 137, 142–43

Jackson, Howard, 139
Jacobi, Jolande, 62, 97, 170, 274, 275, 278
Jaffé, Aniela, xvi, 278
   Memories, Dreams, Reflections and, xii, 94–95, 120, 122, 160–61, 287n
Jaffe, Edgar, 76
Jaffe, Else von Richthofen, 76, 77, 83, 84, 299n
Jaffe, Peter, 77
Jahn, Friedrich Ludwig, 5, 8, 115
James, William, 23, 31, 166
Janet, Pierre, 23, 30, 48, 54
Jerome, 136
Jesus Christ, xvi, 30, 44, 107, 112, 123, 133, 278
   apostles of, 156
   death of, 135, 153
   descent into Hell by, 154
   Pietism and, 9, 10–11
   as Wotan, 146
   see also Aryan Christ
John XXII, Pope, 21
Jones, Ernest, 59, 110, 238, 241
   Freud's correspondence with, 78, 83, 112, 170, 179, 240
   O. Gross and, 71, 75, 78, 83
   CGJ criticized by, 150
   Putnam's correspondence with, 172, 173
Jouret, Luc, 289n
Joyce, James, 231
Judaism, Jews, xv, 25, 72, 143–46, 156, 263–64, 267, 298n
   civilization and, 143, 263–64, 275
   psychoanalysis and, 55, 57, 58, 59, 108–9, 112–13, 238, 259
Judeo-Christian tradition, 30, 64–65, 115
   CGJ's hostility toward, xv–xvi, 61, 99, 106–7, 141–43, 151
   Mithraism as rival of, 132, 141
Julian the Apostate, Emperor of Rome, xv–xvi, 67, 98, 109, 134, 309n
Jung, Agathe (daughter), 25, 69
Jung, Carl Gustav:
   as Aion, *iv*, 121, 123, 124, 139, 143
   anti-Semitism of, 112, 114, 145, 146, 273–77
   betrayals, omissions, and lies of, 40, 50, 88, 94–95, 269–72
   birth of, xii, 7
   bourgeois life of, 69–70, 78, 87, 90, 96
   death of, xii
   diaries of, xii, 123, 290n; *see also* "Red Book"
   doctoral dissertation of, 34, 47–50, 128, 290n–91n, 294n
   dreams of, 20, 94, 99, 100, 101, 105, 122–25, 139, 146–47, 149, 151
   education of, 12, 29, 42, 105, 110
   fame of, xii, 46, 69, 88, 158, 200, 213
   family background of, 6–9, 11–19, 24–30, 157, 291n
   fantasies of, 66, 99, 101, 108, 144
   finances of, 29, 42, 70
   foreign travels of, xii, 40, 42–45, 53, 55, 91, 96, 108, 109, 113, 150–51, 169, 205–6, 207, 234, 239, 242, 246–47, 254–55, 277, 293n, 295n
   in historical perspective, xiii, xiv, xvi, 100, 114–19, 272–77
   initiation and deification of, *iv*, xiii–xvi, 120–25, 133, 138–41, 143, 144, 150, 151, 153, 155–56, 158, 179, 208, 252, 306n

inner fatherland of, 3–21, 41, 109, 287n–91n
lectures and seminars of, xii, 11, 19, 31, 33, 38, 51–52, 100, 109, 120–25, 138–39, 149–60, 171, 239, 246–47, 252, 253, 254, 265, 271, 274, 277, 291n, 292n, 306n
  as Leo, 137
  masks of, 158–60, 251–52, 253
  in medical corps, 181, 188, 211, 242
  military interests of, 42, 43
  myth of, xiii, xiv, 120, 121, 171
  nickname of, 96
  number one personality of, 20, 24
  number two personality of, 4, 24, 50
  paganism of, xv–xvi, 3, 11, 87, 100, 103, 104, 117, 121–25, 133, 148–62, 171–72, 184–86, 239–41, 268, 274–75, 311n–12n
  paintings of, xii, 3–4, 15, 151, 152, 162, 266
  physical appearance of, 22, 62
  polygamy of, 70, 87, 89–97, 158, 191–92, 197, 227
  problems in writing biography of, xii–xiii
  professional disengagement of, 101, 158
  psychoanalysis and, 53–66, 69, 89–94, 102–14, 121, 135, 171, 173, 204
  reading and library of, 11, 30–38, 125–28, 130–33, 289n, 307n
  religion-building proclivities of, xiv–xvi, 64–66, 87, 99–100, 112–13, 149–58, 160, 171–72, 175–77, 180, 184–86, 219, 227–31, 239–41, 251, 268, 277–78
  religious background of, 29, 44
  sexuality of, 3, 61–63, 87, 89–91, 94, 98, 121
  skepticism of, 30, 41, 51, 123
  spiritualism and, 22–41, 51, 54, 58, 64, 87, 108, 121, 290n–92n
  spiritual rebirth of, xiii, 11, 97–100, 104, 120–25, 149–50, 151, 179
  synthesizing abilities of, 102–3, 104, 128, 252
  violent language of, 187
  visions of, iv, xii, 3–4, 45, 94, 102, 121–25, 138, 141, 149, 151, 154, 179, 208, 286n
Jung, Emilie Preiswerk (mother), 24, 29, 40, 42
  death of, 146
  as hysteric, 25, 50
Jung, Emma Rauschenbach (wife), xii, 45, 69, 89, 93, 94, 216, 228, 254, 272
  death of, 97, 146
  CGJ's affairs and, 90, 96, 227
  H. F. McCormick's correspondence with, 232, 235
Jung, Ernst (uncle), 288n
Jung, Franz Ignaz (great-grandfather), 7
Jung, Franz Karl (son), 69, 207, 286n
Jung, Gertrud (sister), 7, 29, 42

Jung, Gret (daughter), 69, 234
Jung, Johann Heinrich, see Jung-Stilling, Heinrich
Jung, Johann Paul Achilles (father), 7, 19, 62
  death of, 23, 24, 27, 29, 30
Jung, Karl Gustav (grandfather), 6–9, 11–19, 28, 157
  baptismal certificate of, 8, 288n
  drawing of, 7, 288n
  exile and homesickness of, 12–13
  as Freemason, 13–16
  as Goethe's illegitimate son, 18, 19
  imprisonment of, 11–12
  religious conversion of, 8, 12, 288n
Jung, Maria Josepha (great-grandmother), 7, 38
Jung, Sigismund von (great-great uncle), 7
Jung Cult, The (Noll), 64, 287n
Jung-Stilling, Heinrich (Johann Heinrich Jung), 11, 30, 32–34
Jung's *Turm*, 3–4, 15, 96, 122–23, 235
"Jung the *Leontocephalus*" (Noll), 306n

Kafka, Franz, 88–89
Kahane, Max, 57
Kandinsky, Wassily, 43
Kant, Immanuel, 23, 30, 31–32, 218
Katz, Fanny Bowditch, 165–99, 236, 255, 259, 312n–13n
  depression of, 167, 196
  descent into underworld by, 195
  diary of, 182–86, 188–91, 193, 194–95, 244
  drawings of, 180–81, 188–90, 193, 194, 195, 197, 199
  family background of, 166–67
  CGJ's analysis of, 167–81, 240
  CGJ's correspondence with, 187–88, 196
  marriage of, 165, 182, 190–92, 194, 197–98
  Moltzer's analysis of, 168, 170, 174, 180, 182, 185–95
  Putnam's correspondence with, 168–70, 172–80, 184–85, 192
  sacrifice of, 182–85
Katz, Johann Rudolf, 182, 186, 190–95, 197–98, 255, 256, 294n
Keller, Adolph, 152, 180, 227, 235
Keller, Tina, 92, 95, 152, 179–80, 186–87, 301n, 311n
Kerner, Justinius, 34–39, 48, 51, 292n
Kerr, John, 64
Keyserling, Count Hermann, 264
Klages, Ludwig, 85, 117
Knapp, Albert, 64–65
König Friedwahn (Borngräber), *164*
Kraepelin, Emil, 73, 81, 83

Krenn, Edwin, 233, 234
"Kreuzlingen gesture" incident, 63
Küsnacht, 3, 70, 96, 101–2, 117, 121, 215, 218, 235, 278

Laban, Rudolph von, 118
Lamarck, Chevalier de, 30
Lamarckian biology, 20, 46, 105, 108, 112, 265
Land of the Dead, 3, 23, 41, 122–25, 129, 146, 154, 159–60, 195, 208
Lao-dze, 218
Lawrence, D. H., 77
Lawrence, Frieda von Richthofen, 76, 77, 84, 299n
Layard, John, 95, 97, 272
Lectures on the Origins and Growth of Religion (Müller), 98
Legge, Alexander, 211
Lenin, V. I., 43
Leo, 137, 138, 139
leo, grade of, 136–38
libido, 98, 99, 105–7, 109–10, 135, 136, 141–42, 181, 194, 241, 245, 246, 249, 251
"Lichtgebet," *68*, 118, 265
"Liebe" (Fidus), *2*
lions, 124, 136–38
Lombroso, Cesare, 31
London Psycho-Analytic Society, 238, 246
Long, Constance, 165–66, 236–60, 264, 316n–18n
  analysis of, 195, 241, 254
  "MKB" and, 243, 253, 255, 256
  diary of, 237, 242–47, 250, 252–60, 317n, 318n
  dreams and visions of, 236, 243, 245, 250, 254, 255
  health problems of, 237, 246, 250, 260
  at International Conference of Women Physicians, 247–50
  CGJ's break with, 255–56
  CGJ's correspondence with, 237, 250–52, 258–59
  CGJ translated by, 241
  Ouspensky and, 255–60, 317n
  in Zurich, 236, 239–41
Ludendorff, Erich, 116
Lusitania, 214, 215
Luther, Martin, 5–6, 9
Lutheranism, 6, 9, 10

McClure's, 72
McCormick, Adah Wilson, 233
McCormick, Anita, 201, 205–6
McCormick, Anne Urquhart Stillman (Fifi), 234

McCormick, Cyrus, Jr., 201–2, 213
McCormick, Cyrus Hall, Sr., 201
McCormick, Editha, 200, 202
McCormick, Edith Rockefeller, 165–66, 195, 200–236, 240, 313n–16n
  agoraphobia of, 201, 205, 207, 218, 224, 231
  analysis of, 200, 204, 206, 207, 213, 218
  as analyst, 200, 202, 207, 224, 231–32, 234
  causes funded by, 224, 225, 226, 231, 234
  death of, 234–35
  divorce of, 202, 233
  dreams of, 218
  in Ellenville, 204–5, 206
  Hungarian trip of, 203, 313n
  intellectual nature of, 201, 202, 207
  return to United States by, 233, 234
  translation of CGJ's works and, 212–13, 225, 241
McCormick, Ganna Walska, 233
McCormick, Harold Fowler, Jr., 200, 202, 203, 207–12, 215, 222–23, 232
  analysis of, 226–27
  CGJ's relationship with, 207–8, 234
  marriage of, 233–34
McCormick, Harold Fowler, Sr., 200–206, 208–24, 226–35, 320n
  analysis of, 195, 212, 226–27
  family background of, 201–2
  CGJ's relationship with, 209, 212, 215, 218
  on Psychological Club, 228–29
  Psychological Club building selected by, 223–24
  return to United States by, 232
  walking trip of, 216–17, 218
McCormick, John D. Rockefeller, 200, 202, 203
McCormick, Mary Virginia, 201, 203, 217
McCormick, Mathilde, 200, 202, 203, 208, 212, 227, 238
McCormick, Medill, 91, 203–4, 205, 233
McCormick, Muriel, 200, 202, 203, 207, 212, 233
  analysis of, 195, 210, 217, 226–27
  education of, 208, 213
  father's correspondence with, 210
  personality of, 208, 209, 211, 217
McCormick, Nancy Fowler (Nettie), 201, 202, 205–6, 211–14, 216–19, 232–33
  Edith's correspondence with, 225
  Fowler's correspondence with, 222–23
  Harold's correspondence with, 204, 208, 211, 212, 213–14, 216–17, 218, 226, 231
McCormick, Ruth Hanna, 91
McCormick, Stanley, 201, 202, 203, 205–6, 226
Maeder, Alphonse, 113, 150–51, 152, 172, 180, 182, 187, 227

Mainz, 7
mandalas, 114, 162, 242, 244, 266, 271
Mann, Kristine, 250, 271
Mann, Thomas, 42, 292*n*–93*n*
Mars, Martians, 39, 48–49
Masculine principle, 118, 189, 194
matriarchy, 72, 74, 85–86, 106
Mazdean religion, 132
Mead, G.R.S. 131, 269–70
Meier, Carl A., 97
Mellon, Mary, 213
Mellon, Paul, 213
memories, 125
  Burghölzli research on, 46–47
  Freud's views on, 56
  hidden, 39, 41–52, 104, 125, 138, 265, 270, 292*n*–95*n*
  "implicit," 49
  organic, 46
Memories, Dreams, Reflections (*MDR*) (Jung), xii–xiv, 7, 24, 29, 160–61, 293*n*
  classical education in, 110
  "Confrontation with the Unconscious" in, 120, 122
  dreams in, 100, 105
  falsifications in, 291*n*
  German edition of, xiii, 286*n*
  hereditary statistics in, 55
  Jaffé's role in writing of, xiii, 120, 287*n*
  "On Life After Death" in, 20–21
  Philemon in, 3, 139
  stone tablets in, 4
  Wiedergeburt testimonies compared with, 11
  Wolff and, 94–95
men, CGJ's problems with, 22, 62–63
Menschwerdung, 155, 156, 157
Mercurius, 278, 312*n*
Metamorphoses (Apuleius), 131–32
Meyrink, Gustav, 74
Miller, Miss Frank, 104, 106, 112
Minder, Bernard, 301*n*
Mithraeums, 132, 136, 137
Mithraic Liturgy, 127, 132, 143, 269–70
Mithraic mysteries, *iv*, 121, 124, 125, 127–28, 132–43, 230, 269–70, 306*n*–9*n*
  Christianity compared with, 132, 133, 308*n*
  initiation into, 132, 136–37, 138
  Philemon and, 3–4, 287*n*
  tauroctony in, 132–36
Mithraic Ritual, A (Mead), 269–70
Mithras, 121, 125, 132
  as *kosmokrator*, 133
  as *Sol Invictus*, 132
  tauroctony and, 132–36

Mithrasliturgie, Eine (Dieterich), 269–70
Moltzer, Maria, 94, 185–98, 239, 241, 245, 311*n*
  CGJ analyzed by, 170
  CGJ's alleged affair with, 94, 170, 191–92, 198, 206
  Katz compared with, 181, 191–92
  Katz's correspondence with, 195–98
  Katz's treatment with, 168, 170, 174, 180, 182, 185–95
  McCormick family and, 206, 207, 217, 227
Monistenbund, 116
Monologen (Schleiermacher), 289*n*
monotheism, xv, 30, 99, 172, 277
  see also God
Morgan, Christiana, 92, 266–68, 302*n*
Morganblatt, 18
Moses, B. Frederick, 240
Mosse, George, 146, 259
"Moth to the Sun, The" (Miller), 106
Mozart, Wolfgang Amadeus, 180
Mühsam, Erich, 74–75
Müller, Friedrich Max, 98, 111–12, 114, 306*n*
Müller, Herman, 234
Mueller, K. O., 307*n*
Munich, 85, 88, 292*n*–93*n*
  O. Gross in, 73–75, 77, 81, 83, 84
  CGJ in, 42–45, 70, 113, 114, 150–51, 300*n*
  1913 psychoanalytic congress in, 113, 114, 150–51, 300*n*
  Schwabing counterculture in, 74–75, 84, 117, 182
Munich Secession, 44, 293*n*
Murray, Henry A., 92, 266–68, 277, 301*n*–2*n*
music, 6, 114
  psychoanalytic interpretation of, 57–58
  Wagner's operas and, 18, 23, 57–58, 116, 145, 155–56, 180, 185, 227, 239, 254, 310*n*
Mutterrecht, Das (Bachofen), 85
Myers, F.W.H., 31
Mysteria (Noll's unpublished anthology), 306*n*
Mysteries of Mithras, The (Cumont), 132, 137
Mysterium Coniunctionis (Jung), 137
mystery cults, xiv, 120–43, 176, 306*n*–9*n*, 315*n*
  at Bayreuth, 145
  Christianity compared with, 130, 132, 133, 308*n*
  of Dionysus, 126, 128, 129, 130, 142, 165
  Eleusinian, 86, 128, 129, 130, 142, 150
  initiation stages in, 129–30, 132, 136–37, 138, 308*n*
  CGJ's sources on, 125–28, 306*n*–7*n*
  Mithraic, *see* Mithraic mysteries
  passion for secrecy in, 131–32, 140–41, 251

mystery of deification, 120–47, 196, 244–45, 306n–10n
  CGJ's account of, 122–25, 306n
  see also mystery cults
mysticism, 9, 21, 30, 115–16, 118, 150, 185, 241
myth, xvi, 10
  Freud/Jung, 53–54
  Greek, 43–44, 86, 98–99, 101, 110, 126
  of CGJ, xiii, xiv, 120, 121, 171
  CGJ's interest in, 64, 65, 81–82, 98–99, 101, 103, 106, 107, 109–12, 125–28, 184, 301n
  of mystery cults, 129, 130, 132
  psychoanalysis and, 57–58
  psychosis and, 102, 103, 104, 127, 142
  Roman, 110, 206
  of Rosicrucians, 14
  solar, 98, 106, 107, 109, 111–12
  in Stuck's work, 44–45

Nabokov, Vladimir, xi
Naeff, Erna Wolff, 93
Nameche, Gene, 63, 90, 95, 272, 273, 274, 276
Napoléon I, Emperor of France, 5, 6
Napoleonic wars, 5, 6, 7, 14
narcissism, 150
nationalism, German, 5–11, 108
  Pietism and, 8–11
nature, 115, 141, 143, 264
Nazism, xvi, 264, 273–77
Nelken, Jan, 103, 127, 142
Neumann, Erich, 274
neuroses, 99, 102, 109, 219
New Age, 238–39, 256
New Man, 155, 158
New Testament, 5, 146
New York Analytical Psychology Club, 250
New York City, International Conference of Women Physicians in, 247–50
Nicoll, Maurice, 246, 254, 257, 258, 260
Nietzsche, Friedrich, 30, 43, 44, 51, 215, 222, 239, 293n
  O. Gross and, 73–74, 76, 77, 78, 79, 84
  as CGJ's source, 126
  Wagner's relationship with, 55, 295n
night-sea journey, 124, 318n
Numa Pompilius, 206

Oczeret, Herbert, 91–92
Odin, *see* Wotan
On Dreams (Freud), 239, 241
"On the Psychology and Pathology of So-Called Occult Phenomena" (Jung), 34, 47–50, 128, 290n–91n, 294n
"ontogeny recapitulates phylogeny," 104–6

Orage, A. R., 238–9, 256–57
Osiris, 143
Otto, Rudolph, 9
Otto Gross (Hurwitz), 299n
Ouija boards, 27–28
Ouspensky, P. D., 255–60, 317n, 318n
Oxford Club, 180

paganism, 10, 43–44, 98–162, 239–41, 302n–12n
  of CGJ, xv–xvi, 3, 11, 87, 100, 103, 104, 117, 121–25, 133, 148–62, 171–72, 184–86, 239–41, 268, 274–75, 311n–12n
  of Stuck, 44
  see also mystery cults; sun worship; *specific deities*
Pallas, 136–37
Pan, 44
Pantheon, xiii
"Paralysis by Analysis," 232
Paris, 12, 13, 40, 50
Parsifal (Wagner), 18, 23, 116, 145, 155–56, 180, 185, 227, 239, 254, 310n
patriarchy, xv, 71–74, 85, 86, 106
Persephone, 129, 150
Persia, ancient, 132
persona, 95, 159, 160, 242, 244, 245
personality, multiple, 30, 34, 48, 49, 50
Peter, Saint, 133, 139
Pfister, Oskar, 225
Philemon, 3–4, 18, 31, 122–23, 134, 139, 149, 151, 160, 161, 254, 287n
philology, 144
  comparative, 102–3, 104, 107, 108, 110–12, 114
Philosopher's Stone (Word of God), 15
philosophy, 110
  CGJ's readings in, 30–32
phylogeny, of psychology, 99, 101–6, 108–9, 126, 133, 138, 142, 303n
Pieta (Stuck), 44
Pietism, 8–11, 19, 29, 30, 107, 175, 288n–89n
plagiarism, unconscious, 51
Plato, 9, 30, 179
Plotinus, 30
Pocantico Hills, N.Y., 206, 212, 213, 222, 233
political liberation, 10, 72, 89, 99
polygamy, 76–79, 85–87, 99, 297n–302n
  of CGJ, 70, 87, 89–97, 158, 191–92, 197, 227
  CGJ's recommending of, 91–92, 204, 233, 267
  of J. R. Katz, 190–92, 197–98
Porphyry, 136–37
Prague, 71, 88–89

Index

Preiswerk, Augusta Faber, 25, 26, 38, 40
Preiswerk, Auguste (Aunt Gusteli), 30
Preiswerk, Bertha, 27
Preiswerk, Celestine (Dini), 28
Preiswerk, Eduard, 29–30
Preiswerk, Hélène (Helly), 23, 25–30, 34,
   37–41, 94, 290n–91n, 295n
  death of, 40, 93
  Ivenes and, 39, 48, 149
  in CGJ's dissertation, 47–48, 50, 51, 128
Preiswerk, Louise (Luggy), 25, 26, 29
Preiswerk, Rev. Samuel (father), 24–27, 38
Preiswerk, Rudolph, 23–24, 25, 27, 29
Preiswerk, Samuel (son), 29, 38
Preiswerk family:
  history of, 24–25, 291n
  CGJ aided by, 29–30
  CGJ's problems with, 29, 40, 50, 51
prisci theologi, 14, 289n
projection, 219, 221
Protestants, Protestantism, xv, 30, 44, 156
  Karl Gustav Jung's conversion to, 8, 12, 288n
  Lutheranism, 6, 9, 10
  Pietism and, 8–11, 19, 29, 30, 107, 175,
    288n–89n
Prussia, 8, 10, 11–12
psychoanalysis, psychoanalytic movement, 45,
  53–66, 69, 87–94, 102–14, 121, 171, 173,
  204, 315n
  Aryan-Semite split in, 103, 108–9, 112–13
  cultural creations and, 57–58, 135
  cultural revitalization and, 54, 84, 99–100,
    104, 113
  in England, 236–41, 246, 257, 258
  O. Gross and, 71, 73–84, 87, 88, 299n
  Jews and, 55, 57, 58, 59, 108–9, 112–13, 238,
    259
  CGJ's enemies in, 150, 177
  CGJ's synthesizing project and, 102–3, 104
  as religion or cult, 58–61, 64–66, 99–100,
    112–13, 150–51
  sexual intimacies with patients and, 56, 59
  as *Weltanschauung*, 54, 57
Psychological Club, 18, 96, 97, 180, 182,
  186–87, 195, 197
  building for, 223–24, 226
  CGJ's 1916 talks to, 149–60, 311n
  E. F. McCormick and, 223–29
  pro-German sympathizers in, 276–77
psychological tests, 47, 49, 69, 71, 102–3, 294n
psychological types, 54, 87–88, 92, 95, 121,
  123, 242–43, 248, 300n
  overcoming limits of, 156
  see also specific types

Psychological Types (Jung), 88, 95, 300n
Psychological Wednesday Evening Circle, 57, 59
Psychologie der unbewussten Prozesse, Die
  (Jung), 159–60
Psychology of the Unconscious (Jung), *see*
  Wanderlungen und Symbole der Libido
Psycho-Medical Society, 239
psychosis, 50, 99, 109, 112
  myth and, 102, 103, 104, 127, 142
Putnam, James Jackson, 167–70
  Freud and, 167, 173, 182, 240
  CGJ's loss of support of, 181–82
  F. B. Katz's correspondence with, 168–70,
    172–80, 184–85, 192

radiolaria, 105
rational thought (reason), xvi, 99, 115, 125
Raub, Michael, 72
Rauschenbach, Emma, *see* Jung, Emma
  Rauschenbach
ravens, as symbol, 146
Read, Herbert, 257
Re-Creating of the Individual, The (Hinkle), 265
"Red Book" (Jung), xii, 4, 123, 134, 139, 151,
  152, 189, 271, 286n
redemption, xiv–xv, 104, 106–7, 153, 185, 239,
  251, 278, 310n
Reimer, Georg Andreas, 8
reincarnation, 18–21
Reitler, Rudolph, 57
Reitzenstein, Richard, 127, 130, 307n
religion:
  CGJ's building of, xiv–xvi, 64–66, 87,
    99–100, 112–13, 149–58, 160, 171–72,
    175–77, 180, 184–86, 219, 227–31,
    239–41, 251, 268, 277–78
  psychoanalysis as, 58–61, 64–66, 99–100,
    112–13, 150–51
  see also specific religions
religious imagery, fin-de-siècle reinterpretation
  of, 44–45, 293n
Renan, Ernest, 30, 107, 109, 111, 112, 114, 141
repression, 72–74, 112, 115, 135, 141, 217, 221
  hysterical, 102
  sexual, 72, 76, 78, 86, 87, 184
resistance, 221, 243
Reventlow, Franziska Gräfin zu (Fanny), 117,
  182
Rhine, J. B., 51, 295n
Ribot, Théodule, 30, 48
Richthofen, Else von, *see* Jaffe, Else von
  Richthofen
Richthofen, Frieda von, *see* Lawrence, Frieda
  von Richthofen

Rieff, Philip, 59
Riklin, Franz, 57, 64, 167–68, 176, 215
Rilke, Rainer Maria, 43, 113
Rintelen, Friedrich, 288*n*
Robinson, Forrest, 92, 301*n*–2*n*
Rockefeller, Edith, *see* McCormick, Edith Rockefeller
Rockefeller, John. D., Jr., 233, 234–35
Rockefeller, John. D., Sr., 200–203, 207, 213–16, 226, 233
   Edith's correspondence with, 210, 214, 222, 224–25, 230–32
   Harold's correspondence with, 202, 203, 205, 209, 211, 215–22, 230
Rockefeller, Laura, 203, 210, 213–14
"Role of the Unconscious, The" ("Über das Unbewusste") (Jung), 259
Roman Catholicism, Roman Catholics, xv, 7, 8, 12, 44, 60, 72, 156, 278, 287*n*
   Jungian analysis compared with, 141, 157
   Mithraism compared with, 132
Romans, ancient, 10, 85, 110, 142, 206
Romanticism, German, 8, 9, 12, 19, 105, 110, 266, 289*n*, 307*n*
Roosevelt, Theodore, 205
rose, as symbol, 5, 14–18, 149, 157, 182, 183
Rosenbaum, Erna, 272
Rosenbaum, Vladimir, 276
Rosicrucians, Rosicrucianism, 7, 14, 15, 130, 157, 289*n*
Rothermere, Lady, 257
runes, 116, 118, 147, 149, 273

Sabazios mystery cult, 129
Sabina (Holtzman), 301*n*
sacrifice, 6, 116, 135–36, 149
   of F. B. Katz, 182–85
Salome, 122, 123, 124, 155, 160
Salzburg, 57, 78–79
Schama, Simon, xiv
Schelling, Friedrich W. J., 30, 37
Schiller, Johann Christoph Friedrich von, 43, 110
Schlegel, August Wilhelm, 8
Schlegel, Friedrich, 8
Schleiermacher, Friedrich, 7, 8–9, 11, 12, 37, 107, 115, 279, 289*n*
Schmid, Hans, 181, 227
Schmitz, Oskar, 264
Schneiter, Carl, 103, 142
Schoenbrun (chemist), 7, 288*n*
Schopenhauer, Arthur, 23, 30, 31, 32, 215
Schubert, Gotthilf von, 37
Schweizer Illustrierten, 234

Schwyzer, E. (Solar Phallus Man), 268–71
séances, 22–29, 38–40, 47–49, 165, 166, 290*n*–91*n*
Sebaldt von Werth, Max Ferdinand, 118, 305*n*–6*n*
Secret Church, 230, 254
Seelenprobleme der Gegenwart (Jung), 268
Seewald, Richard, 74
Seherin von Prevorst, Die (Kerner), 34–39, 48, 292*n*
Semites, 107–12, 142–46
Semon, Richard, 46–47, 294*n*
sensation, 181, 242
Septem Sermones ad Mortuous (Jung), 148–49, 161–62, 186, 251, 253, 311*n*, 318*n*
sexuality, 45, 115, 267
   creativity and, 86–87
   Freud-Jung relationship and, 61–63
   Freud's theory of, 54, 56, 99, 106, 109, 113, 136
   of CGJ, 3, 61–63, 87, 89–91, 94, 98, 121
   repression and, 72, 76, 78, 86, 87, 184
   spirituality and, 87, 95, 99
   tauroctony and, 135, 136
sexual liberation, 70, 72, 76–78, 84, 88
shadow, 95, 242
Sharp, Clifford, 257
Siegfried, 10, 44, 89, 98, 107, 117
"Smith, Hélène," 48–49
snakes, 138, 139
   in CGJ's initiation, 122, 123, 124
   in Stuck's work, 44, 293*n*
Society for Psychoanalytic Endeavors, 168
Solar Temple, 289*n*
"Sonnenwanderer" (Fidus), 262*n*
Sonnwendfest, 114, 115–16, 305*n*
Spielrein, Sabina, 53, 70, 103, 127, 142, 300*n*–301*n*
   as CGJ's lover, 70, 89–91, 94, 98, 170
spiritualism, 19, 22–41, 47–52, 54, 58, 64, 108, 115, 121, 166, 290*n*–92*n*
   animal magnetism and, 32–36, 51
   hysteria and, 33, 34, 48, 50, 51
   CGJ's philosophical reading and, 30–32
   séances and, 22–29, 38–40, 47–49, 165, 166, 290*n*–91*n*
   Seeress of Prevorst and, 34–38
Spring 53, 306*n*
Stark, Rodney, 61
Steiger, Heinrich, 97
Stekel, Wilhelm, 57, 78–79, 88
Stillman, Anne Urquhart, 234
Stoics, 134–35
Stone, Herbert, 214

Strauss, David Friedrich, 30, 37
"Struktur der Seele, Die" (Jung), 268
Stuck, Franz, 44–45, 293*n*
student fraternities, 5, 288*n*
Studies on Hysteria (Freud and Breuer), 56
"Study in the Process of Individuation, A" ("Zur Empirie des Individuationsprozesses") (Jung), 271
suicide, 60, 70, 79, 149, 196, 214
   of Honegger, 63, 93, 269
Sulloway, Frank, 60
Sünde, Die (Stuck), 44–45
sun worship, *68,* 98–119, 194, 263, 265, 302*n*–6*n*
   in German Europe, 114–17
   Mithras and, 133
   Müller and, 98, 111–12, 306*n*
   of Murray, 92
   Renan's views on, 107
swastika, 118, 273
Sweden, psychoanalysis and, 113
Swedenborg, Emanuel, 30, 31, 32, 271
Switzerland, xii
   Freemasonry in, 13, 15
   Karl Gustav Jung in, 12–13
   split in psychoanalytic movement in, 103, 108–9, 112–13
   sun worship in, 114
   Türstkreuze in, 147
   see also specific cities
Symbolik und Mythologie der alten Völker besonders der Griechen (Creuzer), 126
Symbolism, in art, 44–45
symbolism, symbols, 146
   Bachofen's views on, 85–86
   cross as, 5, 6, 14–18, 149, 157
   of Freemasons, 5, 7, 14–18
   Mithraic, 124–25, 133, 135–38, 142
   rose as, 5, 14–18, 149, 157, 182, 183
   Rosicrucian, 7, 14, 15
   of sun worship, 114, 118

Taft, William H., 205
Tannenberg Foundation, 116
tauroctony, 132–36
Taurus, 134, 135, 136
Temple of Solomon, 14–15
Teutons, ancient, 6, 10, 98, 107, 116, 142, 143
Theorie der Geister-Kunde (Jung-Stilling), 32–33, 34
Theosophical Publishing Society, 270
Theosophy, 117, 118, 127, 128, 165, 270, 315*n*, 319*n*
thinking type, 181, 219, 221, 242

Thor, 116
Thuringia, 114
Tieck, Ludwig, 8
Tower:
   of CGJ, 3–4, 15, 96, 122–23, 235
   of Murray, 92, 266, 267
Transcendental Physics (Zoellner), 31
transcendent function, 193, 196, 254
Transcendent Function, The (Jung), 155, 312*n*
transference, 91, 219, 221, 228
   of F. B. Katz, 169, 173, 179–80, 182–83, 190
Tree of Life, 149, 157, 184
Triumph of the Therapeutic, The (Rieff), 59
Trüb, Hans, 152, 227, 235
Trüb, Susanne Wolff, 93, 96, 302*n*
Türstkreuze, 147

"Über das Unbewusste" ("The Role of the Unconscious") (Jung), 259
Übermensch, spiritual, 155
Ulansey, David, 133, 134
Ullman, Regina, 79
unconscious, 41, 150, 220, 244–47
   artistic productions and, 80
   collective, *see* collective unconscious
   evolution of, 99
   Freud's view of, 41, 56
   hidden memories and, 49–51
   CGJ's descent into, 122–24
   myth and, 82
   personal, 159
   plagiarism and, 51
   sources of CGJ's views on, 3, 31
   threats to life and, 95
United States, 9, 166–67, 173, 199, 200, 232–35
   analytic psychology in, 206, 241, 248, 249–50, 265, 277
   CGJ in, 55, 91, 108, 109, 169, 205–6, 207, 234, 277, 295*n*
   in World War I, 226
Urreligion, 126, 143, 263
utopianism, of CGJ, 156, 158, 228–30, 277

Valangin, Aline, 91–92, 276
Vie de Jésus (Renan), 107
Vienna, 42, 53, 57, 78, 88, 108, 181
Villa Stuck, 44
Visible Church, 229–30
visions, 11, 33, 35, 51, 104
   of CGJ, *iv,* xii, 3–4, 45, 94, 102, 121–25, 138, 141, 149, 151, 154, 179, 208, 286*n*
   of F. B. Katz, 189, 195–96
vital force, 40, 292*n*
   see also libido

Volk, Volkish elements, 4–9, 11–12, 18, 21, 24, 115, 252, 259–60, 263–66, 273–75, 277
  Aryan Christ and, 143–46
  CGJ's return to, 109
  F. B. Katz and, 182–85
  mystery cults and, 129
  Pietism and, 9
  sun worship and, 114–17

Wagner, Cosima, 145
Wagner, Richard, 44, 89, 144, 157
  Nietzsche's relationship with, 55, 295*n*
  operas of, 18, 23, 57–58, 116, 145, 155–56, 180, 185, 227, 239, 254, 310*n*
Waite, Arthur Edward, 229–30
Walska, Ganna, 233
Wanderer, 287*n*
Wandlungen und Symbole der Libido (*Psychology of the Unconscious*) (Jung), 44, 93, 98, 103–11, 128, 135–38, 145, 171, 270, 307*n*
  as counterculture success, 104, 117, 118–19
  English translation of, 212, 241
  Mithraism in, 133, 135, 136, 137, 141, 309*n*
  part 1 of, 106–7, 268
  part 2 of, 109–11, 117
  "Sacrifice" in, 135, 136
Wartburgfest, 5–7, 287*n*–88*n*
Watson, John B., 58
Weber, Marianne, 76–77, 84
Weber, Max, 76, 77, 88
Webster, Richard, 59, 60
Weekly, Frieda von Richthofen, *see* Lawrence, Frieda von Richthofen
Weimar, 16
  1911 psychoanalytic conference in, 93–94, 168
Weisz, George, 60
Weizmann, Chaim, 267
Wheelwright, Jane, 278
Why Freud Was Wrong (Webster), 59, 60
Wigman, Mary, 118–19
Will to Power, The (Nietzsche), 222
Wilson, Adah, 233
Wilson, Woodrow, 205, 226
Wolff, Antonia (Toni), 92–97, 151, 160, 216, 232
  as CGJ's collaborator, xii, 70, 93, 95–96, 136, 181

  as CGJ's lover, xii, 3, 70, 93, 121, 170, 197, 227, 234, 235, 267
  CGJ's treatment of, 92–94
women, CGJ's relationship with, 22, 89–97, 165, 170–71, 210, 227
  see also specific women
Woodworth, Robert, 58
word-association test, 47, 49, 69, 102–3, 171, 181, 213, 220, 294*n*
World War I, xiv, 3, 23, 88, 141, 149, 152, 210–12, 214, 231, 232, 241–42
  H. F. McCormick's proposal for ending of, 226
  women and, 247, 249
World War II, 276–77
Wotan (Odin), 98, 116, 274–75, 278, 305*n*
  in CGJ's dreams, 146–47
  F. B. Katz's sacrifice to, 182–85
  as Mercurius, 312*n*
  as psychopompos, 146, 153
  self-sacrifice of, 6, 149

Yale University, 277
Young, James, 254, 257, 258, 260

Zarathustra, 126, 254
Zauberflöte, Die (Mozart), 180
Zeus, 137
Zinzendorf, Count Nikolaus Ludwig von, 9, 107
Zionists, 25, 108
Zoellner, J.C.F., 31
Zofingia Students Association, 23, 29, 31, 38, 292*n*
Zoroastrianism, 126
Zumstein-Preiswerk, Stephanie, 26, 40
Zur Befreiung Deutschlands ("On the Liberation of Germany") (Arndt), 11
"Zur Empirie des Individuationsprozesses" ("A Study in the Process of Individuation") (Jung), 271
Zurich, 24, 88, 119
  CGJ's move to, 30, 31
  see also Burghölzli Psychiatric Clinic
Zurich School, xiv, 3, 18, 96, 97, 117, 121, 142, 149, 150, 165–236, 277–78
  E. R. McCormick and, 165–66, 195, 200–201, 207–35
  F. B. Katz and, 167–95, 199